VERDICTS
OUT OF
COURT

EDITED WITH AN INTRODUCTION BY
ARTHUR AND LILA WEINBERG

ELEPHANT PAPERBACKS

Ivan R. Dee, Inc., Publisher, Chicago

CLARENCE DARROW

VERDICTS OUT OF COURT

Arthur and Lila Weinberg are also the authors of
Attorney for the Damned, *The Muckrakers*, *Instead
of Violence*, *Passport to Utopia*, and *Clarence Darrow:
Sentimental Rebel*. They live and work in Chicago
where Mr. Weinberg is Lloyd Lewis Fellow in
American History at the Newberry Library and
Mrs. Weinberg is a senior editor at the University
of Chicago Press.

First ELEPHANT PAPERBACK edition published
1989 by Ivan R. Dee, Inc., 1169 South Plymouth Court,
Chicago 60605. Manufactured in the United States
of America.

ISBN 0-929587-01-4

In presenting the various lectures, debates and writings of Clarence Darrow, the editors have grouped them into what they believe are natural sections. In the categories which mirror passing events, the editors have given a panorama of newspaper headlines and stories.

Clarence Darrow is generally known as the "attorney for the damned." In this volume the editors present other facets of Darrow—the lecturer, the debater, the writer.

In order to have as large a representation of Darrow material as possible, it was necessary to edit some of the pieces; but in all instances where this has been done, an effort has been made to keep the flavor, color and feeling of each selection.

ACKNOWLEDGMENTS

We thank the Clarence Darrow estate for granting permission to use the various articles, and to the following publishers for permission to use the articles which originally appeared in their publications:

"The Ideal of a Labor Union," reprinted by permission of the Amalgamated Clothing Workers Union of America.

"The Divorce Problem," reprinted from *Vanity Fair*, copyright 1927 by Condé Nast Publications.

"NRA and Fair Competition," reprinted from *The Rotarian*, 1934.

"The Futility of the Death Penalty," reprinted from *The Forum*, 1928.

"Is Man Fundamentally Dishonest?" reprinted from *The Forum*, 1927.

"Who Knows Justice?" reprinted by permission of the Darrow estate from *Scribner's Magazine*, 1937.

"Attorney for the Defense," reprinted by permission of *Esquire Magazine*, copyright 1936 by Esquire, Inc.

"The Foreign Debt and America," reprinted from *Vanity Fair*, copyright 1927 by Condé Nast Publications.

"This Is What I Don't Like About Newspapers," reprinted by permission of the American Society of Newspaper Editors.

"The Myth of the Soul," as it originally appeared in *The Forum*, 1928, with no changes or additions.

We want to thank the numerous libraries in which we did our research: Newberry Library, which has been most helpful; the University of Chicago Library, which houses Clarence Darrow papers; the Chicago Public Library; and the New York Public Library.

We also want to thank various people who in one way or another helped and encouraged us, including Dr. Preston Bradley, minister, People's Church of Chicago; Jacob Potofsky, president, Amalgamated Clothing Workers of America; Judge Michael A. Musmanno of Pennsylvania; Elmer Gertz and Ernest L. Knuti of Chicago, and Charles L. Black of New York.

The editors express their appreciation and thanks to the Clarence Darrow family, including the widow of Paul Darrow, the attorney's only child, as well as his grandchildren Mrs. Jessie Johnston, Mrs. Mary Simonson, and Mrs. Blanche Chase, who were most co-operative in helping us to clear copyrights which they hold. And to our daughters Hedy Merrill and Anita Michelle, age nine, and Wendy Clare, age five, who sabotaged our work as little as possible, and were always ready to bring books and file cards as we needed them.

CONTENTS

"A lawyer without history or literature is a mechanic, a mere working mason; if he possesses some knowledge of these, he may venture to call himself an architect."
Sir Walter Scott, GUY MANNERING

INTRODUCTION

"I BELIEVED THAT THE CAUSE WAS WORTH WHILE."

This was the theme of Clarence Darrow as he trudged from courtroom to courtroom, for more than half a century, in defense of unpopular causes, of the damned, of the unfortunates—poor and rich, weak and strong—who found themselves in trouble.

It was the theme in many of his debates and lectures and writings as he proposed to a materialistic world that some day a new dawn would break when intellectual curiosity, understanding, equality and peace would dominate the world of man.

He was able to envision that future world. He was able to live his own life in accordance with its principles.

"I believed that the cause was worth while."

He believed it when he resigned his position as corporation counsel for the Northwestern Railroad to become attorney for Eugene Victor Debs and the American Railway Union. He believed it when he defended Haywood, Moyer and Pettibone on a murder charge, even though he disagreed with the direct-action philosophy of these officials of the Western Federation of Miners. He believed it as he pleaded his clients, the McNamara brothers, guilty of the *Los Angeles Times* bombing. It was the motivating force behind his defense of Dr. Ossian Sweet when the Negro doctor and his friends protected the doctor's home in Detroit. He believed it in the Leopold and Loeb case when he decried capital punishment and the wail of the mob for the life of these two boys; in the Scopes trial in Tennessee, in which he volunteered his services and paid his own expenses.

If he didn't believe it in the Massie case, he could at least understand what made the lieutenant take the law into his own hands and murder the man who had raped his wife.

"The cause was worth while." This he believed when he attacked man's conformity; when he defended Communists and Anarchists and Socialists, men and women charged with murder, theft, robbery. He believed it as he toured the lecture circuit arguing against free will, against prohibition, against capital punishment, against a prejudiced immigration law; as he debated religion, politics, science.

The question, "Who is this man Darrow?" was raised by a national magazine at the height of the Haywood, Moyer and Pettibone trial in 1907.[1]

The magazine article stated: "As the trial of Moyer and Haywood has proceeded, the country has been asking the question with some degree of interest, for it has been evident that Darrow is more than a hired attorney in this case. He is pleading for a cause as well as arguing for a client, and the cause is one very near to his heart."

And yet Chicago had first begun to ask that question, "Who is this man Darrow?" back in 1888. Darrow had delivered a speech on "Labor and Taxation." Henry George was the featured speaker at that meeting. Among those present were John Peter Altgeld, who four years later became governor of Illinois, and DeWitt C. Cregier. Both were impressed with the young attorney who had just come from the Western Reserve of Ohio. At Altgeld's suggestion, Cregier—who was elected mayor of Chicago a few weeks after the meeting—named Darrow assistant corporation counsel of Chicago.

In 1894, twelve years before the Haywood case, Darrow resigned his position as counsel for the Chicago and Northwestern

1. "Who Is This Man Darrow?" *Current Literature*, August, 1907.

Railroad, to become attorney for Eugene Victor Debs and the American Railway Union. Four years after the Debs case, he defended Thomas I. Kidd and two striking woodworkers in Oshkosh, Wisconsin, who were charged with conspiracy "to injure the business" of a lumber company through their union.

Who is this man Darrow?

He himself answered that question at perhaps the lowest point of his career, when he was on trial in Los Angeles, accused of bribing a juror in the McNamara case.

"What am I on trial for?" he asked the jury. "I am not on trial for having sought to bribe a man. . . . I am on trial because I have been a lover of the poor, a friend of the oppressed, because I have stood by labor for all these years, and have brought down upon my head the wrath of the criminal interests in this country . . . that is the reason I have been pursued by as cruel a gang as ever followed a man. . . .

"I have committed one crime which cannot be forgiven . . . I have lived my life and I have fought my battles, not against the weak and the poor—anybody can do this—but against power, against injustice, against oppression."

The months in Los Angeles, the ordeals of the two trials, fortified Darrow's already avowed pessimism. Jerry Giesler, who worked with Earl Rogers and Darrow in this case, related that Darrow was deeply embittered at the treatment he received in Los Angeles. "When he left town," Giesler wrote, "he shook my hand and said, 'Jerry, I'll never come back here again,' and he never did."[2]

Clarence Darrow is a folk hero; an American legend.

He was born near Kinsman, Ohio, on April 18, 1857, the son of Amirus Darrow, furniture maker, town undertaker, and the "village infidel"—not an inappropriate beginning for the man who was to be called by William Jennings Bryan "the greatest atheist or agnostic in the United States."

2. Jerry Giesler, *The Jerry Giesler Story* (New York, Simon and Schuster, 1960), p. 288.

After graduating from the district school in Kinsman, he attended the Academy, and from there he went for one year to Allegheny College at Meadville, Pennsylvania.

The greatest obstacle to young Clarence's scholastic record was baseball. He loved the game. There was nothing so exciting for him. He was deeply disillusioned, however, when he learned that teams hired the best players from a neighboring town and that local patriotism meant nothing.

He planned to return to college, but the panic of 1873 made it impossible. Instead, he went to work in the town's furniture factory and little store. During the winter he taught in a country school.

It was during his teaching days that he began the study of law. "I am not sure what influenced me to make this choice. I know that I never intended to work with my hands, and no doubt I was attracted by the show of the legal profession," he related years later.[3]

His legal education was one year of law school at Ann Arbor, Michigan, and a second year reading under a lawyer's direction in a law office in Youngstown, Ohio. He passed his examination and became a member of the Ohio bar at the age of twenty-one. He opened a law office first in Kinsman, then in Ashtabula, Ohio.

For a short time in 1878, he considered opening a "lawshop" in McPherson, Kansas. "I was looking for a place that seemed promising for opening a lawshop. I stopped a few days at Newton with old friends and drove one day from Newton to McPherson. . . . I looked the town over, and thought it was all right; so I rented an office, but did not take possession. . . . I never did go back to take that office. I don't know whether they have held it for me all these years," Darrow wrote in 1932, "but I have been a little afraid to go back for fear I would be sued for the back rent."[4]

Darrow did not move to Chicago until 1888, a year after the

3. Clarence Darrow, *The Story of My Life* (New York, Charles Scribner's Sons, 1934), p. 28.
4. Letter to Ralph Johnson, secretary of the Chamber of Commerce, McPherson, Kansas, January 30, 1932.

hanging of the Haymarket Anarchists. All his life he regretted that he had not been able to participate in the defense of these eight men. However, he was active in the amnesty movement. And when Governor Altgeld's political career came to an end because he pardoned the Anarchists, Darrow invited Altgeld to become a partner in his law firm. Altgeld did so, and remained until his death.

Chicago was Darrow's home from 1888 until he died in 1938, although he traveled widely, defending men and women in hundreds of courtrooms and lecturing on hundreds of platforms.

Darrow is remembered by most people as a courtroom hero, a glamorous advocate, the spokesman for "the weak and the poor," for the cause "worth while." But he was more than that. Even in the courtroom he was a social philosopher, a debunker, an educator, a lecturer, an aroused gadfly, a writer penning his words as he addressed juries.

"Men do not build for today; they build for tomorrow," he told the jury in the Kidd conspiracy case in Oshkosh, Wisconsin, in 1898. "They build for the centuries, for the ages; and when we look back, it is the despised criminal and outlaw, the man perhaps without home or country or friend, who has lifted the world upward and onward toward the blessed brotherhood which one day will come."

Darrow received a nominal fee of $250 for his defense in the Oshkosh case. But with it went a promise from the Woodworkers International Union that his jury argument would be publicized and mailed to the membership of the union.

In explaining his defense of twenty members of the Communist Labor Party two years after the end of World War I, Darrow told the jury, "When I entered the practice of my profession years ago I determined that there never should be a case, however unpopular, or whatever the feeling, where I would refuse to do my duty to defend that case; and I can honestly say to this jury that I have kept the faith; that I have never turned my back upon any defendant no matter what the charge. When the cry is the loudest the defendant needs the lawyer most."

Darrow had favored United States participation in World War I; but he decried the government's attempt to shackle the thinking of its citizens. "I shall not argue to you whether the defendants' ideas are right or wrong. I am not bound to believe them right in order to take their case, and you are not bound to believe them right in order to find them not guilty," he told the jury at the Communist trial.

And then he acclaimed the action of rebels throughout history. This approbation, too, is to be found in his writings and lectures. "What do you suppose would happen to the world except for these rebels?" he asked the jury. "You gentlemen," he continued, "owe whatever you have and whatever you hope for to those brave rebels who dared to think and dared to speak and dared to act; and if this jury should make it harder for any man to be a rebel, you would be doing the most you could for the damnation of the human race."

Darrow himself was a rebel. He always stressed the importance of questioning, of doubting, of wondering, of seeking. He was an agnostic student of the Bible; a hopeful pessimist; a sophisticated attorney with the mannerisms of a country lawyer.

He lived by his law practice, not for it.

At the turn of the century, when still a young man, he said, "I want to make my living as a lawyer and devote my leisure to writing stories and essays. And I want to write a long novel."[5]

In 1925, the *New York Times* quoted Darrow as saying: "For twenty-seven years my ambition has been to turn my attention to writing, but the law has so absorbed my attention that I have been unable to do so. I have reached the time when I have to turn away from the law and give my literary ambition a chance for expression."[6]

Yet Darrow had accomplished much in the literary field. His writing, like his speaking, was direct, simple and vigorous. There was little doubt as to what he was trying to say. He combined

5. "Who Is This Man Darrow?" *Current Literature*, August, 1907.
6. August 27, 1925.

realism and romanticism, and made a definite contribution to the development of realistic writing in America.

In all his writing there is an antagonism toward prejudice, ignorance, hate, bigotry. He was a skeptic and a dissenter, but always in defense of what he regarded as the positive right of the individual to liberty of speech, thought, and conduct. His writings express a great love for the universal, for the understanding of man and the longing for a "better day."

Darrow's jury pleas reveal his literary interests; they combine psychology, poetry, philosophy, and literature.

He inherited his devotion to reading and literature from his father. He received much of his education from the books in his father's library. "All his life my father was a visionary and dreamer," Darrow wrote in his autobiography. "Even when he sorely needed money he would neglect his work to read some book."[7]

During his lifetime, Darrow was a contributor to many small and insurgent magazines. One of his earliest articles appeared in the April, 1894, issue of *Current Topics*, where he discussed free trade. Even here there was the emphasis on the philosophy of love and good will to man.

"Protection appeals to the meanest sentiments of man, to the narrowest selfishness and the most sordid greed," Darrow wrote. "It teaches that nations should be enemies instead of friends and that the good of one may be promoted by the disaster and misfortune of the rest."

He continued: "It is in line with the spirit of caste and exclusiveness that has ruled the world; in keeping with the camps and armies, the forts and cannons that have disgraced the earth. It is the doctrine of hatred instead of love, and at war with the rising hope and aspiration of the day, 'when swords shall be beaten into plough-shares and the nations of the earth shall dwell in harmony and peace.' "

7. Darrow, *The Story of My Life*, p. 13.

Darrow's first literary work was a group of essays published in 1899 under the title *A Persian Pearl and Other Essays*. Omar Khayyam was "A Persian Pearl," and "Robert Burns," "Walt Whitman," "The Skeleton in the Closet," and "Realism in Literature and Art" were the "Other Essays."

Darrow felt a kinship with Omar, particularly in relation to the Persian poet's pessimistic philosophy; as a rebel, he sympathized with Burns and understood his dreams; he found in Walt Whitman an emotional tie, a kindred soul. In "The Skeleton in the Closet," he rattled the reader's subconscious mind long before the world heard of Sigmund Freud and psychoanalysis. This is probably the most original and penetrating of the essays.

The *Chicago Evening American* published a group of Darrow's essays in 1902. Called "Easy Lessons in Law," the series was based on actual cases revolving around two points of law which Darrow felt were unjust to the worker: the Doctrine of Assumed Risk, and the Doctrine of Fellow Servants.

Under the Doctrine of Assumed Risk, Darrow pinpoints the problem by telling of Tony Salvador, whose leg was cut off by a train while he was doing his cleaning job on the switches. The judge told the jury that "if Tony did not know better than to work in such a dangerous place, he assumed the risk and they must return a verdict for the defendant (the railroad)."

The employer is not liable if an injury to one employee is caused by the negligence or error of another. This is the Doctrine of Fellow Servants. One of the essays, "The Mystery of Law," tells the story of two men killed during a railroad accident caused by the negligence of the conductor. The widow of wealthy passenger Horace Bartlett was given five thousand dollars compensation. On the other hand, the widow of Robert Hunt, a brakeman on the train, was told that "the road was in no way responsible for her husband's death." She sued. The judge told her that her husband's death was due "to the negligence of the conductor . . . that the conductor and brakeman were fellow servants, and that therefore the company was not responsible."

Darrow concludes: Bartlett's widow went to France to soothe

her sorrow, Hunt's widow "is now doing washing for her neighbors."

"The Breaker Boy" is the story of Johnny McCaffery, who went to work in the coal mines at the age of eleven. It was written after Darrow returned from a preliminary investigation of the anthracite coal mines in Pennsylvania, and before he presented the case of the United Mine Workers Union in an arbitration hearing at Scranton and Philadelphia.

In "The Influences That Make the Law," Darrow pointed out that the essays "are not meant as a criticism to any class of men, but to give plain, concrete examples, generally drawn from real cases, of the way principles of justice have been warped and twisted by our commercial life.

"For some mysterious reason the public has been led to believe that judges were not men, that they were not influenced by the same feelings, training and prejudices that control the ordinary citizen. They have freely admitted that the public acts of all other officials should be subject to criticism, but contended that the judges should be exempt. Free and open criticism of all public acts, measures and policies is the only safeguard of liberty. And no remedy can be found for the unjust, unequal, oppressive laws under which we live except through public agitation and action."

Darrow's sharply delineated characters, his compassion and sensitivity for the despoiled, and his concern over the impersonality of business and the inequities of the legal machinery make these essays an effective exposition of the suffering the working man endures.

William Randolph Hearst did not pay Darrow for this writing. He was Darrow's client, and indulged him by printing his stories. They appeared in the Hearst papers in the same section with features by Tolstoy, Opie Reid, and Finley Peter Dunne.

Irving Stone, in his definitive biography of Darrow, calls these stories "authentic proletarian literature, written when proletarian literature was in its inception. They have a high if not altogether professional quality of literary excellence, for Darrow wrote almost as well as he talked; he wrote only when he was inflamed, and passion is a purveyor of good ink. He was a teacher and reformer; he would have laughed at art for art's sake. Everything he wrote had its purpose: to correct an evil, to avert an injustice, to assuage a suffering."[8]

"Little Louis Epstine" appeared in the December 1903 issue of *The Pilgrim*. The story of the nine-year-old Jewish newsboy from the Chicago slums is an ironic comment on the Christmas scene. In the struggle for bare survival, the poignant hopelessness, the futility of the striving, the bitterness of the story's ending, Darrow is telling the world the brutality of life in the slums.

Darrow's short stories, which today seem exaggerated and sentimental, exhibit the true muckraking style which Upton Sinclair made famous in *The Jungle* in 1905.

Resist Not Evil was published in 1903. At this time, Darrow was under the influence of Tolstoy. He admitted in the preface to the book that it did not contain any new ideas, but that it was inspired by the writings of this Russian "who was the first, and in fact the only, author of my acquaintance who seemed to me to place the doctrine of non-resistance upon a substantial basis."

The initial part of the book deals with the machinations of the state, its nature, the military, and civil government. The second part discusses crime and punishment and is pure Altgeldism, the theories and philosophy of John Peter Altgeld as expressed in his book, *Our Penal Code and Its Victims*. It was this book by Altgeld, given to Darrow by a police judge, which gave the young newcomer to Chicago what he often described as his first sane views on crime and criminals.

In writing an introduction to a reprint of *Resist Not Evil*, more than twenty years later, Darrow again confessed that at the time he wrote the book he was a devoted admirer of Tolstoy and that his ideas were largely influenced by the Russian writer's philosophy. "I still admire Tolstoy and class him as one of the greatest and highest type of literary artists that the world has ever known," Darrow said. "However, my scientific studies have convinced me

8. *Clarence Darrow for the Defense* (Garden City, New York, Garden City Publishing Company, 1941), p. 125.

that man can never reach a state of non-resistance. His structure is fixed . . . and under sufficient inducement the primal emotions will sweep away all the inhibitions and restraints that culture has woven around him. This was fully demonstrated in the great war. In spite of this change of view I am convinced that this book in the main is true."

Within the next two years, Darrow had two more books published. First came *Farmington*, a semi-autobiographical story of Darrow's own childhood in rural America.

At the age of seventy-five, in a preface to the book's 1932 edition, Darrow wrote: "There is no purpose in this story, and no lesson can be gleaned from its reading. It is neither fact nor fiction. But still, I could take my readers to a little rural town in Ohio that is much like Farmington. I could show them the old swimming-hole and the places where the fishes refused to bite. I could point out the boys and girls who are still outside the grave-yard fence, though the few who linger are headed in that direction, and are now quite near the gate that so often opened to let my neighbors in, but never by any chance swung wide enough to let them out. I doubt if any of these old boys and girls will recognize the pictures I have drawn. Their eyes have grown dim, and their memories vague, and they may not recall how important life was then, for our childhood in Farmington lasted such a little while, and was so long ago.

"The years are flying fast, I am going farther and farther from Farmington, but my wandering thoughts are ever returning to that land of dreams, recalling the faces that are no more, and the memories that remain. I need not tell the reader that some of these sketches are real, or were, 'once upon a time.' Nothing is strictly true in a world of constant change. Still, as one who is living beyond his time, I find that the images and recollections of my youth are more alluring than the people and scenes that greet me now. I am aware that this picture of the boys and girls and men and women that I knew really is a composite one, a blend of them all. Even my own form and personality of other days eludes me, and I do not at all realize that I am looking at my face when I scan old photographs of myself, however hard I try to remember just how things seemed and how I really felt."

The book itself concludes with Darrow's typical hopeful pessimism: "All my life I have been planning and hoping and thinking and dreaming and loitering and waiting. All my life I have been getting ready to begin to do something worth the while. I have been waiting for the summer and waiting for the fall; I have been waiting for the winter and waiting for the spring; waiting for the night and waiting for the morning; waiting and dawdling and dreaming, until the day is almost spent and the twilight close at hand."

A modern critic has called *Farmington* "The heart and soul of Darrow; a portrayal of the early influences of his life."[9] *The Dial*, reviewing the book in 1904, said: "It is a book for boys, for women—but above all, it is a book for men who have once been boys."[10]

To Irving Stone, *Farmington* "is perhaps the only one of his dozen books which achieves the artistic symmetry and perfection for which he longed."[11]

An Eye for an Eye was published the following year. This was a sociological novel and may well be the first of what was to be called in later years the proletarian literary school. Here again Darrow showed his compassion for the lower classes, subjected to the brutality of life.

It is the story of a slum dweller convicted of murdering his wife. As he sits in his death cell with his final visitor, hoping that word will come from the governor granting a reprieve, the doomed man relates the story of his life. He tells of the night of the murder. On the way home from work, Jim Jackson decided to get a drink, "and then I thought I could get enough steak for supper for just about what the drink would cost, and the steak would do the most

9. Dr. Preston Bradley, minister of the People's Church, Chicago, speaking at the Clarence Darrow Centennial celebration in Chicago, 1957.
10. *The Dial*, October 16, 1904.
11. *Clarence Darrow for the Defense*, p. 160.

good, and besides she and the kid could have some of that, and I thought it would make her feel pleasanter and liven her up a bit. We hadn't been gettin' along any too well for some time."

He brought the steak home, and "pretty soon I smelt the steak fryin' and went out in the kitchen. When I got there I found the steak fryin' in the skillet all right and her just takin' up the tea kettle to pour water on it. Now this made me mad for that wa'n't no way to fry steak."

This was the beginning of the night's argument which led to Jim reaching for a poker. He "grabbed it, and swung back as hard as ever I could."

But this is only part of the story Jim Jackson tells. He had been an orphan, had lived with an aunt and had completed the sixth grade in grammar school. At fourteen he was already working in the stockyards, then as a switchman for the railroads; he had been a striker, was blacklisted. He married the waitress in the neighborhood restaurant.

Married life was one quarrel after another. Though Jim and his wife agreed that their marriage had been a mistake and that they should be divorced, the settlement house and the priest to whom they turned for help opposed divorce, and they did not have the fifty dollars the lawyer wanted for handling the case.

The court-assigned lawyer who defended Jim Jackson in his murder trial was helpless before a prejudiced judge and jury. Jim was found guilty, and sentenced to be hanged.

As Jim's friend, Hank Clery, started to leave the death cell, he turned to Jim and took his hand. " 'Well, old fellow,' he said, 'I've got to go. I see you're all right, but take that Scotch whiskey when it comes; it won't do you any hurt. I'll look after everything just as I said. Good-bye.'

"Jim seemed hardly to hear Hank's farewell words.

" 'Well, good-bye.'

"Hank went outside the door and the guard closed and locked it as he turned away.

"Then Jim got up from his chair and stumbled to the door.

" 'Hank! Hank! S'pose—you—stop at the—telegraph—office—the

Western Union—and the—Postal—all of 'em—mebbe—might—be somethin'—'

" 'All right,' Hank called back, 'I will! I will!—I'll go to both to make sure if there's anything there; and I'll telephone you by the time you've got through eatin'.' "

Isabel Colbron, a critic for *The Bookman*, said about *An Eye for an Eye*, "If to create an illusion, to attain the effect aimed at, completely and entirely, is literary art, then Mr. Darrow's work is literary art of the highest, in spite of an apparent neglect of all the canons of literary art."[12]

The Independent said the "book is one that will hold the reader's interest from cover to cover."[13]

Professor Abe C. Ravitz, in his book, *Clarence Darrow and the American Literary Tradition*, published in 1962, writes that Darrow "emerged from his bout with Art, however, deserving a trophy not only for sociological veracity but also for genuine literary achievement."[14]

On the other hand, Irving Stone feels that though *An Eye for An Eye* is "repetitious and confused in structure," it nevertheless "contains magnificently written passages." Darrow was "more interested in getting over his ideas than in adhering to an art form." Mr. Stone believes that even Darrow realized that if the story were "better constructed it would have gained a wider public."[15]

Clarence Darrow came into the Haywood, Moyer and Pettibone case in 1907, after the United States Supreme Court had ruled that although the defendants had been extradited illegally from Colorado to Idaho, the case was out of its jurisdiction.

The three union officials were charged with the murder of the ex-governor of Idaho. At the time of the murder, they were in Colorado. The governor of Idaho requested their extradition, but

12. *The Bookman*, February, 1906.
13. October 26, 1905.
14. The Press of Western Reserve University, p. 85.
15. *Clarence Darrow for the Defense*, p. 177.

legal technicalities prevented this, so officials of both states co-operated and "kidnapped" Moyer, Pettibone and Haywood from Colorado into Idaho.

The fifty-year-old Darrow spoke to the jury for eleven hours. It is perhaps the best summation he ever made in his half century of practicing law, next to his plea in his own defense.

"I want to speak to you plainly," Darrow told the jury. "Mr. Haywood is not my greatest concern. Other men have died before him. Other men have been martyrs to a holy cause since the world began. Wherever men have looked upward and onward, forgotten their selfishness, struggled for humanity, worked for the poor and the weak, they have been sacrificed. They have been sacrificed in the prison, on the scaffold, in the flame. . . . But, gentlemen, you shortsighted men of the prosecution, you men of the Mine Owners' Association, you people who would cure hatred with hate, you who think you can crush out the feelings and the hopes and the aspirations of man by tying a noose around his neck . . . Don't be so blind in your madness as to believe that when you make three fresh new graves you will kill the labor movement of the world."

Then, commenting on the state's chief witness, Harry Orchard, who had confessed the actual bombing but implicated the three union officials—a man whom Darrow had described earlier as a "monstrous liar"—Darrow said: "I never asked for a human being's life and I hope that I may never ask for human life to the end of my days. I do not ask for his. And if the time should ever come that somebody pronounces against him the decree of death and nobody else asks to save his life, my petition will be there to save it, for I do not believe in it. I do not believe in man tinkering with the work of God. I do not believe in man taking away the life of his fellow-man."

The jury deliberated for twenty-one hours. Their verdict: not guilty.

With the acquittal, Darrow began to think of retiring; he wanted to do more writing. He returned to Chicago. He developed a diversified practice; he did some writing, lecturing, debating. He represented the strong and the weak, but never the strong against the weak.

Then came the *Los Angeles Times* bomb explosion of 1911, and the indictment of the McNamara brothers. The American Federation of Labor asked him to head the defense.

The McNamara case was a bitter battle and one which almost ended Darrow's career as a lawyer, since it led to his indictment by the state of California on two charges of jury tampering.

As he was preparing the McNamara case for trial, Darrow found evidence pointing to the guilt of his clients. Since he had always been an opponent of capital punishment, it was all-important to him to save his clients from hanging. He felt that the only way to accomplish this was through an agreement with the prosecution that he plead his clients guilty, and in return the state should not ask for the death penalty.

As the jury was being selected, Darrow interrupted the procedure to change the brothers' pleas from not guilty to guilty.

Labor, which had been aroused by what it called another Haywood case, was shocked. Darrow was accused by some of betraying his friends, while others agreed that it was the only thing he could have done.

Darrow's indictment followed soon after the change of plea in the McNamara case. His trial lasted three months. Defending Darrow were Earl Rogers, Jerry Giesler, Harry Dehme, Horace Appel and Darrow himself.

Darrow's argument in his own defense is the best he ever delivered. He pilloried his enemies; he restated his philosophy; he documented the social forces which created the McNamara brothers, and reaffirmed Lincoln Steffens' description of the *Times* blast as a "social crime."

He insisted: "I am tried here because I have given a large part of my life and my services to the cause of the poor and the weak, and because I am in the way of the interests. These interests would stop my voice—and they have hired many vipers to help them do it. They would stop my voice—my voice, which from the time I was a prattling babe, my father and mother taught me to raise for justice and freedom, and in the cause of the weak and the poor. . . .

"I have been, perhaps, interested in more cases for the weak and poor than any other lawyer in America, but I am pretty nearly done, anyhow. If they had taken me twenty years ago, it might have been worth their while, but there are younger men than I, and there are men who will not be awed by prison bars, by district attorneys, by detectives, who will do this work when I am done."

With tears in his eyes, he continued: "I would have walked from Chicago across the Rocky Mountains and over the long dreary desert to lay my hand upon the shoulder of J. B. McNamara and tell him not to place dynamite in the *Times* building. All my life I have counseled gentleness, kindness and forgiveness to every human being, and, gentlemen, at the same time, even speaking for my own liberty, I do not retreat one inch or iota from what I really believe as to this.

"I have loved peace all my life. I have taught it all my life. I believe that love does more than hatred. . . . Men are not perfect; they had an imperfect origin and they are imperfect today, and the long struggle of the human race from darkness to comparative civilization has been filled with clash and discord and murder and war and violence and wrong, and it will be for years and years to come. But ever we are going onward and upward toward the sunshine, where the hatred and war and cruelty and violence of the world will disappear."

Within thirty-four minutes the jury reported a verdict of not guilty.

But Darrow's ordeal was not over; he was tried on the second charge. To this second jury he said: "I have loved my fellow-men. I believe in the law of love. I believe it is the greatest and most potent force in all this great universe. I have loved peace, and I have had to fight almost from the time I opened my eyes—I have been fighting, fighting, fighting. I have grown weary of the fight. I began young. I have loved mercy and kindness and charity and gentleness, and the best I could I have practiced them as the years have come and gone. And it is for this, gentlemen, that I am here today, because I haven't condemned, I haven't judged; I have loved my fellow-man; I have loved the weak; I have loved the poor; I have loved the struggling; I have fought for their liberties, for their rights, that they might have something in this world more than the hard conditions that social life has given them; and I am here today in the hands of you twelve men because of that long fight."

The jury could reach no verdict and was discharged. The second indictment was dropped.

Sixteen months after he left Chicago for Los Angeles, the veteran attorney returned to his home town determined to retire.

But retirement was not for Clarence Darrow—not yet. Still to come were headlined cases in which he would be involved: the defense of Communists in Rockford and Chicago, of Anarchists in Milwaukee, the Scopes monkey trial, Leopold and Loeb, the Sweet case, the Massie trial.

World War I found Darrow forsaking his pacifism. Until this time, he had considered pacifism a sound philosophical doctrine that should rule men and states.

His sympathies from the beginning of the war had been with the French, the English and the Russians, although for several years he argued for American neutrality. But when Germany invaded Belgium, he felt that it was time for the United States to join the war on the side of the Allies.

He did not, however, become a professional patriot. He was skeptical of anyone who made a business of "loving his country." Time and again he said that many of the opponents of the war were idealists. Though he believed them wrong, he nevertheless felt that in most instances they were motivated by higher ideals than many who supported the war. He also confessed "misgivings" when he found that the war became popular in this country.

Many times he went to the government offices in Chicago to save from imprisonment someone who was anti-war, but who Darrow knew was not an enemy of the United States. Frequently he was able to help.

Soon after the Armistice, several states passed an Espionage Act which Darrow described as forbidding "free discussion, either orally or in the press."

At the same time, the Attorney General of the United States began to engage in the notorious Palmer raids, in which radicals of all descriptions were arrested, held incommunicado, indicted, convicted and imprisoned for expressing opinions contrary to popular thought.

It was in this atmosphere that Darrow defended the twenty Communists in Chicago and acted as attorney for Arthur Person in Rockford, Illinois.

Arthur Person worked in the factories of Rockford. He was indicted under an act passed by the Illinois Legislature which made it a crime to aid or assist or join a society which advocated the change or overthrow of the United States government by force and violence.

Person had joined the Communist Labor Party on the invitation of an old-time Socialist, a Dr. Olson, who was a long-time resident of Rockford and had at one time been a park commissioner of that city. Person joined the party; he became the local secretary; he dreamed.

"It may be a fool's dream," Darrow told the jury in his defense of Person in April 1920. "Perhaps all of our ideals and our hopes are fool ideals and hopes, perhaps the human race is destined for nothing better than it has always known; for an eternal struggle in war and peace; for sorrow, for rich and poor; for everlasting contention; for prisons and jails and prosecutors and detectives. Perhaps that is the best the human race can ever get, but if here and there a man or woman has a vision of something else, that the world can be made better and that our weak human nature can be changed and that instead of being wolves fighting for what we can get, there will come a time when the human race will be better and each seek the highest good of all; if men can have that vision it should be cherished because it makes them live in a glorious dream."

Then he told the jury: "If you want to get rid of every Socialist, of every Communist, of every trade unionist, of every agitator, there is one way to do it, and there is only one way to do it, and that is to cure the ills of society."

The jury found Arthur Person not guilty.

In the Communist case in Chicago a few months later, the defendants were intellectuals, many of them educated native-born Americans, including William Bross Lloyd whose mother was a McCormick.

Here again the charge was that of advocating the overthrow of the government. But Darrow had no illusions. It was only a few years after the Russian Revolution, yet Darrow probably could see what was happening there, despite his plea for the Communists' right to free speech in the United States.

"I would like to see the proletariat rule for a while, but I have few delusions left; they might not do any better than the others. I have seen workingmen that were not saints, lots of them. I am not trying to uphold the workingman or his opinion on the ground that he is a saint; he is not; he is human," Darrow told the jury.

The twelve men found the defendants guilty and sentenced them to various terms of from one to five years in addition to fines. But before any of the defendants started to serve their terms, the governor of Illinois pardoned them.

Two years before Darrow defended Leopold and Loeb in Chicago, his book *Crime: Its Causes and Treatment* was published. The theme of the book foreshadowed his plea for the two wealthy boys who committed what they planned as the perfect crime: kidnapping and murder.

Darrow wrote in the chapter "Responsibilities for Crime": "It is only lately that we are beginning to find out anything about the origin and nature of man. Laws have come down to us from old customs and folkways based on primitive ideas of man's origin, capacity and responsibility. It has been generally assumed that man was created different from all the rest of animal life; that man alone was endowed with a soul and with the power to tell good from evil; that in the beginning man was perfect but yielded to temptation, and since then has been the subject of an everlasting contest between the powers of light and the powers of darkness for the possession of his soul; that man not only knew good from evil, but was endowed with 'free will,' and had the power to choose between good and evil; and that when he did wrong he deliberately chose to do so out of an abandoned and malignant heart; and that all men alike were endowed with this power and all alike were responsible for their acts.

"The old indictments charged that: 'John Smith, being a wicked, malicious and evil-disposed person, not having the fear of God before his eyes, but being moved and seduced by the instigation of the devil, etc.' It followed, of course, that John Smith should be punished or made to suffer, for he had purposely brought all the evil on himself. The old idea is still the foundation of the world's judgment of men, in court and out. Of course this idea leaves no room for mercy and understanding. Neither does it leave any chance to give the criminal the proper treatment for his defects which might permit him to lead a normal life."[16]

The *Literary Review* said of the book: "A book of real value. To one interested in the human problem the book is of value because of its clarity. Mr. Darrow tells us in non-technical English what the psychiatrists and criminologists have had to coin new terms to convey."[17]

Darrow was called into the Leopold and Loeb case after the boys had confessed to the murder of fourteen-year-old Bobby Franks. "Save our boys," pleaded the families as newspapers and the state's attorney demanded their lives.

"Why did they kill little Bobby Franks?" Darrow asked in his plea. "Not for money, not for spite, not for hate. They killed him as they might kill a spider or a fly, for the experience. They killed him because they were made that way. Because somewhere in the infinite processes that go to the making up of the boy or the man something slipped, and those unfortunate lads sit here

16. New York, Thomas Y. Crowell, 1922, pp. 28, 29.
17. September 23, 1922.

hated, despised, outcasts, with the community shouting for their blood.

"I would not tell this court," he continued, "that I do not hope that some time, when life and age have changed their bodies, as it does, and has changed their emotions, as it does—that they may once more return to life. I would be the last person on earth to close that door to any human being that lives, and least of all to my clients."

Yet, he did not see the boys fit to be at large in a year, in ten years, in fifteen. "I believe they will not be until they pass through the next stage of life, at forty-five or fifty," Darrow told the judge.

The Leopold and Loeb case gave Darrow a national platform from which to express his views on capital punishment. Many said he had betrayed himself by defending these wealthy youths who admitted their guilt; that he sold his idealistic principles for a million-dollar defense. But to Darrow, this argument was that of a frenzied public clamoring for the life of two sick unfortunate boys.

"In a terrible crisis there is only one element more helpless than the poor, and that is the rich. I knew then, and I know now, that except for the wealth of the families a plea of guilty and a life sentence would have been accepted without a contest," Darrow wrote in his autobiography eight years later.[18]

He confessed to Judge Caverly: "I do not know what it was that made these boys do this mad act, but I do know there is a reason for it. I know they did not beget themselves. I know that any one of an infinite number of causes reaching back to the beginning might be working out in these boys' minds, whom you are asked to hang in malice and in hatred and injustice, because someone in the past has sinned against them."

Turning to the state's attorneys, he said: "Do you think you can cure the hatreds and the maladjustments of the world by hanging them? You simply show your ignorance and your hate when you say it. You may here and there cure hatred with love and

18. *The Story of My Life*, p. 232.

understanding, but you can only add fuel to the flames by cruelty and hate. . . .

"I am pleading for the future," Darrow concluded. "I am pleading for a time when hatred and cruelty will not control the hearts of men, when we can learn by reason and judgment and understanding and faith that all life is worth saving, and that mercy is the highest attribute of man."

After several weeks' deliberation Judge Caverly sentenced Leopold and Loeb to ninety-nine years plus life. Twelve years later, Loeb was killed in a prison fight. In March, 1958, on the twentieth anniversary of Darrow's death, a rehabilitated fifty-two-year-old Nathan Leopold was paroled from the state penitentiary at Joliet, Illinois.

Not quite a year after the Leopold and Loeb case, Darrow met the "defender of the faith" and "Great Commoner," William Jennings Bryan, in Dayton, Tennessee. Darrow had been a friend of Bryan, he had campaigned for him twice in his bids for election to the presidency of the United States. But their paths had drifted apart. The doubter, the questioner, the agnostic was bitter about Bryan's campaign to pass anti-evolution laws.

"Education was in danger from the source that always hampered it—religious fanaticism,"[19] Darrow believed; and for the first and only time in more than half a century as an attorney—always for the defense, never for the prosecution—he volunteered his services to defend the Dayton schoolteacher.

The challenge was simple so far as Darrow was concerned: "If today you can take a thing like evolution and make it a crime to teach it in the public school, tomorrow you can make it a crime to teach it in the private school, and the next year you can make it a crime to teach it from the hustings or in the church. At the next session you may ban books and the newspapers. Soon you may set Catholic against Protestant and Protestant against Protestant, and try to foist your own religion upon the minds of men.

19. *The Story of My Life*, p. 249.

... After a while, Your Honor," he told the judge, "it is the setting of man against man and creed against creed until, with flying banners and beating drums, we are marching backward to the glorious ages of the sixteenth century when bigots lighted faggots to burn the men who dared to bring any intelligence and enlightenment and culture to the human mind."

H. L. Mencken, writing about Darrow and the Dayton events, said: "The marks of battle are all over his face. He has been through more wars than a whole regiment of Pershings. And most of them have been struggles to the death. Has he always won? Superficially, yes; actually, no. Did Darrow best Bryan at Dayton? There, I think, he came closest to a genuine victory. The thing was inconceivably dramatic: two ancient warlocks brought jaw to jaw at last. It was superb to see Darrow throw out his webs and prepare his baits. His virtuosity never failed. In the end Bryan staggered to the block and took that last appalling clout. It was delivered calmly, deliberately, beautifully. Bryan was killed as plainly as if he had been felled with an ax. Imbecilities, you say, live on? They do. But they are not as safe as they used to be. Some day, let us hope, they will be put down. Whoever at last puts them down will owe half his bays to Clarence Darrow."[20]

Again Darrow began to think of retiring.

But in 1926 he was asked to undertake the defense in the Sweet case. A white mob in Detroit attempted to drive a Negro family out of the home they had purchased in a white neighborhood. In the struggle, a white man was killed, and the eleven Negroes in the house were arrested and charged with murder.

To Darrow, this was not a murder case. At the trial, he told the jury: "The State claims there was no mob there that night. Gentlemen, the State has put on enough witnesses who said they were there, to make a mob."

For forty-six hours the jury was in seclusion without reaching a verdict. The judge dismissed them. The defense suggested that each defendant be tried separately, if there were to be any more

20. *Vanity Fair*, 1928.

trials. Five months later, a brother, Henry Sweet, was brought to trial.

Darrow told the all-white jury on that May morning in 1926: "I insist that there is nothing but prejudice in this case; that if it was reversed and eleven white men had shot and killed a black while protecting their home and their lives against a mob of blacks, nobody would have dreamed of having them indicted. They would have been given medals instead. . . .

"I do not believe in the law of hate. I may not be true to my ideals always, but I believe in the law of love, and I believe you can do nothing with hatred. I would like to see a time when man loves his fellow-man and forgets his color or his creed. We will never be civilized until that time comes. I know the Negro race has a long road to go. I believe the life of the Negro race has been a life of tragedy, of injustice, of oppression. The law has made him equal, but man has not. And after all, the last analysis is, what has man done?—and not what has the law done? I know there is a long road ahead of him, before he can take the place which I believe he should take. I know that before him there is suffering, sorrow, tribulation and death among the blacks, and perhaps the whites. . . . I would advise toleration; I would advise understanding; I would advise all of those things which are necessary for men who live together."

The verdict: not guilty.

Darrow returned to Chicago, he continued to practice law, he talked of retirement, he continued to write for magazines and engaged in one of his youthful passions, the love of debate. He toured the lecture platform.

Long before the Volstead Act was passed, Darrow wrote articles and spoke against prohibition. As early as 1909, he delivered talks against prohibition. With biting sarcasm, he said: "Prohibition would not interfere with the rich; it was never meant to interfere with them. Of course, the poor man would be shut off now and then; but why not? What business is there for a poor man to drink? It is his business to work. Anyhow, he is not able to control his own appetite, and he needs his money; he has no right to fool it away."

After the Eighteenth Amendment to the Constitution was passed, Darrow continued to lecture, write and debate the question. As he himself said: "I never missed a chance to speak or write against prohibition." He tagged prohibition as "the damnedest nonsense ever invented by a set of political cowards . . . breeding disrespect for law and for the Federal government itself faster than a horse can trot."

Dr. Clarence True Wilson, General Secretary of the Methodist Board of Temperance, Prohibition and Public Morals, was one of his opponents in a number of prohibition debates. The doctor recalled that he received a wire from the temperance forces in Ohio, asking him to debate Darrow. "I wanted to get at him and accepted the debate," Dr. Wilson said.

If there was any man in the United States whom he abhorred, Dr. Wilson wrote in a magazine article, Darrow was that man. Darrow's views and the doctor's always differed. "The folk I thought a menace to society he championed. I was deeply prejudiced against him."

Describing their first meeting, Dr. Wilson reminisced, "We met in a hotel. I recognized Darrow by his pictures. Unintroduced, I accosted him and gave him my name. We at once walked into the dining room to breakfast together.

"I saw no horns. I saw instead the face of one of the most genial, lovable, friendly, frank men our nation ever produced. We did not conceal any of our differences, but listened tolerantly to the other's views. We spent nearly three hours at that table, and before the debate came that night I dreaded having to attack my opponent, for I was learning to admire him.

"That night before a vast throng the battle royal was waged. I saw the other side of Darrow: the fighter. I took personal thrusts."

Darrow classified Dr. Wilson among the reformers who had never done any good but "curse the earth." He described the Methodist Building, where the doctor lived and had his office, as the Methodist Vatican. The prohibitionists became "the long-haired men and the short-haired women."

"I found Darrow in action one man and Darrow in friendly intercourse another. I liked him in both—heart-warming in friendship and interesting in fight.

"The debate over, I introduced him to my wife. He said to her: 'Your husband debates like a gentleman. If I had known you were here, I wouldn't have been such a ruffian.'

"If kindness and brotherliness, square dealing, fair treatment, doing unto others as you would have them do to you are Christian traits, then Darrow had the Christian characteristics without a Christian creed."[21]

Another man who debated him on prohibition was Dr. John Haynes Holmes, minister of the Community Church of New York. Dr. Holmes said: "Of all the men I have ever known—men rich and poor, literate and illiterate, conservative, liberal, and radical—I would rank Darrow with Gandhi of India as the gentlest, sweetest, most piteous. He had his moments of protest and alarm, his occasions of fierce anger, his furious outbursts of abhorrence and contempt. But, like summer gales, these quickly passed, and pity ruled again. Darrow in his ordered life met the supreme test; he found it easy to forgive his enemies, and love them, for he had great mercy upon them."[22]

Paul H. Douglas, senior United States Senator from Illinois, has photographs of three people hanging in his Washington office, one of them a portrait of Clarence Darrow. He says that "Clarence opened up people's minds and made them more ready to see the difficulties faced by the underdogs of society."[23] The others whose pictures hang in the senator's office are Jane Addams of Hull House, and the insurgent senator from Nebraska, George Norris.

Will Durant first met Darrow in 1921, when he asked Darrow to debate with him on the subject, "Is Progress Real?" The proceeds of the debate were to help Durant meet the deficit on the Labor Temple School in New York City. Darrow agreed, and to

21. Clarence True Wilson, "Darrow, Friendly Enemy," *Forum*, July, 1938.
22. John Haynes Holmes, *I Speak for Myself, the Autobiography of John Haynes Holmes* (New York, Harper and Brothers, 1959), p. 263.
23. Letter to the editors, January 23, 1963.

Durant's request as to what he would charge, replied, "Nothing."

However, while Durant was in Darrow's office, Darrow received a request to give an address in Rochester and quoted a fee of four hundred dollars. "I was overwhelmed by his generosity," Durant writes. "He had never heard of me—it was five years before *The Story of Philosophy*. He just took my word about the work we were doing in adult education."

Durant continues: "As a speaker he was the quietest and most informal talker imaginable; yet people hung so intently on his every word that it carried to the farthest ends of Carnegie Hall, without a microphone. As a man he was one of the gentlest and quietest men I have ever met.

"Several times I debated him—on 'Is Man a Machine?' and 'Is Life Worth Living?' He used to overcome me by brilliance of wit and sheer force of personality. When I asked him the silly question, 'If you think life is not worth living, why do you continue in it?' he answered: 'I continue to live through blind and unreasoning instinct, not through rational intelligence; but if I should happen to die, God help the man who dared to restore me to life!'

"After our debates we used to go and dunk doughnuts together in a nearby café. When he lectured in a Flatbush temple near our home, he spent the night with us, and kept us entranced for an hour, as he sat on the bed in his night dress, reading to us Housman's *Shropshire Lad*. He was especially fond of Mrs. Durant, who loved him this side of adultery. Doubtless he had his faults, but we never found them."[24]

Attorney Morris Ernst knew Clarence Darrow "quite well," and feels that: "his contributions to our culture were substantial though subtle. It was admirable for him," says Mr. Ernst, "to shift from the wealth of acting as a corporate attorney to the defense of the unpopular. In basic historic terms a strong negative value impinged on this shift of stance. He helped decidedly to increase the un-

24. Letter to the editors, December 21, 1962.

fortunate identification of trial lawyer and client, leaving the impression that a lawyer in the United States had no real resemblance to the barrister function in England. I lived through a shameful episode when leading liberal lawyers approached Clarence to reduce his pain when he was to be advised that he wasn't competent to argue the appeal in the United States Supreme Court in the Scopes case. This is part of the same ambiguous symbolism that exists in our legal folkway. Many leading devoted liberal lawyers thought that the case would be prejudiced in our highest court if a lawyer branded as an attorney for the unpopular were to argue the case. They made a pitch which was entirely phony that Clarence knew no law and added, subject to denial by his corporate legal acumen, that he represented big financial interests.

"As a writer," Mr. Ernst continues, "he was soft and generous and without any real punch. He needed the visual symbol of his person, slouching and gangling, thus looking as if he had little spine when, in fact, he was all backbone although many people thought he was just jelly. His technique as an advocate was unique. John Davis used the technique of simplification; Steuer had a bag of tricks, such as remembering a difficult set of statistics to impress the jury; Untermeyer used ego manpower, etc., and Clarence used love, sympathy and human understanding. He identified himself with the harassed witness and by love and affection produced testimony in many situations of aid to the defendant—as the witness dragged those emphases out of his memory and would return to Clarence the affection the witness had for Clarence."[25]

"He was one of the great trial lawyers of our century," attorney Edward Bennett Williams says of Clarence Darrow. "His professional career dramatizes as perhaps no other the safeguards of the Sixth Amendment on the right to counsel."[26]

"Darrow was less of a lawyer in the lawyer sense either of being a profound legal scholar, or even of being a great advocate," is the

25. Letter to the editors, November 29, 1962.
26. Letter to the editors, December 3, 1962.

opinion of attorney Louis Nizer. "He was more of a philosopher, humanist (despite a cynical demeanor), whose views spilled over into the legal realm."[27]

To United States Senator Jacob K. Javits of New York, a member of the Senate Committee on Labor and Public Welfare, Clarence Darrow "first and foremost was a man thoroughly humanitarian in his ideals.

"As a lawyer, he was one of the leaders in our nation's progress toward the world's best working conditions for labor, pioneering in the establishment of collective bargaining as the foundation of our present labor laws; he worked to expose corruption in municipal and state government; and he pressed the courts to modernize their approach to crimes by the mentally ill.

"Clarence Darrow's dream," continues Senator Javits, "was of a world without cruelty where men would be led by their minds rather than by their emotions. But he knew that to win men to his side, he must appeal to their emotions as well as to their minds, and his oratorical style reflected this conviction. He spoke with constant geniality, an ironic humor, and a vigorous imagination. In debate, though, his words were unrehearsed; he could be powerfully convincing.

"Darrow's attitudes towards labor, religion and capital punishment, among other subjects, were considered shockingly unconventional for his time. But already we have sufficient perspective, I think, to recognize the great role he played in bringing to our nation the conditions which made possible our present position of world leadership for freedom. His qualities of vigor and freshness of thought are vitally needed today to meet the challenge to that leadership."[28]

But not all people feel this way about Darrow. Edgar Lee Masters, for example, was for eight years a member of Darrow's law firm. In his autobiography, Masters, referring to Darrow only in the third person or as "this criminal attorney," asserted that

27. Letter to the editors, December 18, 1962.
28. Letter to the editors, January 15, 1963.

though Darrow regarded himself as an altruist, he, Masters, doubted it.

Masters pointed out that he knew Darrow since 1898, when he was instrumental in having Darrow appointed attorney for the receiver of a bankruptcy. "When the time came for us to settle our fees, this criminal lawyer resented my demands and grabbed the larger share of the money, though I had done most of the work."[29]

Masters also wrote that his father-in-law disliked Darrow, doubted his sincerity and honesty of mind, and called Darrow "an immoral fellow," "an anarchist and a disturber." Although Masters wrote one poem in praise of Darrow, he wrote another in which he called Darrow not a "giant" among men, but a "dwarf."

The daughter of Earl Rogers, chief counsel in the Darrow jury bribery case, calls Darrow a "phony" and asserts that "facts are forgotten. Darrow went down in history almost entirely for cases he tried after his escape from the jury bribery charges in Los Angeles; and, to pin it down, few of them had much to do with the poor, the weak and the helpless."[30]

Darrow's debates were always on social, political and religious problems. Even his essays on personalities always concerned the individual and his relationship to the social issues.

In debates he usually took the negative side of the question. Does Man Live Again? Does Man Have Free Will? Is Religion Necessary? Can the Individual Control His Own Conduct? Darrow's answer to all was "No." Is Civilization a Failure? The hopeful pessimist responded in the affirmative.

Perhaps Norman Thomas gave a key to Darrow's "no-sayer" approach in debates. He recalls Darrow's debate with the socialist lawyer Morris Hillquit on American membership in the World Court, on the basis of a protocol approved by Charles Evans Hughes.

29. Edgar Lee Masters, *Across Spoon River* (New York, Farrar and Rinehart, 1936), p. 272.
30. Adela Rogers St. John, *Final Verdict* (New York, Doubleday, 1962), p. 458.

As the debaters were ready to go to the platform, Darrow whispered to Thomas: "Norman, have you got a copy of the protocol of the court?"

Thomas said, "No, not with me. I'm only presiding. Does that mean you haven't read it?"

"Yes," Darrow answered.

"Then how will you debate it?"

"Trust me," Darrow said. "I can debate any question in the negative."[31]

At another debate, this time with T. V. Smith—then professor of philosophy at the University of Chicago, later a congressman-at-large from Illinois, and today professor emeritus of citizenship-philosophy at the Maxwell Graduate School of Syracuse University —Darrow again exemplified his aplomb in debating the negative.

Professor Smith recalls: "While Clarence Darrow, the great criminal lawyer, was still alive and the darling of minority groups in America, somebody failed him as a debating foil for a benefit performance; and I as a young man was asked to go into the arena with the old lion to be eaten alive for some good cause."[32]

The subject was: "Can the Individual Control His Own Conduct?" or, "Is Man a Free Agent, or Is He the Slave of His Biological Equipment?"

Professor Smith argued that the individual can control his own conduct in the same manner that society controls the individual's conduct and the individual controls other people's conduct. He cited Darrow as an example: Darrow, he said, could take almost any jury and persuade them to give the verdict he wanted. Darrow controlled the jury by the mechanism of speech, by talking to them. The same mechanism used to control other people's conduct could be used by the individual to control his own. He added that both Darrow and he knew that the issues they were discussing were actually the questions of freedom and responsibility of man.

31. Norman Thomas, speaking at the Clarence Darrow Centennial celebration in Chicago, May 1, 1957.
32. T. V. Smith, *Live Without Fear* (New York, New American Library, 1956), p. 154.

When it was Darrow's turn to speak, he candidly told the audience that if he had time to think over what the professor had said he "might be able to figure out exactly wherein we disagree. But since I don't, I will proceed to talk about free will and determinism and mechanism just as if I had not heard him."[33]

These debates which Darrow engaged in gave the public who knew him only as a criminal attorney, from newspaper stories and headlines, an opportunity to see and hear him. Wherever and whenever he spoke, the hall was packed; at times many were turned away.

Darrow also co-authored a book on prohibition and co-edited a volume on agnosticism.

The Prohibition Mania, with Victor S. Yarros, published in 1927, presented the authors' case against prohibition. They assert that there is no evidence that "any substantial net good" has resulted from prohibition; that it is an "outrageous and senseless invasion" of personal liberty and that it is "a legislative lie and absurdity."

In 1929, with Wallace Rice, Darrow co-edited *Infidels and Heretics*, in which they presented an agnostics' anthology.

Darrow started to write *The Story of My Life* in 1928 during a trip to Europe. Friends had been urging him to write his autobiography, but Darrow resisted. Actually, *The Story of My Life* is more his philosophy than it is a chronology of events. This book, which was published in 1932, discusses only a few of the thousands of people with whom he came in contact; few of his cases and trials are recorded.

In *The Story of My Life*, which became one of the top ten best sellers in the country, we find his thoughts on the law and lawyers, the Bar Association, child training, World War I, prohibition, the Negro, crime and criminals, religion, capital punishment, and labor.

The *New York Times* said of the book: "It is well worth any intelligent person's cultivating; indeed, he would be worth while

33. Haldeman-Julius Publications, Girard, Kansas.

if only for his simple and often moving prose."[34] A critic in the *Saturday Review* said: "A remarkable book. . . . There are only two defects in the book. One is a certain verbosity and the other is a certain absence of humor."[35]

On the other hand, the *Outlook* critic wrote: "He [Darrow] writes well—simply and with humor."[36]

The same year *The Story of My Life* appeared, Darrow left for Honolulu to defend the Massie case. Lieutenant Massie, with the help of friends, forced a confession from one of the Japanese assailants of his wife and killed him. The victim had been awaiting re-trial on the charges of the rape of Mrs. Massie.

In this case, too, the lawyer presented his fatalistic philosophy of "causes and motives." Before leaving Chicago for Hawaii, Darrow told newspapermen: "It would be very unfortunate if any race issue were injected into the situation."[37]

To the jury, the seventy-five-year-old Darrow concluded: "I have put this case without appeal to the nationality or race of any juror, asking them to pass on it as a human case.

"We're all human beings. Take this case with its dire disasters, written all over by the hand of fate, as a case of your own, and I'll be content with your verdict. What we do is affected by things around us; we're made more than we make."

The jury found the defendants guilty of manslaughter, but recommended leniency. Before the defendants served any time in jail, the sentence was commuted by the governor of the island.

Darrow's last major public appearance was not in a court of law. It was as chairman of a Board of Review of the National Recovery Administration, to which he was appointed by President Franklin D. Roosevelt. Charges were being leveled against the NRA that it was favoring big business though expressing concern for the small business man.

34. February 7, 1932.
35. May 21, 1932.
36. March, 1932.
37. *Chicago Daily News,* March 16, 1932.

The review board conducted almost sixty public hearings, examined thirty-four codes, considered about three thousand complaints, and concluded that the NRA "tends toward monopolies." That report was a prelude to the decision of the United States Supreme Court declaring the NRA unconstitutional.

Darrow died on March 17, 1938. Two years later, Congressman T. V. Smith of Illinois, the man who first met him in debate in 1926, inserted into the Congressional record on April 18, 1940, on the eighty-third anniversary of Darrow's birth:

"Mr. Speaker and Members of the House, this is the birthday of Clarence Darrow, one of Illinois' latest and greatest sons. The biography of every man, even of the most heroic, is but this trinity of sadness: 'Born, troubled, died.'

"Darrow was born eighty-three years ago; he was troubled all his life by man's inhumanity to man; he died two years ago at his home in Chicago.

"Darrow hated to die. Defender of the defenseless, he died to prove, as he lived to argue, that life is accidental and death its slow sure doom. Born in Kinsman, Ohio, Darrow lived in kinship universal and died an undisputed king of human kindliness. Others he saved from the Grim Reaper; himself he could not save. Let the muffled heartbeats of humanity be his fitting elegy as we bethink ourselves of his gallant ashes on this and every birthday."

Smith concluded, "Darrow is dead. Long live Darrow."

ARTHUR AND LILA WEINBERG

PART ONE

ON SOCIAL ISSUES

THE RIGHT
OF
REVOLUTION

All history justifies the right of revolution.
Much that we enjoy was born of revolution.

1895. Japan and China sign peace treaty . . . U.S. Naval officers test Browning automatic gun . . . Terror reigns in Armenia . . . Irish National Convention at Chicago organized to free Ireland from Great Britain by force . . . Empress of Russia gives birth to daughter . . . Bourgeois form conservative radical cabinet in France . . . Admiral says U.S. not prepared to engage in war with any first-class power . . . Oscar Wilde convicted and sentenced to two years hard labor . . . Third daughter born to President and Mrs. Taft . . . Marquis of Salisbury accepts British premiership . . . Debs sentenced to six months in jail.

THE RIGHT OF REVOLUTION IS planted in the heart of man; it is born of the dignity that causes him to feel his personality and defend his right to a free and independent life; it is nurtured and aided by the unjust oppression that comes from without. Except for this, it would have no chance to grow.

In the light of what I know of human nature and history, I cannot think that England has been different from other lands. I cannot think that she is more unjust to the struggling Irishmen than my own country was to the helpless black, or is today to the helpless men, women and little children who toil from day to day for the barest right to live. I am aware that in America the Irish cause is a popular theme; all our political conventions for years have passed resolutions favoring Irish independence. The cause of Poland is popular here. The cause of Hawaii is popular in America. The cause of Cuba is very dear to us. The cause of all the poor of all the earth, except our own, touches the generous and overflowing Yankee heart. I know that with this audience, and perhaps in this country, Irish independence, either with or without force, is a favorite theme. I know, too, that this is not the world, and that Great Britain is very strong. Wiser men than I must counsel such a move, for talking is one thing, fighting quite another.

But here let me say, whether I speak of Ireland or Poland or America, that all history justifies the right of revolution. Much that we enjoy was born of rebellion—of protest against the ruling power, not by resolutions and paper ballots, but with gun and sword. To honor Washington, Franklin, Jefferson and Paine, we must respect the right of revolution for which they so bravely pleaded and fought. Neither will it do for us to say that revolutions were once right, but now are wrong.

The history of the world, like the programs of a theater, presents different names down through the ages, but the part they play in the great drama of life (or the small one) is the same in every land and age. But revolutions are not made, they are born. All the conspirators and agitators of the world, if left free to speak and act and plan, could not produce a respectable rebellion in the smallest kingdom of the world unless the time was ripe. And all the armies and policemen of the earth could not hold one in check when the time has come. I have little faith in deliberate plans for revolution—as well plan an earthquake or tornado. It must be remembered, too, that they who undertake the cause of rebellion take the chances of their cause; with governments as with men, self-protection is the first law of nature; and right or wrong, he who forcibly undertakes revolution must expect to pay the penalty unless he shall succeed. The high motive of the revolutionists is one side, the strength of the government to protect itself is the other.

Again, man is a part of the general scheme; his movements are as much the subject of general law as are the revolutions of the planets in their spheres. A convulsion of society is like any other convulsion of nature; it comes—we may or may not know the reason why. The earth seemed solid underneath Lisbon when the sun rose bright and clear one morning a hundred years ago, but it opened and swallowed her. No doubt the streets of Pompeii were filled with beautiful women and brave men when nature, one day, determined to drive these promenaders out, and use the thoroughfares for red-hot lava instead. It was some higher power than man's that decreed that France and Europe could not be cleansed, unless for a time, instead of water, the sewers of Paris should be flushed with blood.

The Lisbon earthquake, the burial of Pompeii, the French revolution—these are some of the resistless manifestations of the great power which now and then teaches man how weak and futile are all his plans and schemes in the presence of the great Infinite.

The French revolution was not the work of Rousseau and Voltaire; it did not come from teaching theories and making speeches. Through long weary years French kings had wasted the substance of an empire in riotous living and princely indulgence; nobles and favored retainers had grown fat upon the sufferings of the poor; the church and clergy had become corrupt and greedy beyond measure. Beneath all this mass of privilege and vested right the poor peasant vainly struggled and staggered with his load. One day, without premeditation or thought, he arose and shook himself, and thrones and nobles and laws and institutions fell in one smoldering heap.

Victor Hugo, in his immortal work, *Les Miserables*, sends the kind priest to reason with the old dying revolutionist, who sat on the porch of his hermit's cottage, waiting for night and death, which were coming side by side. The priest upbraids him for the cruelty of the revolution; the old man rouses from his dying stupor and says: "You speak of the revolution—a storm had been gathering for fifteen hundred years; it burst, you blame the thunderbolt."

The American Revolution was not the work of Adams or Henry or Franklin or Paine; it was neither any of these nor all who made the revolution of 1776; it was the cruel, unjust restriction of centuries; it was the strong, constant, ever futile effort of conservatism, oppression and tyranny to hold back the resistless tide of progress; to restrain that great sea which ever alternately ebbs and flows, but which, through all, is ever rising higher and higher and sweeping away thrones and empires and states, laws and customs and institutions, and slowly widening the liberty of man.

So Ireland and all the Irish of the world cannot make a revolution; they may hold conventions and assemblies, they may make speeches and pass resolutions, but if grievances are not real, if oppressions are not intolerable, the conflagration will not come. England, however, can bring revolution around her head. If just grievances go unheard and unrelieved; if complaints and demands are answered by the prison and greater coercion laws; if poverty and misery increase with growing wealth, then the thunderbolt will some time fall.

The world is changing; laws and systems are being tried as they never were before. The spirit of freedom is abroad today upon the earth. Germany is a great military camp, but the tramp of her armed soldiers is lost in the cry of her workmen for the right to live. France is being shaken by a revolution of thought more powerful and logical than that which marked the last century's close. Tyrannical Russia, with all her arbitrary powers and despotic, cruel force, cannot make the life of the czar safe in his own domain; and the poor, outraged political prisoner in the Siberian mine is greater and better and more powerful in the world of thought and action than the proudest Cossack whose iron heel rests on the peasant's neck. England, Italy, Spain, Austria and the Netherlands are struggling with this rising mass of discontent that demands a portion of the earth and the right to live and breathe.

The century is closing, the old is dying; the new, let us hope, is coming; the great hostile armies of Europe are no longer kept to be turned against alien lands, but to shoot down discontent at home. All Europe and all Asia are anxiously watching for the general carnage to begin; and when it comes, who can foretell the end, or conjecture the shape of a European map after the war clouds pass away? In this great conflict—if conflict there is to be—will the poor and oppressed join the armies of their kings and fight their brethren of other lands? The workingmen of the world are fast learning the doctrine of the brotherhood of man; they are joining hands regardless of nation and of creed, for the common good; they are looking forward to that universal brotherhood which has been the dream of the poet and the nightmare of the king. In such a cataclysm the opportunity of the disinherited may come. If these lowering, threatening war clouds burst, as some day they must and will, then Ireland may break the chain that holds her an unwilling captive to the British power.

But these reflections must concern us most as they apply to our own native or adopted land. Most of us, I hope, are patriots; patriots not in the meaning in which that word is chiefly used today. The ordinary fair-weather patriot goes out upon the street corners, and in public places, and proclaims his love for American institutions as a cloak for the support of the existing wrongs, which make him rich and great; he uses his patriotism as he does the other tools with which he plies his trade; patriotism to him does not mean devotion to his country and the people's highest good, but a blind, unthinking worship of the things that are; the constitution and the laws, to him, are to be either enforced or broken as it may profit at the time; his is the patriotism that flies an American flag from the schoolhouse, and sacrifices the most vital and fundamental principles of liberty for gain. This patriotism is the patriotism of the demagogue and time-server, and was voiced by Webster, who, with all his greatness, was too small to be brave and true. It found expression in the sentiment which was repeated a few nights since by a United States senator-elect in Chicago, and which is only fit to be quoted at the end of a banquet freely interspersed with wine. Webster and the time-serving patriot said: "My country, may she ever be right; but right or wrong, my country." True patriotism, the patriotism of O'Connell, of Jefferson, of Sumner, of Emerson, so loves its country and prizes her name as to condemn evil the sooner when found at home.

The patriotism that is worthy of a place in any human heart takes little account of mountains and rivers and forests or of boundary lines, but makes much of the men and women and children of the earth. It loves that country best where freedom is the broadest and opportunity the greatest. It holds fast to all the old guarantees of liberty and ever strives to break down the walls and restrictions of the past. It looks eagerly forward to the time when forts and garrisons, swords and cannons, militias and standing armies shall no longer disgrace the earth. It longs for the day when nations and individuals shall learn that peace is more profitable and glorious than war; when the walls and boundaries and restrictions which divide nation from nation, and man from man, shall fade like a cruel dream of the past, and liberty and order shall prevail on earth.

America has furnished a bright example of the beneficence of liberty and the wisdom of opportunity. The fathers here established freedom on the broadest plain the world had ever known, and the wide prairies and rich mountains, unfenced and unowned, gave all a chance to obtain the full reward that should ever come to toil. All the nations of the earth sent their disinherited to find a home, and flowing from liberty and opportunity they builded here a nation that was the wonder of the world. All the greatness of America, all her marvelous wealth, all the wonders that her short national life can show, are a monument to the wisdom of liberty and the power of opportunity. Wealth has been ever owned by the few and produced by the many; but no nation could create it as we once did unless every workman felt the inspiration that can only come through hope.

After all our building and making, shall we now destroy the vital principle which lies at the basis of all our greatness and our power? We stand today in the presence of the same danger that confronted Rome and France and England and all the nations of the past. Our liberty produced prosperity, and this prosperity today looks with doubting eye upon the mother who gave it breath, and threatens to strangle her to death.

Civilization means something more than producing wealth, something besides inventing new ways to make buildings higher and kill hogs faster. More than all things else it means the cultivation of a broad, charitable, humane spirit that makes man feel a closer kinship to his fellow-man. In the light of true civilization, all the wealth of a great city cannot weigh against the barbarism of hanging one lunatic in Chicago or burning one Negro in Texas.

In these changing times we have no right to close our eyes to the dangers and responsibilities of the day. No era of the world has ever witnessed such a rapid concentration of wealth and power as the one in which we live. This is no doubt due to the invention of new machinery for the production and distribution of the world's wealth. But while history furnishes no parallel to the rapid centralization of today, it furnishes abundant lessons of the inevitable result that must follow in its path. As liberty produces wealth, and wealth destroys liberty, so power and tyranny have within themselves the seeds of their own destruction. In Rome every function of government was controlled by the rich and strong. After a time the legislature, the courts, the police and finally the army refused to serve this class unless they received a constantly larger contribution from those who had obtained all the empire's wealth. When the levy of blackmail had commenced, the beginning of the end had come.

Injustice, oppression and wrong may always live, but they cannot exist forever in one form or place; and when the evils are great enough, in some way the end will come. With the land and possessions of America rapidly passing into the hands of a favored few; with great corporations taking the place of individual effort; with the small shops going down before the great factories and department stores; with thousands of men and women in idleness and want; with wages constantly tending to a lower level; with the number of women and children rapidly increasing in factory and store; with the sight of thousands of children forced into involuntary slavery at the tender age that should find them at home or in the school; with courts sending men to jail without trial for daring to refuse to work; with bribery and corruption openly charged, constantly reiterated by the press, and universally believed; and above all and more than all, with the knowledge that the servants of the people, elected to correct abuses, are bought and sold in legislative halls at the bidding of corporations and individuals: with all these notorious evils sapping the foundations of popular government and destroying personal liberty, some rude awakening must come. And if it shall come in the lightning and tornado of civil war, the same as forty years ago, when you then look abroad over the ruin and desolation, remember the long years in which the storm was rising, and do not blame the thunderbolt.

From an address on "The Rights and Wrongs of Ireland," delivered in Chicago, November, 1895.

Clarence Darrow

THE PROBLEM
OF THE NEGRO

*I have no confidence in any plan for improving any class
of people that does not teach man his own integrity and
worth; you must make each man and each woman understand
that they are the peer of any human being on earth.*

1901. 118 legal executions in the North; seventy-one were Negroes and forty-seven were whites. Lynchings total 135, 121 in the South and fourteen in the North; 107 were Negroes, twenty-six whites, one Indian, one Chinese. Alleged crimes of the lynched were murder, criminal assault, theft, cattle and horse stealing, suspected criminal assault, train wrecking, insulting white women. Nine were lynched because of race prejudice, three for unknown causes and one was a case of mistaken identity . . . Pan-American Exposition opens in Buffalo, New York . . . William McKinley, twenty-fourth president of the United States, assassinated . . . Sarah Bernhardt makes extended tour of U.S. . . . Chicago Board of Education adopts provision for free textbooks . . . Verdi dies . . . Booker T. Washington's *Up From Slavery* published . . . J. P. Morgan announces formation of U.S. Steel Corporation.

Probably I do not look at the race problem in as hopeful a way as many of you people do, and I fear that much I shall say this evening will appear discouraging and pessimistic, for I am somewhat pessimistic about the white race, to say nothing about the colored race; when I see how anxious the white race is to go to war over nothing, and to shoot down men in cold blood for the benefit of trade, I am pessimistic about the white race, and when I see the injustice everywhere present and how the colored race is particularly subjected to that injustice and oppression, I admit that I am pessimistic as to the future of the colored race, and fear the dreams we have indulged in of perfect equality and of unlimited opportunity are a long way from any realization. But unless we approach these subjects from the right standpoint and go along the right path there is no prospect of ever reaching a right solution.

Last week I had two conversations with two typical men, and these conversations have done much to arouse in my mind a train of thought in reference to this problem, which is not altogether hopeful, I must say, to the Negro race, and I want to give these conversations, or the substance of them, about as they occurred, and as I go along I will try to draw a lesson from them.

I do not want you to think in the beginning that I endorse either one of them, excepting as they show the thoughts of two men, both of whom were students, both close observers, two men approaching this question from a diametrically opposite standpoint.

The first was born in Virginia upon a plantation, and knew what slavery was—he is one of the ablest men in the United States, a man

Clarence Darrow

who has given his whole life to the cause of human liberty—Mr. Moncure D. Conway. Beginning life as a Methodist minister, he graduated from that to a Congregational minister, and from that he graduated out of all the churches. He had the spirit of abolitionism and, while he was the son of a slave-holder, born with the slaves, he did not believe in slavery. He entered the cause of abolitionism way back when John Brown entered it; he entered it with Wendell Phillips, with William Lloyd Garrison, with Henry Ward Beecher, and with all the great men who made the cause of abolitionism famous, and I may say sacred, as a great cause for human liberty.

He told me with what enthusiasm he entered that cause, how it had been his life, and that when Lincoln issued his proclamation, he thought all had been accomplished, and he felt that he had been one of the warriors in a great battle that had ended in favor of human liberty. He went to England and spent many years there as a teacher and leader of advanced thought. He came back to America a few years ago, went South again, went over the scenes of his early youth and life—an old man still young in his enthusiasm for justice, truth and liberty; but he said, as he looked the field over now, he felt that the abolitionists had been befooled and cheated and defrauded, that this great victory which he believed they had won was not a victory at all, that the enemies of human liberty had really turned victory into defeat, that the colored man today was a slave as much as he was when Moncure D. Conway entered the great fight for human liberty fifty years ago. He said, as he looked over the South and looked over the conditions of the Negro in the South, he believed that they had less—less to eat, less to wear, less comfortable homes to live in, less to satisfy their material wants than they had as slaves—and that some way or other the powers of injustice and wrong which are ever battling in this world against justice, liberty and truth, that these had succeeded and had undone all the glorious work of Garrison, of Phillips, and Conway and Beecher, and that host of men who worked so valiantly for the black man's cause.

The next day I had a conversation with quite a different type of man. This man occupies a high official position in a southern state—he is a man of culture and learning and intelligence. He was born in the South, had all the prejudices of the South, and looked at this question from quite the opposite point of view from the grand old gentleman with whom I had talked the day before. This man said that the Negro in the South was worse off than he was under slavery, that all the schools and colleges in the South were worse than useless, that the Negro had made absolutely no progress and that he never would; that whatever education had been given to the Negro had harmed him and had harmed the whites. He defended all the lynchings and all the burnings; he said the white people were bound to do these things, that it was necessary to protect their property, to protect their lives and especially to protect their women. He said there was absolutely no solution to the Negro question excepting upon the lines of the inferiority of the Negro race; that they were not social equals, never could be social equals, and that every attempt to make them such injured alike the black race and the white.

I have heard this so many times before that I think this statement represents substantially the whole of the white people of the southern states; in the South are a few white people who have been born there who do not agree with this view, but so far as my observation goes, the great mass do agree with it and they form a solid phalanx to fight the cause of the Negro, to keep him where he is, or, if possible, reduce him still further to a position of servitude, so that he simply toils for the race and never expects any reward, or asks for any reward.

Let me tell you some other things that this man said. He said that if they did not lynch Negroes and burn them it would not be safe for white women in the South. I have heard these things before, and you have heard them before. He said there was no such danger in the days of slavery; white men and white women were perfectly safe in the South in the days of slavery, but now they were not; that these Negroes had received ideas that they were as good as anybody else, and that on account of these ideas they had placed themselves in such an attitude towards the whites that they were obliged to lynch them if necessary to protect themselves. He had lived in the South long years before the war, and he said there never was any trouble with the Negro race before the war.

He said that in New Orleans a very strong agitation was setting in to compel companies to have different street cars for the white and colored passengers, and that they would undoubtedly succeed in making the companies carry the colored people on separate cars. He said there were many reasons why this should be; that the white people and the colored people should not mix; and again, he said, of course, the colored people are working people; they go into a car not in proper condition to ride with the people who do not work. Of course I understood that it would be only a question of time when we would get separate cars for working people up here in the North, if this theory was to be universally applied. An aristocrat is an aristocrat, no matter whether you find him in the North or in the South; it is in him and will come out whether he is speaking about colored people, Irishmen, working people, or anyone whatsoever.

There is no use disguising the fact that the colored people are in an inferior position today throughout the South and throughout the North. There is no use to disguise the fact that the South proposes to keep them in that inferior position, and that they do not propose to ever tolerate anything that approaches social equality; they say it openly, at least when they think they are talking to their friends, and they practice it upon every occasion.

This man said to me that it was unpleasant to ride in a street car with a colored person. He said that he did not like the odor of the colored people in the street cars. I had heard that before. I said to him, "You do not refuse to go to a hotel where they have a colored waiter, do you?" "No," he said, "that is all right." "Well," I said, "what is the difference between the odor of the waiter bringing you a dinner and when he rides in a street car?" Well, he said, there was a difference and they could not stand it anyway. Then he went on to tell how he loved his old black mammy. There is nothing wrong about the odor of the old black mammy, providing she is still the same old black mammy, but when the most refined, delicate, clean, colored person in the world meets them

The Problem of the Negro

upon terms of equality, then there is something wrong about their odor. A black woman, no matter how black, may sit all day in a Pullman car if she is holding a white child on her lap; nobody objects to that, but if the white child was not there nobody could possibly stand it to be anywhere near that black woman.

Now, of course, all of these reasons that they give are excuses, pure and simple; they are not truthful statements; at the root it is simply race prejudice, and the prejudices of superiority which we find everywhere in the world, but against which the Negro suffers more than any other race in the world. Nobody can analyze this feeling and arrive at any other conclusion. A man is refused a ride upon a street car in the South not because he is dirty, but because the Lord made his face black, that is the reason. They refuse to eat their dinner beside a woman in a restaurant, a woman whom I could not tell whether she is white or black from her appearance, as I could not tell many of the women here and many of the men here tonight; but they refuse to break bread with them because the Lord happened to put a few drops of African blood in their veins, and of course one drop is just the same as all. There is no excuse for this. No person can place it upon a scientific basis; it is a question of feeling.

When Douglas and Lincoln were debating in Illinois, Mr. Douglas, as his last and unanswerable statement asked, "Would you want your girl to marry a Negro?" and that was the end of it. Well, that is a pretty fair question, and I am inclined to think that really that question is the final question of the race problem; and not merely the catchword of a politician. Is there any reason why a white girl should not marry a man with African blood in his veins, or is there any reason why a white man should not marry a colored girl? If there is, then they are right and I am wrong. Everybody may have his own taste about marrying, whether it is between two people of the same race or two people of a different race, but is there any reason in logic or in ethics why people should not meet together upon perfect equality and in every relation of life and never think of the difference, simply because one has a little darker skin than the other? It does not always follow even that they have darker skins. There are very many people who have some colored blood in their veins and who have a lighter skin.

Is there any reason why an Indian should not associate on terms of perfect equality with the white man? Even our most fastidious people, you know, invite the East Indian gentlemen to come to their dinners and their parties and exhibit them as great curiosities in the best families and the best churches. When the Buddhists came over here at the time of the World's Fair we thought they were great people, and their skin was as dark as any of you people here tonight, and there was no reason why they should not have been treated on terms of perfect equality with the white people of the United States; neither is there any reason why a person of dark skin, who has been born and bred in the United States, should be considered any different whatever from a person of white skin, and yet they are. The basis of it is prejudice, and the excuses given are pure hypocrisy; they are not good excuses, they are not honest excuses.

We hear people say that it is necessary to lynch a Negro in the South, and even to burn a Negro in the South to protect white women, and you find some good, Christian people defending the lynching of Negroes, and even the burning of Negroes in the South, because it is necessary, and I presume they open some of these lynchings with prayer. I do not know why they should not; they defend them.

Now, I do not object to lynchings on account of lynchings especially. We do not always arrive at exact justice in our courts of law; you are not sure because you go through a court that you get at the truth, and I presume that a court organized on the spot, as a body of lynchers are organized, is perhaps quite as apt to get at the truth as a court of justice where lawyers are hired to work a long while to prove that the guilty man is innocent and the innocent man is guilty. I am not especially opposed to the lynchings of Negroes in the South because they do not get a fair trial. A poor man does not get a fair trial anywhere. But this is what I object to: I object to lynching a man because he is a Negro. These men in the South are not lynched because they have committed this crime; they are lynched because the Lord painted their faces black. If the southern people or the northern people would enter into an agreement and would stand by it, by which they would try every black man who assaults a white woman by lynch law, and at the same time try every white man who assaults a black woman by lynch law, I would say, "Well and good, we will stand by it." I do not believe in hanging anybody, much less do I believe in burning anybody, but above all things else I believe in equality between all people, no hypocrisy; treat everybody alike, and if the southern gentlemen, or the northern gentlemen, believe it is necessary to build bonfires to burn colored men for assaulting white women, well and good, but let them also build bonfires to burn white men for assaulting colored women; treat them all alike. These reasons that are given are excuses, hypocritical excuses, which are not true, and which they know are not true. These lynchings in the South and these burnings in the South are not for the protection of the home and the fireside; they are to keep the Negroes in their place. Of course here and there they are done under some provocation. Crimes are being committed always, everywhere, by whites and blacks, but these particular instances are different. When the offenders are Negroes, or are supposed to be Negroes, then they send out to all the world telling what a dangerous class of citizens these poor unfortunate men and women are.

I have traveled somewhat in the South, and I have observed that the Negroes do all the work and the other people have all the property. The South does not want to get rid of the Negroes. Now and then we find some statesman who proposes to solve the Negro question by wishing to send them off to themselves somewhere, as if the Lord made one country for white people and another for black people, and he forgot to sort them out, and as if we should do the sorting—but the South does not propose to send the Negroes away, for if they sent the Negroes away they would be obliged to work themselves. These people all say that the Negroes make excellent servants. This same gentleman with whom I visited and talked upon this question said there were no servants in the world equal to the Negro servants, and they were all right when they were kept in their place. They do not object to the colored man tilling the fields, they do not object to his picking cotton, they do not object to his bringing in wood, they do not object to the colored cook out in the kitchen, they do not object to their waiting on them in restaurants. They simply object to them taking any position in the world excepting the position of inferiors. They do not all of them object to the colored people learning trades, and some of them believe that Mr. Washington is the true prophet of the colored race—I do not care to discuss that question, because I have doubts as to my own position on that point, and I have talked it over with many of my colored friends, some taking one view and some another—but these gentlemen do object to the Negroes becoming lawyers, becoming doctors, becoming preachers, becoming politicians, or anything excepting manual laborers. They are all right to work out in the cotton fields. Some of them perhaps are all right to be stone masons and carpenters, but none of them must be lawyers, none of them must be ministers, none of them must be doctors, they must not rise above manual trades.

Some time ago I was talking with one of the large employers of labor in Chicago, and he said he liked the colored people, because they are so loyal, they are loyal to you, they will stick to you and they don't "strike." "Well," I said, "are you loyal to them?" Well, he answered, as loyal as he could be. I suggested to him that I had seen men like him, and read of other men like him, and that I had noticed when a body of miners left the mines and struck that they would send South and import a lot of Negroes, and when the strike was over would turn the Negroes loose and send them back again. But here was a man who really said he liked the colored man. Now, he did not. He liked their labor because they worked cheap and they did not have spunk enough to strike; he liked them because they had been slaves and they were still; they still bore the attitude of slavery, and it would be very strange if a race should come up from what you people have come and not in a measure bear the stamp of slavery; it should not be expected that you should be otherwise—and here this man liked colored laborers because he could get them at his own price, and if they did not like the price they would take it anyhow and would not strike.

Now these are the sort of friends that you people have among the rich of the North. Now, let us see what can be done for all of this. It is comparatively easy to tell what is wrong; it is not so easy to say what you are going to do about it, and I am not at all sure of my position on these questions.

The path before the colored race is very long and very hard. The first thing to find out is what are you really going to do. I have felt very many times that Booker T. Washington was not on the right path, and I would not say this too positively because I know how devoted he is to the cause of the colored people, and I believe he is honest and sincere, but I want to tell you why I have felt many times that he is not on the right track, and in this I, too, may be wrong, and I may not fairly estimate Washington. This race question can never be finally settled excepting upon one principle, and that is, that all people are equal, that all human beings on the earth, white and black and yellow, men and women, are entitled to the same rights, to perfect social equality, and perfect opportunity, the one with the other. It can never be finally settled upon any compromise whatever. Every man must recognize the right of his brother and his sister upon the earth upon equal terms with himself, and these people who believe, or profess to believe, in the Christian religion, and believe the Lord has made our souls all alike, show they do not believe it when they say that the Lord has made one set masters and the other slaves. This question may be settled in a hundred years, it may be settled in ten thousand years, but if it is not settled for a million years it will never be settled until every human being is the peer of every other human being, and until nobody will dream of asking the color of your skin, or where you were born, or what is your religion, but will simply ask what are you, and nothing else in the world.

I have no confidence in any plan for improving any class of people that does not teach man his own integrity and worth; you must make each man and each woman understand that they are the peer of any human being on the earth. You must respect your-selves or nobody will respect you. No black man, no working man, no red man, ever ought for one single moment to think of himself as being inferior to any human being who treads the earth, no matter who that is. He may be compelled to take an inferior posi-tion because he needs to live, and the strong may starve him if he does not, but he ought to carry within his own breast the con-sciousness that after all he is equal to any man who lives, and if he does not carry that feeling within his breast, then he is not the equal of any man that lives.

And the colored race should learn this: If the white race insults you on account of your inferior position they also degrade them-selves when they do it. Every time a superior person who has position invades the rights and liberties and the dignity of an in-ferior person, he degrades himself, he retards and debases his own manhood when he does it. You may be obliged many times to submit to this, but it must always be with the mental reservation that you know you are their equal, or you know that you are their superior, and you suffer the indignity because you are compelled to suffer it, as your fathers were once compelled to do; but after all, your soul is free and you believe in yourself, you believe in your right to live and to be the equal of every human being on the earth.

Now, I know that many white men believe Mr. Washington is right, and he has gone through the North and through the South, and received a great deal of money on account of it, and I am not saying that his work is not good. I know that the colored people must be taught trades; I know that they must be taught farming; I know that they must be taught to make a living, and so far as that goes I agree with him, but I do not agree in saying that they should have nothing to do with politics. I do not believe in the position that is taken by many of his supporters that in this way the colored people can find a place in society. They can never do it by accepting a subordinate position to the whites; you can never settle this question upon that basis. If it is settled upon that basis you had better go back to slavery from whence you came, and be done with the struggle at once. It must be settled upon a different basis from that. Any education that does not teach the colored person his true dignity and his true worth as a man and as an individual, falls short of the mark. That must be taught first of all and insisted upon in season and out. Now, I know that you people tried your hand at government in the reconstruction days in the South. Sometimes you did not succeed much better than the white people have succeeded, and I suppose it would be expecting a very great deal to think that you could take the reins of government and manage the affairs of state well within a few years of the time of your liberation. We are not doing any too well ourselves, and we have had a good deal of time to practice in. A man's right in a government does not depend upon his color, or his property, but upon the man, that is all, and he should have an equal right, whatever his color, or whatever his property, and every colored person ought to be free, they ought to have every advantage of citizenship that the white people have, and they ought to exercise it, too.

Now, I know that you have stirred up much antagonism in the South by exercising the right of suffrage. How could it be otherwise, because the South wants you to be slaves, they propose to keep you there, and it is perfectly natural that if you wish to be elected to Congress, or to be governor, or take some of the positions which the white people occupy, that you will stir up antagonism in the South, and you will stir it up in the North just exactly the same, as soon as you take an independent position in the North, just as the working man is stirring it up today all over the United States.

There are some things that the colored people can do. Of course, the colored people as a race are poor; they have been slaves for long, weary years. They cannot do all that they ought to do and must do, but after all no people ever were given their liberty from their superiors; you must get it by your own worth, by your own perseverance and by your own work. Nobody will come to boost you up; it is only here and there that some person, out of a feeling of justice, will help you, but you must fight this battle out yourself, many of you must suffer, and many of you must die before the victory will be won. There are some things, however, that you can do, and these poor fellows who have been shot down through the South, and many in the North, have done their work well; they were bound to die, it could not be avoided.

The Negro race, of course, have come from bondage; they have been accustomed to look up to the white race; they have done it for so long that in a way they will keep doing it for some time to come.

They should be taught first of all independence, manhood, integrity. I do not mean to tell the truth. I mean they should be taught the integrity of their own soul, that they are individuals—it may be necessary to tell lies to secure money. If you must tell them, do so; tell them when you have to do so to get along. You will not live very long if you do not tell them.

So far as you people have made your way in independent callings you have done it too much in a servile position. I know you have been obliged to in a way, but you want to get out of it just as fast as you possibly can.

The colored race have been in the habit of being waiters in restaurants, porters on Pullman cars, barbers, working in the kitchen, running elevators, blacking shoes. Now, I know perfectly that you will reply, If we do not do these things, what will we do? I do not know, but I understand that you have worked along the lines of least resistance. The whites have given you a chance to make up beds on the Pullman cars, to be paid in tips; brushing a man's hat when it does not need it. I don't blame you, you can't help it; but, after all, it is a degrading position. You are simply trying to coax a quarter or a half dollar out of a victim. It is the same way in a restaurant, being as polite as you can to a man to see how big a tip you can get—a menial position, where you are depending upon charity, which is the next door to slavery; in fact, I think it is the other side. I would rather be a slave outright than to depend upon the charity of somebody who had more money than I. Being a barber is not very far removed from it.

Now, you cannot all be lawyers, you know. I know too much

about this question to suppose that you can all start a bank; you cannot do that; but you can do the best that is possible. It should be the effort of every colored person to make himself independent as far as he can; do not become anybody's slave any longer than you must; don't live on tips any more than possible, and if you live on tips get as many tips as you can get; brush out as many quarters as you can. Try to be independent. Get a little news stand, a grocery, be a lawyer, a doctor, or an expressman—if you only get an old blind horse that is poorer than you are, and a broken-down wagon, stand on the corner and run your own business; that is better than taking tips. Make your struggle to be independent, just as independent as you possibly can, because you must fight this out yourselves. These fellows are not going to help you, because it means dividing up their money. You people have done all the work and get nothing for it; now, if you go on and do the work and get the money, too, where are they? It is the same problem the working man is facing today, and your cause is the cause of the working man.

You people make a mistake in your friends. The ones who will help you people to any lasting benefit are not the rich, they are the poor every time. They may not be able to give you as big tips—you people who have had to live on them—but after all, the cause of the poor is a common cause all over the world, and when your case is won it will be by uniting your cause with the cause of the common laboring man all over the world; you cannot do it any other way. The rich have been using the working man, making him set you off by yourselves, and they have been using you to cut the working man's throat. The working men organize their trades union for their own benefit, and then, when they have a disagreement, as for instance down at the stockyards, they strike; then the employers send off for a lot of you people to come and take the places of the working men, and that is where you do evil. Perhaps you cannot help it; you cannot always help many things that you do, I understand that; but, after all, you can only grow by the growth of the poor; you can only get your rights by joining in the common cause with all the weak, the poor and the

Clarence Darrow

oppressed, and help them get their rights. No weak man should ever try to get rich by trampling upon some person weaker than himself. They should unite with the weak.

My friends, it is not a question of getting very many people taken care of; that is not the object. It is a question of being recognized. If you have a few members of the Legislature, if you have a few girls in the public schools, if you have a few policemen on the police force, and a few of your girls in public offices, they will begin to recognize you and begin to know you are living, and you will begin to get your rights. You ought to use every opportunity that you can, for let me tell you, you must fight this out yourselves. Help the colored lawyer and the colored doctor—give the colored doctor a chance, even if he does kill you. Give the colored lawyer a chance. Patronize your people all you can, build them up, do not fight each other; do not one get jealous of the other when you know they are doing a little better than you are, as you sometimes do. When one is built up he builds up every other colored person. Of course, I know there are some people who are not building up in a substantial way, some are making money out of crap games, saloons and that sort of thing; they are getting a good deal of money, too.

Now, as fast as you can, get reading rooms, debating clubs, societies like this one, to call your young men away from the crap games and the saloons. Get them together and discuss these questions; let them learn some of the pleasures which come from the mind; and remember all the time you have got to help yourself to make the most of every opportunity, and some time, when I do not know, or how, or where, but some time, there will be perfect equality upon the earth.

Lecture delivered before Negro audience at the Men's Club, May 19, 1901.

The Problem of the Negro

THE OPEN SHOP

*The demand for the closed shop is nothing but the
means that experience has shown is essential to
protect the liberty unions have won and give some
vantage ground for other triumphs yet to come.*

1904. Russians and Japanese at war
. . . Theodore Roosevelt, "no longer
a political accident," elected president
of the United States . . . Mounted police go on duty in New York City
. . . Chicago votes in favor of municipal ownership of street railways . . .
National Association of Clothiers calls
closed shop "un-American," plans to
enforce open shop and resist union
demands . . . "Cy" Young, Boston
American League pitcher, pitches a
no-hit game . . . Best seller for the year
is Winston Churchill's *The Crossing*
. . . Caruso completes his first season
in America.

Clarence Darrow

TRADE UNIONS ARE NOT UNLIKE ANY OTHER CLASS (GROUP). THE
doctors and the lawyers, the brokers and the bankers—in short, all
sorts of trades and professions—organize for their own protection.
Everyone knows how doctors and lawyers regard those members
of their profession who will not be bound by their rules as to
charges, advertising, and generally such conduct as they term
the ethics of their profession, which in its last analysis is the establishment of such rules and regulations as, in their opinion, tend
to the improvement of their own condition. Of course, doctors
and lawyers, like trade unionists, will stoutly insist that these rules
and regulations benefit the public more than their own craft or
profession. Perhaps this is true, but, whether true or not, the instinct of self-preservation causes each member to regard one who
wilfully stands outside as an enemy to his craft.

But the law has never said that even theoretically a man has any
such inalienable right. A man's right to work, like every other
right, has always depended upon what he does and how he does
it. In short, as to whether his means of exercising this right conforms to the public good. Long since the United States excluded the
Chinese from America and forbade employers from going to any
foreign country and contracting to bring labor here. This rests
upon one principle alone, that the maintenance of a certain grade

and scale of living compensation for labor is vital to the interests of our people, and that the protection of workingmen in this rate of wages is the protection of the land.

If it is right to protect American workmen against the cutthroat competition of Chinamen and foreign contract labor, then the same logic makes it right to protect them against unjust competition at home, against the aggressions of the vicious workman, the ignorant workman, the weak workman, the woman and the child. It matters not whether lawmakers have ever carried legislation to this point. The reason for the one is the same as the other, and the workman has the same right to make his own rules and regulations and to protect it by contract in the one case that he has in the other.

But the law, which has never been over-friendly to labor, has gone much further and has recognized every principle for which the union contends in the closed shop. The right to legislate as to the sanitary conditions of the shops and factories, safety of railroad equipment and appliances, hours of work of women and children and even men, and especially conditions in dangerous trades and callings has long been recognized and approved, and without this right the master would be left with the unrestricted power to maim and kill, to possess and destroy and starve, provided he could find men, women and children so weak and helpless that they would choose the hazardous employment rather than be left without work.

The old doctrine of the unrestricted right to buy labor in the cheapest market, unfettered and unhindered by any conditions of sanity, safety or humanity, has long been obsolete in every civilized land. Most countries have gone so far as to protect even animals against abuse and overwork and underpay. Whether man would need this protection if natural opportunities were free and he could exercise his vaunted inalienable right to work, is not worth the while here to discuss. Man has not a right to apply his energy to the bounties of nature until the master gives him a chance to work, and so long as this right is so monopolized that he must look to the employer for a job he is forgetful of himself and recreant to his class, if he fails to impose all reasonable restrictions and conditions, and exact all just terms in the service that he sells.

Clarence Darrow

It is one of the fundamental principles of trade unionism that each member is responsible for his brother's condition. As a nation may go to war to protect one of its subjects, so the duty and concern of the union is to preserve the rights of its humblest member. This it cannot do without an organization of men who are ready and willing to stand or fall together.

That each is responsible for the rest is not a maxim that trade unionism alone has laid upon its members. The law has enforced this responsibility on workmen, sometimes to the most unjust and unreasonable degree. The employer insists that he has the absolute right to employ and discharge at will, and yet the courts always insist that every workman is responsible for the negligence and lack of skill of his fellow workmen, and if he is not satisfied to assume this burden, he must quit his job. The land is full of cripples and widows and orphans whose injuries were caused by the negligence of a fellow servant, whom the employer forced upon the workman. And the courts turn out these cripples and widows and orphans without redress upon the theory that each workman is responsible for his fellow.

In a railroad employing fifty thousand men, each workman cannot personally know all the rest, but so long as the courts have said that they must be responsible for their conduct they certainly have a right to say that they will work only with men who have enough regard for their fellows to join them in a labor union for their self-defense.

The position of trade unionism as to the open shop, as well as to most other questions, is generally misstated and never understood. Of course, the union has no power or right through force and violence to compel the employer to hire only union men. All they can do is to say that they will not work for anyone who employs non-union men either directly in his factory or mill, or indirectly by the material with which he works.

The right of the union to take this position is a question of ethics, not of law. There can be little doubt of the legal right of a workman to refuse to work for any employer for any cause, good or bad, that is sufficient to himself. While it is possible that here and there some judge may have denied this right, these are very few and far between. The courts have uniformly decided that employers may refuse to hire union men and may even boycott union men and send them out to tramp from state to state in search of work, and there can be no doubt of the right of workmen to refuse employment where non-union men are put by their side.

The question, then, is purely one of ethics and of union policy, which latter question is in the province of the organization alone.

One of the chief objects of the trade union is to form such a complete and perfect organization of its craft that through their officers and agents they will be able to make a collective bargain with their employers. To do this the craft must have such a large proportion of organized men as to make it impossible, or, at least, undesirable for the employer to deal with individual men.

That employers always choose to deal with individuals, except where the strength of the union compels its recognition, is proven by the whole history of trade unionism. From the time when the employers were able to make laws absolutely forbidding unionism, down to the present day, every device and means have been resorted to that an individual workman should be obliged, unaided, to make terms with his employer, or, rather, to accept such terms as the master saw fit to impose. The acceptance of collective bargaining by employers in the first instance has always been strongly against their will. This has been fought as every new privilege and right gained by the common people has ever been contested by the ruling class.

But when full recognition of the union has been granted in good faith; when the employer concedes the right to organize, the right to representation, the right to collective bargaining, then there can no longer be any reasonable or honest objection to the closed shop on the part of the employer. Of course, if the union is narrow and exclusive and fixes hard or unreasonable terms of membership or harshly and unjustly limits apprentices so as to work a hardship to the laboring class, then the workman has the right to object. Doubtless, in the history of trade unionism this has many times occurred, but it is not in line with its principles and policies, and has no necessary connection with the closed shop. The rule of trade unions is to urge all members of the craft to join on the easiest terms. No doctrine, or creed, or condition of any kind is required or imposed—except allegiance to the union and a purpose to stand together in making contracts, and fixing terms and conditions for the service of its members.

Of course, too, it must be assumed and agreed, as is always the case, that the union shall at all times be able and ready to furnish a sufficient number of competent workmen, on the agreed terms, to meet the employer's desires. The master does not need to employ any man who comes; he may pick and choose according to his will, subject only to the condition that he must have union men.

The battle waged by trade unions to gain and keep some independence for the workmen has been long and costly, and their rules and regulations have grown from the hard and bitter experience they have passed through. The novice is always ready to criticize every business he does not understand; any person not familiar with the running of trains can readily see how unreasonable are the rules laid down by the railroads charged with the lives and safety of their patrons. A closer examination and a better knowledge show how most of these rules, at least, are not only reasonable and just but essential to the safe conduct of the road.

So the novice, especially the prejudiced novice, finds the rules and regulations of trade unions arbitrary, senseless and unjust. A closer study would show them how all of these have arisen from the necessity to meet conflicting interests and a wily enemy ever on its guard. For the history of trade unionism, as in fact, the history of the rise of the common people toward the measure of independence they now enjoy, is one long tale of struggles, defeats and victories, and every single step in their progress has been against the most stubborn opposition and at the greatest cost.

The demand for a closed shop is nothing but the means that experience has shown is essential to protect the liberty they have won and give some vantage ground for other triumphs yet to come.

To establish a trade agreement, a recognition of the union is a most important step, but to protect it when established is of no less concern. The enemy is ever busy, always resourceful and ready to attack directly or indirectly, plainly or covertly, fully or in detail, and the army of trade unions must carefully guard each point that might be subject to attack. The so-called open shop furnishes the best possible means to drive the organization from every point of vantage, and in the end to disrupt and destroy. The closed shop is the only protection of unionism for its trade agreement and the defense of its individual men.

The master always claims the right to hire and to discharge as he sees fit. This is one of the privileges of being a master. The master can choose his man, but all men cannot choose their masters. This does not come from an agreement alone, it comes from the facts of life. The master can afford to wait, he is not dependent on this man or that. The man must have his job—he cannot wait.

So long as the master has the power to hire and to discharge, human nature dictates that he discharge those whom for some reason he does not want, and that he hire those whom he desires. The men he does not want are the ones who are hostile to his interest, who interfere and hinder and hamper in his one desire— the making of profits for himself. The men he especially does not want are the union men, always the most courageous, the most independent, the most insistent on their rights. And of the union men, those who are the most active, the officers and the agitators, are always marked to "walk the plank." The master is not bound to give excuse. It is his to command; he dismisses the man, because he does not want him. Even if he found it best to give a reason, it is always easy to find a reason for anything you really want to do. No man can long serve any employer without making some mistake; errors of judgment and mistakes are inherent in the nature of man. For instance, a motorman cannot long run a car in a crowded street without accident. For accidents are the common lot. But the mistake of the one servant is overlooked and that of the other met with instant dismissal.

The open shop means only an open door through which to turn the union man out and bring the non-union man in to take his place. This is not theory. The history of unions has shown it

Clarence Darrow

over and over for so many years that even the novice knows that his bread is in constant peril in the open shop. Not only does this system furnish the opportunity to destroy the union by the discharge of its members, but the menace is ever present like a sword above the victim's head. He knows that his job may be and often is dependent entirely upon his lack of interest in the union, which to him is all-important, both to himself and his fellow workmen.

But aside from the question of direct discharge, the open shop is full of annoyance and danger for the workman. Every man desires to do the best he can. He looks for the largest returns for the smallest exertion of energy and strength. In any great institution there are many places of vantage; many jobs that are easy and many more that are hard. Here the employer, or, more often, the boss, has an immense leverage upon his men. As a general rule, the boss is more feared than the employer himself. His term of service depends on the good will of the employer, and his interest is ever leading him to truckle to all of his master's feelings and desires. The employer does not want the union, the boss simply hates the union; thus the promotions, the easy places, the favors, all fall to the non-union workmen, whose presence and whose attitude are ever helpful to the employer and a menace to his fellow workmen. If someone is to be relieved for a day, if a laborer is given extra work, if a workman is specially commissioned for an important duty, and if someone is to be promoted it is always the non-union man. This is his reward for minding his own business. In other words, being unfaithful to his class.

Union men are much like other men. They cannot long be persuaded to pay dues, to make sacrifices for their organization, when they find that others are favored or promoted over them, or receive special privileges because they are non-union men.

The very reason that keeps men from joining the unions of their craft makes them more servile and cringing to their employer; makes them ever subservient to his demands. They have learned well the lesson of the masters that to thrive you need only work hard and do all in your power to get the good opinion of your boss. So this class is ever ready to submit to encroachments; to take longer hours; to consent to poorer conditions; to make no trouble over unsafe tools, and to even let their wages be reduced. If women are employed to take the place of men, and children in turn drive the women out, this is no concern of theirs. Perhaps from their families they may even be able to furnish the women and children to do the work.

It is not so very long since a large part of the coal of England was mined by women, since they were even harnessed to coal cars down deep in the earth, and on their hands and knees drew cars of coal from the darkness up to the point where they were relieved by mules. It is not long since little children from eight years of age were placed in these mines with their fathers and mothers and were penned in the constant whir and din of the spinning wheels of England for ten, twelve and even fourteen hours a day, and it is due to the trade unionism of England that these inhuman conditions are gone forever. But every step of advance was stubbornly fought by employers who violently contended that not only their fortunes, but the safety and glory of the British Empire rested upon the unpaid labor of these helpless slaves. And if trade unionism today should flag or grow weary, should hesitate and falter, should give up its demands for the recognition of its union, its collective bargains, and its closed shop, if the field should be abandoned to the employers and their agents, the great sea of weak and helpless men and women and little children would sweep away the industrial conditions that organized labor has won through its devotion and its struggles, and America would live over the dark industrial history that England passed through.

It will not do to say that employers are too wise and too humane; they are employers and are victims of the markets in which they buy and sell. The market is not patterned from the best employer, but is as stupid and brutal as its worst.

To prevent trade unionism from being conquered in detail; to save its members from being thrown out of the open door to make room for the servile and the weak; to maintain in shop and mill the best conditions that unionism has won, and to look forward to others better still; to save the workman from his once long hours of toil and to provide a day shorter yet, needs every effort of every union man; and without the right to protect themselves by refusing to work with those whose weakness or stupidity makes them recreant and unfaithful to their class, trade unionism can neither hold that which it has won nor look forward to greater victories still.

But aside from the constant aggressions of the employing class, trade unionism cannot be true to its own members without the right to demand the closed shop. The expenses and burdens of the union are no small item to the member who receives but little pay for the work he does. As a price for the protection of the union the members must give up their earnings to support the organization; they must be ready and willing to contribute to any brother on a strike or in need of help; they must be ready at a minute's notice and at whatever inconvenience and sacrifice to self and family to lay down their tools and go out on a strike—a strike always doubtful, dangerous and uncertain; a strike which may be for someone else, and over no grievance of his own; a strike which may bring victory and again may mean not only failure to accomplish the desired result, but the loss of his job, his means of life. It may mean even the blacklist that shall send him branded up and down the land, with no chance to earn his bread.

All these chances and dangers, not less than those of a soldier on the field, the trade unionist assumes for his devotion to his cause and his faith that united action and unbounded loyalty is the duty of every member of his craft. That his devotion through all the years has brought labor no mean reward, and through labor and the humanizing condition for which trade unionism has ever stood brought strength and greatness to the race, is as much an established fact as the effect and influence of a religion or any other social movement of the race.

The dangers that the unionists have encountered, too, have come ever from the non-union workman, who not only refuses to unite with him, but often joins the enemy at the most critical time and gives his energy and his labor to defeat his class. And the hard-won victories of unionism have been won, not only in open contest with the employer, who might be supposed to be on the other side, but have been won against the cowardice and treason of these same non-union men.

But however the non-union man may join the enemy to defeat shorter hours and better wages, when he has lost his fight and the unions have triumphed, he is always the first man to demand the rewards of another's efforts and to profit by the courage and devotion of the men he did his best to defeat and to betray, and the employer, too, realizing that this man has given all the aid he could, is ever ready to pay him for his disloyalty to his class. In the heat of the contest the employer gladly gives this workman more than the union demands, and when the fight is over, of course, places him on at least equal terms.

If the man who not only refused to help, but joined the enemy in time of war, shall be allowed, without danger or cost, to reap the fruits of the union's victory, then few men will be found who will assume the danger and the cost. If the rewards of victory can come to him who made no efforts and took no risk, but profits from the privation and suffering of his fellows, then most men will prefer to take that course. To say that the fruits of victory should come without effort, nay, as a reward for cowardice and disloyalty, is neither right in the realm of ethics nor in the practical work-a-day world.

The reward is for the men who have borne the heat and burden of the day, and unless it shall be reserved for them and those whom they wish to aid, there can be no reason for sacrifice and no reward for fidelity. Men may willingly, even cheerfully, work for the weak and humble, for those not able to protect themselves, but it is asking too much of human nature to require that they shall brave disaster and defeat for the enemies who seek to undermine and destroy their cause.

No one claims that all trade unionists are wise or even honest, much less that they have not made endless mistakes in the past and will not continue to err while time shall last. Neither is trade unionism an ideal institution. It was evolved to serve a purpose and to perform a duty in the upward march of the human race. It was made to fit a condition of society divided into the employing class

Clarence Darrow

and the serving class. Its mission is to protect the weak against the strong. In the great industrial strife that has come down through the ages and which will prevail until the capitalist and the laborer are one, trade unionism has fought the battles of the workman. And in fighting for the wage-earner it has fought for greater liberty to man.

War and strife are not ideal states, but they have been ever present with the human race, and so long as the war of classes shall continue, the weak and helpless must ever look to trade unionism as its chief champion and its most powerful defender. But when its work is done, and class struggles are at an end, trade unionism will be no more. Then all men will be brothers, and the highest good of all will be the fond desire of each.

Pamphlet, 1904.

IF MAN HAD
OPPORTUNITY

We must get rid of the idle poor and the idle rich.

1912. S.S. Titanic hits iceberg; sinks; Guggenheim and Astor among those aboard doomed liner . . . New York Giants pull off triple steal; lose . . . New Mexico admitted as forty-seventh state, and Arizona as forty-eighth state of the Union . . . "Alexander's Ragtime Band" hit song . . . Strike ties up Chicago newspapers . . . Two-count indictment of Clarence Darrow for jury-tampering; acquitted on first charge; jury disagrees in second trial; case dropped . . . U.S. wins the Olympics . . . Theodore Roosevelt bolts Republican Party after Taft renomination; forms Progressive Party. Wilson elected president of United States . . . Theodore Dreiser publishes *The Financier.*

Clarence Darrow

THIS IS THE FIRST TIME IN MY LIFE THAT I HAVE EVER PARticipated in a parade. I never cared much for them. It makes me tired to walk in the dust, and I never liked to ride when the rest are walking.

Neither do I care especially to see the long lines of people marching through the streets representing a cause—and representing it more or less aimlessly, as our parades do.

There were a great many men in this parade who fancied they knew why they were marching; and a great many others who only felt why they were marching; and many, no doubt, who thought marching was all there was to it.

One of the troubles with the working man is that he has done too much walking. And it will take something besides walking to teach him to stop walking.

The great question between capital and labor cannot be solved by marching. It might at one time have served to put some fear in the minds and hearts of those upon the other side, but they have long since learned that marching doesn't mean very much.

We have perhaps accomplished something by parades. We have accomplished a great deal by labor organizations—in fact, about everything that has bettered the condition of the working man.

But back of that have been the thoughtful men and women who have given their devotion and their brains to these great questions,

93
If Man Had Opportunity

and who have taught the working people to march together. Even that is something, after all.

We have done some wise things and some foolish things in the past—some wise things that seemed foolish and some foolish things that seemed wise. If you want to know how serious is the situation and how much cause we have for real thought and real action, it might be well to glance over some of the things we have accomplished by hard work, securing legislation in our legislatures and in Congress, believing the measures passed would help the laboring man, and see how foolish some of these things are.

There is a statute of this state and of the federal government forbidding a man to work more than eight hours a day. We pass laws to keep people from working! You wouldn't be compelled to pass a law to make me stop work—or any other man who had a chance to be idle.

But the industrial condition of the world is in such a serious state today that we are obliged to pass laws to keep people from working! And we seriously go to Congress and to the legislatures and ask them to make it a criminal offense for a man to work more than a certain number of hours a day, as if a man loved to work, and as if he harmed his fellow-man by working!

We want laws to prevent women from working in certain occupations for more than a certain number of hours a day, so that they may be mothers and take care of children. And yet it has been a law of nature for infinite ages for all women that they should be mothers—a law deeper than all human laws.

But now we must pass laws that women may become mothers, lest the human race fail. We might just as well let it fail!

And we passed laws to prevent child labor!

The mothers of the world have so far forgotten their motherhood that they must feed their children to a machine, and we must pass laws that mothers shall not do it. The first instinct of the mother is to care for the child, and the first instinct of the father also is to care for the child. But our industrialism has driven us to the point that we must pass laws to keep fathers and mothers from sacrificing their children!

Man has grown so fond of work in these days. He has come to regard work as a blessing, and if you leave him alone he will work twenty-four hours a day, and we can't let him work but eight for fear there won't be enough work to go around. If we let women alone they will be so busy working they'll stop being mothers.

We have grown so fond of toil and so fearful that other people will do the work for us, so we won't need to work, that we won't let the Japanese and the Chinese in to do any work for us.

The Chinaman likes to work. He wasn't born in a free country like this, and doesn't know anything but work. The East Indian, too, likes to work, and we are so afraid we won't have work enough ourselves we won't let them stay here and work for us.

You've never had to pass a law to keep a lawyer from working —or a doctor—or a preacher—or anybody else who knew better. We only have to pass laws to keep Chinamen and "Japs" and East Indians—and working people—from working, for fear they will work too much and all the work will be done, and then we will have nothing to do but play for the rest of our lives!

Now, I am not saying but that these laws may be good in their time and place. If you can't get the people to go at a thing in the right way, it might be better to go at it in the wrong way than not at all. The human race has always had a faculty for going at a thing in the hardest and most impracticable way, rather than going at it directly and simply.

If every man in the world—or in America—had a chance to turn his time and energy to work and then get what he produces, we wouldn't care to pass laws against work. If, under those circumstances, a man wanted to work himself to death, he ought to be permitted to do it, for then he couldn't hurt anybody else who didn't want to work so long.

Under those circumstances we would not find women in factories and mills, because the instincts planted deep in a woman's heart would keep her out of the factories, and the men would see that she was kept out, because she wouldn't need to work.

If every man and every woman had the opportunity to work and get what they earned, the instincts of motherhood and fatherhood would keep the children out of the mills and factories. These instincts are stronger than any laws ever made, and it is only from our industrial conditions that it is made necessary to pass laws to save children.

How long we had to work to get Congress to pass and enforce a law providing safety devices upon cars and engines, so that when a brakeman coupled two cars, he wouldn't get his hand between the cars!

We pass laws to get safe tools and machinery where working-men go to toil. If every man in the world had a fair chance to labor and to get the full product of his labor, no one could possibly hire him unless the tools and machinery were safe. The working-man would look after the safety of his own machinery a good sight better than any government inspector could or would.

Most of the legislation you talk about today as a solution of your problems would be entirely unnecessary under any fair condition of life. We are busy patching and tinkering, and doing a poor job patching and tinkering at that.

In the last two or three days, Wood, a rich man, president of a powerful association of manufacturers in the East, has been indicted for planting dynamite in such a way that workingmen could be charged with using it—which gives some official recognition to something that workingmen have long known—that not all the dynamite found in the homes or houses of workingmen was placed there by them, but some of it was put there by people of the other side—a large part, but not all.

And what does this mean?

I have no desire to see Mr. Wood punished or sent to the penitentiary. We know that he, like J. B. McNamara and like hundreds of others on both sides, was simply caught in the great industrial machinery and was guilty of social crime, and nothing else.

We know that the conditions under which industry is carried on are responsible for all of this, and that, until we have some fairer and wiser way of adjusting industries, these things will happen over and over.

I believe that J. B. McNamara and others of his kind are simply victims in a great industrial conflict, and that their act was not personal, but social and industrial, and for this they are not to blame. And what is true upon one side is true upon the other.

Until the American people find a wiser and saner means of bringing justice to the world, we may expect these things over and over, no matter how many men we send to the penitentiary.

The world is changing. We are moving from one condition to another, and these things do not change without trouble—in some cases without disaster. No human power can stop the law of progress. In spite of man it will work its way out as best it may.

The human race is not wise enough to go at a thing directly. The wisest of us are not very wise, and the stupidest control. That is one of the things we get out of popular suffrage—the control of the mediocre. A thing of real value can only be seen by the few, and by the time the crowd get up to where they stood they have moved further on and are thinking of something else. So the rule of the masses has always been a stupid rule.

Anybody who supposed we are going to get complete justice because every person has a chance to vote has another guess coming. And it won't be any better since the women vote.

Men have practiced a great many years on this trick and haven't done much. By the time women have practiced as long as men they can possibly do as well. In the meantime we've got to wait and suffer while they practice.

We have so far only tinkered with symptoms and never thought to find out the cause of the disease. When we find a man working ten or twelve or fourteen hours a day that is a symptom. Women working in factories and mills is another symptom. Little children in the mills is still another. When the Japs and Chinese come and take away our precious jobs and leave us nothing to do, and we object, that is another symptom of the disease.

We never dream of setting to work upon the disease and curing that. If the disease was cured the symptoms would fade away and we wouldn't get another in its place.

There is something in human nature which makes a man want to fight whatever is weaker than he is; he never likes to fight the stronger man. When a great railroad company takes all the land, or a great steel trust all the iron ore there is, or a timber trust all the forest, and we catch them at it, we don't go after those men. We don't say to the railroad company, "Take down your fences"; or to a steel trust, "This ore has been stored in the earth for millions of ages and is not for you to take to yourselves—but is for the use of all mankind." We leave the railroad company with all the land, the steel trust with all the iron ore, the coal trust with all our coal, and turn to the Chinaman and the Jap and the East Indian that have come to do the work—our work—for the corporations.

Now are we not intelligent?

If we went at it right, we would take all these resources for the benefit of man, and if the Chinaman wanted to work for nothing, we'd let him do it. We'd even let him work fifteen hours a day if he wanted to.

There is work enough in the world for every man. The trouble with most men is they work too much. Others haven't worked enough—they are the ones who are well off.

A man who really wants to get rich must stop working and get somebody else to work for him.

But we are not only afraid of the Jap, the Chinaman and the East Indians—we are afraid of the machines. Our political economy is founded upon the theory that whatever makes work is a blessing to mankind.

Our industrial conditions are in such a tangle that it was a good thing for our poor people that this city was destroyed by the fire. What a crazy situation that the destruction of property should be good for any human being! There was never a time in Chicago when people were so prosperous and lived so well as after the fire.

Calamity helps the workingman because he hasn't any property to burn down. He built the houses, but he hasn't any. The other fellow's houses burn down, and he has a chance to build more. And we want to keep out the Chinaman and the Jap, so we can build houses to give to the other fellow.

What are we going to do? That labor unions are most important to workingmen every employer and workingman knows. If they didn't understand that, they wouldn't fight you. The best proof of the usefulness of the union is that the employers don't want it. You do many things that are not ideally right. You place limits on the number of apprentices, and of course you don't work as hard as you can. No man is bound to do that. The tendency throughout the organization is to work so that there will be work enough to go around. And that isn't a bad idea—all of which shows how rotten our industrial system is.

There can never be any proper distribution of wealth in the world while a few own the earth—a few men own the mines, the railroads, the forests, while the great mass of men are bound to compete with each other for a chance to toil. There will never be a solution until all men are capitalists and all men workingmen.

However that may come, there can be no peace without it.

We must get rid of the idle poor and the idle rich.

When I was a boy, the village carpenter, the village blacksmith and carriage maker were independent men. That time is past. It can never come again. The wagon is made in a shop, the harness and everything that man uses today is made in great factories, where hundreds of people work together under a common employer.

Men must work in large numbers, and all men cannot be workmen, and all men employers unless there is a joint ownership of the earth and the implements of production. And peace can come in no other way.

When all men are capitalists and all men workers, industrial wars will cease, and we will need no laws to limit child labor, or the hours of toil, or to keep women out of the mills. Then every man who brings his toil into the land will bring wealth, and all men may labor with hand and brain to help their fellow men.

It is for this generation to bring working men together, to learn this is their fight and that they must fight and that they must fight it themselves—to make them stand together in these contests and be brave enough to stand by their own mistakes and not run away from comrades who, they believe, have made a mistake.

You have a right to ask your comrades one question, and only one. That is: "Were you on my side?" and if they were on your side and they stood for you, whether wisely or unwisely, they are your fellow-men and entitled to your sympathy.

You have a right to have them stand by you, and it is for you to stand by them, and with your organization, with your unity. It is for you to study carefully these great economic questions, which this generation must solve, for your sake and for the sake of the little children who have to go as you have gone.

War should not be the natural state of men. Great happiness and prosperity cannot come through war, but only through the co-operation of man with man.

Then it will not matter whether you are an American, a European, an Asiatic or a member of this union, of that union, or no union; if you are a fellow-man that will be enough.

From a Labor Day address at Shell Mounds Park, near San Francisco, on September 2, 1912.

Clarence Darrow

THE IDEAL
OF A
LABOR UNION

*The ideal labor leader, in my mind, is a man who is
practical, who has his mind fixed upon what can be
done today and tomorrow and next week, who is
willing to examine all questions fairly in the light
of the world, as the world is today, who is always
faithful to the men he represents, and who still has a
vision large enough to work for some better condition
of society than the one he is living in now.*

1922. U.S. District Judge Kenesaw Mountain Landis resigns to become baseball commissioner . . . French Premier Briand and cabinet resign . . . Bluebeard Landru guillotined . . . U.S. Supreme Court upholds suffrage amendment to U.S. Constitution . . . Gandhi arrested by British government on charge of sedition . . . U.S. Supreme Court declares Federal Child Labor Law unconstitutional . . . Labor unions call general strike at Mexico City . . . A. E. Housman's *Last Poems* and T. S. Eliot's *The Waste Land* acclaimed by literary critics . . . "Fatty" Arbuckle acquitted on a manslaughter charge . . . British Premier Lloyd George resigns . . . Japanese Diet rejects universal suffrage bill by vote of 243 to 147 . . . Pope Benedict XV dies; Cardinal Ratti elected Pope.

Sidney Hillman, president, Amalgamated Clothing Workers of America, introducing Darrow to union convention: It gives me great pleasure now to introduce a man who is known to all of you, no matter from what part of the country you come—the counsel of our organization in this city, Clarence Darrow.

Clarence Darrow: I presume you are all anxious for us lawyers to get through talking so you can get down to business. I do not know any real good reason for coming here, except I wanted to come and I was invited. When I first met those who in great trouble formed this organization, we did not have any flowers. When I came in today, I did not know whether this was a wedding or a funeral. When I see flowers I am generally afraid to come.

Now, we can all of us give advice. Advice is cheap, unless you go to a lawyer, and it really does not amount to a great deal. I have always been for the union. I shall always expect to be. Not that I think union people are any better than any others, or that they are any wiser, or any fairer, or better companions than any others. I do not think they are. I have no delusions about them. I know them too well. I am for them because the men who make up a union, a real union, never had what they ought to get. After a while, when they get more than they ought to, I will probably be against them.

I know that the unions have a hard time. I know labor leaders have a hard time. I believe that there is no union in this country which has had wiser, more devoted, and more intelligent leaders than your union has. I know that to a large degree the success of this organization, and it has been successful, is due to the wisdom of its leaders. I also note that success is very dangerous. Anybody almost can stand grief, but very few can stand success, and I am always doubtful when I see a man, or an organization, getting too comfortable. It is pretty hard to be well-to-do and successful and keep your ideals. It is pretty hard to be a labor leader and keep your ideals. Your leaders have done it remarkably well. I do not know how long they will hold out, but so far they have done well.

Now, I used to have a great deal of advice upon cases like this, but I have not the same assurance that I once had. In the first place, I know the people never take it, and in the second place, I never know whether it is good advice or not. I used to think that you never got anything unless you got the co-operative commonwealth. I am not so sure any more. I used to think if we did not get the single tax we would not get anywhere. I am not so sure of that any more. In fact, I am not so sure that there is anything that gets you anywhere. The main thing is to be interested in life, to have something to do, to forget yourself. I am inclined to think that there is no plan that can possibly work out to perfection; that all plans are faulty, and due to one thing, that is the people. These you cannot change. They are made a certain way. They will always be made that way and always act practically the same way.

But I do think this, that a man should have ideals. I do not know about myself, but I think other people should have them. They are pretty good things to live on. I think a labor leader should have ideals and I think a labor organization should have ideals. I think that is one thing that has made this organization one of the best and one of the greatest and one of the most dependable organizations of labor anywhere.

The union must be practical, and it is awfully hard work to be practical and have ideals, almost as hard as to be rich and have ideals. Any labor leader, or any organization, cannot get for its members all they want. If they could, nobody else would have anything. Even we lawyers would have to starve or go to work. No leader of working men can get for the working people all that they really ought to have. All you can do is to get as close to it as possible and keep working for it all the time.

Labor is governed by the same laws that govern everybody else, largely the law of supply and demand, and it will be so governed for many years to come, perhaps forever. I know you have to be governed more or less by the conditions of trade. I know that labor unions ought to be in a situation where they are willing to take every advantage to set high wages and where they are willing to meet and discuss the question of lower wages. After all, you must use good judgment when these matters come up, and as a rule those who have the management of the organization understand these questions better than the rank and file.

The ideal labor leader, in my mind, is a man who is practical, who has his mind fixed upon what can be done today and tomorrow and next week, who is willing to examine all questions fairly in the light of the world, as the world is today, who is always faithful to the men he represents, and who still has a vision large enough to work for some better condition of society than the one he is living in now. That is a pretty big bill, but that is an ideal labor leader.

Of course, a good working man, unless he is too much of an idealist for this world, cannot live on the dream of a future co-operative commonwealth. You have got to have something to eat before it comes. Otherwise you would starve while you are getting it. It is well enough to have your dream, and to work for it, and to hope for it. But in the meantime you must have a living, and outside of having a living, we ought to have enough to have some fun out of life. A man who postpones his pleasure until the next world, or until the co-operative commonwealth, is never apt to get any—except in his dreams. So a labor leader must have a vision of the future. He must have practical common sense to get all he can day by day for those who are dependent upon him and upon his energy and his wisdom, because your life is today and tomorrow and next week, and you must live now as well as living in your dreams.

I have always been more or less of an idealist. I like to see people have a vision. I like to see them try. I want to see the Russian people succeed in their great undertaking. Whether they will succeed, nobody can tell, or how long they will succeed nobody can tell, but I believe that every square person ought to wish them well and do what they can to help them. I like to see everybody succeed in his dreams and his visions, and at the same time I do not believe in postponing all that you could get while you are living now to a better society after you are dead. That is just as idle.

I believe that the organization is wise that serves the mind as well as the body, that appeals not only to the present, but to the future. I believe your leaders in intelligence and vision and devotion are far beyond the ordinary leaders. I believe that they know enough to keep ahead of them the vision of a world where labor unions will not be necessary, and still at the same time to know that the only thing in the world which can do anything for the comfort and happiness and the prosperity and the well-being of the men and women who live and work today is a strong union. I believe that this organization, above all the organizations that I know anything about, has that kind of a membership and that kind of a leadership. And so I wish you well.

From the proceedings of the Fifth Biennial Convention of the Amalgamated Clothing Workers of America, Chicago, 1922.

SHOULD THE UNITED STATES
CONTINUE THE POLICY OF
PROHIBITION AS DEFINED IN
THE EIGHTEENTH
AMENDMENT? DEBATE WITH
REV. JOHN HAYNES HOLMES

*Take out of this world the men who have drunk, down
through the past, and you would take away all the poetry
and literature and practically all the works of genius
that the world has produced.*

1924. Prohibition agitates America
... The country has 561 general prohibition agents; 32,611 violations reported by agents; 23,552 arrests and
22,939 recommended for prosecution;
state prohibition directors make 44,609
arrests, seize 2,799 automobiles and
111 boats ... Polish novelist Ladislas
Reymont wins Nobel Peace Prize
... Woodrow Wilson, Joseph Con-
rad, Samuel Gompers, Anatole France
die ... Japan rebuilds after earthquake ... Miriam A. Ferguson of
Texas and Nellie T. Ross of Wyom-
ing first women to be elected governors in U.S. ... Leopold and Loeb
sentenced to life plus ninety-nine
years ... Puccini dies ... *Hell Bent
for Heaven* wins Pulitzer Prize ...
Special Committee on Law Enforcement of the American Bar Association
reports "criminal situation in United
States is worse than in any other
civilized country."

AFFIRMATIVE (Dr. Holmes): *

Democracy does not involve the liberty to "guzzle" when that liberty is a menace to other men, Dr. John Haynes Holmes said in his opening presentation. He stressed, however, that his feeling about this is despite the fact that he believes in absolute liberty of speech, press and assembly—what he calls the "essential liberties."

At the outset, Dr. Holmes defined the terms of the debate. "We are discussing . . . not a specific method of enforcement. . . . We are discussing a policy of social procedure, long sanctioned by public usage and sustained by social precedent and social example." He claimed that prohibition is "as old as democratic society, going back at least to the prohibition of the slave traffic in England, and covering all development in the liquor field during a period of more than half a century."

He added that the topic for discussion is not so much the facts in the case but rather "our" conviction and ideas on the question.

* Arguments by Dr. Holmes have been condensed by the editors.

*The case for prohibition, Dr. Holmes said, is based on the his-
torical experience that laws are necessary for the life and happiness
of society.*

*Dr. Holmes analyzed the various types of laws passed in a
democratic society. These included: administrative, which define
how government shall be conducted; sumptuary, which affect the
standards and the habits of individuals. "Sumptuary law," he explained, "is the state invading the individual life to interfere with
those standards and habits that belong absolutely to the individual
life." He then pointed out that there are many habits of individual
life, however, which "overflow" into the social realm and affect
other individuals. He cited: "When a person lives in the open
prairie, it doesn't make any difference what he does with his garbage. When a man lives in New York City, he can't throw his
garbage into the back yard."*

*The "overflow" of individual conduct into society involves
public welfare, thus creating the third type of legislation: social
legislation.*

*The Eighteenth Amendment is social legislation, Dr. Holmes
contended, because liquor is dangerous to the public safety and because it creates poverty, encourages crime, and establishes social
conditions generally which are a burden to society.*

*"Liquor legislation is social legislation," he continued, "because
liquor constitutes a deliberate exploitation of the weak by the
strong." He said the liquor business is in the hands of a few for
the "amassing of great millions which preyed upon the weaknesses
of the people as a tenement house owner would prey upon the
weaknesses of the people if he were allowed to do so in the absence
of tenement house legislation."*

NEGATIVE (Mr. Darrow):

I thought for a few moments that the doctor had this house
packed on me.

I will say this: that it has been a long time since I have participated in a debate where I have had an opponent who has stated the position as fairly and as clearly as Dr. Holmes. And I shall agree with a good deal he said—but not all of it.

I could present miles and miles of statistics to show that everybody was richer and happier and behaved better when they had a chance to drink. Those statistics wouldn't be worth a continental —m-m—continental. He can produce just as many to show that they are happier and better and richer if they don't drink. He is quite right in saying statistics are of no value.

And then, I don't care a continental which way a man gets rich. I am not interested in getting rich—any longer.

This question is not a question of statistics. I have been in statistic factories. I know how they are made. It is, as Dr. Holmes stated, a pure question of the philosophy of government. And I am very glad indeed to have this question presented by the able man that I know Dr. Holmes to be. I have never yet found a debater or prohibition speaker who would do it. They talk about little Johnny's father, who wouldn't come home and take care of his sick mother; and they tell you how many prisoners are in jail, who all got there by drinking, and they tell you all these things from which you can draw no conclusion whatever.

This is a question of the philosophy of government. I will go slightly further than he goes. I know how accurately he described government. A great many people in this world, unless they act with a certain kind of organization, are apt to bump into each other. And if there is too much organization, why, they can't move at all. And it is better to have some bumps than no movement, and you have got to take it all together. How tight you are going to tie a people and how much you are going to let them bump is a question of practice and theory. If Dr. Holmes knows of any way in the world to draw the line that will include all cases, why, he would contribute something to me, if not to the rest, if he would tell what that way is.

I know that there isn't any—that is, I know up to this time. It is a question of infinite trial, of infinite mistake, of infinite going in and coming out. It depends upon the people. It depends on where they live. It depends on the kind of people they are. It depends upon ten thousand things as to how close the organization should be knit together. You may knit it so close that they will all suffocate. You may leave them so far apart that they can't move without bumping, and there you are.

Now, where is the line? I don't know. Does Dr. Holmes know?

I am one of those, I will admit in starting, whom he has more or less defined as doubtful and suspicious of authority. I don't like it. I think the less we have, the better. He describes that as bordering on the philosophical anarchist view. I would speak for that as against the extreme socialist view, which says that everything on earth should be regulated or controlled. Society is always moving between those two views. And as a practical matter, neither one is correct. Society will never submit to an organization, in my opinion, where there is no authority of any sort by one man or another or by collective organization over others; and it will never, for long, submit to what is still more intolerable, the complete enslavement of the unit by the mass.

Now, you can't find where the line is—and I can't find where. I am here to say that prohibition is 'way over the line in reason, in logic, in human experience. There are other things that are clear beyond the line. They have been wiped out gradually. Then the people got a brainstorm—and they have come back again.

If there were any line that could be drawn, people haven't got the intelligence and tolerance to draw it. They are like a flock of sheep. All go one way at one time and another way at another time.

One mistake that we make is assuming that human beings are reasoning animals. Human beings do not reason. They act from the strictest personal motives and are influenced by the mob, first of all, and sometimes they go one way and sometimes they go another. That is one of the main reasons why I am so suspicious of authority. And I think that to preserve any liberty whatever to the individual, we must watch carefully to prevent the encroachments of what we call the state or organized society.

Now, let me refer specifically to some of my friend's remarks.

Clarence Darrow

He says that he doesn't object to a man drinking if he goes off alone. Well, that is the way I do it generally. But he objects to society drinking. Well, society doesn't drink—only individual men and women drink.

I object to a man being drunk if he gets in the way of anybody else. I don't mind his being drunk alone. But if I want to take a drink and do not get drunk where I interfere with anybody else, should society then tell me that I can't drink? Or, if Brother Holmes—no, I will not use him; I will take the chairman—if he hasn't got any more sense than to get drunk, is that any reason why I, who do not get drunk, shall not have anything to drink? Now—is it?

He says that, of course, to forbid us smoking would be sumptuary legislation and nobody would stand for it. Wouldn't they? There is a big movement in this country today to pass legislation against smoking—and every man and woman in it is a prohibitionist.

Now, I don't believe in encouraging prohibitionists. There isn't anything that they would stop at. They would pass a law to make you go to church—as they have done. They did that in New England, and they picked out the church. They would send you to jail if you didn't go to it. And then they passed a law against your sleeping in church—and that took all the pleasure out of religion.

I say that nobody in their right senses would trust their individual liberty to the people who believe in that sort of legislation.

My friend says he believes in liberty—liberty of speech, liberty of the press. I can talk about beer, but I can't drink it. What is the use of talking about it? All that makes it worse when I can't drink it. Right now in this discussion I get thirsty just talking about it.

Can you have any liberty without liberty of action? Liberty of thinking and liberty of talking—well, everybody doesn't like to talk as well as my friend and I do.

Of course, I know perfectly well that a man isn't absolutely free. In fact, I don't know that he is free at all. He imagines he is, and that is something. I know that everybody gets tied up in all sorts of ways.

He says that in matrimony a man sacrifices fifty per cent of his freedom. I think he has got the percentage rather low. Somewhere around one hundred would be better. But if a man does it—why, he does it. I would object to the state forcing it on us—forcing us either to get in or stay in.

If a man goes on a steamboat, he sacrifices some liberty, if it is out on the ocean; but that is different from putting him on it. Men may voluntarily accept certain conditions, but that isn't the state's affair, and the state should not have anything to do with putting you there or making you stay.

Now, let's see whether we can get any kind of basis here on this question—and it isn't easy when one meets the issue fairly and openly, as my friend does. Shall we support a theory of government where the majority, by a vote, may make anything criminal if they do not believe in it?

Now, they can do it. I never talk about the "rights" of anybody. There is no such thing as "rights," anyhow. It is a question of whether you can put it over. In any legal sense or any practical sense, whatever is, is "a right." If you can put it over, all right!

I don't believe in the Eighteenth Amendment, but it is here. And I wouldn't believe in it if I knew that the people in this country could get richer under it; I still don't believe in it. Of course, they would get richer without coffee, in which he seems to believe, and he probably drinks it. Everybody believes in what they want and they are not interested in what the other fellow wants, unless they want it, too.

I am not interested in making the people richer or even healthier. I don't know about making people better. Maybe, if I made them better—what I think is better—they would be worse. I am rather interested in letting the individual do his own thinking, if any, but he would have more fun while he was doing it.

Now, let me admit for the sake of argument. He has told you what area was dry in the United States—a great area, but not much besides area. All the desert—that is dry. All the South—that is dry, as far as the Negroes are concerned. Railroad employees are dry. That doesn't mean the presidents, mind, or the general managers or any of the officers. Oh, no, I know them myself. It doesn't mean them. The prairies are dry and the farmers—I never count them either.

But the vast centers of population, where all the feeling for liberty that still persists in this country is kept alive, the great centers of tolerance and independence and thought and culture, the cities—all of them were wet before prohibition, and since.

It isn't a question simply whether prohibition would be good if there ever was any such thing. Of course, we don't know whether it would be good or not, yet. I never knew anybody with money who couldn't get a drink. Do any of you? I would agree to find places here, although I am a stranger. I wouldn't have to look far. They would come to me. I never knew anybody in this land of ours, under the Amendment and under the Volstead Act, to go thirsty.

Of course, it has raised the price. It hasn't placed it within the reach of all. It has substituted whiskey for beer to many people—which I think is a poor substitution. It has made people drink gin and whiskey where they once chose wine—which is a poor substitution. It has done all of those things. And I imagine there is no system of prohibition under which it will not always do those things, and that is practically the only thing it will do.

Now, suppose we admit, for the sake of the argument, that sixty per cent of the people of this country would vote dry. If sixty per cent of the people do not believe in something that the other forty per cent believe in, should they send the forty per cent to jail for what they do?

Now, there is your question. What proportion of a population should believe that certain acts are criminal before passing a criminal statute? If forty per cent of the people of this country believe that a thing is innocent, do you think that the sixty per cent who do not believe it would send that forty per cent to jail if they were tolerant people?

I assume that sixty per cent of the people in this country believe in either the Protestant or Catholic religion, or think they do, and believe that it is very necessary to man's welfare on earth and absolutely necessary to his welfare in the hereafter. Are they justified in passing a criminal statute and sending heretics to jail?

They have done it, and they may do it again, because intolerance is just as strong in the world today as it ever was. And when we permit it to have its way, nobody knows who will be the victims. Intolerance is ever vital and living. They not only have sent them to jail for heresy, but they have burned them at the stake for it. They broke them on the rack. They visited every means of torture upon them, simply because of a difference in religious opinion.

I suppose my friend will say those were sumptuary laws. What is a sumptuary law? A law regulating your personal habits or your personal conduct. He says it would be a sumptuary law if you passed a law against drinking coffee. Then why not if you passed one against drinking beer? It is a sumptuary law if it is against drinking coffee, but it is not a sumptuary law if it is against drinking beer. Why didn't he tell us why that was? Nobody could tell us which of the two is better or worse for the constitution. And if it is worse, what of it? I might take a little chance on my constitution for something I wanted to do. What is the use of taking such good care of your constitution, anyhow?

What is a sumptuary law? Here is the state of New York, that forbids the playing of professional baseball on Sunday. They may have changed it lately, I don't know. They are getting wickeder and wickeder, every day in every way. But Pennsylvania is so good that they can't do it yet. They would forbid you going out in your automobile (if the law were strictly construed) on Sunday.

He says that liquor is in the way of automobiles. Well, then, let's get rid of the automobiles. Now, he might prefer having an automobile. Well—I have no automobile, so I would rather have beer.

It all resolves itself into a question of either you getting your ideas over or the other fellow getting his ideas over. And that seems to be the common idea of government. Instead of tolerating each other's frailties and getting along as best we can with each other's peculiarities, we say that if it is right for me it is right that you should do the same thing, because I know what is right and you don't know what is right.

Now, if it is a sumptuary law to forbid the one thing, why it is a sumptuary law to forbid the other thing. Some fellow might forbid eating johnnycake. Well, it wouldn't hurt me, but I would hate to have them tackle pie. Yet pie, I know, isn't nearly as healthy as johnnycake. Perhaps that is the reason I like it better. Really, I never did like anything that was healthy or anybody that was healthy. It is—well, kind of too healthy—there is not enough excitement about it.

Is this glorious state of ours—and all the wisdom isn't in Congress, although I sometimes think that all the ignorance is—to appraise a human being, measure him up and figure out his appetites and his tastes and his capacity, and then just determine what sort of food and what diet will keep him alive the longest? We would have a fine time, wouldn't we?

Now, if we put this question to the members of the Women's Christian Temperance Union, I know I would be out my beer. But I know that all of them would stick to coffee and tea—every last one of them—and it wouldn't change their minds a bit if we told them it was killing them by inches; they would keep it because they like it.

And, after all, that is mostly why we eat and drink. Is anybody going to change this human race so that it will be rational according to what will produce the most muscle and the most fat and the least brains?

Take out of this world the men who have drunk, down through the past, and you would take away all the poetry and literature and practically all the works of genius that the world has produced. What kind of a poem do you suppose you would get out of a glass of ice-water?

Why, there is nothing to it. Who is the fellow that is going to measure up the human being and tell him what he needs—what will make him stout like a horse, or make him live long like an elephant—and then pass laws to see that he conforms?

Do not the desires and the emotions and the feelings of the human beings count? Why, by the time the state, moved by the reformers, makes every man over in its own likeness, what do you suppose he will look like?

That is what they have always done. Haven't we had enough experience in the past? Let anybody look at the long trail through which the world has wended its way, and then say whether the fight for liberty is worth while, whether we should meekly surrender because, forsooth, somebody tells us we can live longer and we can drive an automobile better if we don't have a drink.

What have we done in New England, for instance? We have had laws against witchcraft, and old women have been put to death for being witches. Of course, if they had put young women to death, there would be some sense in it.

It was made a criminal offense to go to a theater. It was a criminal offense to dance—although, of course, everybody was going to have the privilege of dancing in the hereafter if they were bad, much to the pleasure of the Puritans. It was a criminal offense to go anywhere on Sunday, except to church. And it was a criminal offense not to go there, else they wouldn't have gone.

The prohibitionist is the lineal descendant of the Puritan. I didn't know it before, but even my friend here says that he came from Massachusetts. But he believes somewhat in freedom. He believes in the liberty of speech and of the press. Well, there are some people that like to do something besides talking and writing. That doesn't cover the whole range of liberty. Almost every sort of conduct has been hedged around in this world by fanatics.

Now, I will tell you what is back of it all. It may take some time for it to get into some of your heads, but I will tell you. It is this old heaven-and-hell idea that God, somehow, levels things up, and if you are happy in this world you are going to be tortured in the next. They all believe in futures. They are going to be happy somewhere else. There is a large percentage of the population of this country and the world that have got it into their heads that happiness is sinful. They must not go to the theater, they must not

116
Clarence Darrow

drink, they must not do anything they want to do, but just something they don't want to do. Now, that is the basis of it all.

Let's see about this question of liquor. It has always been on the earth and always been used—many times to excess, of course. Food has also been on the earth and also used, generally to excess. I never saw anybody that didn't eat too much, if he could afford it. And if you go down to the graveyard and look them over and learn their history, I will guarantee you will find that there are ten funerals pulled off where the corpses would have lived longer if they hadn't had so much to eat, to every one that would have lived longer if it hadn't drank so much.

Suppose the question of eating certain kinds of food or drinking certain kinds of liquid were put up to the community, and forty per cent of the people thought it was right. Who are the other sixty per cent who would have the audacity to send those forty per cent to jail for doing something the sixty didn't believe in?

On how many questions do two people think alike? They can go only a certain way, when they branch off and leave each other. Men ought to hesitate a long time before they vote that a certain thing is a crime—and prohibition means crime.

I have been raised, we'll assume, to drink beer. Nature ferments the cider and the grape-juice, and the world has always used it—the good and the bad alike—in churches, also. They have used it on all occasions. They have used it for the festivity of the wedding and the sorrow of the burial, for all time. And probably three-fourths of the people of the earth believe they should have a perfect right to use it—and at least forty per cent of the people of the United States.

If the doctrine should prevail that when sixty per cent of the people of a country believe that certain conduct should be a criminal offense and for that conduct they must send the forty per cent to jail, then liberty is dead and freedom is gone. They will first destroy the forty per cent, and then turn and destroy each other.

In this world of ours we cannot live with our neighbors without a broad tolerance. We must tolerate their religion, their social life, their customs, their appetites of eating and drinking, and we should be very slow, indeed, when we make criminal conduct of what is believed by vast numbers of men and women to be honest and fair and right.

This prohibition law has filled our jails with people who are not criminals, who have no conception or feeling that they are doing wrong. It has turned our federal courts into police courts, where important business is put aside for cases of drunkenness and disorderly conduct. It has made spies and detectives, snooping around doors and windows. It has made informers of thousands of us. It has made grafters and boodlers of men who otherwise would be honest. It is hateful, it is distasteful, it is an abomination, and we ought to get rid of it, and we will if we have the courage and the sense.

AFFIRMATIVE REBUTTAL (Dr. Holmes):

Dr. Holmes refuted Darrow's assertion that because a certain practice or institution has existed from the beginning of the world one should be tolerant of it.

"I never have thought that antiquity was any reason for reverence or that the age of a thing necessarily meant that the thing was right or should be accepted in the name of liberty," Dr. Holmes said. He pointed out that the same argument was applied in the days of slavery—that the Negro was always enslaved to the white man and "therefore it was the part of tolerance to recognize that that institution was right!"

He accused Darrow of arguing as if the Eighteenth Amendment were "put over on the people of the United States by a lot of Methodists or a lot of moralists."

Dr. Holmes contended that prohibition was a "scientific progress. . . . The final argument in demonstration of that proposition was the experience that came to us during the war (World War

1). *In every one of the great nations of the world it was discovered, before the war had been proceeding more than a few months, that victory was impossible if the liquor traffic was allowed to go without interference."*

NEGATIVE REBUTTAL (Mr. Darrow):

Let me just see how logical my friend is. He said that if he lived in a flat and some family got to playing the piano and dancing and having a good time until three or four o'clock in the morning so that he couldn't sleep, wouldn't he be justified in having them arrested for breaking the peace? Yes. But that isn't what he would do. He would get a constitutional amendment passed to destroy every piano in the United States.

Now, he says that he wouldn't bother people who drink coffee, although he doesn't drink it himself. Well, that is good of him. I wish he wouldn't bother about the people who drink beer. But he says the trouble comes when a thing slops over into the community. None of mine ever did. He says, "If you do it alone, all right." Let's see about that. I never got drunk in my life. I never drank much—before. And I don't believe I ever disturbed any neighbors on that account—and I don't believe there is one in a thousand who ever drank, that did. Now, I don't object to his bothering the one in a thousand. Arrest him, send him to jail. With me it doesn't slop over, and yet you are going to take care of that fool fellow who gets drunk and disturbs the peace, by not giving me any beer.

Who did put over this fool prohibition business? Was it the killjoys? I came from the country, and up to the time I was ten years old, I used to be dragged to church on Thursday nights to listen to a prohibition meeting, and I will bet I signed the pledge a thousand times. There wasn't anything to drink within fifty miles of me, but I signed the pledge, and everybody else did. That was all we had to do in the country. The meetings were always held in churches, Presbyterian, Baptist or Methodist, as a rule. I am not crazy about them—I might just as well admit it. I don't mind their going to heaven in their own way, but I want them to let me go to hell my own way, in peace. God will take care of me after I get there. These are the backbone of the prohibition movement of America today, and they always have been.

Is there any question about all this? Let's see. You have heard of the Anti-Saloon League, haven't you? They have been holding meetings in this country, in the churches, for years. They have an organization, and whenever a congressman would rise with a little bit of intelligence, they would pick him off. Of course, that ought to be a good reason for picking off a congressman. But if a man were "dry," even though he might be a thief, a crook, or the worst enemy the world ever had, every blooming fool fellow who belonged to that League would vote for him. If he were a statesman, a philosopher, a historian, a wise man, but took a drink, he would have to go. So they loaded up the Congress of the United States with nincompoops, with brainless people who would take their commands and sell their souls for votes—and they voted this country dry while these congressmen had liquor salted away in their cellars. A set of hypocrites and vote-mongers who voted this country dry while they had liquor in their cellars, and they have had it there ever since. There is no question about it; not the slightest.

Science? Did anybody ever do anything from science? No. Science never affected the opinions of men. We have had science, plenty of it, for fifty, sixty or a hundred years, but Billy Bryan and Billy Sunday still draw crowds. Nobody cares about science— never did, unless they are going to make some chemical compound.

How did they get this law through? Everybody knows how they got it through. Under false pretenses. They got it through by, first, a system of regulations which might have been all right in wartime, to save food and save labor, and so they cut down on the liquor supply. For quite a while I didn't have any sugar, either. Why didn't you prohibit that? Also butter, and a whole lot of other things.

They fixed up that law in wartime, when everybody but the prohibitionists were fighting—and they were policing the camps to see that the soldiers didn't get a drink, because they said they couldn't fight if they had something to drink. Didn't the Germans fight? Didn't the French fight? And even our fellows, when they got over there, where things were free, and they were in a land of some kind of liberty, and had something to drink.

And so the things which came purely as a war measure, they foisted on the country in time of peace, and these trafficking, miserable politicians voted for it, scarcely one of them believing in it. And they never did submit it to the people. They passed it through state legislatures, under the threats of this League that held the whip above their backs, and is doing it today, until nobody dares speak. That is how it came here.

What I say is this: No man who has in him the spirit of tolerance, or any regard for the opinions of others, would pass a criminal statute which would make criminals of forty per cent of the people of the United States. He would hesitate and doubt whether he was right. He might elect a president, he might elect an official, but when it comes to sending a man to prison for an opinion or a habit or a custom or a practice, no man who has any regard for the rights of other men would do it when forty per cent were one way and sixty per cent the other way. If such were the case, what would become of most of us on some things? I know that more than sixty per cent of the people of this country would be against my religion. If we didn't keep the other fellows so busy fighting amongst themselves, it might be dangerous for us. You might land in the midst of the forty per cent at any time.

What would my friend do if they should pass a law in the United States that he couldn't enjoy the religious privileges which he enjoys today? And there has been many a time in the history of the world when he would have been burned at the stake for it if he had held out that long, and I think he is one of the kind who would. What would he think if the religious fanatics of this country should say that he couldn't preach freedom of thought, freedom of religion, obedience to conscience? It would be easy to get sixty per cent to say that, if they ever got their minds on it. And they don't ever need minds—they need votes, that's all. Do you suppose he would obey it? I don't believe he would. Do you suppose he would think it was right because a bare majority said so?

And yet all that he has said, in every position he has taken upon this question, is encouraging the bigotry that has made this world run red with blood. I don't care what a man believes, and I am not interested in his habits. He seems to be tricked more than anybody else by those two words, "white slavery." I wonder where he got them? Must have been at church. Of all the fool things ever put over in the United States that foolish talk was the worst. It never amounted to anything. Never was anything —just simply catchwords.

Social organization—control of men—regulating their diets and regulating their habits. For what? You are getting pretty close to the danger line when you begin it. And who are the ones that would do it? Have they the knowledge, the information—have they the scientific training to do it? Have they the wide tolerance, the spirit of "live and let live," which ought to prevail with any and all before they undertake the regulation of their fellow-man?

Now, my friend has tried to be fair about his statements, and I want to be fair about mine. I know that all the human ills cannot be cured, cannot be regulated, etc. Some fellow will get drunk and run an automobile, and somebody will get killed. Well—he would have died anyhow, sooner or later. My experience is that a very large majority of the human race die some time, and in some way. And I do not believe in picking out this thing or that thing or the other thing, which may have caused some particular death, and destroying it in a moment of anger or a moment of fear, regardless of what consequences will follow from it.

Now, suppose you were in trouble and wanted a real, human-being friend, and you knew that here was a prohibitionist and

Clarence Darrow

over here was a fellow who drank. Which side would you take a chance on? Haven't the prohibitionists been the joy-killers since the very beginning of time? I cannot understand how my friend here, with his broad views and his intelligence, came to be one of them, except that he came down through the preacher line, and some of it lingers. For you know, "You may break, you may shatter the vase if you will, but the preacher psychology sticks around still."

Am I right in saying that they are the joy-killers, who look with envy upon people who have a good time? The people who would forbid you to drink, would forbid you to dance, would forbid you to go to the theater. I will guarantee that half of the prohibitionists in this country would close the theaters on Sunday—no, nine-tenths of them would, and most of them would close them every day. They would forbid dancing. It is a question of joy.

Now, I don't mean to say that books were written and pictures were painted because of alcohol. But it takes a certain kind of nervous system, a certain kind of imagination, a certain kind of temperament to write a book or paint a picture—a book that anybody will read or a picture that anybody will look at—and that same kind of a nervous system has always craved some liquor, and always will.

If you could gradually kill off anybody who ever drank, or wanted to, and leave the world to prohibitionists—my God, would any of us want to live in it?

Debate held in New York City on December 14, 1924.

THE
DIVORCE
PROBLEM

Almost invariably, when separation or divorce is sought,
matters have gone so far that living together is no longer possible.

1927. Sacco and Vanzetti executed
. . . "The sex instinct is not to be set
free but to be held under control,"
urges a report of the Federal Council
of Churches of Christ in America . . .
1,200,694 marriages reported against
1,202,574 in 1926; 192,037 divorces
against 180,853, and 4,252 annulments
versus 3,825 in 1926 . . . Federal Ra-
dio Commission created with authority to license broadcasting stations
. . . Agitation for a uniform marriage
and divorce law.

Clarence Darrow

M ARRIAGE IN THE UNITED STATES IS SIMPLY A CONTRACT. LIKE many other agreements, the law provides the method of attesting it and likewise of bringing the partnership to an end. In a country where there is no established religion, it could not well be otherwise.

In America, if one religion could fix the terms and conditions of marriage, then all could do the same, and there would be no uniformity in the requirements that the state should make. But nothing with us prevents any religious or other organizations from prescribing conditions additional to those required by the state, such conditions, of course, serving to affect the conscience of those who are members of the organization. So long as men are able to think there will be a great diversity of opinion on most subjects, and in connection with the marriage contract, or its dissolution, there has been unusual diversity of opinion. However, the tendency amongst the enlightened states has been, undoubtedly, to make it easier and easier to dissolve the marriage contract. The close relations under which married people live, and the fact that these relations generally involve the welfare of children, have always led to sharper divisions of opinion as regards both the making and the dissolution of the contract.

Few marriages are entered into for the sole or even the main purpose of raising a family. The moving consideration is almost invariably the desire of the contracting parties for the ultimate companionship that goes with this union. Most of these contracts are made in youth and often by those who are legally incompetent to enter into many binding contracts that are of slight importance in comparison with marriage. The marriage contract is prompted by the strongest desires and longings for the association that both parties are anxious to enjoy. As a rule, the relation soon becomes one in which association and close intimacy form the major part. This not only involves the most intense feelings, but likewise mental and emotional adjustments that begin in youth and last for many years.

In any relation, human beings are rarely the same at forty as they were at twenty. Their emotions change, their ideals and ambitions change, their knowledge generally increases; and, because of these changes, it is almost impossible for the mature person to realize how he could once have been interested in the the things, thoughts, feelings, and ambitions that he had in youth.

It is rare, indeed, outside of marriage, that two people change and develop together. One needs only to look back at the companions of his youth to realize how few, if any, are congenial in his mature life. Each human being is an individual, with his individual structure, individual potentialities and individual ambitions. He is molded and changed by life and experience. Some men become wiser as they grow older. Some form new ambitions, some stand still or retrograde; but it is almost a miracle when two persons change in the same way. The marriage that does not bring companionship brings practically nothing, and sometimes less than nothing.

Every person should have some chance for happiness and some opportunity for individual development. All intelligent people know that many marriages do not furnish that chance. Since women have insisted upon having a life of their own and a chance to develop themselves and live as the equals of men, there can be little doubt that the number of unhappy marriages has increased. When woman had no thought except to minister to her husband and children, and was willing to accept whatever condition the husband imposed, the chance for friction was less. Instead of women going back to their old conditions, they will no doubt insist more and more upon their individual rights and their determination to live their own lives. No man with imagination or a sense of justice can fail to sympathize with them in this. Inevitably women will hold fast to what they have and fight for more.

Until comparatively recent times, only men had the right to ask for divorce. Today in America most divorces are requested by women. This tendency will naturally grow as women come to be more and more self-sustaining, and as a constantly greater number insist on managing their own lives.

It is plain from the nature of things that a large percentage of marriages must bring more pain than pleasure. The growth and change of the individual from youth to age could not bring any other result. Without the feeling of companionship which should go with close relationship, the association becomes unbearable. Some people resign themselves to a life of misery, accepting the situation, through religious feelings or social conventions, and live in blank despair as they see the years go by and all hope of happiness fade away. Others seek relief in the divorce courts, but most of these take this step only as a last resort. There are some, of course, who never can take marriage seriously, and these go into court without much regret. Their cases usually receive the most attention from the press. Still, very few cases reach court until all possibility of any tolerable relation is gone. The great majority fear public opinion and dread scandal. The church, the law, the conventions hold them back. They may know that life is passing and neither the present nor the future furnishes a chance for happiness, and still they refuse to seek relief in court.

In many cases, children are involved, and the opponents of divorce always use these as an argument against separation, but the child that is brought up in a home where husband and wife are not congenial always suffers grievously from the situation. Children readily understand the relations of their father and mother. Their sympathies are torn by everlasting conflict. There is none of that peace and serenity that ought to come in a proper home. As a rule, therefore, it is much better for the children if a divorce is granted, and one parent or the other has the responsibility of rearing them. Where people are reasonably well disposed, this can be done, and in that case the children not only have respect for both parents, but have the advantage of their co-operation and help.

Every reason for the proper bringing up of a child, therefore, demands that where the husband and the wife cannot agree or live happily together, the children should be spared the trouble and suffering that inevitably grow out of ill-adjusted marriages. There are too many children who have been well reared and thoroughly cared for by divorced persons to make this any longer a matter of doubt. Besides, the court always has jurisdiction of the children, and can change their surroundings at any time and provide for their maintenance. But court intervention is seldom necessary. In spite of the common idea of divorce, most parents are fond of their children and anxious to provide for them, whether they live together or not, and many instances can be pointed to where parents have taken more pains to see that the children are well reared after divorce than before.

The parties to every marriage are entitled to a chance of happiness. It by no means follows that, because a man and his wife are unhappy while living together, both of them could not form other relations that would make life pleasanter and sweeter and further their legitimate ambitions. It is well known that most people find happiness and contentment after a marriage relation has been severed. There are, of course, those who cannot find contentment in any situation whatever. That is incident to their mental and emotional nature, and in such cases it is not only useless, but cruel, to decree that a person who can adjust himself to life shall be forever tied to one who cannot. It must be remembered that all of these questions are subject to the sound discretion of the court, and that a judge has to be satisfied before granting a divorce that it will be better if the relationship is severed.

Often lawyers and judges seek to bring men and women together after an application for divorce, or at least after a consultation which precedes an application. It is very seldom, however, that they accomplish any good by persuading men and women to live together after one or both of them have reached the point of even seeking a separation. Almost invariably, when separation or divorce is sought, matters have gone so far that living together is no longer possible.

All sorts of evils have resulted from preventing divorce when one or both parties really desire separations. Such a condition brings despair into the lives of the parties, destroys all healthy ambition, and not infrequently results in murder. The criminal cases that reach our courts, where either the husband or wife has killed the other, almost always follow an attempt to live together when the desires and character of the two are too inharmonious to make that possible or endurable. These murder cases arise when neither the husband nor the wife would otherwise have dreamed of committing such an act. They grow out of hopeless despair, thwarted ambition or sudden and violent quarrels. The situation of the children when this fatal situation is reached is, of course, almost hopeless. Under greater freedom of divorce most of these cases would be prevented.

Marriage has a very definite psychology all its own. Unfortunate marital relations often produce the feeling that the situation cannot possibly be remedied, and must be endured forever, and that there is no further opportunity for peace and joy. Many men and women would be happier if they knew that the relation could be severed without scandal, unpleasantness and severe condemnation by the public, which last is always a bugbear with most people.

It is not infrequent for divorced people to remarry each other.

This is due to the feeling that they are free once more and able to exercise their choice. The proportion of divorced people remarried to each other is very large, and, as a rule, at least, the second attempt at matrimony is much more successful than the first.

A formidable and pestiferous part of the community is always anxious to regulate other people. Nothing so annoys this class as to see individuals pursue freely their own lives, even where this pursuit in no way interferes with anyone else. The constant tendency is to forbid and deny. Whatever one really wishes to do is inevitably wrong, and the offenders must be restrained. The meddlers always annoy and pester. Their tyranny affects the destiny of men and states. But they might as well seek to regulate the revolution of the earth on its axis, or its annual flight around the sun! These same meddlesome people are constantly harping about divorce. If the court records show that a growing number seek and obtain relief from galling fetters, this to them is a sign of the decadence of the state. It calls for protests against courts and lawmakers that dare to release bonds that have become burdensome and galling. But the increasing number of divorces really shows the growing demand for individual happiness and the right to live one's own life. Especially does it show that women will no longer accept the semi-slavery that custom and law have so long forced upon them.

The people who have always protested against individual free- dom have done much to make divorce laws crude, tyrannical and barbarous. Marriage is the only contract that the courts will not annul on the request of both parties to the agreement. In fact, so crude is our law that if both parties request a divorce, the court will not and may not grant it, even if there are no children, or if full and fair provision has been made for all parties interested in the case. A divorce will only be granted if one party objects to the decree. This makes it necessary that ugly charges be made, whether true or not. It makes it needful to hurt or pain one for whom you may have the kindliest feeling and the greatest respect, even though marital relations can no longer exist. It turns a plain and simple case, where justice could be done to all parties with the best of feelings, into a chamber of horrors for the torment of sensitive men and women, and, what is still worse, it helps heartless litigants to practice blackmail and extortion by threats of disgrace and outrageous publicity.

All of this is unfortunate for children and for parents, and all of it is done in obedience to laws that should be modified in the interest of common sense, common humanity and common decency.

If marriage were looked upon as any other relation is regarded, no one would ever question the wisdom of the policy of granting relief where both parties wished it and where the courts were satisfied that the children would be properly provided for. Judges who have observed the workings of the law are, as a rule, more ready to grant divorces for adequate cause where they feel that both parties desire a divorce and that both would be the better for its granting.

On the part of conventional persons there is a more or less persistent demand for uniform divorce laws and their administration in the federal courts. Often some ambitious novelist, who may have exhausted all other subjects, finds some special case where the laws of the different states created an anomalous situation, as, for instance, one party being legally divorced and the other not. Out of this situation can be made hysterical, blood-curdling melodrama to foster and promote the idea that divorce should be controlled by federal courts. While some cases of this sort have occurred, while the law is naturally replete with all sorts of anomalous situations in many relations, wisdom in changing state laws would remove the few divorce anomalies now possible.

Laws should be adjusted to individual communities. This is the basic idea of the system favored by the founders of the American Republic. Those men knew perfectly well that individual happiness cannot be conserved by making the same laws cover a territory as large as the United States. They provided for local self-government by making the state the unit for most human affairs and relations. Men and women dissatisfied with certain state laws are always rushing to the federal government to try to give it jurisdiction over all citizens of the various states regardless of the grave and numerous evils that inevitably follow such centralized jurisdiction.

The United States has been settled by all sorts of people from all parts of the world. They have come here with their different religions, their different customs, their different habits, and their different views of life. The states can and do pass laws measurably adapted to their own populations. There are states that grant divorces only for one cause, and one at least that refuses to grant them for any cause; some states grant them for seven or eight different causes. These provisions have been made to fit the ideas of the populations of the various states. It is plain that no federal statute could be passed that would not seriously violate the sentiments, opinions, habits and customs of practically every state in the union. No such law could be passed that would not be a compromise and work serious injustice and oppression to those who have other views of the domestic relation.

Then too, the federal courts should not be burdened with this sort of litigation. Prohibition has added vastly to their work, having practically turned the federal courts into police courts. To transfer to them the business of divorce as well would well-nigh destroy the purpose for which these federal courts were created. It would likewise necessitate an increase in the number of judges and of other government officials.

Practically every movement to increase federal power is dangerous to individual liberty, but to demand that one divorce law should be applied to all the diverse elements that make up a country as large as this, is to demand a policy that could not fail to produce incredible mischief and tyranny.

Some day, perhaps, people will learn to respect individuals; some day they may learn that the state should protect freedom and the aspirations of the members who make up the state; some day they may understand that government should not be a tyranny, but an agency for the development and self-realization of the citizens. When these rational principles are applied to the question of divorce, much of the cruelty, misery and despair now inflicted on innocent people will be prevented and averted.

Vanity Fair, *August, 1927.*

IS THE IMMIGRATION LAW BENEFICIAL? (RESOLVED: THAT THE IMMIGRATION LAW DISCRIMINATING IN FAVOR OF THE RACES OF NORTHERN EUROPE AS OPPOSED TO THOSE OF SOUTHERN EUROPE IS AN ADVANTAGE TO THE UNITED STATES.) DEBATE WITH DR. LOTHROP STODDARD

I am a foreigner; my people didn't get here until about 1710. They got here, and now I am asked to close the doors to the people who came over on a later ship.

1929. Stock market crash . . . Congress votes to retain national origins clause in the immigration law . . . Hoover appoints Wickersham of New York as chairman of a commission to investigate the reasons for the breakdown of law enforcement . . . King calls J. Ramsay MacDonald to form a new cabinet because of British Labor Party gains . . . *All Quiet on the Western Front* is the "outstanding" novel of the year.

Clarence Darrow

AFFIRMATIVE (Dr. Stoddard):*

Self-preservation was the driving force behind the enactment of the immigration law of 1924, which promoted immigration from northern and western Europe and restricted it from eastern and southern Europe, said Dr. Stoddard in his opening presentation.

"It is by no means a matter of race feeling," he added. "The northern European aliens in this country had nearly half a century of very wide and increasingly acute experience with the

* Arguments by Dr. Stoddard have been condensed by the editors.

*immigration which was pouring in in ever-increasing numbers
from the southern and eastern sections of Europe. This situation
became more and more evident and more and more disturbing
until finally it crystallized public opinion and put over the law,"*
the doctor explained.

What are the factors which led to the enactment of the law?

*(1) Economic. This was "really the first and foremost. . . .
The great majority of immigrants from southern and eastern
Europe were from the poorest classes of a poor and backward
race. They came to this country with low living standards, and
they came with strange business and social customs which produced a very serious and a very aggravating and annoying dis-
turbance in the economic life of the country," Dr. Stoddard
claimed.*

*(2) Social. They "had different habits, manners, customs, at-
titudes, and domestic relations between themselves and their
neighbors and their community as a whole. This led to a whole
series of difficulties which inevitably made trouble both among
themselves and between them and the Nordic element in the
population."*

*(3) Political. They "have different traditions. They do not
accept democratic self-government and trial by jury." The doctor
cited an average Sicilian immigrant as an example.*

*"The average Sicilian differs with us in his attitude toward
courts and the law. . . . He does not trust the law, and there is
a good reason for it. Italy has never had good laws; their justice
is not always just. . . . You may be sure that a man coming from
a country like that, where heroes are brigands who rob the rich
and give to the poor, would not fit into our communities."*

*Dr. Stoddard admitted that some of the results of the law have
been "unfortunate." "It has hurt the feelings of the southern
Europeans in this country. But why look exclusively at that side
of the picture? What about the feelings of the older stocks?"*

*The National Origins Plan gives proper importance to all the
immigrants in this country at the present time, and to their descendants, Dr. Stoddard said.*

NEGATIVE (Mr. Darrow):

I am glad my friend wants to meet this question squarely. Facing things squarely is what I believe in doing, and he does also.

The law as it stands today, passed in 1924, provides that 150,000 immigrants may come to the United States annually, and that the number should be fixed for each country according to the number of citizens of that country who had emigrated to the United States, but that it should be the number of citizens who had emigrated previous to 1890—thirty-five years before the law was passed. Instead of using 1924 as the basis of immigration quotas, they dated it back thirty-five years. Why? So they could get Nordics from England and Scotland, and Norway, and Sweden, and exclude the people from Italy, France, and the Balkan states, and Russian Jews.

The problem is clear. Our friend does not dodge it. To him and to some other people here who claim to be old stock, the northern European Nordics are the salt of the earth. I am a foreigner; my people didn't get here until about 1710. They got here, and now I am asked to close the doors to the people who come over on a later ship. I am not for it, for several reasons.

Our friend talks about the right of countries to do things. Countries have rights only when they have power to enforce them. I don't agree with him because I have imagination; that is all. I can imagine myself being an Italian and wanting a better chance, or being a Russian Jew and wanting a better chance, or being an Austrian and wanting a better chance. It is hard for me to forget that there are other people on earth besides the stock I came from.

He speaks of the people in the United States now as if they owned this country. Why, the first of them came over on the Mayflower. They couldn't stay at home without going to jail for debt. They were selfish, superstitious, and bigoted in the extreme. They came over here to get a chance. The real American was the Indian, and they solved that problem by killing him. The land was occupied, but they took it, and then our Puritan fathers proceeded to pass the most outrageous laws that any country ever knew anything about.

What are our institutions, anyway? He spoke of trial by jury. There is a very strong, active element in the United States now who are trying to destroy trial by jury, and every last one of them is a Nordic, and they are rich. I know of some of these Nordics who have taken the best mines and the best buildings, and the land of America, and they want to keep every last one of the rest of us out. My ancestors came here to get a better chance, and I don't believe in closing the doors on the people who would like to come for the same reason now.

We are told that the laboring man is against immigration. I don't know what he is for and against this year, and he doesn't know what he is for and against next year. I have always been for the poor man, but I am not for injustice as I see it either for the rich man or the poor man. Who are these working men? Most of them haven't been here as long as I have. I have been here so long that I don't need to work. Is it justice to allow these late comers to close the doors and allow nobody else to come? If there is anything like justice, and the rules are not strict, I don't want to believe that stuff. And I am not going to, because even if I haven't found any clear idea of justice I have a clear idea of imagination, of common barnyard sympathy, and it tells me that the people of the world must be treated somewhat alike.

We are told that we must not have the Sicilians here because they are people who rob the rich; well, I should worry. Where do you suppose these rich people get all the money they are getting robbed of? The reason for this is that a few of them think they own America and they want to reduce the people to slavery, and they are doing it almighty fast. They are doing it while they talk of elections and fake prosperity. It is only people who have had prosperity who are prosperous. They own all the mines, all the coal, all the lumber, and everything else that is worth owning. They will soon own all the stores, and the little corner storekeeper can go and tramp the streets, and I wouldn't care much, for they have always been fooled by the very people who are now trying to get their property away from them.

They are combining one thing with another, until they will soon have it all. If the people from southern Europe can help us equalize it, I am for them. But I have no feeling of the divine right of property; not a particle. These things are arranged in this world in a particular way partly because it happened so and partly because they who are on top are the strongest.

Are these descendants of the Mayflower such wonderful people? I don't know. They used to hang old women in New England for being witches, and everybody knows that an old woman couldn't be a witch. These Mayflower descendants are the most devoid of human sympathy of any people on the earth today. What do they care about people? They like to work; that is all.

And do you talk about labor unions being interested in this question? Well, I expect you can fool all the working people as you can the farmers. I think I read in your book, Mr. Stoddard, that the machine power of the United States is equal to the labor of three billion people. Well, at least that statement was correct. A lot of others may have been. We have three billion man-power in the nation, and the working man is afraid to have one hundred and fifty thousand people come into this country in a year. When we learn to take care of the production of these machines, we can take care of the whole world if we want to.

And there is another point. This country isn't a quarter settled, nor a tenth. If it were, and we had the proper social order, would we be poorer than we are now? Three men at work will probably produce more than three times as much as one can now; probably six times as much. Then with proper systems of distribution we shall be so rich that we will die of fat. We can produce now infinitely more than we can consume because the poor people haven't a chance to buy anything. To me, this whole idea is narrow, selfish, unimaginative, and cruel; somehow I can't believe it is a good thing. I think it would be a good thing for the United States to get a little idealism into her.

My friend is entirely wrong when he says that this act was brought about by a bright light which dawned in 1920 and grew until in 1924 it resulted in the most unjust law that America ever passed—and that is going some. Do you suppose it was passed because there was any need on the part of the working man? Did it grow out of any idea of political expediency? No; it came from the mistaken idea of patriotism. This kind of patriotism is a heritage from the war; it was handed down by the army, the navy, and now it is being dispensed throughout Rotary Clubs, the Eagles, and other clubs that are shouting themselves hoarse about patriotism; they know nothing about it.

The whole movement is narrow, stupid, mean, contemptible. I can, I believe, point out a few broad principles that should affect human beings. We have wandered from the ideas of the past; we used to encourage people to come here. The only habit or custom they have that is different from ours is that they take a drink of wine in the open, whereas we have to hide to drink ours. I have traveled quite extensively abroad and some in America, though I prefer to travel in Europe because of the present drought in America. Of course, Canada will do.

Are our political institutions any different than theirs? Before the war the king of Italy had no power; Italy was governed completely as England is governed by Parliament. Today she has a usurper who is an absolute tyrant, but the Italians don't like him any more than we do, and some day he will forget to put on his steel shirt, and it will be the last of him.

And was there any difference between the Italian government and the British government before the war? They sent their boys and had them killed for democracy, just as we did. And now that the war is over we say, "You can't come and associate with us descendants of the old Puritan fathers who hanged old women as witches."

When was it that that load of Pilgrims came over? That was

Clarence Darrow

about 1620, I believe. And they landed on Plymouth Rock; that was a tough day. What is there about those people that isn't true about everybody else? What else was different or is today different about these southern Europeans? Their family life? No. They have five wives at once, and we have them one at a time.

I knew my father and my mother; I knew two of my grandparents; back of that I have only heard; I know nothing further. How far can you go back and still know that pure Nordic blood is running in your veins? Why, we are mixed with all the animal species. Did you ever take out your blood, drop by drop, and say, "Here is a drop of English blood; here is one of Swedish; I am sorry, but here is some Italian blood." And one time, to be a Roman was to be greater than to be a king. Can you sort it out? I don't think so. If I could, I would turn out the Nordic.

There is no such thing as a race. There are people who are isolated in certain communities for a long time and they take on particular characteristics, but spread them out over a long period of time and they vanish. What do we know about the origin of things, anyhow?

Let us look at the history of the world. First the Chaldeans, then the Babylonians, then the Egyptians. Coming down to the modern world, we get a great deal from the Greeks—perhaps the greatest people who ever lived. Of course the Nordics would have been greater if they had lived then. And then the Romans, the Italians whom we speak of so lightly; the great colonizers and empire builders. Then we come down to the English; and now the Americans. Where are we going? We are probably on our way. Soon we shall land in the dust heap and something else will take our places.

When you try to interfere with the working out of the laws of nature, you get hurt, and for our puny minds to say that this is good and that is bad, and that this is better and that is worse for the short time that we shall be here on earth is just foolishness.

Immigration restriction is the order of the day, answered Dr. Stoddard.

"Everywhere you see protective measures taken by countries with high living standards against countries with low living standards, and for that very reason it has become very much more imperative for us to keep up our barriers, otherwise immigrants will come from all parts of the world by the tens of millions. And then what will remain of our . . . opportunities here? We shall be swamped economically as well as every other way," he claimed.

Dr. Stoddard contradicted Darrow's assertion that the Founding Fathers believed in having the doors wide open. Dr. Stoddard said that Washington, Patrick Henry and the "arch-democrat Thomas Jefferson" were against a wholesale immigration from foreign sources.

Put the immigration law on a permanent basis, he urged. "Give everybody a chance who is already here in this country and then let the differentiation of the birth rate take care of the future."

NEGATIVE REBUTTAL (Mr. Darrow):

I may say that my friend seems to meet this issue squarely, but it seems that there is no discrimination. Is the present law which discriminates against the southeastern European a good policy? If there is no question, then what is this all about?

Just because somebody comes here and raises more food, should that make me poorer? No; it ought to make me richer. There is no excuse for a poor man in America. And yet Secretary Davis estimates that eighty-five per cent of the people in America are poor. Well, they didn't all vote for Al Smith; some of them voted for the high-priest of efficiency—because of prosperity. These folks are not poor because America is over-populated. If our population were reduced to ten million, eighty-five per cent of them would be poor. If it were increased to five hundred million, still eighty-five per cent of them would be poor.

I do not know why my friend is interested in the unborn millions who have a right to be born. These millions of unborn Americans consist of the trillions of cells in the future women of the race down the course of perhaps a million years, and the septillions of male cells that might possibly happen to fertilize those particular cells if certain accidents should turn out that way. I never asked to be born; that isn't the way we got here. Now you are here; what are you going to do about it? We all have some intelligence. We have a little common idealism to let other people live, and about all we can do to settle a question rightly is to settle it upon what little light we have.

We drove the Indian out because there wasn't room here for both races, and the Indian was already becoming crowded. What right had we to say to the people of the rest of the world that they can't come? Why can't they come? Because away down the course of time, perhaps a million years hence, the unborn babies are struggling to get born in America.

Now I have one kind of imagination; my friend has another. I can't for the life of me understand anybody who is worrying about what is going to happen to him in five hundred thousand years. There won't be any America to me in fifteen years; perhaps a little less. I have looked up the obituary tables. Why should I worry about what is going to happen in America a thousand years from now? I don't. I have children, but they must take their chances with all the other children of the world. They need expect no pile of money to be left by me. I can help them best by trying to make the world decent so that every child who lives may have a chance.

There is no excuse for poverty, especially in America, and

there is no use for it anywhere else. Is England poor? Why? Because a few people own all of it. Need France or Germany be poor, barring a war they have just been through? Why have they been poor? Just for the same reason that a few people in the world take it all. Are the people of China poor? Yes. The older a country is and the more thoroughly organized it is, the poorer the people are.

If an old Italian comes to America and gets three dollars a day, does that make you poorer? It is not production that causes poverty; it is lack of distribution. If we ever get to the point where the captains of industry turn their attention to the distribution of things instead of production, this question will be solved.

I have done everything about labor except work. I have tried many of their cases, and I sympathize with them on account of their conditions of labor. Have you ever a time when working men seeking higher wages or better conditions were not met by the combined wealth of the rich, or by a machine? The rich never did care, and they never will care; they are interested in keeping America for the Americans, and to keep out bolshevist ideas. They don't even know what these words mean. They say the same old fool things over and over again, without a single thought as to what the words mean. They are all organized for a common purpose—to keep things as they are.

I am not in favor of keeping things as they are; I would like to make them better, but I do not like to make them better by forgetting the poor of other lands, by injustice, by oppression, by wrong. I don't think justice can ever grow on injustice; I don't believe that kindness and humanity can ever come from selfishness. I do not believe that because we get to a place first where there is plenty of room, that we should say to others like ourselves, "You can't come."

Are these men afraid of Russian working men or Russian ideas? Are they afraid of Russian laborers or Russian Jews? Why is it, if American machinery is equal to three billion men, that we can't live in comfort and plenty? There is just one reason, that's all—

Clarence Darrow

the horrible injustice of an unfair division of wealth. We have forgotten all about it; we have lost all sense of proportion; we have lost all sympathy with our fellow-men.

Isn't that a fine picture here in America? With our great natural resources we can produce enough to feed the whole world. Here in America, and we must keep everyone else out because of the unborn millions. Germany, France, and England are doing the same thing. What is it? Is it anything less than the backsweep of a great war that carried with it all the human feeling that man has acquired? All over the world we find that the war for democracy made everybody cruel and hard. We told everybody to fight for democracy, and now we are fighting for the spoils.

I find again that nothing will pay in the long run unless it meets our feeling of kindness, of humanity, of universal sympathy, of the brotherhood of man which Christians talk about on Sunday but whose gates they close up on Monday.

Why, if Jesus Christ, as the story has been told, should land in Wilmington tomorrow, he would be deported. He would be lucky if he got off with that.

I tell you, this world has grown soggy and cruel since the Great War. I was a near-patriot myself. I believed in the war, and fought for it with oratory, if this is oratory, but I am beginning to realize that I was not quite logical in my arguments. I see the direct result that comes to every country on the earth —tyranny, oppression, filled jails, prohibition, and every other plague that infested Egypt.

Now let us see if we can't settle this question. Are you going to have less because somebody else comes here and works? If you do, something is wrong with distribution, isn't it? I remember when that great statesman, the inspired president who was given to the United States as a direct act of the Almighty, Calvin Coolidge, had his attention called to the troubles the southern farmers were having about the price of cotton. He said, "Well, we will try to do something for you, but you mustn't raise so much again." The same is true of the farmers in the West. But when the manufacturers are stumped on account of over-production they don't have any trouble. They own the mills, and they can shut them down until the demand catches up. The trouble with our world is that we are suffering from too much.

There isn't any need for poverty. There is room on the earth for all the people who are here. Although population may overtake the food supply, it hasn't done so yet. And we may be able to make food out of the primary elements more cheaply than we can raise it. We may be able to make everything we need, and much more cheaply than at present. If the work of three billion people can be done by the machines invented in the last generation, what difference can be made in our economic organization by having one Italian or Russian Jew come over here?

There are such people as descendants of Nordics; they are hounds for the Nordics. And now we have a law, unjust in every way you look at it, dated back to 1890 because at that time the southern European hadn't come in such great numbers.

Why is an Englishman so much better than an Italian? The Italians have produced wealth on the old abandoned New England farms. I suppose they will own New England some day; and I know they will be more tolerant than the Puritans ever were. Why should we cut out anybody? Isn't one as good as another?

I suppose I am a Nordic. I am not bragging about it; I am apologizing for it. Of course, I am not a Puritan in much. I believe in taking a drink; I believe in letting everybody else take a drink. But I am broadminded about it; I don't believe in forcing a Puritan to take a drink if he doesn't want it. And I am of Puritan stock, but from so far back that I can't trace it.

Men can't be separated on kinds of blood any longer. As you know, all kinds of blood circulate in all human beings who live. We go back to Europe; they go back to Asia; for a million years men have been tramping up and down over the face of America. I can't know all my ancestors; I can't know all the kinds of blood that are mixed in me.

Clarence Darrow

Who am I to say that my kind alone shall come to America and all the rest must stay away? I believe this earth is big enough for the human race. When it gets so crowded that they can't all live, if I am here I will be willing to cast lots to decide who shall die and who shall stay, and give everybody an even break.

Debate held in 1929.

THE NRA
AND "FAIR
COMPETITION"

*It is all well enough to talk about fair competition and
unfair competition, but the opportunity of the small businessman
to compete with the large concerns on equal terms is about
as fair as would be a contest in the arena between
a thoroughly equipped prizefighter and a child.*

1934. Marie Curie dies . . . Russia,
Greece, Yugoslavia and Turkey sign
non-aggression pact . . . Upton Sin-
clair, Democratic Party candidate for
governor of California, offers his
"End Poverty in California" plan . . .
Darrow appointed by F.D.R. to head
National Recovery Review Board . . .
Dionne quintuplets born in Callander,
Ontario . . . F. E. Townsend intro-
duces his Old Age Pension plan . . .
"The Drunkard," originally produced
in 1843, is revived . . . Protocols of
the Elders of Zion denounced by
Swiss expert as "scandalous literature
of the worst species" . . . William
Saroyan attracts attention with *The
Daring Young Man on the Flying
Trapeze* . . . American actress Marie
Dressler and author-diplomat Brand
Whitlock die.

Clarence Darrow

THE SHERMAN ANTI-TRUST LAW WAS PASSED BY CONGRESS AND approved July 2, 1890, by Benjamin Harrison, president of the United States, nearly forty-five years ago. This statute, as passed, was drastic in its terms and far-reaching in its scope. It provided for both civil and criminal prosecutions against any individuals or combinations offending the act. It also called for the forfeiture of property by those found guilty, and the right to bring civil cases by those injured through the violation of this law.

During all these years since the passage of that act, cases have been constantly pending in various jurisdictions of the federal courts. Almost every conceivable question of the meaning of the law has been passed upon and construed in the various courts of the country. Repeated efforts, in Congress and out, have been made to abolish and nullify or vitally amend the act. Friends of monopoly have used all sorts of measures to get rid of this statute; while some of its provisions have been modified, still, on the whole, it has been sustained by the courts and has remained a serious obstacle against monopoly. The Anti-Trust Act, even in its present form, should

NRA and "Fair Competition"

remain in the statutes as an important deterrent to the unrestrained liberty of Big Business to trample down and crush all competitors who stand in its way.

The National Industrial Recovery Act (NIRA) provided for the repeal of the Sherman Anti-Trust Law, and this act no doubt is largely responsible for the fact that the large corporations were almost unanimous in their support of the NIRA. With the repeal of the Sherman Anti-Trust Law, and the Clayton Act subsequently passed, there is nothing left in the United States forbidding monopoly and extortion, which ran riot in the days of unrestrained corporate rule. Before the passage of the NIRA, the rights of the people had been closely guarded by the Clayton Act and the Anti-Trust Law, aided and watched by the Federal Trade Commission.

It is hardly necessary to discuss the question of whether the Sherman Anti-Trust Law and the Clayton Act conflict with the NIRA. If large corporations, which for years have been fighting the Anti-Trust Law, in court and out, had not believed it necessary to have these laws repealed before treating with the National Recovery Administration (NRA), then why did the statute which created the NRA provide for the repeal? None of the large corporations that have accepted the NRA could have been forced to come under the jurisdiction of this Recovery Act. For more than forty years, these and other corporations have strenuously fought the Sherman and Clayton Acts, and the courts have never released them from the control of these laws.

Likewise it is evident that the NRA offered the long-desired release from the Sherman Law in exchange for accepting the NRA. Had there been any strong sentiment in the country for the repeal of the Sherman Act it would have made itself manifest in an effort to have Congress repeal this law.

The enemies of the Sherman Law are the large combinations which are the foundation and the backbone of the NRA. In the past forty-five years, a large percentage of the chief offenders among the large corporations have been prosecuted under the Sherman Law or the Clayton Act for monopolistic practices. It is perfectly plain that the large concerns were promised the repeal of the

Sherman Anti-Trust Law on condition that they would support the NRA. However objectionable some provisions of the NRA might be to Big Business, its representatives were willing to assume the risk in order to be released from the restrictions of the Sherman Anti-Trust Law.

A direct effort of Congress to repeal these anti-trust laws would have met overwhelming defeat. If by any chance or ill fortune such an effort could have been successful, a great majority of senators and congressmen who voted for the repeal would have found their seats occupied by others at the following session.

These statutes have so long been a part of American law that they could not have been repealed by a frontal attack; they could only have been wiped out by a large organization like the NRA, that had succeeded in making Congress believe that the promised blessings of the NRA would justify the overthrow of these two well-established protective laws. It is passing strange that a law against monopoly should have been repealed by an organization supposed to have been created for the benefit of the common people.

The Sherman Anti-Trust Law was passed after much discussion and long consideration. It grew out of the feeling and understanding of the people at that particular time. For a great many years, intelligent men and women had observed and felt the growing power of monopoly; the division between the rich and poor was constantly widening; new methods of business, the growth and development of railroads, and the power of concentrated wealth called for heroic remedies. And the Sherman Anti-Trust Act was a heroic measure.

True it is that the courts had for years been modifying and chipping away at this law until it lost much of its original virility, but still the Act itself has remained one of the chief obstacles to monopoly through forty-odd years. During all this time it was either feared or respected by the great majority of the American people. It was left for the NRA to destroy the statute after the monopolists had failed.

The NRA itself was the result of dire distress in the land, which now after four years of ills and evils is still unrelieved. The poverty and dread of our people drove them to such desperation that they willingly accepted any promised panacea. While American citizens had carefully protected the Sherman Anti-Trust Law through more than forty years, they threw it away without protest or objection to induce Big Business to adopt the NRA.

It is true that competition has many times caused distress and failure; for competition does not think or feel; still, thus far, we have found nothing to take the place of competition excepting monopoly, which is but a modern form of slavery. Unrestricted business tends toward monopoly. It gives an advantage to the strong, the clever, the selfish and unscrupulous. It is the rule of the jungle. The problem in business, and in life, has always been to preserve freedom without monopoly. This is an old, old question; and it bids fair to plague mankind for a still longer time to come. We have solved it as we do most questions by taking both courses at the same time.

The backbone of the NRA is made up of the big institutions of the United States; these monopolies were permitted by the NRA to frame their own codes, and they fixed their own rates for what they wished to sell: oil, steel, coal, lumber, moving pictures, electrical appliances, and, in short, all Big Business. Practically every officer and director of each one of the big corporations now in charge of the management are the same officers who had charge of their affairs before. Each concern made its own code, and fixed its prices for itself. This price was not the maximum that they could charge, but it was the minimum that they could take. They could sell no lower than the price fixed, but the sky was the limit if they cared to go the other way.

Small concerns in the same lines of business likewise were permitted to fix their own prices, with the same provisions that they could not lower them but could raise them if they wished; but the price for each, large and small, was ordered to be the same in each line of business. This seeming fairness disposed of the "chiselers" but left the big operators to fix the rates.

The wealthy institutions, generally located in the large cities, could afford to spend whatever they chose in advertising, soliciting, or in making a show. The small manufacturer or dealer, generally living in towns or the smaller cities, could hire labor cheaper, dispense with extravagant advertising and many kinds of overhead and all elaborate show, and be content with smaller profits. It is impossible for any small dealer to compete with Big Business and mass production. The smaller concerns as a rule furnish the only competition that Big Business could encounter, and it is obvious that this institution alone is rapidly driving all small business out of the field.

Since this policy has been adopted and carried into effect, the so-called "chiselers" are fast going into bankruptcy, and the large concerns are taking the field to themselves. It is all well enough to talk about fair competition and unfair competition, but the opportunity of the small businessman to compete with the large concerns on equal terms is about as fair as would be a contest in the arena between a thoroughly equipped prizefighter and a child. The statute creating the NRA declared that one of its purposes was to establish fair competition, the very aim and object of the Anti-Trust Law, which the NRA has nullified. No one knows the meaning of the term "fair competition"; all business dreads and fears competition; all business seeks to prevent and destroy it when it appears. Still, competition exists in all trades and commerce, and so far, we have not found a way to protect society without it.

The claim of those supporting the NRA that they are seeking to eliminate unfair competition raises the question of why the NRA should want to encourage competition when in the very law that they have produced they have eliminated the Sherman Anti-Trust Law. Senator Gerald P. Nye of North Dakota has called attention to numerous instances where corporations and trusts, pretending to comply with the codes, or even daring to ignore their rulings, have put up prices to exorbitant points, and thus driven small business out of the field.

Everyone familiar with current events knows something about the amount of money that has been lavishly scattered broadcast over the western prairies of the United States to revive the farming industry, which is in a grave dilemma. The effect on the agricultural element clearly shows the disastrous results of price-fixing as we know it. For instance, land has been laid waste, animals have been sacrificed, crops plowed down beyond the danger of any one using them, all in the name of prosperity-to-come. Scarcity boosted prices, but the drought came, which even the shrewdest schemers could neither anticipate nor avert, the supply was still further diminished, the market depleted, and the income thus made practically non-existent. Now the prices are higher, but the farmer has nothing to sell or to spend.

Then, too, the farmer pays an undue share of taxes, direct and indirect; his land cannot be hidden away out of sight, and he is an easy mark for tax-gatherers and creditors. And he keeps the farm because no one will take it. All told, the farmer is worse off than before prices were raised for him. Meanwhile, the farmer has been made aware of changes. The farmer is both a buyer and seller. He knows that for all he buys, from overalls to gasoline, prices have soared all the way from sixty-seven to one hundred twenty per cent, determined by industrialists who apply themselves to "huddling" around tables somewhere and wisely deciding such matters.

The farmer can scarcely buy an article that is not regulated and priced by some trust or monopoly, from farm implements to gasoline, and such gain as has resulted from his products has landed in the hands of those whose profits were already too high in proportion.

Cotton towels have risen eighty-seven per cent, according to a recent compilation; women's hosiery, sixty-three per cent; children's stockings, ninety-four per cent; men's socks, sixty-seven per cent; ribbed undersuits, seventy-three per cent; cheap shirts, a fraction more than seventy-two per cent; and overalls more than one hundred per cent.

At such a rate, it is not possible for the farmer to meet taxes, mortgages, and living expenses. Not alone the farmer, but all working people and small manufacturers and small dealers and their families, who represent about ninety per cent of the population of the United States, are victimized by present-day conditions, faring no better where fewer business hours are permitted for earnings with which to meet the increased cost of the necessaries of life. For this vast majority of the citizens of the United States, the standard of living has everywhere been greatly lowered. It seems like adding insult to injury to force people to abstain from producing those things that all must have if they are to exist; to compel them to consume less than usual, to resign themselves to poverty, in order that the little that is allotted and allowed shall stretch just short of the breaking point.

The Anti-Trust Law may not be the perfect and complete checkmate for all economic evils of today, but it has long served as a strong and potent factor toward discouraging and deterring many impositions on the humbler competitors for a chance in the business world, and has kept open the avenues furnishing a livelihood for those who depend on their labors, without inflicting compulsory idleness, non-production, and curtailed earnings leaving them destitute. The Anti-Trust Law and Clayton Act safeguarded against such domination as today forces many heretofore self-supporting men and women into breadlines and humiliating visits to the counters of local relief associations. The Anti-Trust Law and the Clayton Act, "suspended" by the NIRA, if not killed outright, are made helpless and useless under an anaesthetic that renders them little better than buried unless something can be done to revive and restore them. They should not be tamely surrendered. They are too important as factors against price-fixers and their new co-operators, scarcity-dictators.

The Rotarian, *November, 1934.*

PART TWO

ON MEN

ROBERT BURNS

Burns was a natural leveler, and while men still
believed in the "divine right of kings," he preached
"man was the divine king of rights."

IT IS DIFFICULT TO ACCOUNT FOR a genius like Robert Burns. His life and work seem to defy the laws of heredity and environment alike. The beasts of the field were scarcely bound closer to the soil than were the ancestors from which he sprang; and from his early infancy he was forced to follow the stony path his father trod before. As a mere child, he learned how hard it is to sustain life in the face of an unfriendly nature and a cruel, bitter world. He was early bred to toil; not the work that gives strength and health, but the hard, constant, manual labor that degrades and embitters, deforms and twists and stunts the body and the soul alike. Burns was denied even the brief years of childhood—those few short years which most of us look back upon from our disappointments and cares as the one bright spot in a gray and level plain.

It is not by the works he has left us that Robert Burns is to be truly judged. Fortune endowed him with a wondrous brain and a still rarer and greater gift: a tender, loving, universal heart. But as if she grudged him these and sought to destroy or stunt their power, she cast his lot in a social and religious environment as hard and forbidding as the cold and sterile soil of his native land; and from these surroundings alone he was obliged to draw the warmth and color and sunshine that should have come from loving hearts, generous bounties, and bright, blue southern skies. In measuring the power and character of Robert Burns, we must remember the hard and cruel conditions of his life, and judge of his great achievements in the light of these.

Measured by the standards of our day and generation, the life of Robert Burns was a failure and mistake. He went back to the great common mother as naked of all the trappings and baubles which men call wealth as when she first placed the struggling infant on its mother's breast.

The great masterpieces of his genius were not created in the pleasant study of a home of refinement, luxury, and ease, but were born in the fields, the farmyard, the stable, while the "monarch peasant" was bending above the humblest tasks that men pursue for bread. Only the most ordinary education was within the reach of this child of toil, and the world's great storehouses of learning, literature, and art were sealed forever from his sight; and yet, with only the rude peasants with whom his life was spent, the narrow setting of bleak fields and gray hills which was the small stage on which he moved, and the sterile Scotch dialect with which to paint, he stirred the hearts of men with the sweetest, purest melody that has ever moved the human soul.

Olive Schreiner tells of an artist whose pictures shone with the richest, brightest glow. His admirers gazed upon the canvas and wondered where he found the colors, so much rarer than any they had ever seen before. Other artists searched the earth, but could find no tints like his; he died with the secret in his breast. And when they undressed him to put his grave-clothes on, they found an old wound, hard and jagged, above his heart; and still they wondered where he found the coloring for his work. Robert Burns, perhaps more than any other man who lived, taught the great truth that poets are not made but born; that the richest literature, the brightest gems of art, even the most pleasing earthly prospects are less than one spark of the divine fire which alone can kindle the true light. Robert Burns, like all great artists, taught the world that the beauty of the landscape and the grandeur and pathos of life depend, not upon the external objects that nature has chanced

Clarence Darrow

to place before our view, but upon the soul of the artist, which alone can really see and interpret the manifold works of the great author, beside which all human effort is so poor and weak.

Millet looked at the French peasants standing in their wooden shoes, digging potatoes from the earth and pausing to bow reverently at the sounding of the Angelus, and saw in this simple life, so close to nature's heart, more beauty and pathos and poetry than all the glittering courts of Europe could produce. And Robert Burns, whose broad mind and sympathetic soul made him kin to all living things, had no need to see the splendor and gaiety of wealth and power, to visit foreign shores and unknown lands; but the flowers, the heather, the daisies, the bleak fields, the pelting rains, the singing birds, the lowing cattle, and above all, the simple country folk seen through his eyes, and felt by his soul, and held in his all-embracing heart, were covered with a beauty and a glory that all the artificial world could not create, and that his genius has endowed with immortal life.

Robert Burns did not borrow his philosophy from the books, his humanity from the church, or his poetry from the schools. Luckily for us he escaped all these, and unfettered and untaught, went straight to the soul of nature to learn from the great source the harmony and beauty and unity that pervades the whole; and he painted these with colors drawn from his great human heart. His universal sympathy gave him an insight into life that students of science and philosophy can never reach. Contemplating nature, and seeing her generous bounties lavished alike on all her children, he could not but contrast this with the selfishness and inhumanity of man, which crushes out the weak and helpless and builds up the great and strong. Burns was a natural leveler, and while men still believed in the "divine right of kings," he preached that "man was the divine king of rights." None knew better than he the injustice of the social life in which he lived, and in which we live today. Burns knew, as all men of intelligence understand, that worldly goods are not and never have been given as a reward of either brains or merit.

It's hardly in a body's power
To keep at times, frae being sour,
*   To see how things are shared;*
How best o' chiels are whiles in want
While coofs on countless thousands rant
*   And ken na how to wair't.*

The voice of the French Revolution could not fail to move a soul like that of Robert Burns. This great struggle for human liberty came upon the world with almost the suddenness of an earthquake, and with much of its terror, too. Here the poor and the oppressed felt the first substantial hope for freedom that had pierced the long, dark centuries since history told the acts of men. To the oppressors and the powerful, who hated liberty then as they ever have, before and since, it was a wild, dread threat of destruction and ruin to their precious "rights." When the struggle commenced, Burns was enjoying the munificent salary of fifty pounds a year as a whiskey gauger in the village of Dumfries. He had already spent a winter in Edinburgh, and had been fêted and dined by the aristocracy and culture of Scotland's capital without losing his head, although at no small risk. An acquaintance and entertainer of the nobility and an incumbent of a lucrative office, there was but one thing for Burns to do; this was to condemn the Revolution and lend his trenchant pen to the oppressor's cause; but this course he flatly refused to take. He openly espoused the side of the people, and wrote the "Tree of Liberty," one of his most stirring songs, in its defense.

Upon this tree, there grows sic fruit,
*   Its virtues a' can tell man;*
It raises man aboon the brute,
*   It mak's him ken himsel' man.*
Gif ance the peasant taste a bit,
*   He's greater than a lord man.*

King Louis thought to cut it down
*   When it was unco sma' man;*
For this the watchman cracked his crown,
*   Cut aff his head an' a' man.*

Clarence Darrow

It is perhaps as a singer of songs that the literary fame of Burns will longest be preserved. No other poet has ever breathed such music from his soul. His melodies are as sweet and pure as the bubbling spring, and as natural and spontaneous as ever came from the throat of the nightingale or the lark. These songs could not be made. The feeling and passion that left his soul bore this music as naturally as the zephyr that has fanned the strings of the Aeolian harp. The meter of these songs was not learned by scanning Latin verse, or studying the dry rules that govern literary art, but it was born of the regular pulsebeats, which in the heart of nature's poets are as smooth and unstudied as the rippling laughter of her purling brooks.

> *John Anderson, my jo, John,*
> *When we were first acquent,*
> *Your locks were like the raven,*
> *Your bonnie brow was brent;*
> *But now your brow is beld, John,*
> *Your locks are like the snow;*
> *But blessing on your frosty pow,*
> *John Anderson, my jo.*

> *John Anderson, my jo, John,*
> *We climb the hill tegither,*
> *And mony a canty day, John,*
> *We've had wi' ane anither;*
> *Now we maun totter down, John,*
> *But hand in hand we'll go,*
> *And sleep tegither at the foot,*
> *John Anderson, my jo.*

Who was this Burns that sang these sweet songs and whose musical soul was stirred by every breeze and moved to poetry by every lovely face and form that came within his view? Biographers and critics and admirers have praised the genius and begged excuses for the man. Without asking charity for this illustrious singer, let us view him in the light of justice, exactly as he was.

It is not difficult to understand the character of Robert Burns.

His heart was generous and warm and kind; his mind was open as the day, and his soul was sensitive to every breath that stirred the air. These qualities have made the poet loved in every land on earth, and brought more pilgrims to his grave than were ever drawn to the tomb of any other poet or author that has ever lived and died. And yet the shortsighted, carping, moralizing world, with solemn voice and wisdom ill-assumed, has ever told how much better and holier he could have been and should have been. Poor, silly, idle world, can you never learn that the qualities that make us strong must also make us weak; that the heart that melts at suffering and pain is made of clay so sensitive and fine as to be moved and swayed by all the emotions of the soul? Would you serve the weak, the suffering and the poor—would you calm their fears and dry their eyes and feel with them the cruel woes of life—you must wear your heart upon your sleeve, and then of course the daws will peck it into bits. Would you keep it safely hidden from the daws, you must hide it in a breast of stone or ice and keep it only for yourself. Perhaps we may admire the man that walks with steady step along a straight and narrow path, unmoved by all the world outside. He never feels and never errs. But we cannot ask of either man the virtues that belong to both, and when our choice is made we must take the strength and weakness too.

We look at the mountaintop, lifting its snow-crowned head high into the everlasting blue, and are moved with wonder and with awe. Above is the endless sky; below, the world with all its bickering and strife, the clouds, the lightning and the storm; but the mountain, cold, impassive, changeless, unmoved by all the world, looks ever upward to the eternal heavens above. Again we gaze on the peaceful, fertile lowlands, rich with their generous harvests yet unborn—beautiful with their winding streams and grassy fields, ever ready to bestow bounteously on all that ask, demanding little and lavishly returning all; and we love the quiet, rustic, generous beauty of the scene. The mountain is majestic and sublime, and the yielding, generous lowlands are beautiful and pleasing too. We love them both, but we cannot have them both at once and both in one.

Clarence Darrow

Robert Burns, and all men like him that ever lived, were always giving from their generous souls. In the cold judgment of the world, Burns wasted many a gem upon the thoughtless, worthless crowd, who consumed a life he should have spent for nobler things. But the flower that never wastes its fragrance has no perfume to give out. If it is truly sweet, its strength is borne away on every idle wind that blows. Robert Burns with lavish bounty shed his life and fragrance on every soul he met. He loved them all and loved them well; his sensitive, harmonious soul vibrated to every touch, and moved in perfect harmony with every heart that came within his reach. The lives of men like him are one long harmony; but as they pass along the stage of life, they leave a trail of disappointed hopes, and broken hearts, and vain regrets. But of all the tragedies great and small that mark their path, the greatest far and most pathetic is the sad and hopeless wreck that ever surely falls upon the exhausted artist's life.

The life of Burns was filled with wrecks—with promises made and broken, with hopes aroused and then dashed to earth again. It was filled with these because one man cannot give himself personally to all the world. The vices of Robert Burns, perhaps like those of all the rest that ever lived, were virtues carried to excess. Of course, the world could not understand it then, and cannot understand it now, and perhaps never will, for slander and malice and envy, like death, always love a shining mark.

The life of Burns is the old Greek fable told again. Achilles' mother would make him invulnerable by dipping him in the river Styx. She held him by the heel, which remained unwashed and vulnerable and finally brought him to his death. To whatever dizzy height we climb, and however invulnerable we seek to be, there still remains with all the untouched heel that binds us to the earth. And after all, this weak and human spot is the truest bond of kinship that unites the world.

It is difficult to understand our own being; it is impossible to know our fellow man's, but I have faith to think that all life is but a portion of one great inclusive power, and that all is good and none is bad.

Robert Burns has been dust for a hundred years, and yet the world knows him better now than the neighbors that lived beside his door. I look back upon the little village of Dumfries—not the first or the last town that entertained angels unawares. I see poor Robert Burns passing down the street, and the pharisees and self-righteous walking on the other side. The bill of indictment brought against him by the Dumfries community was long and black: he was intemperate, immoral, irreligious, and disloyal to the things that were. The first two would doubtless have been forgiven, but the others could not be condoned. And so this illustrious man walked an outcast through the town that today makes its proudest boast that it holds the ashes of the mighty dead, who in life was surrounded by such a halo of glory that his neighbors could not see his face.

A hundred years ago Scotland was held tightly in the grasp of the Presbyterian faith. Calvinism is not very attractive even now, especially to us that live and expect to die outside its fold, but even Calvinism has softened and changed in a hundred years. Burns was too religious to believe in the Presbyterian faith, and to the Scottish Covenanter there was no religion outside the Calvinistic creed. How any man can read the poetry of Robert Burns and not feel the deep religious spirit that animates its lines is more than I can see. True, he ridicules the dogmas and the creeds that held the humanity and intellect of Scotland in their paralyzing grasp; but creeds and dogmas are the work of man; they come and go; are born and die; serve their time and pass away; but the love of humanity, the instincts of charity and tenderness, the deep reverence felt in the presence of the infinite mystery and power that pervade the universe: these, the basis of all the religions of the earth, remain forever, while creeds and dogmas crumble to the dust.

Scotland of a hundred years ago measured Burns' religion by "Holy Willie's Prayer," "The Holy Fair," and kindred songs. The world a hundred years from now will not make these the only test. Dumfries and all the unco' guid of Scotland could not forgive Burns for writing:

O Thou wha in the heavens dost dwell,
Wha, as it pleases best thysel',
Sends ane to heaven and ten to hell,
  A' for thy glory,
And no for ony guid or ill
  They've done afore thee!

I bless and praise thy matchless might,
When thousands thou hast left in night,
That I am here afore thy sight,
  For gifts an' grace,
A burnin' and a shinin' light,
  To a' this place.

Lord, hear my earnest cry an' pray'r,
Against that presbt'ry o' Ayr;
Thy strong right hand, Lord make it bare
  Upo' their heads!
Lord, weigh it down, an' dinna spare,
  For their misdeeds.

But, Lord, remember me and mine
Wi' mercies temp'ral and divine,
That I for fear and grace may shine,
  Excell'd by name;
And a' the glory shall be thine,
  Amen, Amen.

It was not enough that Robert Burns taught a religion as pure and gentle and loving as that proclaimed by the Nazarene himself. Its meaning and beauty and charity were lost on those who could not see. Long ago it was written that, "Inasmuch as ye have done it unto one of the least of these my brethren, ye have done it unto me." If this is any test of a religious life, then few men will stand as high in the Great Beyond as Robert Burns. This poor poet has melted more hearts to pity and moved more souls to mercy, and inclined more lives to charity than any other poet that ever dreamed and sung. Not men and women and children alone were the object of his bounteous love and tender heart,

but he felt the pain of the bird, the hare, the mouse, and even
the daisy whose roots were upturned to the biting blast. Hear
him sing of the poor bird for whom he shudders at the winter's
cold:

> Ilka hopping bird, wee helpless thing
> That in the merry month o' spring
> Delighted me to hear thee sing,
>   What comes o' thee!
> Where wilt thou cow'r thy chilling wing
>   And close thy ee?

Few men that ever lived would stop and lament with Burns,
as he shattered the poor clay home of the field mouse with his
plow. No matter what he did; no matter what he said; no matter
what his creed; the man that wrote these lines deserves a place
with the best and purest of this world or any other that the
universe may hold:

> Wee, sleekit, cow'rin, tim'rous beastie!
> O, what a panic's in thy breastie!
> Thou need na start awa sae hasty,
>   Wi' bickerin' brattle;
> I wad be laith to rin an' chase thee,
>   Wi' murd'ring prattle.

In a world which still enjoys the brutal chase, where even
clergymen find pleasure in inflicting pain with the inhuman gun
and rod, these lines written a hundred years ago, on seeing a
wounded hare limp by, should place Burns amongst the blessed
of the earth:

> Inhuman man! curse on thy barb'rous art,
> And blasted be thy murder-aiming eye;
> May never pity sooth thee with a sight,
> Nor ever pleasure glad thy cruel heart!
>   *   *   *
> Oft, as by winding Nith I musing wait
> The sober eve, or hail the cheerful dawn,

Clarence Darrow

I'll miss thee sporting o'er the dewy lawn,
And curse the ruffian's aim, and mourn thy
hapless fate.

This was Robert Burns—and yet Dumfries, which held this gentle soul within its walls, and the Protestant world of a hundred years ago, looked at John Calvin piling the faggots around Servetus' form, and knelt before him as a patron, religious saint, while they cast into outer darkness poor Robert Burns with his heart bowed down at the suffering of a wounded hare.

Will this world ever learn what true religion is? Will it ever learn that mercy and pity and charity are more in the sight of the Infinite than all the creeds and dogmas of the earth? Will it ever learn to believe this beautiful verse of Robert Burns:

But deep this truth impressed my mind,
Through all his works abroad;
The heart benevolent and kind,
The most resembles God.

Dear Robert Burns, to place one flower upon your grave, or add one garland to your fame is a privilege indeed. A noble man you were, knighted not by king or queen, but titled by the infinite Maker of us all. You loved the world; you loved all life; you were gentle, kind and true. Your works, your words, your deeds, will live and shine to teach the brotherhood of man, the kinship of all breathing things, and make the world a brighter, gentler, kindlier place because you lived and loved and sung.

From A Persian Pearl and other Essays, *1899*.

WALT WHITMAN

*No one ever fell in love with Whitman's work for
its literary art, but his work must live or die because
of his philosophy of life and the material he chose
from which to weave his songs.*

THE WORK OF WHITMAN STANDS
alone in the literature of the world. Both in substance and construction, he ignored all precedents and dared to be himself. All the rules of form and taste must be unlearned before the world can accept his style as true literary art. Still, it may be that Walt Whitman was a poet, and that some time the world will look back and marvel at the mechanical precision and glittering polish that confines and emasculates for the sake of a purely artificial form.

Measured by the common rules, Whitman's work is neither poetry nor prose; it is remotely allied to the wild chanting of the primitive bards, who looked about at the fresh new marvels of earth and sky and sea, and unhampered by form and rules and customs, sang of the miracles of the universe and the mysteries of life. Whitman seems one of those old bards, fresh from the hand of nature, young with the first creation, the newest handwork of the great Master, untaught in any schools, unfettered by any of the myriad cords which time is ever weaving about the brains and hearts and consciences of men as the world grows gray; a primitive bard of nature, born by some chance or accident in this old, tired, worn-out world, dropped into this nineteenth century with its machines and conventions, its artificial life, its unnatural morals and its fettered limbs. He alone in all the ages seems to have been specially given to the world, still fresh with the imprint of the Creator's hand, and standing amid all our false conventions, natural, simple, true, "naked and not ashamed." To the world with its crowded cities, its diseased bodies, its unnatural desires, its narrow religion, and its false morals, he comes like a breeze of the morning, from the mountains or the sea. Aye, like a breath of that great, creative life, which touched the fresh world and brought forth the green grass, the sparkling waters and the growing, beauteous, natural earth.

No one ever fell in love with Whitman's work for its literary art, but his work must live or die because of his philosophy of life and the material he chose from which to weave his songs. It is in his whole point of view that Walt Whitman stands so much alone. No one else has ever looked on the universe and life as this man did. If religion means devotion to that great unseen power that is ever manifest in all of nature's works, then Walt Whitman was the most reverent soul that ever lived. This man alone of all the world dared defend the Creator in every part and parcel of his work. The high mountains, the deep valleys, the broad plains and the wide seas; the feelings, the desires, and the passions of man; all forms of life and being that exist upon the earth, were to him but several manifestations of a great creative power that formed them all alike, made each one needful to the whole, and every portion sacred through its Master's stamp.

> *And I will show that there is no imperfection in*
> *the present and can be none in the future,*
> *And I will show that whatever happens to anybody*
> *it may be turn'd to beautiful results,*
> *And I will show that nothing can happen more*
> *beautiful than death.*
>
> *And I will thread a thread through my poems that*
> *time and events are compact,*
> *And that all the things of the universe are perfect*
> *miracles, each as profound as any.*
> *I will not make poems with reference to parts.*

> *But I will make poems, songs, thoughts, with*
> *reference to ensemble,*
> *And I will not sing with reference to a day, but*
> *with reference to all days.*

Whitman's philosophy knew no evil and no wrongs. The fact of existence proved the right of existence; in the great workshop of nature every tool had its special use and its rightful place.

The imperfections of the world come from the narrow visions of men. If the perspective is right, the universe is right. From the narrow valley the house may look old and worn, the fences decayed, the fields barren, the woods scraggy and the cliff ragged and bare; but climb to the only place where either life or landscape can be rightly seen, the mountaintop, and look once more. The hills, the valley, the stream, the woods, and the farms have melted and blended into one harmonious whole, and every imperfection has been swept away.

The universe is filled with myriad worlds as important as our own, each one a tiny floating speck in an endless sea of space— each whirling, turning, moving on and on and on, through the countless ages, past and yet to come. No one can tell the purpose of their tireless, endless flight through space; but still we know that each has an orbit of its own, and every world is related to the rest, and every grain of sand and the weakest, feeblest spark of power has its needful place in the balance of the whole. So all of good, and all of bad, and all of life, and all of death, and all of all, has the right to be and must needs be. Walt Whitman did not even know how to divide the evil from the good, but he sang them both alike.

> *I am not the poet of goodness only, I do not decline*
> *to be the poet of wickedness also.*
> *What blurt is this about virtue and about vice?*
> *Evil propels me and reform of evil propels me, I*
> *stand indifferent.*

Happy is the man that has climbed to the height on which Walt Whitman stood. Happy is he that has mastered the haste and impatience of youth, and is content to bide his time. Happy is he that has so far solved the problem of life as to know that reward is not received from others and cannot be withheld by others, but can be given only by ourselves. Such a man has struck the subtle harmony which unites his soul with the universal life, and he knows that no one but himself can cut the cord.

To a great mass of men and women, Walt Whitman is known almost alone by that portion of his work called "Children of Adam." These poems have called forth the fiercest opposition and the bitterest denunciation, and if the common judgment is correct, they are obscene and vile. While this portion of his book is by far the smallest part, still, before the court of public opinion, he must stand or fall upon these lines. In one sense public opinion is right, for unless these stanzas can be defended, his point of view is wrong, and Walt Whitman's work will die. We need not accept all he did, or give unstinted praise to all his work, but his thought and his point of view will determine the place he shall fill in art and life.

It is in his work that the courage and personality of Whitman towers so high above every other man that ever wrote. It is easy for the essayist to speak in general terms and glittering phrases in defense of Whitman's work. His defenders have been many, but he alone has had the courage to speak.

It is not difficult to insist that his "A Woman Waits for Me" is a tremendous work, and as pure as nature's generating power. Still, perhaps few would dare to read it aloud in an assembly of men and women. If Whitman is right, the world is wrong. This poem, and others of its like, in plain words deals with the deepest, strongest, most persistent feelings that move the sentient world. In proportion as they are deeper and stronger than any other, they should the more be the subject of thought and art. And still ages of established convention have made the world pretend ignorance, until no one dares defend his right to life but this brave and simple man.

In both England and America, narrow interpretations of morality have almost stifled art. As remarked by a leading novelist,

"All our literature is addressed to the young schoolgirl." If it will not pass muster before her eyes, it has no right to live, and almost no English or American author has been great enough to rise above these narrow conventions and write the natural and true. The artists of continental Europe have been less fettered and have taken us over a broader range and a wider field. Still, while these authors have told more of life, they have treated these tremendous subjects by drawing the curtain only a little way aside, and giving us a curious, perverted, half stolen look, as if they knew that the picture was unholy and therefore tempting to the gaze. But Walt Whitman approached the human body and the mysteries of life from an entirely different view.

> *If any thing is sacred, the human body is sacred,*
> *And the glory and sweet of man is the token of*
> *manhood untainted,*
> *And in man or woman a clean, strong, firm-fibred body,*
> *is more beautiful than the most beautiful face.*

If Walt Whitman could have drawn the veil from the universe and shown us the living God in all his majesty and power, he would have approached his throne with no greater reverence than when he stripped the human body and pointed to its every part fresh and sacred from its Maker's hand.

No true system of life and morals will exist until the holiest feelings and most potent and eternal power are openly recognized and discussed with neither jest nor shame.

Walt Whitman was the great bard of democracy and equality; not simply the vulgar democracy of political rights and promiscuous familiarity, but the deep, broad, fundamental democracy that looks at all of nature and feels the unity and kinship that makes the universe a whole.

To Walt Whitman there could be no thought of class or caste. Each one held his certificate of birth from the same infinite power that, through all the ages and all the false and criminal distinctions of man, has yet decreed that all shall enter helpless and naked through the same gateway of birth, and each alike must go back

Clarence Darrow

to the fundamental mother, shorn of every distinction that man in his vainglorious pride has sought to make. Whitman placed the works of nature above the works of man. He had no faith in those laws and institutions which the world has ever made to defraud, and enslave, and deny the common brotherhood of all. He believed that every child that came upon the earth was legitimate, and had an equal right to land, and sea, and air, and all that nature made, and all that nature gave.

> *Each of us is inevitable,*
> *Each of us limitless—each of us with his or her*
>   *right upon the earth,*
> *Each of us allow'd the eternal purports of the earth,*
> *Each of us here as divinely as any is here.*

Let this stanza speak to our conscience face to face—is it true or false? Can any but a blasphemer deny the divine right of every man upon the earth? And yet if this simple stanza is true, every law book should be burned and every court abolished and natural justice, unfettered and undenied, should be enthroned above the forms and conventions and laws, which, each and all, deny the integrity of the soul and the equal rights of man.

Through all the injustice and inequality of the world, the vision of democracy has still prevailed and ever must prevail as long as nature brings forth and takes back the master and the slave alike. But the aspiration for democracy is not always high and noble. It is easy to demand for ourselves the same rights enjoyed by our fellow men, but Whitman's democracy was on a higher plane.

> *I speak the pass-word primeval, I give the sign of*
>   *democracies,*
> *By God! I will accept nothing which all cannot*
>   *have their counterpart of on the same terms.*

These lines breathe the spirit of true humanity, the spirit that will one day remove all barriers and restrictions, and liberate the high and low alike. For nothing is truer in life or more inevitable in the economy of nature than this sage thought:

Whatever degrades another degrades me,
And whatever is done or said returns at last to me.

It is a sad mistake to believe that injustice and wrong can injure only the poor and the weak. Every mean word and narrow thought and selfish act degrades the aggressor, leaves its mark upon his soul and its penalty in his life. So, too, no good effort is really lost, however it may seem to be. The kind word may be spoken to the deaf, the righteous effort be wrongly directed, the alms unworthily bestowed, but the heart that feels and the soul that tries has grown greater by the act.

Walt Whitman's work is not of the old, timeworn sort. When he speaks of love it is the love of life, the love of reality, the strong love of men, the intense love of women, the honest love that nature made, the love that is; not the unhealthy, immoral, false, impossible love told in erotic prose and more erotic verse, and given to young girls and boys as the truth, to poison and corrupt with its false and vicious views of life.

But he sings of the common things, the democracy of every day; for it is the small affairs that make up life, and its true philosophy is to see the beauty and greatness and relation of these little things, and not to pine for the seemingly momentous events which can rarely come. The Alexanders, the Caesars and the Napoleons are scattered only here and there in the great sea of human existence, and yet every life measured by just standards may be as great as these; and the soul that is conscious of its own integrity knows its own worth regardless of the world.

I do not call one greater and one smaller,
That which fills its period and place is equal to any.

Walt Whitman felt the music of the hammer and the axe as he felt the harmony of the symphonies of Beethoven, and he understood the art of the plow-boy in the field as well as the glorious creations of Millet.

The young mechanic is closest to me, he knows me well,
The woodman that takes his axe and jug with him
shall take me with him all day,

Clarence Darrow

The farm-boy plowing in the field feels good at
   the sound of my voice,
In vessels that sail my words sail, I go with
   fishermen and seamen and love them.

The soldier camp'd or upon the march is mine,
On the night ere the pending battle may seek me,
   and I do not fail them,
On that solemn night (it may be their last) those
   that know me seek me,
My face rubs to the hunter's face when he lies down
   alone in his blanket,
The driver thinking of me does not mind
   the jolt of his wagon,
The young mother and old mother comprehend me,
The girl and the wife rest the needle a moment
   and forget where they are,
They and all would resume what I have told them.

Walt Whitman's democracy did not end with sex. Man is not always a logical animal. Most of the practical democracy of the world has stopped with men, and generally with white men at that. The political equality of woman has only barely been considered; the still more important question, her economic independence, is yet a far-off dream. But Walt Whitman knew no limit to equality. With him equality meant equality. It could mean nothing else.

I am the poet of the woman the same as the man,
And I say it is as great to be a woman
   as to be a man,
And I say there is nothing greater
   than the mother of men.

Probably Walt Whitman would not have raised his hat to a woman on the street, nor given her his seat in the car, simply because she was a woman. Both these may be well enough, but they grow from false ideas of women, and of course through these false ideas women lose the most. Injustice and oppression can never be made up by chivalry and pretended courtesy. And the evil always is and must be the false relation which these create. Men expect to pay women for their political and economic freedom in theater tickets and by taking off their hats in public, and in the end women become willing to receive this paltry and debasing bribe.

Walt Whitman's democracy was more inclusive still. It is almost becoming the fad to forgive the evil in others and to insist that, after all, their good qualities give them the right to kinship with ourselves, but this is only one side of true democracy. The felon is my brother, not alone because he has every element of good that I so well recognize in myself, but because I have every element of evil that I see in him. Walt Whitman was wise enough to see the feelings and passions that make others sin, and he was just enough and great enough to recognize all these feelings in himself.

> *You felons on trial in courts,*
> *You convicts in prison-cells, you sentenced assassins*
> *chain'd and handcuff'd with iron,*
> *Who am I too that I am not on trial or in prison?*
> *Me, ruthless and devlish as any, that my wrists*
> *are not chain'd with iron, or my ankles with iron?*
>
> *You prostitutes flaunting over the pavements*
> *or obscene in your rooms,*
> *Who am I that I should call you more obscene*
> *than myself?*
> *O culpable! I acknowledge—I expose!*
> *(O admirers, praise not me—compliment not me—*
> *you make me wince,*
> *I see what you do not—I know what you do not.)*
> *Inside these breast-bones I lie smutch'd and choked,*
> *Beneath this face that appears so impassive*
> *hell's tides continually run,*
> *Lusts and wickedness are acceptable to me,*
> *I walk with delinquents with passionate love,*
> *I feel I am of them—I belong to those*
> *convicts and prostitutes myself,*

> *And henceforth I will not deny them—*
> *for how can I deny myself?*

These lines are not a burst of poetic feeling, they are the sincere utterances of a brave philosopher and poet, who tells the truth about himself and about you and me. Let us be honest about sin. How do you and I differ from the murderer on the gallows, the prostitute in the street or the burglar in the jail? How wide a breach is there between coveting the house or home or sealskin coat of your neighbor and taking it if you can? How great a difference between making a sharp trade with your neighbor, getting more from him than you give to him, and taking outright what he has? Yet one is business, the other larceny.

What is the distance between hating your neighbor, and wishing him dead: how great a chasm between feeling relief at his death, and killing him yourself? So far as the man is concerned, it is not the act that is evil, but the heart that is evil. There is no difference between the committed and the uncommitted crime. Every feeling that makes every sort of crime is in the heart of each and every one.

Nature has made the blood of some of us a little cooler, and has developed caution a little more, or fate has made the temptation a trifle less, and thus we have escaped—that is, managed to conceal the real passion that boils and surges in our hearts. Until this is dead, evil is in our souls. Away with all this talk of superiority and differences. It is cant—pure, simple cant.

> *I will play a part no longer, why should I exile*
> *myself from my companions?*
> *O you shunn'd persons, I at least do not shun you,*
> *I come forthwith in your midst, I will be your poet,*
> *I will be more to you than to any of the rest.*

Has man the right to be less kind than nature is? Have we the right by word or deed to pass judgment on our fellow-man? Can we not learn of love and charity and hope from the sun, the rain, the generous earth, and the pulsing, growing spring? Hear Walt Whitman's word to a common prostitute:

Be composed—be at ease with me—I am
Walt Whitman, liberal and lusty as Nature,
Not till the sun excludes you do I exclude you,
Not till the waters refuse to glisten for you and the
leaves to rustle for you do my words refuse
to glisten and rustle for you.

Neither was it the magnanimous soul of Whitman that was charitable and kind, but it was the truthful, honest man who saw his own goodness in the woman; and her sin, which after all was only an excess of kindness, in himself.

The regenerated world will be built upon the democracy Walt Whitman taught. It will know neither rich nor poor; neither high nor low; neither good nor bad; neither right nor wrong; but:

I will establish in every city of these states
inland and seaboard,
In the fields and woods, and above every keel,
little or large, that dents the water,
Without edifices or rules or trustees or any argument,
The institution of the dear love of comrades.

Walt Whitman was always and at all times an optimist. He never struck a despairing note or voiced a doubting strain. His hope was not anchored in blind faith or narrow creed. His optimism was not that of the cowardly fanatic who stubbornly shuts his eyes to avoid an unpleasant view. He looked abroad at all the world and called it good.

Optimism and pessimism in their last analysis are questions of temperament. They depend upon the eye that looks out, not upon the object that it sees. The pessimist points to the sunset, casting its lengthening shadows on the earth, and tells of the night that is coming on; the optimist shows us the rosy dawn, the golden promise of a glorious day. The pessimist tells of winter, whose icy breath chills and deadens all the world; the optimist points to springtime with its ever-recurring miracle of light and life. Is the pessimist right or is the optimist right—does the night precede the day, or the day precede the night? After all, are our

Clarence Darrow

calendars wrong—does the winter with its white shroud and cold face mark the ending of the year, or does the springtime with its budding life and its resurrecting power awaken the dead earth to joyous, pulsing life again?

Above the view of the optimist, who sees the morning and the spring, and the pessimist, who sees the evening and the closing year, stand a few serene souls, who look on both with clear eye and tranquil mind, and declare that all is good. The morning is right and the evening is right. It is beautiful to pass through the joyous gates of birth; it is good to be clasped in the peaceful arms of death. Rare Walt Whitman at thirty-seven, full of health and vigor and strength, with the world before him, and conscious of his genius and his power, sings in a burst of optimism:

> *I celebrate myself, and sing myself,*
> *And what I assume you shall assume,*
> *For every atom belonging to me as good*
> *belongs to you,*
> *I loafe and invite my soul,*
> *I lean and loafe at my ease, observing*
> *a spear of summer grass.*
>
> *My tongue, every atom of my blood,*
> *form'd from this soil, this air,*
> *Born of parents born here from parents the same,*
> *and their parents the same,*
> *I, now thirty-seven years old*
> *in perfect health begin,*
> *Hoping to cease not till death.*

Again at seventy, looking back on a life well spent, conscious that the last few sands are running out, a confirmed invalid with palsied limbs and failing strength, looking death squarely in the face and just before him; with the same sweet smile, the same lovely nature, the same all-embracing philosophy, sings once again his optimistic song:

> *Not from successful love alone,*
> *Nor wealth, nor honor'd middle age,*
> *nor victories of politics or war;*

But as life wanes, and all the
    turbulent passions calm,
As gorgeous, vapory, silent hues
    cover the evening sky,
As softness, fulness, rest, suffuse the frame,
    like fresher, balmier air,
As the days take on a mellower light, and the apple
    at last hangs really finish'd and
        indolent-ripe on the tree,
Then for the teeming, quietest, happiest days of all!
The brooding, blissful halcyon days!

It must be that somewhere is a serene height where life triumphs over death. It must be that nature does not jar, and that the close of a lovely life is really as peaceful and as beautiful as the decline of a perfect day; that each day rightly lived and every year well spent must bring the pilgrim more in harmony with his journey drawing to a close.

Whitman had solved the eternal riddle; he had conquered death; he looked at her pale form and saluted her as he would welcome a new birth. No bard ever sang a more glorious hymn than Walt Whitman sang to death.

Come, lovely and soothing Death,
Undulate round the world,
    serenely arriving, arriving,
In the day, in the night, to all, to each,
Sooner or later, delicate Death,
Praised by the fathomless universe
For life and joy, and for objects
    and knowledge curious,
And for love, sweet love—but praise! praise! praise
For the sure enwinding arms of cool—
    enfolding Death,
Dark Mother, always gliding near with soft feet,
Have none chanted for thee a chant
    of fullest welcome?
Then I chant for thee, I glorify thee above all,

Clarence Darrow

I bring thee a song that when thou
must indeed come, come unfalteringly.
Approach, strong deliveress,
When it is so, when thou hast taken them
I joyously sing the dead,
Lost in the loving, floating ocean of thee,
Laved in the flood of thy bliss O Death.
From me to thee glad serenades,
Dances for thee I propose, saluting thee,
adornments and feastings for thee,
And the sights of the open landscape
and the high-spread sky are fitting,
And life and the fields, and the huge
and thoughtful night,
The night in silence under many a star,
The ocean shore and the husky whispering
wave whose voice I know,
And the soul turning to thee, O vast and well veil'd Death,
And the body gratefully nestling close to thee.
Over the treetops I float thee a song,
Over the rising and sinking waves, over the myriad
fields and the prairies wide,
Over the dense-pack'd cities all,
and the teeming wharves and ways,
I float this carol with joy,
with joy to thee, O Death.

Whitman in his wheel chair, physically shattered and broken, but with a mind strong and serene, and at peace with all the world, waiting for the sun to set, is a lesson in optimism better than all the sermons ever preached. Without faith in any form of religion that the world has ever known, he had brought his life so in harmony with nature that he felt every beat of the great, universal heart, and with the confidence of certain knowledge he looked upon the fading earth and caroled a song as he sailed forth on that great unknown sea, which is hidden in perpetual night from all but the few great souls, whose wisdom and

183
Walt Whitman

insight have given them the confidence and trust of a little child.

When a man has grown simpler and saner and truer—when the fever of civilization has been subdued and the pestilence been cured; when man shall no longer deny and revile the universal mother who gave him birth, then Walt Whitman's day will come. In the clear light of that regenerated time, when the world looks back to the doubt and mist and confusion of today, Walt Whitman will stand alone, the greatest, truest, noblest prophet of the age, a man untainted by artificial life and unmoved by the false standards of his time. In a sodden, commercial, money-getting age, he enjoyed all the beauty of the earth without the vulgar lust to own. In a world of privilege and caste, he felt and taught the brotherhood of man and the kinship of all living things. In an age of false modesty and perverted thought, he sang the sanctity of the body with the divinity of the soul. Against the agnostic and the Christian too, he defended every part and portion of the faultless work of the creative power. Above the doleful, doubting voice of men, through the dreariest day and darkest night, in the raging of the storm and the madness of the waves, his strong, optimistic, reassuring note was ever heard above the rest, proclaiming to the universe that all is well.

He saw that in a wise economy and a great broad way, that the false was true, the evil good, the wrong was right, and that over all the universe, pervading all its teeming life, a power omnipotent, beneficent and wise was working to uplift, conserve and purify the whole.

The poor, the weak, the suffering, the outcast, the felon, all knew him for their comrade and their friend. His great, inclusive, universal heart left no soul outside, but all alike he knew, the life of all he felt, and one and all he loved. In his vocabulary were no words of bitterness and hate, and in his philosophy no right to censure or to blame. In his every deed and thought he seemed to say:

> So I be written in the book of love,
> I have no care about that book above.

Clarence Darrow

Erase my name, or write it as you please,
So I be written in the book of love.

As the shadows lengthen and the daylight wanes—as the hair whitens and the passions cool—more and more do we learn that love is the true philosophy of life. More and more do we revise the sterner judgments of our earlier years. More and more do we see that pity should take the place of blame, forgiveness of punishment, charity of justice, and hatred be replaced by love. When old familiar faces awake the memories of bygone days, often and often again do we fear that our judgments were cruel and unjust. But every deed of mercy and every act of charity and every thought of pity is like the balm of Gilead to our souls. We may none of us be wise or great, fortune may elude us and fame may never come; but however poor or weak or humble, we yet may inscribe our names in the fairest, brightest book—the book of love. And on its sacred pages, earned by the glorious truths he taught, by his infinite, ever present love of all, upon the foremost line will be inscribed Walt Whitman's name.

From A Persian Pearl and other Essays, *1899.*

LEO TOLSTOY

*He could find no refuge in blind creeds, whether of the
church or state. He boldly stood in the clear light of day,
with his feet upon the earth, unbound by the traditions
of the world in which he lived, and took counsel of his
conscience and his judgment and of nothing else.*

IT IS NOT ALONE FOR THE GOOD
he has done, or even the good he has sought to do, that the life
and work of Leo Tolstoy shine so brightly through the mists and
darkness of the world. Since man was born upon the earth, there
have been the rich and poor, the strong and weak, the master and
the slave. One class has ever had the power to rule and the humble
millions been forced to do its bidding and its will. These poor and
weak and suffering ones have been hewers of wood and drawers
of water, not because they wished it so, but because they had no
power to choose. Patiently, through all the ages, they have bent
their backs to receive the heavy burden which earth's favored ones
have decreed that they should bear, and yet through the long, dark
centuries they have groaned and muttered and cursed the fate
which doomed them and theirs to suffer for the world.

When one of these bondmen slays his master, or cries out against
oppression, or boldly strikes for freedom against fearful odds, we
sympathize with the cause and man, and feel regret that he must
fail; but still we know that he is battling for himself; that for the
time he feels the injustice which the centuries have heaped on him,

Clarence Darrow

and rebels against the cruel, heartless fate that yoked him to his endless task. But when a ruler leaves his favored class and takes his place beside the humble and the weak; when the driver lays aside the goad which the world has placed ready in his hand, and, stepping from the cart where he was wont to ride, bares his shoulder to the heavy yoke that rests upon his fellow's neck; when one of earth's pampered, favored sons refuses to ride upon his brother's back, but bravely takes a humble place to work with him, to live with him, to die with him, then may the world well marvel and stand amazed at what it sees.

Leo Tolstoy was born a count. Before he came upon the earth the laws and customs of his native land had decreed that he should rule while other unborn babes should serve. Nature, ages since, had spread out the Russian plains and in their broad and fertile breast had stored the food and shelter for a mighty host of men. Nature, too, had contrived and planned that the race should never fail, and that each individual child should be born alike naked and helpless, and turn to her endless bounties to sustain its life. But the laws of Russia had divided up this broad domain and carved out a large estate waiting ready for Count Tolstoy's birth, and still more kindly had decreed that many other unborn babes should have no place to live upon the earth except on Tolstoy's land, and on such terms as he was willing to allow.

Tolstoy was reared and educated like others of his class. He found a title waiting ready to distinguish him from his humble fellow-man, and his early training served to separate him still further from his natural kith and kin. On leaving school he followed the only profession that is open to the favored class—the trade of war. For civilization carefully divides man from man. Some of course must toil, else none could live, but such toil as sustains life and produces useful things for man has ever been called menial labor and fit only for slaves and earth's humble ones to do.

Tolstoy learned the trade of war. He was a brave soldier, he risked his life as one would risk a pawn upon the board, as the man made drunk with patriotic pride will vie with other brutes to kill.

He rose to distinction in the army, was endowed with genius, money, social position, and the whole world seemed ready to be conquered by his touch.

But the useless life of a mere soldier could not satisfy a soul like his. Genius had touched him with her divine gifts, and this inspiration was to kindle a light that would shine to the remotest portion of the earth.

Tolstoy's career as a man of letters began during his military life. Then were written some of his marvelous short stories which made him famous throughout the literary world. Then too he produced his great work—*War and Peace*—which, with *Anna Karenina*, proves Tolstoy one of the greatest masters of fiction that the world has ever known. Perhaps no author living, excepting Zola, has such power of creation as Tolstoy's earlier writings show.

But it is not by these novels that he wishes to be judged, and if Tolstoy's philosophy is true, his fame and usefulness will not rest upon this work of his earlier years. It will rest upon his life, upon the message that he speaks to man, upon what he tells us of the duty that each owes to his kind, of the true solution of that endless, awful, ever-present mystery, the purpose and the meaning and the end of life.

At the age of fifty, Tolstoy had gained all the world can give. He had wealth, high social position, had won distinction as a soldier and was acknowledged one of the greatest authors of his age. Tolstoy at fifty stood upon the high pinnacle on which fate and genius and his fellow-men had placed him, and looked abroad upon the world. At fifty the sun is well past the meridian, and the calm evening twilight seems only a little way beyond the quickly waning afternoon. It is very rarely that a career is commenced after fifty years are lived. Traits of character may be modified or intensified, but the man will be the same. After fifty the harvest time has come. And whether we have sown wisely or foolishly, we must reap the fruits of life, and these ripen fast upon the whitening head.

But Tolstoy at fifty began a new career. He looked abroad over his country and the world. He saw wealth and poverty—luxury and squalor—vice above and vice below—men dying from bestial excess, and the thin, wan faces of the overworked and the underfed. He looked at his brilliant career, at his marvelous work, and pronounced it bad; and then with the weight of half a century upon his head he turned his feet into a strange, almost unbroken path, and commenced a toilsome, thankless, hopeless journey all alone. He turned his back upon the luxury and ease his life had known—fine clothes, ready servants, delicate viands, sensual pleasures, ease, indolence, idleness; all of these he left behind, and with a lofty soul and brave purpose consecrated his remaining years to toil.

At fifty Tolstoy came face to face with the old, old question, ever old, ever new—what does life mean? This question has been put in endless ways by unnumbered souls. Tolstoy asked it plainly, simply, like an honest fearless man.

"Suppose I should come to possess ten thousand acres and three hundred head of horses, what then? Suppose I become more famous than Gogol, Pushkin, Shakespeare, and all the writers in the world, what then?"

Leo Tolstoy met this question like a man. He met it in his thought and he met it in his daily life. He could find no refuge in blind creeds, whether of the church or state. He boldly stood in the clear light of day, with his feet upon the earth, unbound by the traditions of the world in which he lived, and took counsel of his conscience and his judgment and of nothing else.

Every man is the product of heredity and environment. Scientists may always differ as to the relative weight of these influences in the lives of men, but that both are factors in human character is almost beyond dispute. Each fact of life appeals to each separate man according to the heredity and environment that have made his life. And thus it is that the same scenes do not move all men alike.

Leo Tolstoy was not the first great Russian who has seen the misery of the poor, the pathetic, hopeless struggle of the weak, the indolence and vice of the powerful and strong. Other men had looked at the same human tragedies that confronted him; others had looked at these pathetic scenes and had painted pictures true to life and sold them to the rich, to satisfy a vulgar craving and fill an idle hour. But Tolstoy looked upon the peasant life and felt the kinship that binds all souls in one, and sought to learn his true relation to the rest.

Even in his early writings Tolstoy shows that genius was not the only heritage that was his. Nature had touched him with a rarer and diviner gift—the power to suffer and to feel.

Genius has not been rare upon the earth. In every age and land men have stood high above their fellow-men, and in almost every case these favored ones have used their power and strength to serve their selfish ends; but it is only now and then, in periods far apart, that fate has sent mighty men whose grand, broad souls have been devoted to the service of mankind, and when these men have come, they have been crucified in one age, to be resurrected and glorified in the years to come.

Here and there, both in *Anna Karenina* and in *War and Peace*, Tolstoy shows that nature placed within his soul the divine power to work and suffer for the world; and that under right conditions this holy feeling would dominate his life.

Tolstoy was fifty years of age when he opened wide his eyes and looked upon the world, and one broad, full view convinced his soul that all his life he had been fast asleep. He was not content to ask the lawyers and clergymen what was right and wrong. He knew that the institutions of his land protected and defended the injustice and misery on which rested Russian social life. He asked himself the question how he and other men became possessed of the power to buy the labor and the lives of the millions who served the great and strong.

Political economists holding chairs in endowed universities may see no wrong in this statement which Tolstoy makes, but the man with a conscience and no master whom he watches for a crust, cannot overlook the injustice of which it speaks.

"It is an evident fact that when I have in my pocket three rubles to spare, which I am not in need of, I have only to whistle, and in every civilized town I obtain a hundred people ready for these three rubles to do the worst, most disgusting and humiliating act I require, and this comes not from money, but from the very complicated conditions of the economical life of nations."

Clarence Darrow

But aside from the obvious fact that money should have no such influence, Tolstoy asks himself the question by what right he is possessed of this power to dominate his fellow-men.

"And, indeed, what is my money, and how did I come by it? One part of it I collected in the shape of rent for my land, which I inherited from my father. The peasant sold his last sheep or cow in order to pay it to me.

"Another part of my money I received for the books I had written. If my books are harmful, and yet sell, they can only do so by some seductive attraction, and the money which I receive for them is badly earned money; but if my books are useful, the thing is still worse. I do not give them to people, but say, 'Give me so many rubles, and I will sell them to you.' "

In Tolstoy's great work, *What To Do*, he has carefully and thoroughly discussed the pressing problems of capital and labor, and the meaning of human life. Although most of the so-called reformers who have closely identified themselves with any particular school of radical thought are inclined to criticise this book as not clearly based on scientific grounds, still I believe that as the years go by and the various schools and sects shall come and go, the world will more and more regard this book as one of the most profound and searching works on social science that the century has produced. The future will rank Tolstoy by this work, and long after he has passed away, all men in whom conscience yet remains will be startled and aroused by the searching questions which this book asks of their inmost life.

Tolstoy looks at the conditions present everywhere about, and knows that these conditions must be wrong. It needs no logic to convince, only a simple appeal to the heart and conscience of men based upon these patent facts. One illustration is enough to condemn the whole social system under which he lives—this simple sketch of Tolstoy could not be true if justice ruled on earth.

"On the day I wrote this, there was a ball in Moscow. On the same night I left home at eight o'clock. I left home after the factory whistle had sounded, and when, after a week of incessant work, people were freed for their holiday. Factory men passed by me and

I passed by them, all turning their steps to public houses and inns. Many of them were already tipsy; many more were with women.

"Every morning at five I hear each of the whistles which means that the labor of women, children and old people has begun. At eight o'clock another whistle—this means half an hour's rest; at twelve another whistle—this means an hour for dinner. At eight o'clock the fourth whistle, indicating the cessation from work. By a strange coincidence, all the three factories in my neighborhood produce only the articles necessary for balls.

"One may, on hearing these whistles, attach to them no other meaning than that of the indication of time. 'There, the whistle has sounded: it is time to go out for a walk.'

"But one associates with them also the meaning they in reality have—that at the first whistle at five o'clock in the morning, men and women, who have slept side by side in a damp cellar, get up in the dark, and hurry away to the noisy building, and take part in a work of which they see neither cessation nor utility for themselves, and work often so in the heat, in suffocating exhalation, with very rare intervals of rest, for one, two, three, or even twelve and more hours. They fall asleep, and get up again, and again do this work, meaningless for themselves, to which they are compelled exclusively by want. And so it goes on from one week to another, interrupted only by holidays.

"And now, from every side, carriages appeared, all going in one direction. On the coachbox sat a coachman, sometimes in a sheepskin coat; and a footman—a dandy with a cockade. Well-fed trotters, covered with cloth, ran at the rate of fifteen miles an hour; in the carriages sat ladies wrapped in shawls, and taking great care not to spoil their flowers and their toilets. All, beginning with the harnesses on the horses, carriages, gutta-percha wheels, the cloth of the coachman's coat, down to the stockings, shoes, flowers, velvets, gloves, scents—all these articles have been made by those men, some of whom fell asleep on their own pallets in their mean rooms, some in nighthouses with prostitutes, and others in a police station.

"The ball-goers drive past these men, in and with things made by them; and it does not even enter into their minds that there could possibly be any connection between the ball they are going to and these tipsy people, to whom their coachmen shout so angrily. With quite easy minds, and assurances that they are doing nothing wrong, they enjoy themselves at the ball.

"Enjoy themselves!

"From eleven o'clock in the evening until six in the morning, in the very depth of night, while with empty stomachs men are lying at night-lodgings, or dying, as the washerwoman had done."

This is a story of Russian life, and it is equally true in New York, Chicago, and in fact wherever civilization has cast its blighting curse. This was the story of Rome in the days of her wealth and pride, before the conquering hordes came down with fire and sword to destroy the corrupt and rotting empire that was once the marvel of the world. It was the tale of France, through the long years of oppression and wrong that were followed by the red retribution, when the heads of nobles and kings were used as footballs by the long-suffering, frenzied poor. It is the story which can be seen by all who have eyes, and heard by all who have ears, and upon which the blind and selfish have ever turned their backs.

Tolstoy looked upon this picture of human life, and his soul was revolted at the sight; he could not gather his ill-gotten goods around him and pray that the deluge might not come until he and his had passed away. He sought to find a solution for this pressing problem that has been the riddle and the destruction of all the civilizations that have gone before. He turned to the books and the professors and the preachers to give him light, and he found that the books had been written for the rich, the professors were teaching for the rich, and the clergy were praying for the rich. After seeking for light amongst others of his class, he gave up this method in despair, and, to use his own words, determined that "if he desired to live and comprehend the meaning of life, he must find this meaning not among those who have lost it, who long to get rid of life, but among those thousands of men who create their life and ours, and who bear the burden of both."

Above all the men who had helped him, Tolstoy gives credit to two simple, wise, uneducated peasants, who lived near his estate.

Leo Tolstoy

These taught him that he should live with the peasants, that he should be of them, eat from the same bowl with them, remove the social distinctions and class barriers that have separated them—in short, live the simple, plain life that the common people live.

Before this time the liberation had given political freedom to the serfs of Russia, and Tolstoy had conceived it his duty to go to these emancipated slaves and teach them to be good and useful men. Tolstoy soon found what many other sincere teachers have discovered—that the rich have more to learn from the poor than the poor can learn from the rich. He soon sees that even his own desire to help the peasant is not genuine and sincere, that he does not believe in the equality which he has come to teach. Speaking of the peasant, he says:

"I should like to become intimate with him; but I am afraid to sit down upon his bed for fear of lice or some infectious disease; I am also afraid to let him come into my room; and when he comes to me half-dressed, he has to wait—if fortunate, in the entrance hall, but oftener in the cold porch."

He soon discovers too that he really has nothing to teach the peasant, that all he knows is useless, and that in valuable information bearing upon the real, honest burdens and duties of life, the peasant is richer than himself.

"I go to help the poor. But no one is poorer than myself. I am a weak, good-for-nothing parasite, who can only exist in very peculiar conditions, who can live only when thousands of people labor to support this life which is not useful to anyone. And I, this very caterpillar which eats up the leaves of a tree, wish to help the growth and the health of the tree, and to cure it."

Tolstoy soon finds that the world is divided into two classes, those who sow and those who reap, those who toil and those who live upon their fellow-men. Early in the development of the race the leisure class evolved. This leisure class determined that it should do no useful work. To till the soil, to tend the herd, to work the mine, all ministered to the material wants of man, and therefore no one could follow these pursuits free from the suspicion that he was bound to work. But war and statecraft, and church craft, together with games and sports, were free from taint of useful work, and could therefore safely engage the time and strength of the favored leisure class. Through the progress of the ages the constant pressure of man has been to find a place in the leisure class, and even when want has made it necessary for men to do some useful work, the constant tendency has been to do the least useful labor that can take care of life, and the law of compensation has ever been that the more useful the labor, the smaller the share the toiler gets. Some must work, or man cannot live, and it must therefore follow that the greater the leisure class, the harder must be the task which the laborer performs. That some men may be idle and live worthless lives, many men and women and children must be condemned to endless, hopeless toil.

Tolstoy looked at the thousands of profligates and idle rich who were consuming the lives and products of the poor, and declared that no man had the right to demand the service of his fellow man. Each human being should perform the labor needful for his life or else should die.

With merciless logic Tolstoy examines the old excuse for idleness, the division of labor. The worthless parasites who consume the hard-earned product of their fellow-man are ever saying that the law of the division of labor makes it right that one class should do the drudgery of the world for scantiest pay, while the other should contribute the labor of the mind. This brain work in the main has always consisted in exercising the wits to devise means to live in idleness and ease. The excuse of the division of labor cannot avail except upon the theory that all mankind enters into a free compact to work together for the common good, and that in this compact certain work is fairly and voluntarily assigned to each to do. Of course no such compact exists or ever did exist. The so-called brain workers have used their wits to control the earth, and place the balance of mankind with the animal kingdom subject to their will. The brain workers have taken possession of the earth, the mines, the forest, all means of life. They possess all the implements and tools of trade, and have left the countless millions stripped and starving, with no chance to live except to enter a heartless competition with each other for the right to serve.

No body of laborers have ever freely assembled and offered to raise so much corn for the author who will write a book, or to make so many pairs of shoes for the artist who will transcribe the sunset with his brush, or dig so much coal in exchange for the arduous labor of holding the title deeds to the uncreated earth. Instead of this, these so-called brain workers have appropriated to themselves all the bounties of the earth, and in exchange pretend to give the toilers things they do not need and cannot buy or use.

Tolstoy saw what all honest men must understand, that the service the toiler gives the thinker is positive, necessary, disagreeable and constant. The wealthy are absolutely dependent on the poor. From them, they get food, drink, shelter, raiment, and the personal service that satisfies their pettiest want. And in return the poor receive only the privilege of being ruled by an iron rod. The poor are made to think that the idle rich confer a favor when they grant them nothing but the right to serve.

Tolstoy looked at the great estates of Russian nobles and the luxurious homes of Moscow's favored few. He knew the extravagance and dissipation of the idle rich. He saw that the labor of scores of men and women was destroyed to sustain each worthless life. He saw the old and feeble, the young and innocent, the sick and helpless, all forced by the bitter whip of want to give their lives to satisfy the whims and pampered tastes of an idle, vicious crew.

"Around us people are dying from want and overwork; and we destroy the food, clothes, labor of men merely in order to amuse ourselves. And therefore the conscience of a man of our circle, though he may have but a small remainder of it in his breast, cannot be stifled, and poisons all these comforts and charm of life which our suffering and perishing brethren procure for us."

When his eyes were opened, Tolstoy could no longer take this forced tribute of the poor. He had come to understand that his luxury and ease were purchased by the miseries and denials of the weak. He had learned to know that the idle bread he ate was the peasant's flesh, and the red wine he drank was his helpless neighbor's blood.

When he understood these facts, there was but one thing left to do, and he faced the issue like a brave and honest man.

"I came to the following simple conclusion, that, in order to avoid the suffering and depravity of men, I ought to make other men work for me as little as possible, and to work myself as much as possible.

"It was by this roundabout way that I arrived at the inevitable conclusion at which the Chinese arrived some thousand years ago, and which they express thus: 'If there is one idle man there must be another one who is starving.'

"I came to the simple and natural conclusion, that if I pity the exhausted horse on whose back I ride, the first thing for me to do, if I really pity him, is to get off of him, and walk."

Tolstoy points out that parasitic life has reduced the vast body of humanity to beasts of burden with nothing to hope for but the grave. It has rendered sordid and worthless the class who live upon their brother's toil. It has debased and degraded art, and brought literature, science and religion to serve the most unworthy ends. The leisure class, supported by the ceaseless toil of human slaves, must be amused. This class has all the wealth and favors of the world. It must read books, hear music, see pictures, attend the theater and speculate upon the world to come. It must hire a great army of artists who give their time and energies, not to the highest creation that their souls conceive, but to producing those objects that will amuse and satisfy the ruling class. The artist lives from the labor of the poor, and to them he can give nothing in return. All the creations of his brain and brush must go to adorn the mansions of the rich. The author must write the books that pander to the things that are, else there are none to read and buy; and the church must teach that it is easier for a camel to go through the eye of a needle than for a rich man to miss the kingdom of heaven.

The millions have no place in art. A peasant might be made to pose for a picture by Millet, but the canvas would find its place

Leo Tolstoy

upon the rich man's walls to amuse an idle hour. The theater is for the rich. The creations of the modern stage cost endless toil. This work, for the most part, is done for the scantest pay. It matters not the subject of the scene, the audience is the same from night to night, the pampered idle class who go to be amused. Upon the stage the star struts back and forth to please the crowd and get a portion of the wealth that it has wrung from toil. The ballet girls who sing and dance and smile through powdered faces have exposed their persons to the vulgar crowd for bread. They are faint for want of food, and no one knows or cares whether the pittance that they get will provide them with a bed when the glare of the footlights is turned off. And the cheering crowd upon the stage that hangs upon the brave utterances of the star—these were picked up on the street, and when the play is done will return to the vulgar mob from which they came. The play from beginning to end was made to serve no purpose, to help no soul, to make better no human life, but to amuse men and women who do no work and who give a portion of their wealth to him who provides a new sensation for their idle hours.

The artists who today with pen and brush are selling their genius to the rich have no right to live. They are prostituting their powers for the rich man's gold. Tolstoy truly says:

"If men are really called to serve others by mental labor, they will have to suffer in performing this labor, because it is only by sufferings that spiritual fruit is produced. Self-denying and suffering are the lot and portion of a thinker and an artist.

"A thinker and an artist will never sit on the heights of Olympus, as we are apt to imagine; he must suffer in company with men in order to find salvation or consolation.

"Thinkers and artists cannot be sleek, fat men, enjoying themselves and self-conceited. Spiritual and mental activity and their expression are really necessary for others, and are the most difficult of men's callings—a cross, as it is called in the gospel."

No true art exists that does not have as its fundamental purpose the desire to better and to serve mankind. The prophets and seers and saviors of the earth have given freely of their power and genius to help their fellow-man. Ever and ever again have the rulers of the world taken them to the top of a high mountain, and pointing to all the kingdoms of the earth have offered these in payment for their souls. Few have been so brave and strong as to resist the proffered bribe. Few have cared to stand with the outlawed and oppressed against the powerful and the great.

For the story of mankind is never new—injustice, oppression and wrong are ever fortified and entrenched. Here are lawyers with specious arguments and endless briefs, to prove that black is white, that wrong is right. Here are judges in high places ready to maintain existing things. Here is the state which protects the strong and subverts the liberties and natural rights of the disinherited and despised. And here is the press with its million brazen tongues—its tongues of malice, of envy, and of spite, ready to defile the truth, to proclaim falsehood and error to the world, and to lash to madness the passions and the hates of men. And here is the church raising its voice with the cry of the mob, and proclaiming to the world that whatsoever ye bind on earth shall be bound in heaven, and that whatsoever ye loose on earth shall be loosed in heaven. And now, as of old, truth, crushed and bleeding and helpless, has no tongue to speak and no voice to raise.

Well may Tolstoy say that we must turn back from the false, unwholesome luxury of today to the patient, toiling, simple poor. Well may he turn from his disciples, as another reformer ages since, from the closed doors of the great and the barred temples of the God of Hosts to the peasants, the fishermen, the publicans, the sinners, and the wandering, homeless Magdalens.

Leo Tolstoy has the brain to see and the strength to do. Amid the universal clamor of the crowd he has raised his voice for justice and for right, and his strong words and brave message will be borne by other tongues and upheld by other lives until righteousness shall rule upon the earth. In that day no man will compel the service of his fellow-man, but each will gladly labor for the whole, moved by the righteous power of love. The great artist will paint no more to adorn the mansions of the rich, but earning his right to live by the labor of his hands, and knowing humanity as he knows himself, will draw his inspiration from the great eternal source of life and art, and dream such dreams and do such work as the world has never known. Then art will become a part of daily life, and daily life a part of art. To make one pair of shoes for weary feet will be as worthy in the sight of man as to write an epic poem, or compose a deathless song; to thatch one roof, as great as to paint the brightest hues that the sunset ever wrought; and to cool one parched tongue or hold out one hand to guide your fellow mortal through the dark, more than all the sermons ever preached by man.

From The Rubric, *January, 1902.*

Clarence Darrow

FACING LIFE
FEARLESSLY:
OMAR AND
HOUSMAN

We hear a great deal said by the ignorant about the
wickedness of the youth of today. Well, I don't know:
some of us were wicked when we were young. I don't
know what is the matter with the youth of
today having their fling.

IT IS HARDLY FAIR TO CALL THE
Rubaiyat the work of Omar Khayyam. I have read a good many
different editions and several different versions. I never read it in
Persian, in which it was first written, but I have read not only
poetical versions but prose ones. The beauty of the *Rubaiyat* is
Edward FitzGerald's. He evidently was more or less modest, or
else he wanted to do great homage to Omar, because no one would
ever have suspected that Omar had any more to do with the book
than they would have suspected Plato. But under the magic touch
of FitzGerald, it is not only one of the wisest and most profound
pieces of literature in the world, but one of the most beautiful pro-
ductions that the world has ever known.

I remember reading somewhere that when this poem was thrown
on the market in London, a long time ago, nobody bought it. They
finally put it out in front of the shop in the form in which it was
printed and sold it for a penny. One could make more money by

buying those books at a penny and selling them now than he could make with a large block of Standard Oil. It took a long while for Omar and FitzGerald to gain recognition, which makes it rather comfortable for the rest of us who write books to give away, and feel happy when somebody asks us for one, although we suspect they will never read them. But we all think we will be discovered sometime. Some of us hope so and some are fearful that they will be.

Neither Omar nor FitzGerald believed in human responsibility. That is the rock on which most religions are founded, and all laws —that everybody is responsible for his conduct; that if he is good he is good because he deliberately chooses to be good, and if he is bad it is pure cussedness on his part—nobody had anything to do with it excepting himself. If he hasn't free will, why, he isn't anything! The English poet Henley, in one of his poems, probably expressed this about as well as anybody. It looks to me as if he had a case of the rabies or something like that. But people are fond of repeating it. In his brief poem about fate he says:

> *I am the master of my fate,*
> *I am the captain of my soul.*

A fine captain of his soul; and a fine master of his fate! He wasn't master enough of his fate to get himself born, which is rather important, nor to do much of anything else, except brag about it. Instead of being the captain of his soul, as I have sometimes expressed it, man isn't even a deckhand on a rudderless ship! He is just floating around and trying to hang on, and hanging on as long as he can. But if it does him any good to repeat Henley, or other nonsense, it is all right to give him a chance to do it, because he hasn't much to look forward to, anyway. Free will never was a scientific doctrine; it never can be. It is probably a religious conception, which of course shows that it isn't a scientific one.

Neither one of these eminent men, Omar or Housman, believed in free will. There is eight hundred years between Omar and Housman, and yet their philosophy is wondrously alike. It is not a strange and unusual philosophy, except in churches and Rotary Clubs and places like that. It is not strange in places where people

think, or try to, and where they do not undertake to fool themselves. It is rather a common philosophy; it is a common philosophy
where people have any realization of their own importance, or,
rather, unimportance. A realization of it almost invariably forces
upon a human being his own insignificance and the insignificance
of all the other human atoms that come and go.

Men's ideas root pretty far back. Their religious creeds are very
old. By means of interest and hope and largely fear, they manage
to hang on to the old, even when they know it is not true. The
idea of man's importance came in the early history of the human
race. He looked out on the earth, and of course he thought it was
flat! It looks flat, and he thought it was. He saw the sun, and he
formed the conception that somebody moved it out every morning
and pulled it back in at night. He saw the moon, and he had the
opinion that somebody pulled that out at sundown and took it in
in the morning. He saw the stars, and all there was about the stars
was, "He made the stars also." They were just "also." They were
close by, and they were purely for man to look at, about like
diamonds in the shirt bosoms of people who like them.

This was not an unreasonable idea, considering what they had
to go on. The people who still believe it have no more to go on.
Blind men can't be taught to see or deaf people to hear. The
primitive people thought that the stars were right near by and just
the size they seemed to be. Of course now we know that some of
them are so far away that light traveling at nearly two hundred
thousand miles a second is several million light years getting to the
earth, and some of them are so large that our sun, even, would be
a fly-speck to them. The larger the telescopes the more of them we
see, and the imagination can't compass the end of them. It is just
humanly possible that somewhere amongst the infinite number of
infinitely larger and more important specks of mud in the universe
there might be some organisms of matter that are just as intelligent
as our people on the earth. So to have the idea that all of this was
made for man gives man a great deal of what Weber and Fields
used to call "proud flesh."

Man can't get conceited from what he knows today, and he

can't get it from what intellectual people ever knew. You remember, in those days the firmament was put in to divide the water below from the water above. They didn't know exactly what it was made of, but they knew what it was. Heaven was up above the firmament. They knew what it was, because Jacob had seen the angels going up and down on a ladder. Of course, a ladder was the only transportation for such purposes known to Jacob. If he had been dreaming now, they would have been going up in a flying machine and coming down in the same way.

Our conceptions of things root back; and that, of course, is the reason for our crude religions, our crude laws, our crude ideas, and our exalted opinion of the human race.

Omar had it nearer right. He didn't much over-estimate the human race. He knew it for what it was, and that wasn't much. He knew about what its power was; he didn't expect much from the human race. He didn't condemn men, because he knew he couldn't do any better. As he puts it:

> But helpless Pieces of the Game He plays
> Upon this Chequer-Board of Nights and Days;
>   Hither and thither moves, and checks and slays
> And one by one back in the Closet lays.

Compare that conception with Mr. Henley's, with his glorious boast that he is the captain of his soul and the master of his fate. Anyone who didn't catch that idea from the ordinary thought of the community, but carved it out for himself, would be a subject for psychopathic analysis and examination. When you have an idea that everybody else has, of course you are not crazy, but if you have silly ideas that nobody else has, of course you are crazy. That is the only way to settle it.

Most people believe every day many things for which others are sent to the insane asylum. The insane asylums are full of religious exaltants who have just varied a little bit from the standard of foolishness. It isn't the foolishness that places them in the bughouse, it is the slight variations from the other fellows' foolishness

Clarence Darrow

—that is all. If man says he is living with the spirits today, he is insane. If he says that Jacob did, he is all right. That is the only difference.

Omar says we are simply "impotent pieces in the game He plays"—of course, he uses a capital letter when he spells "He," which is all right enough for the purpose—"in the game He plays upon this chequer-board of nights and days." And that is what man is. If one could vision somebody playing a game with human pawns, one would think that everyone who is moved around here and there was moved simply at the will of a player and he had nothing whatever to do with the game, any more than any other pawn. And he has nothing more to do with it than any other pawn.

Omar expresses this opinion over and over again. He doesn't blame man; he knows the weakness of man. He knew the cruelty of judging him.

> The Moving Finger writes; and having writ,
> Moves on: nor all your Piety nor Wit
>   Shall lure it back to cancel half a line,
> Nor all your Tears wash out a Word of it.

Whatever the impulse calls one to do, whatever the baubles or the baits that set in motion many acts, however quickly or emotionally, the consequences of the acts, as far as he is concerned, never end. All your piety and all your wit cannot wipe out a word of it! Omar pities man; he doesn't exalt God, but he pities man. He sees what man can do; and more important still, he sees what he cannot do. He condemns the idea that God could or should judge man. The injustice of it, the foolishness of it all, appeals to him, and he puts it in this way:

> O Thou who didst with pitfall and with gin
> Beset the Road I was to wander in,
>   Thou wilt not with Predestin'd Evil round
> Enmesh, and then impute my Fall to Sin!

Nothing ever braver and stronger and truer than that! Preachers have wasted their time and their strength and such intelligence and learning as they can command, talking about God forgiving man, as if it was possible for man to hurt God, as if there was anything to be forgiven from man's standpoint. They pray that man be forgiven and urge that man should be forgiven. Nobody knows for what, but still it has been their constant theme. Poets have done it; Omar knew better. Brave and strong and clear and far-seeing, although living and dying eight hundred years ago. This is what he says about forgiveness:

> *O thou, who Man of baser Earth didst make,*
> *And ev'n with Paradise devised the Snake:*
> *For all the sin wherewith the Face of Man*
> *Is blacken'd—Man's forgiveness give—and take!*

"Man's forgiveness give—and take!" If man could afford to forgive God, He ought to be willing to forgive man. Omar knew it. "Ev'n with paradise devised the snake." Taking the orthodox theory, for all the sin with which the earth is blackened, "Man's forgiveness give—and take!" That is courage; it is science. It is sense, and it isn't the weak, cowardly whining of somebody who is afraid he might be hurt unless he whines and supplicates, which he always does, simply hoping that some great power will have compassion on him. Always cowardice and fear, and nothing else!

Omar was wise enough to know that if there was any agency responsible for it, that agency was responsible. He made us as we are, and as He wished to make us, and to say that a weak, puny, ignorant human being, here today and gone tomorrow, could possibly injure God or be responsible for his own weakness and his ignorance, of course is a travesty upon all logic; and of course it does great credit to all superstition, for it couldn't come any other way.

Housman is equally sure about this. He knows about the responsibility of man. Strange how wonderfully alike runs their philosophy! Housman condemned nobody. No pessimist does—only good optimists. People who believe in a universe of law never condemn or hate individuals. Only those who enthrone man believe in free will, and make him responsible for the terrible crudities of nature and the force back of it, if there is such a force. Only they are cruel to the limit.

One can get Housman's idea of the responsibility of the human being from his beautiful little poem, "The Culprit," the plaintive wailing of a boy to be executed the next morning, when he, in his blindness and terror, asked himself the question, "Why is it and what does it all mean?" and thought about the forces that made him, and what a blind path he traveled, as we all do.

Nobody lives in this world to himself or any part of himself. Nobody fashions his body, and still less is responsible for the size or the fineness of his brain and the sensitiveness of his nervous system. No one has anything to do with the infinite manifestations of the human body that produce the emotions, that force men here and there. And yet religion in its cruelty and its brutality brands them all alike. And the religious teachers are so conscious of their own guilt that they only seek to escape punishment by loading their punishment onto someone else. They say that the responsibility of the individual who in his weakness goes his way is so great and his crimes are so large that there isn't a possibility for him to be saved by his own works.

The law is only the slightest bit more intelligent. No matter who does it, or what it is, the individual is responsible. If he is manifestly and obviously crazy they may make some distinction; but no lawyer is wise enough to look into the human mind and know what it means. The interpretations of the human judges were delivered before we had any science on the subject whatever, and they continue to enforce the old ideas of insanity, in spite of the fact that there isn't an intelligent human being in the world who has studied the question who ever thinks of it in legal terms. Judges instruct the jury that if a man knows the difference between right and wrong he cannot be considered insane. And yet an insane man knows the difference better than an intelligent man, because he has not the intelligence and the learning to know that this is one of the hardest things to determine, and perhaps the most impossible. You can ask the inmates of any insane asylum whether it is right to steal, lie, or kill, and they will all say "No," just as little children will say it, because they have been taught it. It furnishes no test, but still lawyers and judges persist in it, to give themselves an excuse to wreak vengeance upon unfortunate people.

Housman knew better. He knew that in every human being is the imprint of all that has gone before, especially the imprint of his direct ancestors. And not only that, but that it is the imprint of all the environment in which he has lived, and that human responsibility is utterly unscientific, and besides that, horribly cruel.

Another thing that impressed itself upon all these poets alike was the futility of life. I don't know whether a college succeeds in making pupils think that they are very important in the scheme of the universe. I used to be taught that we were all very important. Most all the boys and girls who were taught it when I was taught it are dead, and the world is going on just the same. I have a sort of feeling that after I am dead it will go on just the same, and there are quite a considerable number of people who think it will go on better. But it won't; I haven't been important enough even to harm it. It will go on just exactly the same.

We are always told of the importance of the human being and the importance of everything he does; the importance of his not enjoying life, because if he is happy here of course he can't be happy hereafter, and if he is miserable here he must be happy hereafter. Omar made short work of that, of those promises which are not underwritten, at least not by any responsible people. He did not believe in foregoing what little there is of life in the hope of having a better time hereafter.

He says, "Ah, take the Cash and let the Credit go." Good advice that: "Ah, take the Cash and let the Credit go." If you take the "Credit," likely as not you will miss your fun both here and hereafter. Omar knew better.

It is strange how the religious creeds have hammered that idea into the human mind. They have always felt there was a kinship between pleasure and sin. A smile on the face is complete evidence of wickedness. A solemn, uninteresting countenance is a stamp of virtue and goodness, of self-denial that will surely be rewarded. Of course, the religious people are strangely hedonistic without knowing it. You couldn't expect them to know it. There are some of us who think that the goodness or badness of an act in this world can be determined only by pain and pleasure units. The thing that brings pleasure is good, and the thing that brings pain is bad. There is no other way to determine the difference between good and bad. Some of us think so; I think so.

Of course, the other class roll their eyes and declaim against this heathen philosophy, the idea that pain and pleasure have anything to do with the worthwhileness of existence. It isn't important for you to be happy here. But why not? You are too miserable here so you will be happy hereafter; and the hereafter is long and the here is short. They promise a much bigger prize than the pagans for the reward of conduct. They simply want you to trust them. They take the pain and pleasure theory with a vengeance, but they do business purely on credit. They are dealers in futures! I could never understand, if it was admissible to have joy in heaven, why you couldn't have it here, too. And if joy is admissible at all, the quicker you get at it the better, and the surer you are of the result. Omar thought that: "Ah, take the Cash, and let the Credit go!" Take the Cash and let the other fellow have the Credit! That was his philosophy, and I insist it is much better, and more intelligent philosophy than the other.

But Omar had no delusions about how important this human being is. He had no delusions about the mind, about man's greatness. He knew something about philosophy or metaphysics, whatever it is. He knew the uncertainty of human calculations, no matter who arrived at them. He knew the roundabout way that people try to find out something, and he knew the results. He knew the futility of all of it.

> Myself when young did eagerly frequent
> Doctor and Saint, and heard great argument
> About it and about: but evermore
> Came out by the same door where in I went.

That is what Omar thought. Man evermore came out by the same door where in he went. Therefore, "take the Cash and let the Credit go!" He put it even stronger than this. He knew exactly what these values were worth, if anything. He knew what a little bit there is to the whole bag of tricks. What's the difference whether you were born seventy-five years ago, or fifty or twenty-five? What's the difference whether you are going to live ten years, or twenty or thirty, or whether you are already dead? In that case you escape something. This magnifying the importance of the human being is one of the chief sins of man and results in all kinds of cruelty.

If we took the human race for what it is worth, we could not be so cruel. Omar Khayyam knew what it was, this life, that we talk so much about:

> *'Tis but a Tent where takes his one day's rest*
> *A Sultan to the realm of Death addrest;*
> *The Sultan rises, and the dark Ferrash*
> *Strikes, and prepares it for another Guest.*

" 'Tis but a Tent where takes his one day's rest"—is there anything else, if one could just make a survey of the human being, passing across the stage of life? I suppose man has been upon the earth for over a million years. A million years, and perhaps his generations may be thirty to thirty-five years long. Think of the generations in a thousand years, in five thousand years, in a hundred thousand, in a million years! There are a billion and a half of these important organisms on the earth at any one time. All of them, all important—kings, priests and professors, and doctors and lawyers and presidents, and one hundred per cent Americans, and everything on earth you could think of—Ku Kluxers, W.C.T.U.'s, Rotarians, Knights of Columbus and Masons, everything. All of them important in this scheme of things! All of them seeking to attract attention to themselves, and not even satisfied when they get it!

What is it all about? It is strange what little things will interest the human mind—baseball games, fluctuations of the stock market, revivals, foot races, hangings, anything. Anything will interest them. And the wonderful importance of the human being!

Housman knew the importance just as well as Omar. He has something to say about it, too. He knew it was just practically nothing. Strangely like him! The little affairs of life, the little foolishnesses of life, the things that consume our lives without any result whatever; he knew them and knew what they were worth. He knew they were worth practically nothing. But we do them; the urge of living keeps us doing them, even when we know how useless and foolish they are.

That is what life is, rising in the morning and washing and dressing and going to recitations and studying and forgetting it, and then going to bed at night, to get up the next morning and wash and dress and go to recitations, and so on, world without end.

One might get a focus on it from the flies. They are very busy buzzing round. You don't exactly know what they are saying, because we can't understand fly language. Professors can't teach you fly language. We can't tell what they are saying, but they are probably talking about the importance of being good, about what's going to happen to their souls and when. And when they are stiff in the morning in the autumn and can hardly move round, the housewife gets up and builds the fire, and the heat limbers them up. She sets out the bread and butter on the table. The flies come down and get into it, and they think the housewife is working for them. Why not?

Is there any difference? Only in the length of the agony. What other? Apparently they have a good time while the sun is shining, and apparently they die when they get cold. It is a proposition of life and death, forms of matter clothed with what seems to be consciousness, and then going back again into inert matter, and that is all. There isn't any manifestation that we humans make that we do not see in flies and in other forms of matter.

Housman understands it; they have all understood it. Read any of the great authors of the world—any of them; their hopes and their fears and their queries and their doubts are about the same.

Housman saw it. He knew a little of the difference between age and youth—and there is some. The trouble is, the old men always write the books; they write them not in the way they felt when they were young, but in the way they feel now. And they preach to the young, and condemn them for doing what they themselves did when they had the emotion to do it. Great teachers, when they grow old! Perhaps it is partly envy and the desire that no one shall have anything *they* can't have.

We hear a great deal said by the ignorant about the wickedness of the youth of today. Well, I don't know: some of us were wicked when we were young. I don't know what is the matter with the youth of today having their fling. I don't know that they are any wickeder today. First, I don't know what the word wicked means. Oh, I do know what it means: it means unconventional conduct. But I don't know whether unconventional conduct is wicked in the sense they mean it is wicked, or whether conventional conduct is good in the sense they mean it is good. Nobody else knows!

But I remember when I was a boy—it was a long time ago—I used to hear my mother complain. My mother would have been pretty nearly 125 years old if she had kept on living, but luckily for her she didn't. I used to hear her complain of how much worse the girls were that she knew than the girls were when she was a girl. Of course, she didn't furnish any bill of particulars; she didn't specify, except not hanging up their clothes, and gadding, and things like that. But at any rate, they were worse. And my father used to tell about it, and I have an idea that Adam and Eve used to talk the same fool way.

The truth is, the world doesn't change, or the generations of men or the human emotions. But the individual changes as he grows old. You hear about the revolt of youth. Some people are pleased at it and some displeased. Some see fine reasons for hope in what they call the *youth movement*. They can put it over on the old people, but not on the youth. There is a revolt of youth.

Well, youth has always been in revolt. The greatest trouble with youth is that it gets old. Age changes it. It doesn't bring wisdom, though most old people think because they are old they have wisdom. But you can't get wisdom by simply growing old. You can even forget it that way. Age means that the blood runs slow, that the emotions are not as strong, that you play safer, that you stay closer to the hearth. You don't try to find new continents or even explore old ones. You don't travel into unbeaten wilderness and lay out new roads. You stick to the old roads when you go out at all.

The world can't go on with old people. It takes young ones that are daring, with courage and faith.

The difference between youth and old age is the same in every generation. The viewpoint is in growing old, that is all. But the old never seem wise enough to know it, and forever the old have been preaching to the young. Luckily, however, the young pay very little attention to it. They sometimes pretend to, but they never do pay much attention to it. Otherwise, life could not exist.

Both of these poets saw the futility of life: the little things of which it is made, scarcely worth while. It is all right to talk about futility. We all know it, if we know much of anything. We know life is futile. A man who considers that his life is of very wonderful importance is awfully close to a padded cell. Let anybody study the ordinary, everyday details of life; see how closely he is bound and fettered; see how little it all amounts to. Think; that is all there is to it, and it is what everybody is trying to do, without fully realizing it. Many are taking the Credit and letting the Cash go.

That is why I have so little patience with the old preaching to the young. If youth, with its quick-flowing blood, its strong imagination, its virile feeling; if youth, with its dreams and its hopes and ambitions, can go about the woodland "to see the cherry hung with snow," why not? Who are the croakers who have run their race and lived their time, who are they to keep back expression and hope and youth and joy from a world that is almost barren at the best?

It has been youth that has kept the world alive; it will be, because from the others emotion has fled; and with the fleeing of emotion, through the ossification of the brain, all there is left for them to do is to preach. I hope they have a good time doing that, and I am so glad the young pay no attention to it!

Of course, Housman and Omar and the rest of us are called pessimists. It is a horrible name. What is a pessimist, anyway? It is a man or a woman who looks at life as life is. If you could, you might take your choice, perhaps, as to being a pessimist or a pipe dreamer. But you can't have it, because you look at the world according to the way you are made. Those are the two extremes. The pessimist takes life for what life is: not all sorrow, not all pain, not all beauty, not all good. Life is not black; life is not orange, red, or green, or all the colors of the rainbow. Life is no one shade or hue.

It is well enough to understand it. If pessimism could come as the result of thought, I would think a pessimist was a wise man. What is an optimist, anyway? He reminds me of a little boy running through the woods and looking up at the sky and not paying any attention to the brambles or thorns he is scrambling through. There is a stone in front of him and he trips over the stone. Browning said, "God's in his heaven and all's right with the world." Others say "God is Love, Love is God," and so on. A man who thinks that is bound to be an optimist. He believes that things are good.

The pessimist doesn't necessarily think that everything is bad, but he looks for the worst. He knows it will come sooner or later. When an optimist falls, he falls a long way; when a pessimist falls it is a very short fall. When an optimist is disappointed he is very, very sad, because he believed it was the best of all possible worlds, and God's in his heaven and all's well with the world. When a pessimist is disappointed he is happy, for he wasn't looking for anything.

If I had my choice, I would not like to be an optimist, even assuming that people did not know that I was an idiot. I wouldn't want to be an optimist because when I fell I would fall such a terribly long way. The wise man "trains for ill and not for good."

214
Clarence Darrow

He is sure he will need that training, and the other will take care of itself as it comes along.

Of course, life is not all pleasant; it is filled with tragedy. Housman has told us of it, and Omar Khayyam tells us of it. No man and no woman can live and forget death. However much they try, it is there, and it probably should be faced like anything else. Measured time is very short. Life, amongst other things, is full of futility.

Omar Khayyam understood, and Housman understood. There are other poets that have felt the same way. Omar Khayyam looked on the shortness of life and understood it. He pictured himself as here for a brief moment. He loved his friends; he loved companionship; he loved wine. I don't know how much of it he drank. He talked about it a lot. It might have symbolized more than it really meant to him. It has been a solace all down through the ages. Not only that, but it has been the symbol of other things that mean as much—the wine of life, the joy of living.

From a lecture at the University of Chicago, 1929; sponsored by the Poetry Club and the Liberal Club.

PART THREE

ON CRIME
AND
CRIMINALS

THE
HOLDUP MAN

The season of the holdup man will wane as the winter
gaieties fade away . . . when the nights again grow short
and the days grow long, when the price of coal goes
down and the sun comes back once more and warms the
poor and homeless, without money and without price.

1909. Taft inaugurated as president
. . . American Institute of Criminal
Law and Criminology founded . . .
Prohibition laws become effective in
Alabama, Mississippi and North Caro-
lina . . . William Allen White's *A
Certain Rich Man* a "best seller" . . .
Francisco Ferrer, Spanish educator
and anarchist, executed . . . Forty
thousand young women shirtwaist
makers, mostly Jewish and Italian
from New York's East Side, strike
for union recognition, fifty-two-hour
week and pay hikes . . . Clemenceau
retires as French premier . . . Philhar-
monic Society of New York begins
its sixty-eighth season with Gustav
Mahler as its new conductor . . .
Abbott Lawrence Lowell installed as
president of Harvard University . . .
First wireless message sent between
Chicago and New York . . . Orville
Wright sets record; plane carries passenger, flies for one hour, twenty minutes and forty seconds.

THE SEASON OF THE "HOLDUP man" and the "anti-holdup man" is once more at hand. This period comes annually at the same time of year, just after the flower show, the horse show, and along with the college football games. It begins with the season of gaiety, when the days grow short and the nights grow long, when the first sharp, tingling frost of winter drives the people off the streets and huddles them around their fires, and when the price of coal goes up.

The season of the "holdup man" will wane as the winter gaieties fade away—soon after Lent—when the nights again grow short and the days grow long, when the price of coal goes down and the sun comes back once more and warms the poor and homeless, without money and without price.

Lawyers, mayors, doctors and policemen freely give their advice as to the best way to treat the "holdup man." There is scarcely a topic of the day in which all classes of society so generally agree —one remedy is prescribed by all—more police, more revolvers, more clubs, more jails—this is the remedy for the "holdup man." One able lawyer advises every citizen to carry a revolver and to shoot at every suspected holdup—to aim at the abdomen, presumably the most fatal spot. Why the "holdup man" should be treated differently from other men who transgress the moral law is not quite clear. If all sinners were to be shot at sight few would be left to bury the dead. A doctor, generally humane and wise, declares that the mayor is responsible for all the holdup men, that there is no excuse for a burglary on "Maple Street," and some other street. What the residents of these streets have done to exempt them from the holdup man is not made clear.

It has not occurred to any of these eminent people to find the cause for the "holdup man," and yet most of them know that nothing in this world exists without a cause.

Of course no one but a crank or a fanatic could find any necessary connection between the brilliant costumes of the horse show, the cold blasts of winter, the price of coal and the holdup man; yet after all, many men whom the world has called wise—and even orthodox—have associated these causes and brought not only arguments but long tables of figures to show that there is a law which governs even the actions of the holdup man and relates him to every other living thing upon the earth.

There are many other facts that students have learned while policemen were wielding their brutal clubs.

The number of homeless girls who patrol the streets of our large cities grows greater, they walk more briskly and waste less time negotiating with the prospective customer as the nights grow long and cold—to most people this is an accident like all other things on earth. There are those who know that the rooms where these girls sleep are poor, that they are not all heated with steam, that most of them are cold, and that to say nothing of food, these wanderers must do something to keep warm.

There are other facts, too, which the "crank" and sentimentalist has found out. Our jails and police stations are fuller in winter than in summer. The Salvation Army and other bodies of evangelists who have warm rooms and nice bowls of hot soup make many more converts in winter than in summer. The winter "Christian" is known to all who do this sort of work. Our poorhouses, wood yards, orphan asylums, and even art galleries and public reading rooms are well patronized in winter. This last would teach some profound thinkers that cold weather conduces to literature and art. Pawnshops and second-hand furniture men get better bargains in winter than in summer—but still, what of it?—do not lawyers, doctors, policemen and clergymen all say that the panacea for all ills is the policeman's club?

There are other facts which dreamers and visionists are wont to note—those people have so little to do with the practical side of life that they must needs dream. In good times tramps are scarce, jails are empty, criminal courts not over busy, street-walkers few, holdup men very rare.

The early winter is the time that frugal men and frugal beasts lay up their stores for the cold days and nights coming on. The thrifty mine owners lay in their stocks by marking up the price of the coal which the Lord placed in the earth long ages since; the lawyer and merchant telephones his dealer to put twenty tons of coal in his cellar to feed his furnace through the winter months —the poor seamstress works farther into the black night to buy a few bushels to keep her fingers from growing stiff. Old, bent, haggard women take huge sacks upon their shoulders and wander up and down the railroad tracks for the stray lumps that may drive away a portion of the frost, and lean, dirty little boys pull their carts through the streets and sweep up what the rich man leaves; and the holdup man, he, too, goes out to lay in his winter stock against the ice and cold.

The holdup men are not the ones who mark up the price of coal and gas and beef—these would take no such chances as fall to the lot of the holdup man. The holdup man comes from the home of the wretched and the poor. Who think you is this holdup man—was he born this way? If so, don't fire as you meet him on the street, but turn your gun on God Almighty who made him as he is. But he was not born—he was made—he might have been an unsuccessful merchant who could not compete with the department store—or a railroad man whose name is on the black-list because he dared to strike. He grew more and more desperate year after year until he became a "holdup man."

It is fifty years since the great philosopher and historian Buckle gave his monumental work to the world. In this work he showed not alone by reason and logic, but by statistics covering long periods of time, that the suicides, the defalcations, and the crimes of all kinds increased and decreased in England, and have for years, exactly as the price of bread went up and down. This was not new when Buckle wrote it down; it was known before and has been shown by almost every good economist since then.

Clarence Darrow

There are many other facts that cranks often cite. Australia was settled by exported criminals, but they went to a country where land was cheap and opportunity great, and became industrious, hard-working men; the next generation became respected, high-toned citizens. Take a thousand of our low-class crooks and a thousand of our commonest prostitutes, and put them on an island where land is cheap and opportunity great, and in the third generation their descendants will be civilized, well-mannered citizens, with houses and barns, books and pictures, churches, policemen and jails.

The holdup man of today is the same man who lurked around the mansions of the rich in Rome fifteen hundred years ago. He was sent to jail, but he battered away at the civilization of Rome until the rich and poor went down in common ruin and despair. He is the same holdup man that Louis XV and Louis XVI were wont to club and kill in France a hundred years ago, but one day all the disinherited holdup men crept out from the alleys and caverns and marched on the king's palace and took possession of the state. Then these men made the rules of the game, and the nobles and princes went into the back alleys and took the place of the holdup men—that is, those who did not move to the catacombs.

Every increase in the price of coal makes "holdup men." Every time the price of meat goes up, some women go upon the streets, and some men get burglars' tools. Every extortionate penny taken by the gas trust makes holdup men. In their last analysis these despised criminals are men whom our social system has frozen out—who cannot live—who have no place upon the earth. Even the prostitute who plies her trade for the love of the trade, and the criminal who loves crime (if any such there be) have come to their present place through years of misfortune or hard environment, and would surely disappear under fairer conditions and with anything like a decent chance.

The rescue missions save many girls from prostitutes' lives, but they only make room for some other girl whom society is starving and freezing until she takes her place. So you may kill all the holdup men, but back of these are a long line of other men standing on the border, waiting for a chance to take their place.

Chicago is fairly well-to-do for jails and lockups. We have just built a fine, large addition to our county jail—the building has steam heat and electric lights and many boarders are found therein, especially in winter time; but has crime decreased as the jail increased in size? No one seems to expect this—it is taken for granted that this will grow as fast as any other institution of the town. If a pestilence of typhoid fever should break out in town the wise, humane doctors would advise us to build more hospitals—the cranks and visionists would tell us to boil the drinking water and stop the scourge. Thank God, the practical man has always ruled the world—with clubs!

With a small handful of men controlling all the earth and every opportunity for life, and the great mass forced into hopeless want, it will take more jails, policemen and clubs to keep the disinherited at bay. There is one way, and only one, to treat the holdup men—feed them, or rather let them feed themselves.

But more grim and farcical still than the senseless talk about the holdup man is one other fact. Chicago has hundreds of Christian churches—we are a Christian people. It is nineteen hundred years since Christ's teachings were given to the world—we profess to be the disciples of that lowly man who believed in no jails or clubs—who taught infinite love and infinite mercy—who said if a man asked for your coat, give him also your cloak—and yet today we know nothing better than hatred, repression, brute force, jails and clubs. We single out a considerable class of our fellow-men to shoot on sight. Of course, the world will continue to treat its so-called criminals in this enlightened human way. Therefore would it not be well to rechristen our churches, and stop calling them after Christ?

The International Socialist Review, *February, 1909.*

THE FUTILITY
OF THE
DEATH PENALTY

*The state continues to kill its victims, not so much to
defend society against them . . . but to appease
the mob's emotions of hatred and revenge.*

1928. Hoover elected president . . .
Emperor Hirohito ascends to the
Japanese throne . . . Chief Justice
Benjamin Cardozo of the New York
Court of Appeals urges revision of
penal code as it relates to insanity
in crime and to the law of homicide.
"Adjustment of some sort there must
be if we are to fulfill our duty to
defective human beings. The sin, in
truth, is ours, the sin of a penal system that leaves the victim to his fate
when the course he is going is written
plainly in the files of the courts," said
the judge . . . Railway president and
U.S. Senator Chauncey DePew dies.

LITTLE MORE THAN A CENTURY ago, in England, there were over two hundred offenses that were punishable with death. The death sentence was passed upon children under ten years old. And every time the sentimentalist sought to lessen the number of crimes punishable by death, the self-righteous said no, that it would be the destruction of the state; that it would be better to kill for more transgressions rather than for less.

Today, both in England and America, the number of capital offenses has been reduced to a very few, and capital punishment would doubtless be abolished altogether were it not for the self-righteous, who still defend it with the same old arguments. Their major claim is that capital punishment decreases the number of murders, and hence, that the state must retain the institution as its last defense against the criminal.

It is my purpose in this article to prove, first, that capital punishment is no deterrent to crime; and second, that the state continues to kill its victims, not so much to defend society against them—for it could do that equally well by imprisonment—but to appease the mob's emotions of hatred and revenge.

Behind the idea of capital punishment lie false training and crude views of human conduct. People do evil things, say the judges, lawyers, and preachers, because of depraved hearts. Human conduct is not determined by the causes which determine the conduct of other animal and plant life in the universe. For some mysterious reason human beings act as they please; and if they

Clarence Darrow

do not please to act in a certain way, it is because, having the power of choice, they deliberately choose to act wrongly. The world once applied this doctrine to disease and insanity in men. It was also applied to animals, and even inanimate things were once tried and condemned to destruction. The world knows better now, but the rule has not yet been extended to human beings.

The simple fact is that every person starts life with a certain physical structure, more or less sensitive, stronger or weaker. He is played upon by everything that reaches him from without, and in this he is like everything else in the universe, inorganic matter as well as organic. How a man will act depends upon the character of his human machine, and the strength of the various stimuli that affect it. Everyone knows that this is so in disease and insanity. Most investigators know that it applies to crime. But the great mass of people still sit in judgment, robed with self-righteousness, and determine the fate of their less fortunate fellows. When this question is studied like any other, we shall then know how to get rid of most of the conduct that we call "criminal," just as we are now getting rid of much of the disease that once afflicted mankind.

If crime were really the result of wilful depravity, we should be ready to concede that capital punishment may serve as a deterrent to the criminally inclined. But it is hardly probable that the great majority of people refrain from killing their neighbors because they are afraid; they refrain because they never had the inclination. Human beings are creatures of habit; and, as a rule, they are not in the habit of killing. The circumstances that lead to killings are manifold, but in a particular individual the inducing cause is not easily found. In one case, homicide may have been induced by indigestion in the killer; in another, it may be traceable to some weakness inherited from a remote ancestor; but that it results from *something* tangible and understandable, if all the facts were known, must be plain to everyone who believes in cause and effect.

Of course, no one will be converted to this point of view by statistics of crime. In the first place, it is impossible to obtain reliable ones; and in the second place, the conditions to which they apply are never the same. But if one cares to analyze the figures, such as we have, it is easy to trace the more frequent causes of homicide. The greatest number of killings occur during attempted burglaries and robberies. The robber knows that penalties for burglary do not average more than five years in prison. He also knows that the penalty for murder is death or life imprisonment. Faced with this alternative, what does the burglar do when he is detected and threatened with arrest? He shoots to kill. He deliberately takes the chance of death to save himself from a five-year term in prison. It is therefore as obvious as anything can be that fear of death has no effect in diminishing homicides of this kind, which are more numerous than any other type.

The next largest number of homicides may be classed as "sex murders." Quarrels between husbands and wives, disappointed love, or love too much requited cause many killings. They are the result of primal emotions so deep that the fear of death has not the slightest effect in preventing them. Spontaneous feelings overflow in criminal acts, and consequences do not count.

Then there are cases of sudden anger, uncontrollable rage. The fear of death never enters into such cases; if the anger is strong enough, consequences are not considered until too late. The old-fashioned stories of men deliberately plotting and committing murder in cold blood have little foundation in real life. Such killings are so rare that they need not concern us here. The point to be emphasized is that practically all homicides are manifestations of well-recognized human emotions, and it is perfectly plain that the fear of excessive punishment does not enter into them.

In addition to these personal forces which overwhelm weak men and lead them to commit murder, there are also many social and economic forces which must be listed among the causes of homicides, and human beings have even less control over these than over their own emotions. It is often said that in America there are more homicides in proportion to population than in England. This is true. There are likewise more in the United States than in Canada. But such comparisons are meaningless until one takes into consideration the social and economic differences in the countries compared. Then it becomes apparent why the homicide rate in the United States is higher. Canada's population is largely rural; that of the United States is crowded into cities whose slums are the natural breeding places of crime. Moreover, the population of England and Canada is homogeneous, while the United States has gathered together people of every color from every nation in the world. Racial differences intensify social, religious, and industrial problems, and the confusion which attends this indiscriminate mixing of races and nationalities is one of the most fertile sources of crime.

Will capital punishment remedy these conditions? Of course it won't; but its advocates argue that the fear of this extreme penalty will hold the victims of adverse conditions in check. To this piece of sophistry the continuance and increase of crime in our large cities is a sufficient answer. No, the plea that capital punishment acts as a deterrent to crime will not stand. The real reason why this barbarous practice persists in a so-called civilized world is that people still hold the primitive belief that the taking of one human life can be atoned for by taking another. It is the age-old obsession with punishment that keeps the official heads-man busy plying his trade.

And it is precisely upon this point that I would build my case against capital punishment. Even if one grants that the idea of punishment is sound, crime calls for something more—for careful study, for an understanding of causes, for proper remedies. To attempt to abolish crime by killing the criminal is the easy and foolish way out of a serious situation. Unless a remedy deals with the conditions which foster crime, criminals will breed faster than the hangman can spring his trap. Capital punishment ignores the causes of crime just as completely as the primitive witch doctor ignored the causes of disease; and, like the methods of the witch doctor, it is not only ineffective as a remedy, but is positively vicious in at least two ways. In the first place, the spectacle of state executions feeds the basest passions of the mob. And in the second place, so long as the state rests content to deal with crime in this barbaric and futile manner, society will be lulled by a false sense of security, and effective methods of dealing with crime will be discouraged.

It seems to be a general impression that there are fewer homicides in Great Britain than in America because in England punishment is more certain, more prompt, and more severe. As a matter of fact, the reverse is true. In England the average term for burglary is eighteen months; with us it is probably four or five years. In England, imprisonment for life means twenty years. Prison sentences in the United States are harder than in any country in the world that could be classed as civilized. This is true largely because, with us, practically no official dares to act on his own judgment. The mob is all-powerful and demands blood for blood. That intangible body of people called "the public" vents its hatred upon the criminal and enjoys the sensation of having him put to death by the state—this without any definite idea that it is really necessary.

For the last five or six years, in England and Wales, the homicides reported by the police range from sixty-five to seventy a year. Death sentences meted out by jurors have averaged about thirty-five, and hangings, fifteen. More than half of those convicted by juries were saved by appeals to the Home Office. But in America there is no such percentage of lives saved after conviction. Governors are afraid to grant clemency. If they did, the newspapers and the populace would refuse to re-elect them.

It is true that trials are somewhat prompter in England than America, but there no newspaper dares publish the details of any case until after the trial. In America the accused is often convicted by the public within twenty-four hours of the time a homicide occurs. The courts sidetrack all other business so that a homicide that is widely discussed may receive prompt attention. The road to the gallows is not only opened but greased for the opportunity of killing another victim.

Thus, while capital punishment panders to the passions of the mob, no one takes the pains to understand the meaning of crime. People speak of crime or criminals as if the world were divided

Clarence Darrow

into the good and the bad. This is not true. All of us have the same emotions, but since the balance of emotions is never the same, nor the inducing causes identical, human conduct presents a wide range of differences, shading by almost imperceptible degrees from that of the saint to that of the murderer. Of those kinds of conduct which are classed as dangerous, by no means all are made criminal offenses. Who can clearly define the difference between certain legal offenses and many kinds of dangerous conduct not singled out by criminal statute? Why are many cases of cheating entirely omitted from the criminal code, such as false and misleading advertisements, selling watered stock, forestalling the market, and all the different ways in which great fortunes are accumulated to the envy and despair of those who would like to have money but do not know how to get it? Why do we kill people for the crime of homicide and administer a lesser penalty for burglary, robbery, and cheating? Can anyone tell which is the greater crime and which is the lesser?

Human conduct is by no means so simple as our moralists have led us to believe. There is no sharp line separating good actions from bad. The greed for money, the display of wealth, the despair of those who witness the display, the poverty, oppression, and hopelessness of the unfortunate—all these are factors which enter into human conduct and of which the world takes no account. Many people have learned no other profession but robbery and burglary. The processions moving steadily through our prisons to the gallows are in the main made up of these unfortunates. And how do we dare to consider ourselves civilized creatures when, ignoring the causes of crime, we rest content to mete out harsh punishments to the victims of conditions over which they have no control?

Even now, are not all imaginative and humane people shocked at the spectacle of a killing by the state? How many men and women would be willing to act as executioners? How many fathers and mothers would want their children to witness an official killing? What kind of people read the sensational reports of an execution? If all right-thinking men and women were not ashamed of it, why would it be needful that judges and lawyers and preachers apologize for the barbarity? How can the state censure the cruelty of the man who—moved by strong passions, or acting to save his freedom, or influenced by weakness or fear —takes human life, when everyone knows that the state itself, after long premeditation and settled hatred, not only kills, but first tortures and bedevils its victims for weeks with the impending doom?

For the last hundred years the world has shown a gradual tendency to mitigate punishment. We are slowly learning that this way of controlling human beings is both cruel and ineffective. In England the criminal code has consistently grown more humane, until now the offenses punishable by death are reduced to practically one. There is no doubt whatever that the world is growing more humane and more sensitive and more understanding. The time will come when all people will view with horror the light way in which society and its courts of law now take human life; and when that time comes, the way will be clear to devise some better method of dealing with poverty and ignorance and their frequent byproducts, which we call crime.

The Forum, *September, 1928.*

PART FOUR

IN A
PHILOSOPHIC
MOOD

THE SKELETON
IN THE CLOSET

It is the skeleton in the closet, pointing ever to the
mistakes and maladjustments of our past, the skeleton
standing there before our gaze that makes us still
remember where our lives fell short.

THE CLOSET HAS SO LONG BEEN allotted to the skeleton that we have come to regard this room as its fit and natural home; it has been given over to this guest because it is the darkest, the closest and least conspicuous in the house. The door can be securely fastened, and only now and then can the grating bones be heard by the world outside. Still, however secluded and unused this guest chamber seems to be, and however carefully we bolt the door and darken every chink and crevice in the walls, we are ever conscious that the occupant is there, and will remain until the house is closed, and the last tenant has departed, never to return.

The very fact that we try so hard to keep the skeleton in its proper room makes it the more impossible to forget that it is there. Now and then we awake with a start at the thought of what might happen should it break the door and wander through the house, and then stray out into the wide world, and tell all the peaceful, trusting neighbors from what house it stole away; and yet we are somehow conscious that the rumor of its dread presence has already traveled as far as we are known.

Man is a wonderfully adaptable animal; he fits himself easily into the environment where he is placed. He passes from infancy to childhood and from childhood to boyhood as smoothly as the placid river flows to the waiting sea. Every circumstance and surrounding of his life seems to have been made for him. Suddenly a new desire takes possession of his soul; he turns his back on the home of his childhood days and goes out alone. In a little time a new family is reared about him, and he forgets the group that clustered round his father's hearth. He may lose a leg or a fortune, and he soon conforms to his changed condition, and life goes on as naturally and as easily as before. A child is born beneath his roof; it takes a place within his heart and home, and in a little while he can scarcely think of the day it was not there. Death comes, and a member of his little band is carried out, but time drops its healing balm upon the wounds, and life goes on almost unconscious that the dead has ever lived.

But while we adjust ourselves naturally to all things living and to ever-varying scenes, the skeleton in the closet is always an intruder, no matter how long it may have dwelt beneath the roof. Even though we may forget its actual presence for a little time, still no scene is so perfect and no enjoyment so great but we feel a cloud casting its shadow across our happiness or the weight of some burden on our soul; and when we stop to ask the cause, the grinning skeleton reminds us that it is with us even here.

This specter stands quite apart from the other sorrows of our life; age seems powerless to forget, and time will not bring its ever-fresh, recurring scenes to erase the memory of the past. With every breath we insist that there is nothing in the room. We refuse to take it to our hearts and homes and acknowledge it as our own. We seek to strangle it to death, and each fresh attempt not only shows our murderous design, but proves that the skeleton is not a pulseless thing but is endowed with immortal life. The brighter the firelight that glows around our hearth, the more desolate and drear sounds the wail of the wind outside, for through its cold blasts wanders the outcast whose rightful place is in the brightest corner of the room.

Our constant annoyance and sorrow at this dread presence is not caused by the way the skeleton behaves to us, but from the way we treat our guest. If we looked it squarely in its grinning skull, it might not seem so very loathsome to the sight. It has the right to grin. It may be but a grim smile over the consciousness that it has sounded the last sorrow and that henceforth no greater evils are in store; it may be a mocking, sardonic grin at the thought of our discomfiture over its unwelcome presence and the knowledge that we cannot drive it out.

There is no truer index to real character than the way we treat the skeletons with which we live. Some run to the closet door, and try to lock it fast when a neighbor comes their way. If perchance any fear of discovery is felt, they stand guard outside and solemnly protest that there is nothing in the room. Their anxiety and haste plainly show fear lest their hated guest shall reveal its face; and of course there rises in the neighbor's mind a vision of a skeleton more horrible by far than the one inside the door. If the luckless jailer really fears that the rattle of the prisoner's bones has been heard outside, he feels it his duty to carefully explain or tediously cover up every detail and circumstance that caused the presence of the specter in the house. All this can only show that the guest is terrible to behold, or that the jailer is so poor and weak that he himself is a helpless prisoner to his foolish pride and unmanly fear. It can only serve to emphasize the presence he tries so vainly to deny.

There are also those who know that their skeleton has been seen, or who, having lost all else but this persistent, grinning guest, drag it out and parade it in the world to gain the sympathy or the money of their neighbors and their friends, like the crippled beggar standing on the corner holding out his hat to every passerby. The true man neither guiltily conceals nor anxiously explains nor vulgarly parades. He lives his life the best he can, and lets it stand for what it is. A thousand idle tales may be true or false. One may have seen but certain things, and placed him with the saints. Another little soul, who never felt the breadth and depth of human life, may have seen his scars alone, and cast him out.

But standing by his side, or clasping his strong, sympathetic hand, no one thinks of halos or scars or asks an explanation of this or that, for in his whole being is felt the divine presence of a great soul, who has lived and loved, sinned and suffered, and been strengthened and purified by all.

The skeleton is really kind that it only grins as we look it in the face. Of all our household it has received the hardest treatment at our hands. It has helped us more than any of the rest, and been locked in the closet for its pains. It may perchance have come at our own invitation, bringing us the keenest, wildest joy our life had ever known. We gladly drained the pleasure to the dregs, and then coolly locked the memory close in the darkest hole that we could find. The day it came has well nigh faded from our minds, and the mad, wild joy we knew can never more be awakened from the burned-out passions of the past, but the skeleton, which rose up grim and ghastly from the dying flame, remains to mock and jeer and make us sad. And now when the day is spent and the cup is drained, we charge the poor specter with our lasting pain, and forget the joy it brought. We look with dread at these mocking, grinning bones, which we cannot drive away, and we forget the time, long ago, when those dry sticks were covered up with beautiful and tempting flesh.

It may be that we shall always shudder as we hear the rattle of the bones when we pass the closet door, but in justice to the inmate, we should give him credit for the joys of long ago. And this brings us back to the old question of the balancing of pain and pleasure, good and evil, right and wrong. It may be that in the mysterious adjustment of nature's balances, a moment of supreme bliss will outweigh an eternity of pain. Which is the greater and finer, the blameless life of the patient brute, or the winding, devious path of a human soul? It is only the dull level that brings no sorrow or regret. It is a sterile soil where no weeds will grow, and a bare closet where no skeleton will dwell.

Neither should we remember the skeleton only for the joy it brought; from the day it came, it has been the greatest benefactor that our life has known. When the mad delirium had passed away, and the last lingering fragrance was almost spent, this despised skeleton remained as the sole companion, whose presence should forever bind us back to those feelings that were fresh and true and straight from nature's heart, and that world which once was green and young and filled with pulsing life. As the shadows gather round our head, and our once-straying feet fall mechanically into the narrow path so straight and even at the farther end, we may shudder now and then at the thought of the grim skeleton whose life is so far removed from our sober later selves; but with the shudder comes a spark, a flash of that great, natural light and heat that once possessed this tottering frame, and gave a glow of feeling and a strength of purpose so deep and all-controlling that the artificial life of an artificial world seems no more than a dim candle shining by the glorious sun.

It is the exhausted emotions of age, which men call prudence, that are ever warning youth of the follies of its sins. It is the grinning skeleton, speaking truly from the memory of other days, that insists that life's morning held the halcyon hours. Does old age outlive the follies of childhood, or does the man outgrow the wisdom of youth? The most vociferous preachers are often those whose natural spirits have led them to drink the deepest of life. They are so foolish as to think that others can be taught by their experiences, and mumbling greybeards endorse the excellence and wisdom of the sermons they preach. They are not wise enough to know that their prattle is more vain and foolish than the babblings of their childhood days. It was the growing, vital sap of life that made them children years ago; it is the icy, palsying touch of age that makes them babbling, preaching children once again.

As well might the calm and placid lake teach the beauty of repose to the boiling, seething cataract that thunders down Niagara's gulf. When the troubled waters shall have reached the lake they shall be placid too. Nature is wiser far than man. She makes the first childhood precede the second. If the age of prudence came with youth, it would be a dull and prosy world for a little time; then life would be extinct upon the earth and death triumphant over all.

But these are the smallest reasons why we should venerate the neglected skeleton, which we have ruthlessly cast into the closet as if it were a hideous thing. This uncanny skeleton, ever thrusting its unwelcome bones into our presence and our lives, has been the most patient, persistent, constant teacher that all our years have known. We look backward through the long dim vista of the past, back to the little trusting child that once nestled on its mother's breast, and from whose loving lips and gentle soul it first was a benediction to the life that was once a portion of herself. We remember still this mother's words teaching us the way to live and telling us the way to die. We always knew that no selfish thought inspired a single word she said; and yet, time and time again we strayed and wandered from the path she pointed out. We could not keep the road, and after while we did not try.

Again, our teacher told us of the path. He, too, was good and kind and knew the way we ought to go, and showed us all the bad results of sin; and still we stumbled on. The preacher came and told us of the beauteous heaven, straight at the other end of the narrow path, and the yawning gulf of hell to which our shifting footsteps led; but we heeded not his solemn tones, though they seemed to come with the authority of God himself.

As the years went on, our mother's voice was stilled, the teacher's words were hushed, the preacher's threats became an empty, hollow sound; and in their place came the grinning skeleton, born of our own desires and deeds; less loving than the gentle mother, more real and lifelike than the teacher, saner and truer than the preacher's idle words. It was ever present and persistent; it was a portion of our very selves.

We detested and feared the hated thing; we locked it in the closet, and denied that it was there; but through the brightness of the day and the long and silent watches of the night, we heard its rattling bones and felt its presence at our side. No teacher of our youth was like that grim and ghastly skeleton, which we tried to hide away. The schoolmaster of our early life took our fresh, young, plastic minds and sought to crowd them full of useless, unrelated facts that served no purpose through the years that were to come. These lessons that our teacher made us learn by rote filled so small a portion of our daily lives that most of them were forgotten when the schoolhouse door was closed. When now and then we found some use for a trifling thing that we had learned through years at school, we were surprised to know that the pedagogue had taught us even this. In those early days it seemed to us that life would consist of one long examination in which we should be asked the names of states, the rule of three, and the words the Romans used for this and that. All that we were taught of the great world outside and the problem that would one day try our souls, was learned from the copy books where we wrote the same old maxim until all the paper was used up. In after years, we learned that, while the copy book might have taught us how to write in a stilted, unused hand, still all its maxims were untrue.

We left school as ignorant of life as we commenced; nay, we might more easily have learned its lesson without the false, misleading theories we were taught were true. When the doors were opened and the wide world met us face to face, we tested what we learned, and found it false, and then we blundered on alone. We were taught by life that the fire and vigor of our younger years could not be governed by the platitudes of age. Nature was ever present with her strong and earthly grasp, her keen desires, her white-hot flame. We learned the precepts of the books, but we lived the life that nature taught.

Our pathetic blunders and mistakes, and the skeleton that followed in their wake, remained to teach us what was false and point to what was true. This grim, persistent teacher made but little of the unimportant facts that the schoolmaster sought to make us learn, and it laughed to scorn the preacher's doctrine, that in some way we could avoid the results of our mistakes and sins. It did not preach; it took its place beside us as another self and by its presence sought to make us know that we could not be at peace until we clasped it to our breast and freely accepted the unwelcome thing as a portion of our lives.

Only the smallest fraction that we learned in youth was assimilated and made a portion of ourselves; the rest faded so completely that it seemed never to have been. The teacher soon became a dim, uncertain memory of the past, whose voice had long since died away; but the skeleton in the closet never wearied nor grew old. It ever made us learn again the lesson we would fain forget; opened at each succeeding period of our lives the pages we would gladly put away, until, at last, the ripening touch of time and the specter's constant presence made us know. From the day it came beneath our roof, it remained the liveliest, wisest, most persistent member of the family group, the tireless, watchful teacher, who would neither sleep nor allow its pupil to forget.

It may be that there are lives so barren and uneventful that this guest passes ever by their door, but unfortunate indeed is that abode where it will not dwell. The wide vistas can be seen only from the mountain top, and the infinite depths of life can be sounded only by the soul that has been softened and hallowed by the sanctifying touch of misery and sin.

Life is a never-ending school, and the really important lessons all tend to teach man his proper relation to the environment where he must live. With wild ambitions and desires untamed, we are spawned out into a shoreless sea of moving molecules of life, each separate atom journeying on an unknown course, regardless of the countless other lives it meets as it blindly rushes on; no lights nor headlands stand to point the proper way the voyager should take; he is left to sail an untried bar across an angry sea. If no disaster should befall, it does not show that the traveler is wise or good, but that his ambitions and desires are few or he has kept close inside the harbor line.

At first we seek to swim the flood, to scale the rocky heights, to clutch the twinkling stars. Of course we fail and fall, and the scars our passions and ambitions leave remain, though all our particles are made anew year after year. We learn at last to leave the stars to shine where they belong, to take all things as they are and adjust our lives to what must be.

The philosophy of life can come only from those experiences that leave lasting scars. Rather than seek to cover up these gaping wounds, we should accept with grace the tales they tell, and show them as trophies of the strife we have passed through.

No life can be rounded and completed without the education that the skeleton alone can give. Until it came we never knew the capacities of the human soul. We had learned by rote to be forgiving, kind and true. But the anguish of the human soul cannot be told—it must be felt or never known. The charity born of true comradeship, which is the highest and holiest sentiment of life, can be taught by the skeleton alone. The self-righteous, who prate of forgiveness to their fellow-men and who look down upon their sinning brothers from above, are hypocrites or fools. They either have not lived or else desire to pass for something they are not. No one can understand the devious, miry paths trodden by another soul unless he himself has wandered through the night.

Those placid, human lives that have moved along a narrow, even path; that learned by rote the lessons that the churches and the schools have ever taught; whose perfection consists in refraining from doing certain things in certain ways; who never had a noble thought or felt a great desire to help their fellow-men—those blameless, aimless, worthless souls are neither good nor bad. They neither feel nor think; no skeleton would deem it worth its while to come inside their door.

Though accursed, doubted, and despised, nature ever persists in her relentless plan. She would make us learn the lessons that youth so easily forgets. She finds us headstrong, unreasoning, and moved by the same feelings that sway the brute. She decrees that every act, however blind or wilful, must leave its consequences on our lives, and these immortal consequences we treat as skeletons and lock them up. But these uncanny specters wrap us closely in their bony arms; they ever peer with sightless eyes into our soul; they are with us if we sleep or wake, and their persistent presence will not let us sleep.

It is the hated, imprisoned skeleton that we vainly sought to hide away, that takes an untamed, fiery soul within its cruel, loving clasp, and holds it closely in its unforgiving grasp until the vain longings and wild desires of youth are subdued and cooled, and the deeper harmonies of life are learned. It is the hated skeleton that finds within our breast a heart of flint and takes this hard and pulseless thing and scars and twists and melts it in a thousand tortuous ways until the stony mass is purged and softened and is sensitive to every touch.

However blind and stubborn we may be, however long we deny the lesson that the skeleton would teach, still it will not let us go until with perfect peace and harmony we look at all the present and the past, at all that was, and all that is, and feel no regrets for what is gone, and no fears for what must come. It may be that our stubborn, stiff-necked soul will still persist until the hair is white and the heavy shadows hang about our heads, but the skeleton with his soothing, softening ally, time, sits with the last watchers at our suffering bed, and goes if need be to the silent grave, where alike the darkest crimson spot and the softest, purest clay are reunited once again with the loving, universal mother who has forgiven all and conquered all.

All triumphs are futile without the victory over self; and when the triumph over self is won, there are no more battles to be fought, for all the world is then at peace. It is the skeleton in the closet pointing ever to the mistakes and maladjustments of our past, that makes us still remember where our lives fell short; that teaches us so slowly but surely to turn from the unworthy victories and the dire defeats of life to the mastery of ourselves. It is the skeleton from whom we learn that we can live without the world, but not without ourselves.

Without the skeleton we could never feel another's sorrow, or know another's pain. Philosophy and theology cannot tell us how another's life became a hopeless wreck. It is ourselves alone that reveal the precipice along which every footpath leads. It is from life we learn that it is but an accident when we fall, and equally an accident when we keep the path. The wise and good may forgive the evil and the wrong, but only the sinner knows that there is no sin.

Let us do simple justice to this neglected, outcast guest, the useful, faithful teacher of our lives. Let us open the closet door, and let the skeleton come out, and lock the schoolmaster in its place. Let us leave this faithful friend to roam freely at its will. Let us look it squarely in the face with neither fear nor shame, but with gratitude for the lessons it has taught. It may be that the jeering crowd will point in scorn as they see us with the gruesome figure at our side, but when we fully learn the lesson that it came to teach, we shall need to look no more without for the approval or disapproval of our acts, but seek to satisfy ourselves alone.

Let us place a new chair beside the hearth, in the cosiest nook, and bid the skeleton take its place as the worthiest guest. Let us neither parade nor hide our new-found friend, but treat it as a fact of life—a fact that is, a fact that had the right to be, and a fact that taught us how to find ourselves.

Let us not forget the parents who watch us in our youth, and the friends that were ever good and true. But above all, let us remember this grim and silent teacher, who never neglected or forgot, who showed us life as only it could show, who opened up new vistas to our soul, who touched our human hearts, who made us know and love our fellow-man, who softened and mellowed and purified our souls until we felt the kinship that we bore to all living things. Until it came we knew only the surface of the world. Before it came, we had tasted of the shallow cup of joy and the bitter cup of pain, but we needed this to teach us from the anguish of the soul that there is a depth profound and great, where pain and pleasure both are one; that there is a life so deep and true that earth's rewards and penalties alike are but a hollow show; that there is a conquest of ourselves, which brings perfect peace and perfect rest.

From A Persian Pearl and other Essays, *1899.*

CONDUCT
AND
PROFESSION

Nature has room for all the matter and all the
motion that the universe can hold, and however
unimportant any particle may seem to be, its life
and existence is necessary to the whole.

Nothing in human action is more striking than the almost universal conflict between the conduct of life and the philosophy of life. So well recognized is this apparent inconsistency that men are rarely judged by their sentiments alone. It is always understood that no man is a hero to his valet, and it is universally believed that to approach a man is to find his imperfections and shortcomings and to be disillusioned of any glamour that distance and sentiment may have lent. It is presumed that we will live in our kitchen and receive our guests in the finest room the house affords; and however careless and easy the morning toilet, yet when the work of the day is done and evening brings us to public view we will deck ourselves anew for the stranger's unfamiliar gaze.

So well accustomed are the wise to this seeming dual quality of man that they rarely wish to see the hero whom they love. They rather choose to read his fine sentiments or hear them from the platform, and shroud the man in that mist and cloud which gives birth to heroes and saints, and the legends taught to young and trusting souls. If, perchance, the hero is really seen when not on dress parade, how great the shock felt by the devotee! What a rude awakening to find that, after all, he is but a man with all the human feelings and imperfections that are the common heritage of life.

It is for the glamour that cannot be dispelled, the mist that can never rise, that our real heroes are the long since dead—those men and women whose great struggles, triumphs or defeats stand out in bold relief above the imperfections and spots that claimed the chief attention of the common crowd who hovered round them while they lived upon the earth. These heroes gave their greatness to history, which has left unchronicled the faults their neighbors knew.

Endless pains have been taken to account for this seeming great discrepancy between philosophy and life. The thoughts, emotions and actions which make up human existence are too many and complicated to be easily explained or brought under one fixed and general rule. No doubt much of the disappointment and shock of the ordinary mind comes from its incapacity for fine sentiments and desires and the inability to see that these may be found in a house of clay. However just or unjust his opinions of other men may be, still in every verdict that he renders on another, man unconsciously judges himself, and this judgment is always the true measure of his own mental and moral worth. The outlook on landscape and life simply tests the vision of the eyes.

But, after all, the better portion of the world is kindly and generous in its judgments, and after much discussion and great marvel, the common explanation is generally indulged that the weakness of the flesh here and there triumphs over the higher sentiments of man. *The Strange Case of Dr. Jekyll and Mr. Hyde* is familiar to us all. The case is no longer strange; we see it in every life; we know and recognize it perfectly in our own. The world in its charity has generally accepted Mr. Stevenson's philosophy and generously believed that the real man was Dr. Jekyll and that Mr. Hyde was some sort of a demon who drew him down.

The modern human philosopher stands after all with the religionist of the Middle Ages who believed that the life of man furnished a battleground for angels and demons, each striving for the mastery of his soul. In this conflict the man himself took little part; he must stand or fall in accordance with the strength and weakness of these contending powers.

In this view of human conduct there is some element of truth. Man is born of the soil, and his highest aspirations show the marks of his birth. However he may keep his head above the mists in the realm of the ideal life, he still must plant his feet upon the earth, for in the economy of nature, unless the man still keeps his feet upon the solid vulgar soil he must surely die. It is those who know only the mud and mire who insist that because his feet are on the ground he must keep his whole body prostrate on the earth.

According to the judgment of the common soul, living men are of two kinds, the hypocritical and the base. Those whose common tendencies are untouched with higher thoughts and sentiments are simply vile—and those whose nobler sentiments are mixed with common deeds are but masquerading knaves. Legend and fable alone contain the names of great souls, and those who pretend to imitate these heroes are the most to be despised. Man in his critical judgments of men is influenced by various emotions, most of all by malice and envy. It is difficult to live the high ideal of which the dreamers tell. It is so impossible to the common soul that it does not try. It is infinitely easier to insist that the dreamer is false and that after all he is like the ordinary man except that he pretends to be something else. Of course if these unworthy souls should succeed in raising their shrill cries to such a pitch as to affect human life, it would mean that men must abandon the ideal and all live together on the carper's plane, without even an aspiration to lift them up and urge them on.

But the ordinary philosophy of life in its judgments of character is sadly wrong. Its whole data for the estimation of conduct is entirely at fault. It is first at fault in setting up empirical rules to judge between right and wrong. This it persistently will do in spite of the whole teaching of history and philosophy that there are no fixed rules by which the righteousness or evil of a human thought or action can be judged. And these empirical rules when established no matter by what school of thought, whether by the narrow religious zealot or the broadest moralist, ever have the same basis, and that foundation is the common concept of right and wrong which rules the particular time and place. It is idle to point out that this concept has ever changed and must ever change, and that every man in the past who has risen to supreme excellence has violated the common concept of his time and thus brought the world forward to a broader morality and a higher life. Man is ever ready to worship the dead iconoclast, but is equally impatient to stone the living one to death.

Every higher morality is born not only of man's ideals for a more perfect order and his impatience of the hard rules and restrictions that the past has imposed upon him, but still more of the reckless daring of those who by their actions have defied the common concept. These have beaten themselves to death and must ever beat themselves to death against the cruel bars of conservatism that the past has welded to fetter them; for progress has ever demanded its victims; and these victims have been not alone those whose philosophy taught them the higher life, but those others, weaker or stronger, for whom the commands of nature were more potent than the conventions and forms of man.

But whatever the justice or injustice of the world's concepts and acts, the philosopher has no right to quarrel with his fate. He knows that the present is builded on what is gone, and that as he gives his life in protest against the past, so in time must others yield up theirs in combat against the better system that he would live and teach, a system which, whether he will or not, another generation will mould into stone, and universally believe is the sum of all goodness and the perfection of all life. It is not alone that the heart of man is cruel, intolerant and brutal, that it ever sacrifices its greatest and bravest and most rational souls. This is due still more to the fact that nature preserves the species not through the strongest and the greatest and the best, but through the average which makes up the great weight of human life.

But still more than in its judgment of character and its canons of right and wrong is humanity at fault in its estimation of conduct and life.

All philosophies have placed too much weight upon action and too little upon thought, have believed too much in things and too little in ideals. This is but a different statement of the truth that all philosophy is too material, and that it too persistently refuses to believe in or appreciate the spiritual or the ideal. That which can be seen and felt and heard has ever been thought the substance. All the rest is but an image, an unsubstantial mist, a waking dream. It is ever assumed that there is a total difference between thought and deed, and that when these are in conflict, the deed is the man and the thought the pretense. It is never understood that thoughts, like deeds, are rooted in human life; that not alone the mind of man, but its every change and manifestation are a portion of the man. The convolutions of the brain from which come the thoughts and ideals of man are no more creations of caprice and chance than the movements of the arms or the comings and goings of the physical man. Even this statement is not quite strong enough. Every movement of the body is hampered and obstructed by the objects that hedge it in. It is only the mind which can be tolerably free to show the real life which animates the soul.

Then once more, we come back to the incontestable truth that man in his human judgments but passes judgment on himself. As the physical eye cannot look beyond itself, but sees only the image that is mirrored on its surface, so the human judgment reveals only the action of the judge's brain. Whatever the surface indications to the superficial mind, there is or can be no real inconsistency in the complete life of any human being, howsoever that life may be made manifest to the world. The thoughts and aspirations of man, together with his acts and deeds, grow from the same soil, are both rooted in the same eternal life, and are alike governed by the laws of being. Each is not only the natural product but the only possible fruitage of that mysterious incomprehensible entity, a human life.

The real oneness of nature does not lapse in the formation of a man. Here, as everywhere in the universe, all is taken together and must be so taken to make up the whole. The naturalist would form but a poor judgment of the earth if he should ascertain only the weight of the soil, the resistance of the rocks, the substance of the plants, and make no account of those mighty hidden forces which permeate its every atom; which throw up its mountain ranges, cause its crust to heave and open, and, instinct with energy and power, build up and destroy life upon the earth. It is not enough to weigh and measure the sun, but the scientist must know and recognize those eternal forces which urge it on its endless path through the universe, which make up the seasons of the year in far-off planets, and which each day, through direct and reflected forces, move every drop of water in all the mighty seas of earth.

Nature has room for all the matter and all the motion that the universe can hold, and however unimportant any particle may seem to be, its life and existence is necessary to the whole. The day is the complement of the night—the mountain of the valley—the water of the land—the summer of the winter—force of matter—life of death. Each and all in their proper place and quantity make up the whole. The existence of each and all is not only consistent with, but absolutely necessary to the whole.

The thoughts and aspirations of man are a portion of his being, and as real as any other part. So long as life endures, these mental manifestations will remain as persistent and constant as any other that marks his life. From his physical being, his heredity and environment, from all of life, his thoughts are born. And these thoughts and aspirations mark the man and determine his character, and are as much the individual as the familiar face we know so well.

That the daily life or casual transgressing may seem inconsistent with the thoughts he gives to the world or to his open deeds does not show the man himself untrue. Both deeds and thoughts are born of infinite causes reaching back to infinite time and outward to every influence that moves and makes a life. The open and secret sources of thoughts and acts are beyond the power of any soul to trace. Like the hidden channel of the spring, it has flowed through long and devious ways, been turned aside, its pathway blocked, compelled to wander far and wide before it comes to view. However wandering its course, its acts have been consistent from the time the first drop groped blindly through the earth until it burst from the rock, a living spring.

But the laws that control the mind of man are most difficult to solve. The noblest thoughts and purest aspirations may be born not from the fruitfulness but the poverty of life. For with all the fetters and obstacles that confine the man, the mind is often the only faculty that has the power to do the master's will. Our day dreams, like our night dreams, may not be formed of our daily life, but of what we wish it might have been. Our thoughts and aspirations are what we would be; our deeds are what we must be.

Imagery and poetry are the stories of those far-off ethereal lands that are visited by the human soul. The feet are heavy, the limbs are weary, and the flesh is sore; and these must abide in the valleys shrouded by the mist. But from the overhanging clouds, from the frail body so longing to be free, are born the grand visions which tell us what the soul desires. It may be that had the body lived upon the heights the soul would have been content and never spread its wings to find a higher peak from which to rest and view the world.

The poor captive with his pinioned body may lie down upon the cold stone of his cruel cell. The weary years may come and go, and he, fettered and chained and penned, may have no power to move except a few halting paces up and down; and yet the grandest songs of freedom may be born from this living grave. His body is chained, but in the damp seclusion of his narrow walls, he dreams of the broad green earth, the generous sun, the free and sparkling brook and the great blue dome which alone confines the world. His grandest vision of freedom is born of the cramped walls that fetter his body but cannot confine his soul.

It may be that only the ideal really is. We can describe the landscape only as it looks to us. We can tell of truth, of justice, of love, of charity, only as our minds conceive that these should be. All the facts of life are not what are, but what seems to us to be. Our conception may be born not only from our personal intimacy with the highest ideal that we conceive, but from poverty and want of these ideals in the environment in which we live. We may conceive of justice and long for its ideal life because

Clarence Darrow

of the injustice that everywhere abounds. We may love truth even though constrained to lie.

If the idealities could come only from the ideal life, then man could never grow from a lower to a higher state. It is the stern realities that bind us to the soil, that make us dream of nobler things. The yearnings of the human soul come not from satisfied ambitions, but from failures and defeats, from vain struggles and hopeless conflicts.

The philosophy of life is learned not alone by worthy examples of duty done, not wholly by the brave words and oft-repeated lessons of the school, but by sharp conflicts and bitter fruit. Instinctively the human mind turns from what it has to what it needs. The everyday experience of the common humdrum life can but leave a quenchless longing in the soul.

Be not surprised when the placid quiet life shall sing the glories of strife and of conquest. The human soul that is born within a narrow vale surrounded by the mountains and the hills, and still more fettered and confined by the ties which life is ever weaving day by day to confine the body and impede the will; this human soul that does its humble task day after day and week after week, and waits and watches while the seasons come and go, with endless measured step, year after year, the same waiting, the same humble daily task, the same nightly sleep, this soul you may not know. It seems a calm and peaceful life; almost without a change, the peace of life passes to the profound quietness of death. The casual observer may believe that this plodding sleeping life was all there was of that existence that seemed to move so placidly and calmly by.

The casual observer has not the subtlety to deal with human life. Beneath this quiet face, hidden deep within that seeming placid breast, was the greater portion of the man, whose outward form alone his neighbors knew and saw. True, this quiet man was wont to drag his leaden feet in the furrows of the plow that went before. True, he seemed at night to fall asleep and live again the quiet simple incidents of the day. But while the weary years could only bring his daily round of humble toil and recuperating sleep, still his soul was filled with wild longings and vain dreams for a life that could not be. While he made the weary rounds behind his plow, he dreamed of fierce battles and wild conflicts which he bravely fought with sword in hand, and even while he slept his seeming quiet sleep, he dreamed of war and strife and stirring scenes, of thrilling victories that a cruel fate with its pinions and fetters had forbidden him to taste.

So too the weary warrior dreams of peace. In his early youth the legends and stories of strife and conquest and victory lured him from his quiet home to the battlefield. Over and over again his teachers told in song and story the glories of victory and the honors of strife. His wild imagination was one great canvas covered over with battle scenes, and this picture shone brighter as the years passed by. But the experiences of life untaught the lessons of youth. War to the soldier meant long and toilsome marches with weary limbs and bloody feet; war meant cold wet nights upon the cheerless ground; war meant disease and death in countless ways; war was blood and pain and shattered limbs and brutal thoughts. But in the thickest of the strife, amidst the shot and shell and flowing blood, his troubled mind roamed backward to that far-off peaceful spot his youth had known. Once more he saw the fresh green grass, the blossoming trees, the lowing cows, the quiet country hillside, as the evening hours stole on. The blood-stained, shattered, toiling, fighting body was on the field of strife, but the homesick, weary, struggling soul was filled with visions of the holy joyful life of peace.

Each sphere of life knows its own joys and tastes its own pleasures; it rejoices in the triumphs and victories it holds, but it likewise knows its sufferings and pains, its disappointments, its trials and its sins. From the hardship of our daily task, from the grievous burdens incident to the life we know, we turn to other prospects which seem brighter and fairer from afar. Neither the doubtful pleasures nor the ever-present pains can be truly seen from this far-off spot, but in the glamour and symmetry that distance lends to every prospect, the evil is blended in the good, and the whole is alluring and inspiring to the view.

It is only the fettered soul that truly yearns for the untrammelled life. From the narrow paths and hard conventions of the world it turns with longing eyes to a life left free to pursue its chosen way. There just beyond the reach are great tangled woods, where sturdy giant trees stretch out their strong broad arms to embrace the wanton breeze. There fern and creeping vine and flowering bush with wild abandon and unpruned grace entice it with their lavish charms. There the uncaged bird is pouring out its soul in untaught song, and there the wild, free brook is gladly rushing to the sea. Beyond are green fields and wide views and fair prospects, and bending over all the cloudless heaven with its infinite blue expanse unfettered and unconfined. And here where it is forced to dwell are long straight sanded paths, pruned and tended trees with not a branch awry, beds of flowers laid out with the precision of the compass and the rule, and a close-clipped grassy lawn on which you must not tread.

But the sojourner who leaves the beaten path has yet another view. The dense, untraveled woods are alluring to the sight, they appeal to that free soul of man which has ever led him onward to fairer prospects and to untrammelled heights. But out there in the dark wood where the foot of man had seldom trod are unknown dangers and unlooked-for pains. The great forests are trackless; thorns and briers grow with the fairest flowers. The creeping vines which glisten so brightly in the sun are poisonous to the touch; strange mocking voices jeer him as he passes by—rude unfriendly eyes glare with hate and malice and envy, and tell of fierce hard claws that long to reach his quivering heart. The sound he hears is not the laughter of the brook or the free birds' song, but the hiss of poisonous serpents who would strike their fangs into his tender flesh. The glory of the sun departs, the night comes on, the rains descend. There is no shelter for the soul that will be free. In the darkness and despair far, far beyond his reach, he sees a vision of a plain, straight path, between green glowing lawns; the flowers bloom on either side, and their sweet perfume is wafted on the breeze. The straight sanded path leads to the friendly open door where meat and drink and rest are waiting ready for the soul that has not wandered from the path.

The child of the city, whether rich or poor, dwells forever in a human hive. The streets are stone; great walls of solid brick and mortar meet his view on every side; the black smoke of toil hangs ever like a dark pall above his head. A selfish, heartless, careworn crowd, in endless procession pass upon the street—each hurrying, jostling, fighting atom intent upon his own concern, and moving, rushing on and on, without a thought to the other countless souls they meet, without the raising of an eye to look into another's face, without reaching out a hand to give one touch of help or fellowship to the tired pilgrim with his burden of care and sorrow which seems more than he can bear. The roar and grime and dust of a great heartless, cruel, toiling, surging mass of men have driven peace and joy and quiet from the world. Only the stars in the hushed and sleeping night look down to remind the pilgrim of that vast and restful nature which the schemes of men have blotted from the earth. In the midst of the toil and grime and weary endless strife the mind soars off to great untrodden mountains, to wide valleys, to quiet hillsides, to clear streams and blue skies, to a fairyland where nature reigns supreme. How gladly would the weary body leave the endless strife and din of the great city for the green fields and blue sky, and the trackless woods, amid the deep peace where nature dwells alone.

But from the countryside the scene is changed. Here are barren rocks and sterile soil. Here are forests and swamps to be subdued. Here is wearying toil and scant return. Here is poverty and self-denial, a lonely life, a premature and comfortless old age. From the endless monotony of a hard battle with the soil, a life of small events, of daily commonplace, the weary soul turns to the city with its wealth, its activity, its honor, its conquests, and its strife. It would exchange an eternity of quiet and peace for one taste of that conflict which really animates the soul.

In their squalid homes, the poor dream of the joys of wealth; from their humble room they build gorgeous palaces and furnish them in a royal way. They dream of luxury, of possession, of all the treasures of the world which their hard life has forbidden them to have. But the voluptuary, with his uncounted gold, turns vainly from bauble to bauble, each serving only to further sicken his clogged and sated soul, worn with the weariness of the world and tired with the endless fetters that a complex civilization has placed upon his hands; borne down by the weight of things, he dreams of that freedom and simplicity which would emancipate life from the net in which civilization and luxury have entangled and ensnared the soul. The yearnings for the simple, the natural and the true cannot be born from naked walls, bare floors, rude benches and a sterile, hopeless life.

Would you learn the truth that nature teaches to the comprehending soul, then listen to the singing of the bird. Here is music fresh and pure from nature's matchless lute. As you listen to the overflowing of the soul, you need not ask the history of the bird. This matchless song may be but the echo of the forests and the fields wherein it dwells, of the clear blue sky and the wild free breeze it loves so well. The bird may be but pausing here to tell you from his bursting soul the hopes, the loves, the life it brings from tree and earth and sky. But it may be too that this singing bird is confined in bars of steel, that its poor eyes have been put out to add to the sweetness of his song. But whether the music comes from the free air of heaven and an untrammelled soul, or is born of the hopeless sadness of the poor captive, who with sightless eyes looks through the hard wire of his cage into endless night, it is the same true eternal voice that speaks to every soul attuned to know and feel.

The poet and the dreamer and the idealist are instruments through which the infinite conveys his message to the world. The soul that understands this message will ask no questions as to the kind of clay through which he chose to speak. It will listen reverently to the message and be content. It may be that the prophet told of the sights that his clear vision made plain to him, of the pure heavens in which he dwelt, of the ideal life he knew and loved and lived. It may be too that his divine message was born of sin and sorrow, the defeated hopes and vain strivings of his fettered soul. It may have come from his exultation over victory achieved, or been born of the helpless agony of despair. But however learned or wherever born, it was the true voice of that infinite power which sometimes speaks to man, and the human soul through which the message came, however scarred or imperfect, had still that divine quality which made it the bearer of truth imperative to the world. The soul which rightly hears this message will ask no question as to the instrument through which it came or the motive which inspired the thought, but will listen reverently to the voice and thank the infinite source of life for the power to know and feel its everlasting truth.

The Rubric, *1901.*

Clarence Darrow

THE THEORY OF
NON-RESISTANCE

*The theory of non-resistance does not, necessarily, say
that a man cannot be restrained, although very likely that
would not be necessary under any decent law of society.*

As THIS IS A SUNDAY MORNING,
and a semi-religious question, I take for my text the thirty-eighth
and thirty-ninth verses in the fifth chapter of Matthew. I cannot
quote it literally. It is quite a time since I have read it. But I know
the import of it.

"Ye have heard that it hath been said (I am quoting from
Matthew): An eye for an eye, and a tooth for a tooth. But I
say unto you, resist no evil. But whosoever shall smite you on
the right cheek, turn to him the other also."

I do not quote this because Matthew wrote it. I really do not
know whether he did or not; and I care a great deal less. But I
quote it because throughout all the western world this has been the
accepted statement of the doctrine of non-resistance. It is, perhaps,
as good a statement of that theory as one can find in a few short
sentences. Matthew had no patent on it, of course. There are very
few thoughts in this world that are patented, and those are not
worth it. It was undoubtedly very old before Matthew lived—if
he lived. And it has been repeated a great many times since he
died—if he died.

The theory of non-resistance is taken, generally, as the opposite to the theory of punishment, or the theory of vengeance, which, up to the time of the Christian religion, was the theory of the world—and since that time has been doubly the theory of the world. Its announcement, as generally admitted by those who have written and spoken upon the subject, has reference, first, to the treatment of those whom society calls criminals; next, perhaps, to governments in their relations to each other and to their subjects; and then to women and children, insane, prisoners, and the like. It relates to the way those who have the power have generally exercised that power in relation to the rest of the world.

Now, I might say in the beginning that I am not quite sure of this theory, or of any other theory. I used to be a good deal more positive than I am today. And especially, I am not at all sure that there is any theory in philosophy, or morals, or laws, that works out in sociology. The science of society, if there is such a science, is not an exact science. You cannot demonstrate any theory of society the way you can demonstrate the multiplication table, unless it is Socialism—and you cannot demonstrate that in the same way unless you are speaking to an audience of Socialists. You might demonstrate Single Tax to a Single-Taxer, but you could not do it to anybody else. Exact science has little to do —something to do, but little to do—with the ways in which man organizes himself on the planet. He does not move in straight lines, or in regular curves, or even in crooked lines, that can be depended upon. When he learns what the crooked line is, he goes straight. And no theory of life, no theory of society can be worked out as to communal life, in the same way that you can work out the science of mathematics, or of astronomy, or geology, or any science dealing with anything that keeps still.

But the question is, whether the theory of punishment, as opposed to the theory of non-resistance, is most in harmony with life, and tends to the progress of the world; whether human life in its slow evolution is going toward the theory of non-resistance, or is going toward the theory of violence, and force, and punishment.

If one looks back at the origin of the state we do not find

that it had the immaculate birth that most people believe. It was born in force and violence. The strong took a club, and made a state for himself. It was a simple state, kept there by the force of the strong man's club and his will. From that it has gone on until it takes a good many strong clubs, together with a good many armies, navies, policemen, lawyers, judges, etc., to keep the state in order. But through it all has run the theory of force, and through it all the power has come not from the people who asked it, but from the people who took it because it was the stronger. In the beginning the chief preserved order and the law, by saying what should be the law and enforcing order himself with his club.

In modern society the controlling forces arrange things as they want them, and provide that certain things are criminal. Sometimes those things have a semblance of natural crime, and sometimes not. The largest number of crimes are crimes against poverty. Sometimes you may trace them more or less directly to violation of some law that is in the natural world. But the fact is that the class which rules society come together and say what men must do, and what they must not do. And the man who violates it commits crime.

There are in society, and always have been, a large number of people, due mainly to conditions of society, who are what we call defectives; who are anti-social in their nature; whose life and conduct tend toward the disintegration of society, instead of the life of society. Very largely the treatment of crime is a question of treatment of these anti-social individuals. It is a question of treatment of those who persevere, in one way or another, in violating the rules of the game which society has made.

Way back under the Mosaic law—and Moses did not have a patent on it either—but under the law of the world, the doctrine of "an eye for an eye, a tooth for a tooth" prevailed. If a man killed another his life should be taken. If he stole something he should be punished. If he burglarized, then it meant something else, generally death. If he did something, the world would do something to him. And they would do that something that the world at that time thought was the right thing to do to him. In this way, even down to a hundred years ago, there were in England about two hundred crimes punishable by death. Almost everything that could be conceived of was punished by death. And the lawyers, and judges, and preachers of that day had no thought that society could hang together if men were not hanged regularly for stealing sheep and anything that happened. The old doctrine of an eye for an eye, and a tooth for a tooth, was the common doctrine of the world, and that doctrine prevails today.

All penal codes are really built upon that doctrine. When you trace penal codes back to the beginning, they mean one thing, and only one, *i.e.*, vengeance. A man has done something. He has caused someone to suffer. Therefore society will do something to him. In the early stages, if someone slew another, the members of his tribe had the right to go and take the life of any member of the other tribe in return. It did not matter whether he had been guilty or not. It was the law of vengeance, the law of punishment —and punishment and vengeance have always meant the same thing in the world, no matter where it has been.

Punishments of crimes have always been arbitrary. One man would say that for stealing a horse the somebody stealing it should go to the penitentiary for a year; another would say five years; and somebody else would say he should be hanged by the neck until dead. Punishments have never depended upon the act done, but upon the man who saw the act done and the mind possessed by the ruling power. Of half a dozen judges given authority to administer punishment for a certain act, no two judges would administer the same kind of punishment. One would say thirty days, another thirty years; just according to the mind he has. Some judge might give you less after breakfast than he would before. And another judge might give you more if he had attended a banquet through the small hours in the morning preceding, and did not feel well when he administered the sentence. All those things enter into it, and when you come to sum it all up, the real theory of it is a question of vengeance: The individual has done something. How much shall we do to him in return?

How much will we make him suffer, because he has made some-one else suffer?

Now, the non-resistant says, there is no such thing as crime, *i.e.*, some of them say that. And they say that all punishment is bad, not heavy punishment alone, but all punishment; that man has no right to punish his fellow-man, that only evil results from it; that the theory of vengeance and the theory of punishment is wrong; that it cures nobody, it does not tend to benefit society, it does not tend to change the defective, it does not tend to build up society. It is wrong and untrue in its whole theory; and the theory of non-resistance is the true theory as to crime. Whatever you may think of the theory, the world has been steadily going that way. It has been abolishing the death penalty, until today in most civilized countries there are only one or two crimes punish-able by death; and it is very rarely that death is meted out for those.

Punishment has been growing less severe, and the methods of inflicting punishment are less severe. Of course, in the old days when men were less squeamish and more honest they had their hangings in broad daylight. Today we do not do it, not because we are better, but because we are squeamish. We have hangings in the jail, so that the effects of the punishment will be entirely lost to the community.

Our terms of imprisonment are not so long. Our methods of treating the imprisoned are more humane. We sentence a man to prison. Of course, in the old time he used to be put in a vile place, where he would be covered with rags full of vermin, and where he would suffer all sorts of physical pain. Today we send him to jail, and we have the jail steam heated and electric lighted. We have a doctor to take care of him so if, perchance, the penalty is death he won't die before his time comes; and if he is to be hanged he gets better food than he ever did before. So far as men are entrusted with the power of carrying out these provisions they do it as humanely as they can do it.

In the old times the insane were treated like criminals. They were locked up in cells; they were loaded with chains; they were criminals, because the rest of the world did not understand them. We have gotten over that. We have learned to treat them as human beings, and to treat them as those suffering from ailments, whereas once in the history of the world they were visited with the old law of vengeance, the law of force. The world some time will learn to treat all of its defectives, and all those who violate the code, the same as they treat the insane and the ill today. And we are learning it, more and more, every day.

The theory of non-resistance does not, necessarily, say that a man cannot be restrained, although very likely that would not be necessary under any decent law of society. It is possible there are some who are so born, and have been so treated by society, that they would need to be restrained just as those afflicted with smallpox may be restrained in a hospital. But to restrain them and treat them until cured is one thing; to say that men because of some inherent wickedness deserve punishment is another thing. It would be absurd to restrain men suffering from smallpox and turn them out from a hospital in six weeks, whether cured or not. If hospitals were run in the same way as jails, we would send them up for thirty days; and if they got well in a week we would keep them there.

The whole theory of punishment, so far as there is any theory in it—and there is not much in it, except the idea of vengeance— but the whole theory, so far as there is one, comes from the religious conception that some people are made inherently bad, that their minds are evil, or their soul for that matter, or whatever the intangible thing about them that makes them evil. And they deserve punishment, because they have a wicked, abandoned, and malignant heart. We always have to put that "wicked, abandoned, and malignant heart" in the indictment; otherwise it is no good. If he has that in his heart he can be punished. When twelve jurors and a judge get together, how can they tell whether his heart is bad or not? You could tell better if you dissect him.

It goes upon the theory that man is apart from all the other beings that inhabit the universe; that he is a free moral agent;

Clarence Darrow

that he is a sort of a wild train running at large through the universe; that he is not governed by rules and conditions like the rest of the universe about us. But that the Lord created him, put a mind in him, a good heart in some of them; a wicked, abandoned, and malignant heart in others; and sent them out to run wild independent of all the universe about them. And whenever the good people catch up with these wicked, abandoned, and malignant people then we punish the wicked, because intrinsically they are bad, because they chose the evil instead of the good. They could be better if they wanted to be better, but they did not choose. Society sends them to jail, just as brutal parents whip their children because they are bad instead of good.

As a matter of fact, science and evolution teach us that man is an animal, a little higher than the other orders of animals; that he is governed by the same natural laws that govern the rest of the universe; that he is governed by the same laws that govern animal life, aye, and plant life; that free moral agency is a myth, a delusion, and a snare. It teaches us that he is surrounded by environment, the product of all the past, the product of the present; that he is here just like any other subject of natural law; and that it is not goodness, it is not badness, that makes him what he is. It is the condition of life in which he lives. And if he lives unwisely, if he is a defective, if he is anti-social, it is not that he chose it, but it is due to a thousand conditions over which he has not the slightest control. And the wise society seeks to change his environment, to place him in harmony with life. They know that they can only change the man by changing the conditions under which he lives; that good and evil, so far as he is concerned, do not exist; that right and wrong are religious myths; that it is a question of the adaptability of the individual to social life, and a gradual change of the environment under which he lives.

With the state it is the same thing. The theory of force and violence applied to the state has drenched the world in blood. It has built great navies and great armies. One nation builds a great navy and a great army, and destroys the resources of its people to build armies and navies. And another nation must build a greater navy and a greater army, because of the first. It makes of the people of the earth armed camps, and the stronger the one arms itself, the stronger must the rest. England builds her wonderful navy out of the toil of the poor, out of what should buy food for the men who produce it. And when she builds it, then Germany must build one as large, and so must France, and so must Russia build one, too. And of course patriotic America must build one. We need a navy for fear that a band of Senegambians might send a fleet to devastate Chicago some night. The theory of force and violence as applied to political states has built up the navies and armies of the world, and has caused most of the bloodshed of the human race.

Is there any doubt but what nations would be stronger if they burned their battleships instead of building new ones? Can you increase the power of one nation by building ships, when you simply make others build larger? You never change the relative proportion, which alone makes the strength. If instead of adding to the navies the world over, we gradually got rid of them, the relative strength would be what it was before.

In industrial life it is the same thing. The reign of force and the reign of violence means competition, means industrial strife; it is responsible for the greed and selfishness and avarice, for the fortunes of the great and the poverty of the poor. It is only in these later days, when the world is looking to something better, when they are learning that force and violence is wrong, that it is wrong that merchants compete and cut each other's throats, and workmen compete against each other to show how much less they can work for; and that it is better to organize society on a co-operative basis where each man is to help his fellow-man instead of fighting his fellow-man.

The dreams of the world may be far off, and we must fit every dream to every reality. For the world is imperfect. But if, as society progresses, there shall one day be a civilization better

Clarence Darrow

than the world has known, it will be a society where force and violence and bloodshed and cruelty have disappeared. It will be a world of brotherhood. A world not of destruction, of competition, of violence, of hatred, of enmity; but a world of co-operation, of mutual help, of love, of brotherliness; and that alone makes for the progress of the world.

From a debate with Arthur M. Lewis, 1910.

Theory of Non-resistance

RESPONSE TO
BIRTHDAY GREETINGS,
SIXTY-FIRST
BIRTHDAY ANNIVERSARY

*I have always yearned for peace, but have lived a life
of war. I do not know why, excepting
that it is the law of my being. I have lived
a life in the front trenches, looking for trouble.*

IF I HAD KNOWN JUST WHAT I
was to run into here I would have worn a gas mask. A man is
never painted as he is. One is either better or worse than the picture that is drawn. This is the first time that I have felt that I
was worse. No one ever gave me a dinner like this before, and
I really do not know how my friends happened to take into
their heads to do it this time. I am sure it has been pleasant, although in spots more or less embarrassing; still on the whole I
prefer the embarrassments incident to this dinner, rather than
the ones I often get.

Like most others who reach the modest age of sixty-one, I
have hardly noticed it. Still this morning for the first time in
more than twenty years I felt a twinge of rheumatism, a gentle
reminder on this birthday that I am no longer a "spring chicken."
On the whole the years have passed rapidly. Some of them, it is
true, have dragged, but mainly they have hurried as if anxious to
finish the job as soon as they possibly could. So quickly have

Clarence Darrow

they sped that I hardly realize that so many have been checked off, in fact I have scarcely thought about it as they went by.

I have been congratulated a good many times today, no doubt on the fact that I am so nearly done with it all. One scarcely feels as they go along that they are getting—well, older. Of course I know my intellect is just as good as it ever was; I am sure of that. Everyone tells me that I am looking younger. I had my hair cut about a month ago; a friend remarked, "It makes you look ten years younger," so I had it cut again. Perhaps I shall keep on getting it cut. Of course, one more or less doubts the truthfulness of these old friends, when they say you are getting younger, but at the same time you try to believe them and do not contradict.

Perhaps it would be proper at a time like this to reminisce more or less, but I am always afraid to do it. I am never quite sure whether I might not have said the same things before. Neither am I certain that I shall not say something I had better leave unsaid. If one has lived an active life, as he grows old he finds that he has gathered a large fund of facts and fictions that he should keep to himself; and yet he always feels an urge to tell. Then I have had Tolstoy's frightful example before me all my days. You know he lived a busy, useful life, getting about all there was out of it, and then after he got—well, past sixty-one, he grew good and began to moralize. I presume Tolstoy did not know just what was the matter with him.

Now, of course, allowance should be made for the actions and habits of life of a man when he grows old. No doubt you will some time need to make allowance for mine, but if ever I begin moralizing, I trust I shall have some good, kind friend who will hit me on the head with an axe. It is all right to be as you are and feel as you feel when you are old, but it is silly to moralize. It gives you away. So I trust I shall die before I begin moralizing.

One at sixty, or even younger, begins to take on airs; or at least most people do. I am so inherently modest that I haven't commenced taking them on. I remember the first case I had after I began practicing law, just before I was twenty-one. An old country pettifogger, the terror of the community, was on the other side. I intended to overwhelm him, but the first time he noticed that I was present he called me "bub." This dampened my ardor. For many years I never met a lawyer as young as I. These older lawyers always patronized me, excused my innocence and ignorance—especially my ignorance. Now I seldom meet a lawyer as old, and I hope I do not patronize the young ones as the older lawyers once patronized me.

For after all, it is a foolish habit of old people to patronize the young and to advise them what to do, whether the young are children or only a little younger. The fact is that age does not necessarily bring wisdom; it may here and there bring caution, but not always that. If the child behaved as the grown people, there would be no children. The child or young person has as good reason to think that he is right as the old person; perhaps better. The young person has a better guarantee that he is right than the old person who believes that the child would be right if he followed the advice of the old. Still, the world is full of moralizing and teaching and preaching to the young. The only satisfaction is that the young pay no attention to it.

Parents, teachers, preachers and the like are forever condemning in children the things they once did themselves. They have so little imagination that they cannot bridge the space of years between them and childhood, and understand that the emotions and feelings of youth are right for youth, and without them the child could never come to be the man. The law for youth is one thing, and the law for old age is quite another; and it is idle and senseless for age to lay down precepts for youth. The young would not keep them if they could, and they could not keep them if they would. Each must work out the experiment of life according to his own age, his own experience, and the emotions and tendencies that are incident to his own machine.

Perhaps in some respects my life has not been quite the same as others. I have always had a feeling that I was doing what I wished to do, but a certain knowledge that I never did anything I chose to do. I have always had an ambition for freedom, but

Clarence Darrow

I know that I never had the slightest influence over myself. I am sure that I have everlastingly been controlled by the influences before me and the infinite influences around me, and that I have never known what freedom is. I keep on working for it and hoping for it and wanting it, but I know that I never shall have it. In this, no doubt, my life has been like the life of every being that ever lived. Even while I have fought for freedom, the freedom of others and the freedom of myself, I have always had a consciousness that I was doing it to amuse myself, to keep myself occupied so I might forget myself; which after all is the best thing that any of us can do as we go along.

I remember reading a while ago a statement of Anatole France. He said that the chief business of life is "killing time." And so it is. What is the difference if we gather all the facts of the universe into our brains for the worms to eat? They might give the worms indigestion. What matters it how much we get together? It lasts but a short time. It never brings what we expect. All we get from it is the self-forgetfulness that comes from gathering it. We get from the gleaning the loss of self-consciousness, which after all is the only thing that makes life tolerable to the ordinary person, or the extraordinary for that matter. One can imagine nothing more tiresome and profitless than sitting down and thinking of one's self. If you are bound to work and cannot avoid work, and can be lost in the work, it is the most tolerable life after all that one can have.

Now, I never was industrious. I could prove that by a number of people here tonight. Still, I have always worked. Some task is always waiting for me and someone always calling to me. And I could not avoid the task or ignore the call. So the sixty-one years of my life have slipped by and I have scarcely known it.

In spite of the manifold troubles and cares that go with living, still life is not bare of joys. When I was a boy the thing that gave me the greatest pleasure was baseball. I would always leave school when I could, and of course work if I could, to play baseball. I once thought that when the time should come that I could no longer play ball there would be nothing left in life. But

I passed that age and then found that there were other things quite as interesting as baseball to fill my time. And when I wonder what can take the place of the ones I have still to leave behind, I remember the past and feel that later there will yet be other things as interesting as the ones that I must give up.

I used to wonder what old people could find to do that would bring them any joy—of course I am not old, I am still quite young. I am not boasting. I used to wonder what boys could do to have fun after they were twenty years old; then I raised it to twenty-five; then I raised it to thirty. I have been raising it ever since, and still wondering what people can do for pleasure when they are old. But we are there with the same old illusions and the same old delusions, with fantasies promising us and beckoning us; with castles that we begin to build, never stopping to think whether these castles will be finished; we get our satisfaction and we kill our time listening to the voices and building the castles. Whether the voices fade in the distance or the castles tumble down does not seriously matter. I fancy it would be as much fun to tear down the Masonic Temple as to build it, if we really wished to do it. The main thing is to be occupied with our work.

There is not so much difference as you get older; at least so far I can see but little. I am not sure how it would be if I really should get old. There is not so much difference in life. As I have remarked, my intellect is all right. Of course I need to watch my diet more carefully than I once did; and then the Lord never did seem to know much about teeth. This is one place where he especially fell down. I visit the dentist oftener than I used to. But there are very clever dentists to take your money away from you, and they fix you up all right. I remember when I found that two teeth on each side were not doing good service, and that I should get some store ones to take their place. The dentist fixed up a contrivance so that I could put these in to take the place of the imperfect ones that nature furnished. These new ones did good work. I never had any trouble with them and they never hurt me. I generally wear them in my pocket. I seldom have a proposition so tough that I cannot handle it with the ones

I have left—and then there are always the store ones to fall back on in case of need.

Of course as you grow older, you can't run so fast. But what is the use of running so fast? You would have to come back anyhow. And then one can learn to stay where he is; the place he would run to is no better than the one that he would leave. Nature, by taming your ambitions and cooling your blood, steps in and helps you out, and you hardly know what is happening as the years crowd around you.

Then I fancy that if one really grows old, nature is able to handle that job too. She rather fools you. As Oliver Wendell Holmes once said, nature has a sort of an anodyne that she begins giving to her children along when one is older than I am; I don't know just how much older—probably never shall. This dose is something like the black drop the doctors once gave. It has a deadening narcotic effect; it stuns your sensibilities and leaves you to doze and dream. Oliver Wendell Holmes was right. Nature does not temper the wind to the shorn lamb, but she tempers the shorn lamb to the wind. So after all I fancy that age does not cut so much figure as the young suppose.

I am inclined to think that young people are more apt to suicide than the old. Of course I know that life is not worth while, but I have never got ready to end it all. I never could see much to be gained by dying today. Better wait until tomorrow and save the trouble and the muss of it all.

On the whole I think young people get less comfort out of life than older people. The fact is, when we are young we expect too much; we haven't the experience to temper our emotions. If it is raining today, the child cannot temper his disappointment with the thought that the sun will shine tomorrow; no more if the sun shines today can he repress his emotion by the thought that tomorrow it will rain.

I have always felt that older people commit great crimes against children. I fancy that one who has in his power the destiny of a child should do what he can to make that child's life happy. Childhood is the time of the greatest illusions, and these should not be denied. Children are almost helpless in the hands of older people.

Neither the old nor the young can live long without pleasure, or the hope of pleasure. The denial of this is death or worse than death. Of course, I have done my best to have my full share of pleasure as I lived. I could never resist temptation. As Heine said: "It was very well for Kant to say, 'Act so that your conduct may be a law for all men under similar conditions.' But Kant forgot that YOU are a part of the conditions. Suppose you happen to be one of those fellows to whom all the roses nod and all the stars wink," then what are you to do? Everyone is the heir to all that has gone before; his structure and emotional life is fixed, and no two children of nature have the same heredity. I believe everyone should and must live out what is in him. So no two lives can be the same.

Perhaps strong emotions are a grievous burden. If they sometimes lead to the depth of despair, they likewise take you to the mountain top where you see the rising sun in all its glory and its strength. Some of you may hear me preach ten years from now. You will think that I have passed into senile dementia—but what I say now goes! One should live out his life according to the law of his being, for why live without joy? Why live for pain and suffering? Of course the good man, the altruist, says you should live to make your fellow-man happy. But why should you make your neighbor happy if it is wicked to be happy yourself?

The one thing that gets me, perhaps more than anything else, is the terribly cruelty of man. Someone here said that I loved my fellow-man. I don't know whether I do or not. It depends on whether you are speaking intellectually or chemically. Intellectually, I think human beings are a pretty poor lot. Here and there no doubt is nobility of character, but the human race is not a proper subject for worship. It has always taken itself too seriously. It amounts to little. If it should die, it would doubtless be as well or better for the rest of creation. The thing I see everywhere present is the cruelty of man. Men torturing animals, regardless of the suffering of the weak. Men torturing each other, simply for the joy of doing it. Man is cruel, one of the cruelest animals of the brute creation. I remember the great naturalist, Fabre, said that there is no other species that devours and enslaves members of its own species; this is left for man alone.

We seem to get pleasure in torturing our fellow-men. And here with you, who I am sure are higher intellectually than the average people, or you wouldn't be my friends and appreciate me—even here I venture to say that most of you enjoy telling or hearing some disagreeable thing about your fellow-men. Why is it? There must be some philosophy back of it all. You go home to the old town of your birth and ask, "How is John Smith?" "Why, John Smith has been in the penitentiary." This is the first news you will get of John Smith. "How is Mary Jones?" "Mary Jones has just been divorced." How is it that with the great majority of men and women, the first thing that occurs to them about their neighbor is something disagreeable or unkind? As far as I can see, there is no exception to it, for as wise and good as I am, I like to hear these things. I enjoy hearing them, with this exception: When the persons spoken of are so near to me that to hurt them hurts me, then I do not like to hear these remarks. If a man is nothing to me, if I am indifferent to him, or do not like him, then I am quite sure I am glad to hear them.

Life is an everlasting struggle. It is filled with cares and sorrows of all sorts. Of course, when you come close to your real friends, you find solace and rest. Still, life is hard, and all who really live know that it is hard. Man is continually moving between his desire to do certain things and his regret that he has done them. He is always resolving that in the future he will be better and more thoughtful than he has been in the past. We are all makers of resolutions. I "swear off" smoking several times a day, but I smoke again. "Swear off" doing many things, but not seriously. Habits are too strong for me and life is too strong for me. As old Omar said:

"Indeed, indeed repentance oft before
I swore, but was I sober when I swore?
And then, and then came spring and rose in hand
My threadbare penitence apieces tore."

My penitence would last if spring did not come; if temptation did not come. In the warmth of spring and the odor of violets, it fades away.

Most of life is hard for those who think. No doubt there are those who believe that "God's in his heaven and all's right with the world." If one can live on this delusion, he would be foolish to awaken from his dream. But if we really think and feel, life is serious and hard. All who live a full and long life without illusions, at times involuntarily look with almost longing eyes to the last release. The plaintive, wistful, mournful words of Swinburne are not unwelcome music to his ears:

From too much love of living,
From hope and fear set free,
We thank with brief thanksgiving
Whatever Gods may be;
That no life lives forever,
That dead men rise up never;
That even the weariest river
Winds somewhere safe to sea.

From the sterner things of life and death men have turned always to illusions to make things seem what they are not. For those mortals who must look life in the face and cannot dream, there is nothing left but a sense of humor and hard work. Hard work is good. It is good because it brings a loss of consciousness. It makes man live an intuitive, automatic life, where he forgets that he is living. Hard work, like sleep, is an interruption of life; it is unconsciousness and death and is, therefore, peace.

No doubt some things bring deeper and more lasting happiness than others. Perhaps, too, we learn a little as we live. I want to testify as I get older that the greatest comfort I have is in the

Clarence Darrow

companionship of friends. I am deeply sensible of the compliment you pay in gathering here tonight. I have enjoyed this evening. I am willing you should be deluded all you wish as to who I am and what I am. I am willing to delude myself.

Some of you have wished that I might live to be a hundred. Well, I shall not—I am sure of that. Still, we listen to those things and like to hear them, even while we know better. We can pick up the mortuary tables of the life insurance companies and find out almost to a day when the bobbin will be wound up. But we do not do it. We know that, given a million people, the average of death is fixed and we can linger only a few days beyond the rest. We could find the time for ourselves if we would. We try to think that our fate will be unlike the rest, when we know that it will not.

As other pleasures disappoint us and fail us, we turn more and more to friends. I am frank to say that it is a comfort and consolation to me to have so many as you who are here tonight. I am not sure how much I have done to deserve them. Of course all friends are not always true. Human nature is too weak; men are machines and can stand only a certain pressure.

Perhaps I may be pardoned for saying just a little for myself. I may have earned them as well as most men have. I have tried to play the game fair. I have never judged any man. I have harmed no one consciously. I have had sympathy for all. I have done my best to understand the manifold conditions that surround and control each human life. I have always wanted friends and tried to get them, but I have tried to get them honestly, with no pretense of being something that I am not; and to know that I have so many as you who are here tonight is a deeper consolation than anything else could be.

As we grow older, friends mean more and more. There are not many who have the capacity for true friendship. The world does not permit it. We have too much to do. We are too busy getting a living and getting money. We are too busy keeping out of the poorhouse and the jail. I have often told young men starting out in business not to make acquaintances, but to make friends. Acquaintances are of little value unless you want to run for office, and I know that each of you have an ambition higher than that. But friends are of value as you go through life. They are of value in an infinite number of ways and places that you can never see in advance. They give consolation, comfort, and help which nothing else can bring. I have often said friendship is like agriculture—the intensive kind is the sort that pays. Our American farmer will take five hundred acres and cultivate it poorly and let the weeds grow with the grain. The French farmer will take ten acres and cultivate it with thoroughness and care and get more profit from his ten than the American will from five hundred. One cannot reach the whole world. We should intensively cultivate our friends, find out the capacities, the sympathies, the depths of nature of those around us and cultivate them until they are our friends and we are theirs. More and more as we grow older we find friendship the chief thing in life.

Of course we fight and we work. I have always yearned for peace, but have lived a life of war. I do not know why, excepting that it is the law of my being. I have lived a life in the front trenches, looking for trouble. The front trenches are disagreeable; they are hard; they are dangerous; it is only a question of days or hours when you are killed or wounded and taken back. But it is exciting. You are living; and if now and then you go back to rest, you think of your comrades in the fight; you hear the drum; you hear the cannon's voice; you hear the bugle call; and you rush back to the trenches and to the thick of the fight. There, for a short time, you really live. It is hard, but it is life. Activity is life. Peace is death; and there is no complete peace excepting death. However hard, if it is the law of our being it cannot be changed.

I have always believed that man has little or nothing to do with himself. He is born without willing. He dies when his time is up. He is influenced by everything about him, helpless from the beginning to the end.

This is life and all there is of life; to play the game, to play the cards we get; play them uncomplainingly and play them to the end. The game may not be worth the while. The stakes may not be worth the winning. But the playing of the game is the forgetting of self, and we should be game sports and play it bravely to the end.

April 18, 1918.

THE CONSOLATIONS
OF PESSIMISM

*The pessimist takes life as he finds it, without
the glamour that false creeds and false teachers and
foolish people have thrown about it.*

THERE ARE TWO SORTS OF PESSI-
mism, at least—one which refers to emotions and the other which
refers to intellect. Really, emotions and intellect have very little to
do with each other. Whether one is happy depends largely upon
his makeup. Mark Twain put this very well in his remarkable little
volume, *What Is Man?* If a man is a pessimist, he is born a pessimist, and emotionally you cannot make him an optimist. And
if he is an optimist, you can tell him nothing to make him a
pessimist. You might as well talk about telling an idiot something
to make him wise as to tell an optimist something to make him a
pessimist. It comes to pretty nearly the same thing. What we think
and how we feel are different matters.

I fancy, as the world goes, I am about as happy as anybody. I at
least am not much more miserable, which is a safe way of putting
it. I never had any complaint to make about myself. The way I do
is to compare myself with others who are worse off, which is a
good way. I get other consolations in various ways. I do not get
very cold in the winter. I keep fairly cool in the summer—and at all
other times. I cannot say that I suffer much, except perhaps intellectually, and I have got used to that, so it does not bother me.

Clarence Darrow

I speak of pessimism as an intellectual theory. Is life worth while? Wouldn't it be better—if you could imagine it—for the human race if it had never been born? Is there more pain or more pleasure in life? Those are the questions that determine whether one is a pessimist or an optimist. Are there more pleasurable sensations or more painful sensations?

If you had a friend whom you really cared for, not wholly in a selfish way, and he should die, would you bring him back to life if you could? Would you bring him back to life, not because it would make you happier but because it would be better for him? Many people will do something to make themselves happy and think they are doing something to make someone else happy. These things are more or less mixed, and not easy to separate. But if you are thinking of a friend you really care for and to whom you wish the best, and who is safely dead and out of it, would you think you would be doing him a favor by bringing him back? I fancy if I really went dead, if anybody would awaken me and tell me to begin living again, I would kill him. And I can say that and still not wish to die. For the desire to live goes with living. The will to live, at least, goes with living. One cannot live without willing to live. When one is ready to die, of course, the will to live is gone—if one dies in a natural way—just at the time of death.

It is an intellectual question: Would it be worth while to wake me up for the short time I should be awake and let me go back to clay? That is the problem. It seems to me that, to the intellectual person, there can only be one answer; and all the optimists show us that there is only one answer. All optimists are dope fiends. And everybody is encouraged to take dope all through life. There has come to be an attitude in the world where the optimist thinks it is a crime if you will not take dope, or if you cannot take it. I repeat, there is not an optimist who is not essentially a dope fiend. And if he is a fairly intelligent optimist—if you can use those two words together—he takes dope consciously; he wants to take it, just as many of us, when we are enjoying a pleasant dream and on the point of waking, try the best we can to keep on dreaming; we do not want to waken. And so the less ignorant of the optimists—I pretty nearly said the most intelligent—consciously keep on dreaming.

I find no fault with all that. If one can fool himself, all right. I have tried it, but I cannot. Perhaps, when I get older, I will be glad to become an optimist and think that "God's in his heaven" and "all's right with the world." You cannot tell what you are going to do. I trust they will take me away before that time, but you cannot tell.

The conspiracy to optimism is so general that you cannot speak the language without using dope. They come to you and tell you your friend has "passed on," when they mean he has passed off. There is not a shred of intellectual honesty in all of it. We are taught from the time we are children not to see life as life is, but to live and die in an opium dream. Perhaps that is wise. That question I am not discussing. But for us who are more or less intelligent and cannot fool ourselves, the question is still here. And it is only intelligent people who can discuss this question or who can consider it; nobody else will consider it. So I say again, as I have often said before, as Mark Twain and some other wise men have said, that intelligence is a curse. Intelligence and happiness do not go together. Mark Twain, you remember, makes his hero, Satan, promise to make a good priest happy the rest of his life; and he fulfilled his promise by putting him in a padded cell where he thought he was king of the universe, as many insane people think. Satan said that was the only way he could make him happy forever. So it is, the only possible way that it can be done. Of course, some are born crazy and others have it thrust upon them.

Now, broadly, you can take just one statement and show that optimism is entirely false—unless you take what the priests do. The priests believe in immortality. I am not saying whether there is, or is not, immortality. All I am saying is that all the investigations of the science of the world have never shown one shred of evidence that there is; while all the analogies of nature seem to show perfectly plainly that there is not. But in order to get out of the universal pessimism of the world, the world has created a heaven. Of course, if you can get into that state of exaltation where you see that life is a serious matter, has more pain than pleasure, and you believe that you can go down into the grave and be mixed with the earth and then come up again and be happy ever after, why you might be an optimist. If you believe this, then there is room for optimism. It is not a pessimist who says that life is not worth while. All the religious optimists say the same thing—that there is nothing in the world unless there is a heaven, and, I suppose, a hell. Otherwise, there is nothing in life that is worth while.

But suppose we take life as life is—"an unpleasant interruption of a peaceful nothingness," as Schopenhauer put it. It is short. The average, we will say, is forty years. I have passed the average. I do not believe I have been treated right. But assume that is all there is of us. What does forty years amount to in eternity? You could not measure it. Take forty years for a numerator and eternity for a denominator, and where do you get? You might as well have a numerator that is zero. It is not a pinprick in time; and it furnishes no sort of basis for optimism because at best it is nothing. And that must be at least the attitude of every person who assumes the perfectly obvious—that life is only while the organism persists.

Even if we say that we go back into the great well of human life, it does not help the individual. I don't want to get into the common reservoir—see whom I have to mix with! And man—who necessarily is egotistic while he lives, because he can only think of himself, for he thinks through himself—man must have a personal immortality or he has none. That is, after his brain is destroyed, he must remember that he was a man here on earth before he became an angel.

Now, whence came this idea of optimism? I fancy that the brute is neither an optimist nor a pessimist; neither is a blade of grass or a tree an optimist or pessimist. They are just a manifestation of matter and force. They live instinctively and intuitively, and that is all there is of them. Whence comes this idea? So far as we can see we cannot find it in the brute creation. Of course the brute draws back at death; but so does the plant. The instinct of life, the will to live, makes it draw back at death. It is a simple reflex action, and mechanical. Probably, when we get to the end of it, all human actions, whether they come through the body or through what we call the mind—which is a function of the body—are purely mechanical actions. Man is just as much a machine as an automobile; some of them Packards, but most of them Fords.

Now, for living organisms that think, to contemplate the end of life—especially the lives of those near and dear to them—calls forth unpleasant emotions, and a manifest desire to find something else. None of us are free from it. I confess that I have it, although, intellectually, I know the best thing that could happen would be to have it finished. But we feel it while we live. It is emotional and mechanical. Death is, by all odds, the most important and overshadowing thing that confronts man. Of course, we do not talk much about it because it is unpleasant. And perhaps one of the chief reasons why it is so unpleasant is because we do not talk about it. I fancy that the sexton does not think so much about death as the fellow who is always going to church or to dances. The sexton buries the dead every day and does not think much of it. The optimist might once in a while think of "passing on," but this is the most.

Of all the phenomena of nature that confront man, there is nothing else of any great importance when placed beside death— if death is death. And from that idea has come a feeling that we can, in some mysterious way, bridge that chasm. Of course this feeling has been helped out by more or less natural influences, like the dreams and visions producing the thought of the reappearance of the dead and all that sort of thing. But after all, the controlling feeling so far as semi-intelligent people are concerned is the dread of death. Every religion in the world is based on the idea that death is not death. You do not need to convert a Christian to pessimism. He will say: "If life is so short, what is the use?" And every creed that I know anything about is based on pessimism, assuming death is death.

We start with the cruder religions held by Billy Sunday and Billy Bryan, and that sort. To them, hell is hell; it is fire and brimstone. And if it is not, there is no use to get scared about it and join the church. And heaven is heaven—some fun there, if not in this world. The only reason they drive pleasure out of earth is so that they can have it some other time.

Starting with men like that, men of arrested development, assuming they ever had any, and coming down to the world religions like Christian Science and Unitarianism, we find them still based on the idea that we are going to get paid for it, and that death is not the end. The only serious effort ever made by intelligent people in the other direction that I am familiar with, is stoicism—the denial of pleasure to themselves so they can get used to disappointment and death. But the Christian is not a stoic. He is only a usurer. He is like the miser who hoards up gold and loans it to somebody at ten per cent interest, so that he can get it later. He gets along without a drink on earth because he is going to have so much in heaven. It is essentially sensual. All you need to do is to postpone pleasure. It is a plain bargain, with the odds a million to one in your favor if you believe, and not losing much if you do not. But it has no relation to stoicism. It is a plain matter of barter and sale. There are the wares; you know what you are getting. Now, you may take all the orthodox religions, which, so far as the Christian world goes, include most all people, and it is a plain question of bargaining. And optimism is based entirely upon the idea that the one who foregoes will be happy.

But there are people who get away from that idea; who cannot take these crude and crass doctrines. Take Christian Science, which is purely a religion of words and means nothing. Why do Christian Scientists believe in it? Because they are afraid to face the facts, that is all.

You may ask whether science is everything. Perhaps not. But when you approach a question from the intellectual side, you must take facts as facts are ascertained, and it has nothing to do whatever with these superstitions which are based purely upon faith. Assume you go down into the grave and come up again, just as good as new. Science knows nothing about it; and when we reason we can take no account of it. A man or woman who wishes to use his reason, or who must use it because he has found nothing to chloroform it with, has to take life as it is; he must face facts. And when you face facts, then the question occurs, "Is life worth while?" And I know no one who says it is worth while, if he considers facts.

I cannot too strongly urge that there is no orthodox church that is not built upon the idea that life can be of no value unless there is a future. Strike from the belief of the Christian the idea of immortality, and he would be paralyzed by terror and forget about going to church. Not only is religion full of this, but literature is full of it. We are taught about it in the nursery. All the imbecilic utterances of the world are of that sort. Art is full of it; poetry is filled with it; novels are full of it; every nursery book is full of it. They say, "Look upward, not downward, forward, not backward. Look outward, not inward." Well, why? They might just as well say: "Close your eyes." That is what they do say. Every cheap catch phrase that can be invented by the half-wits of the world has been used to make people optimists; to make them see things; to dream dreams and have visions. All right; I am not complaining of it. Perhaps that is just as well; but if this won't work on me, what am I to do about it?

I happened to be born queer. If you ask me whether I believe in this spook or that, I want you to tell me about the spook, then I will tell you whether I believe in it or not. If I had a way of making myself believe something that I did not believe I would probably do it. But I cannot do it by saying backwards and forwards, "God is love, or love is God," any more than by saying, "Dickory, dickory dock." One would mean just the same as the other, and neither would mean anything to me. I take life as life is, and with all of the light that experience and science can throw upon it. I ask myself the question—Is it worth while?—and there is only one answer to it, if you take it as it is.

This optimistic idea has gone so far that good people think it is evil to be a pessimist! Some sort of a moral obloquy attaches if you don't believe God's in his heaven and all's right with the world. Optimism is, somehow, mixed up with goodness, and yet the last thing an optimist does is to be good. Why should he be good?

God is enough to do the whole job! Really there is no doctrine that I know anything about that has been so persistently intertwined with every idea, with every thought, with every religion, as optimism. Children have been dosed with it as early as they took Mother Winslow's Soothing Syrup. It is the same kind of stuff, a chloroform preparation.

The question between optimism and pessimism is this: Are the painful emotions more than the pleasurable emotions in the brief time that we are awakened out of a perfectly tranquil sleep? Which had you rather do: sleep an hour or two longer, or get up and go to work in the morning? How many would be willing to knock off their job and go to bed an hour earlier? How many think life is as pleasant as sleep? Well, of course, the optimist, with his words, will say: "You are not achieving anything while you are asleep." Well, I am not while I am awake; and if I was, what of it? Before you can achieve, you must know what you are trying to achieve and what it all means. Alexander, and Caesar, and Jesse James, and a lot of the rest of them were great achievers. Billy Sunday is quite an achiever. He has probably sent more people to the "bughouse" who were almost ready for it, than any man we have a record of.

Well, what of it? When is a man doing best for himself? When he is asleep or when he is achieving? How many optimists have taken chloroform to go to sleep?—to say nothing about it, when they are awake. How many of them take it for the toothache? How many of them take it for all kinds of pain and suffering? How many of them want to get along without an opiate if they are going to have an operation? Even the thought of heaven is not enough for them. They need dope, and need it badly, when the time comes.

What do they talk about? I don't know that I am such a gloomy fellow. Perhaps I am. I never indulge in self-pity, and I think I get on all right. But an optimist does not talk much about graveyards, does he? That is not healthy. Of course, it is unavoidable, but it is not healthy. He would rather talk about "God's in his heaven," and "all's right with the world"; God is love, and love is God; that is a great deal better. You cannot go into a company gathered together for a good time and talk about death. You never hear of any social gatherings assembled in a graveyard. They don't hold dances there. They have no saloons there—excepting to take care of the mourners so that they cannot think.

There is a universal conspiracy to close your eyes to all disagreeable things. Suppose we go out to dinner and have a talk about cancers. Isn't a cancer a beautiful thing? It is as wonderful as a rainbow. So it is, but it is not a rainbow. Doesn't the world universally avoid everything that makes them think, not only of what is disagreeable, but of what is utterly inevitable? The whole idea of optimism is a huge bluff, which no sane people entertain for a minute. Why should I avoid graveyards, hospitals, jails and all the disagreeable subjects of life, if I am a real optimist? Why, just exactly as we boys that used to whistle while we went through the graveyard. That is what the optimist does, going through life. And you think it is wicked not to whistle. He goes through life blindfolded. I do not object to his doing it, but I can't go through it that way unless he can tell me how.

I have examined, with considerable patience, many schools of Christianity, even Christian Science, and New Thought, and Spiritualism, to say nothing about the Single Tax and Socialism. And I haven't lost consciousness yet. What am I to do for a delusion? What am I to do for chloroform, especially since the good people have shut up the saloons? I cannot take their dope. It is too silly. And then, the optimist makes me sick anyhow, prating of dreams, repeating phrases that have absolutely no relation to life.

Can we get any good in any other way? What does pessimism do for us? Well, it saves our self-respect, to start with. It prevents my saying a lot of muddling words I don't believe in, and that nobody else can define; terms that mean nothing to a man or to a woman. Did you ever see any of these people who could give you a definition of God? What is he? What does he look like? The human mind cannot imagine something unless it is in the image of the known. Does he look like a man or a horse or a rainbow? We have had gods in all these shapes. Or is he love? God is love— what does that mean? Then, what is love? Why, love is God. There

Clarence Darrow

you have it. There is the most intelligent religion in the world, because it has made the most converts, in what seems to be the most intelligent period of the earth—Christian Science. Look at it: God is love and love is God. Does it mean anything to anyone who has a brain? You might as well say: God is pale blue and pale blue is God. If one cares to, or rather, must look facts in the face, is there anything in any of it that a man can cling to while he is a man? And if not, there are two things; one is to die and the other is to harmonize your life, so far as you can, with the facts, and make the best you can of it; and that is all there is to it.

Now, there is only a small fraction of people who will kill themselves; I don't care whether optimists or pessimists. I think of the two, an optimist is more apt to commit suicide than a pessimist because he expects more, and gets disappointed. There is nothing to make a pessimist suicide, because he knows he is going to die anyhow; he is used to the thought of it—nothing except serious disease, accompanied by pain.

What has pessimism to offer? Really, it is a more cheerful belief than people ordinarily suppose. Just look at me. I know I am not an optimist. Some people try to tell me, in a kindly way, that my pessimism is just a pose. Very complimentary to a man to tell him he really knows better; that he is talking to hear himself talk. They are good about that. I can see nothing in life to glorify; I can see nothing in life to justify an intelligent, decent being in awakening a piece of senseless clay, and implanting in it feelings, emotions, hopes, and then making it clay again. I can see nothing in life to compensate for all the misery and suffering that is incident to the human race. And if I were an optimist, life would be still harder. Because if I felt that life to me and to others was one long dream of joy, then the thought of death would make life harder still. The thought of death to one who believes all life is simply a manifestation of matter, not necessarily painful or pleasurable, but a manifestation of matter like the growing of a tree, is nowhere near so hard as the thought of death to the man who is filled with these dreams and illusions.

Now, what can pessimism do for us? Here as everywhere we

must turn back to nature. You people know I am not a worshipper of nature. Nature is a horrible taskmistress. Not only does she know no good and no evil, but she is devoid of all emotions and has no sort of sympathy. She rides across life in the most brutal and ruthless way. But you cannot change her. Nature is your boss, and she is mine, and we must learn to make life tolerable, to conform to her as closely as we can. Now, what does nature do? There is a passage which says: God tempers the wind to the shorn lamb. Now, God does no such thing. What God does is this: He tempers the shorn lamb to the wind. It is a good deal easier to temper the shorn lamb than the wind. Along toward fall or winter, its fleece begins to grow, and when it begins to get cold and icy, it gets a pretty good coat of wool, which nature uses to keep him fairly warm in the winter time. Nature starts us out in life with easily digestible food—milk. We have no teeth and cannot eat beefsteak. We have no mind because the brain is just a piece of clay, ready for impressions; and that is where the optimist gets in his work, because clay is very plastic when it is young. Nature gradually develops strength until the child can eat beefsteak or something like that, and gradually his emotions grow. His ambition comes; he thinks of conquering the world. Of course, he gets a whole lot of hard knocks. As he begins to get older, he has trouble with his teeth, and has to consult a dentist, and tell his friends that he doesn't care so much for meat; he likes bread and coffee and things like that. And he is not so ambitious. He lives nearer the shore, as you might put it. And after a while he gets rid of his teeth, or nature does for him, and then he gets back to milk again, and his brain is just what it was when he was born, except that it has been through the process. He does not fear death very much. Nature is taking care of him and fitting him for it.

Now, that is what nature does with the animal. I fancy the animal never thinks anything about death, excepting an involuntary shudder as he comes up against it when man kills him, or an effort to save his life; but that is mechanical. But the idea of old age does not enter its head. The dog runs faster when it is young than when it is old, and is more ambitious, that is all. And man follows the same course. Nature takes care of him—very poorly, of course—but she adjusts him in a way to the hardships inevitable to life. And in that time of his life when he is strongest, come certain ambitions and strength to meet them, and they gradually die away, and he goes out. That is all there is of that.

Now, we ought to learn something from nature. Nature prepares all animal life in the summer for the winter that is coming. She prepares the animal with plenty of covering to carry it through the winter. The optimistic cricket sings, "Why worry about winter?" and dies. Just like the human optimist—although as a rule his optimism does not prevent him from gathering in all the money he can; he might need it over there. Nature tempers us; she tempers the shorn lamb to the wind.

To my mind, there can be no question but that the right philosophy of life is to temper ourselves the best we can to the facts of life, if we cannot take dope. We know what is coming; we know that pain is everywhere incidental to life. We know the only inevitable thing is death, and we all ought to have brains enough to know it, even if we shut our eyes and refuse to look at it. The best way is to live on; to conform as near as possible, to temper ourselves to the facts of life, to pain and death.

Now, the optimist is the most unfortunate of human beings when he awakens. Of course, most of them never awaken. The optimist, if he believes what he preaches, goes singing on his way through the world, excusing and explaining all the sorrow of the world, until he stumbles into a grave that he might have seen if he had been looking downward instead of upward. The optimist, of course, is silly. You ask him to explain the pain and suffering of the world, and he says: "Oh, well, God is good." Yes. Why did God kill the young child in my neighbor's house? "Oh, well," he says, "God is good and he thought it would be better for the child." That would be no excuse for a man, but is an excuse for God. Why did God put a cancer on a beautiful woman's cheek? "Oh, well, he thought she would be too vain; anyway, God knew." Why does he shake down a city with an earthquake? "Well—oh, you are using human judgment to judge God." Well, with my human judgment, I judge man; why not God? It is better to judge God than man, because if your premises are right, he has the power to act and man has not. Anyhow, all I have is my human judgment; and that is all you have, and you will not use it. Why does God send an earthquake, or a volcano, or sink a ship at sea; or why consign some to hopeless disease and long suffering until death? Well, I have been defending people in the criminal courts for a long, long time, and making excuses for people, but I wouldn't know how to make any excuses for this; neither would anybody else that had any sense.

There is no judgment with nature. With nature it is just inevitable, and we must conform life to it; that is all. We must live in the summer with the thought of the winter. We cannot sing our way through life like the grasshopper, and forget there is a cold winter coming. The pessimist is not filled with elation; we are not overly happy, and then we are not overly miserable. When we have serious trouble, we don't tell it to everybody, because we have sense enough to know that others have theirs, too, and will not be interested in ours. We know that life is filled with pain and trouble, and that it is incidental to everything that lives.

The only consolation at the thought of death, to one who is not a dope fiend, is that you will lose nothing. If someone were to tell you today, in full health, that you would die before tomorrow night, what consolation would you have—assuming that you could not take dope? Of course some of you might say: "Well, I will see Jesus." But I am not interested in seeing Jesus. Neither are they. People who talk about him don't want to see him. They are willing to have him prepare a mansion for them, but they are not willing to move in. The only consolation is, "Well, I will have no further trouble; it will be like going to sleep at night." For many, many years it has been the best thing I could think of after a day's labor and a day's trouble. It is the pleasantest thought that a sensible man can have; I know, for I have it. Pessimism keeps an even balance in life. If I am happy today, all right. I will not get too elated, because I know I will be unhappy next week; and I will temper it as I go along.

Man, if he is intelligent, takes into account the future and past,

Clarence Darrow

and there is nothing sure about luck, as Bret Harte says, except that it will change, whether it is good luck or bad luck. For, after all, pain is a feeling that is contrasted with pleasure, and pleasure is contrasted with pain, and you must have both, or you have neither.

When the optimist falls, he has farther to fall than the pessimist. It is a long, hard fall. It is a good way from the clouds down to the earth, a long way, and he lives always in the clouds. You have all seen the sorrows of childhood and had them. The sorrows of the child are almost hopeless. The night is entirely black; every star is blotted out, because he lives for the present, and he forgets the past, and the future he cannot see. The animal is the same. The grown-up child is the same. We reach with our imagination, forward and backward, and we know that pain, however great today, will not last forever; and we know that joy, however strong today, cannot last forever; and that thought tempers the joy and it tempers the pain. We know we cannot even take the emotions of men, and say one is good and another bad. Take that one which produces the deepest joy—love—and has perhaps the most permanent effect on the human race, it brings, too, the deepest grief. Nothing brings the pain that love brings. If it brought no other, it brings the pain of loss, which is deep in proportion as the love is great.

The pessimist takes life as he finds it, without the glamour that false creeds and false teachers and foolish people have thrown about it. He knows he must meet this thing day after day, year after year. He knows that it is not good. He knows that it is not entirely bad. He knows it is life. And he adjusts life to meet those conditions. He does not live in the clouds. He does not live with the thought that he will be happy in another world. He lives it from day to day in the knowledge of what it means, and as a rule, he is a better man and a kindlier man than the optimist.

If you need friends, don't go to optimists; they are always too busy optimising, and they don't have time for you; go to the pessimists. Schopenhauer says: "You ask me to love my fellow-man because of his nobility, his greatness of character. I cannot do it, for I know better. But if you ask me to love him because of his helplessness, because of his weakness, that are common to him and to me, then I can sympathize with him and I can help him." The optimist says: "Love man because he is inherently noble; he is the work of God and must be noble." According to his theory, everything is the work of God. Love him because he is noble? He is not. He is neither bad nor noble; he is a manifestation of matter. Awakened to consciousness for a moment; gone forever; necessarily filled with limitations; some nobility, and much that is not. The pessimist takes him as he is. He is sorry for him; sorry for him as a member of a shipwrecked boat on the waves would be sorry for the rest who were floating in the open ocean with him—fellow-sufferers, without reason, or justice, but still fellow-sufferers, with a common, human bond between them.

The pessimist expects nothing. He is prepared for the worst. It is something like getting vaccinated so you will not get the smallpox. If you are well vaccinated with pessimism, nothing much troubles you. You say, "Oh, well, it might be worse." Whenever the pessimist is disappointed, he is happy, for it is better than he thought.

Now, it is all a question of taking life as life is. If you have tried all kinds of dope, as most of us have, and none of it will work, and you are bound to look at life as life is, then look at all of it, and prepare for the worst. It takes away the shock. A man figures on a trip to Europe next summer, and is building on it all winter. When he gets there, it will not be half so nice as if he had come upon it without thinking of it. And you are figuring on death and bankruptcy and disease and loss of your friends, and you get pretty well used to it before it happens to you, and you hardly know it. It is the most consoling to my mind for an intellectual person. Perhaps that is the only reason why I have taken it.

Lecture, January 11, 1920, before the Rationalist Educational Society, Chicago.

IS MAN
FUNDAMENTALLY
DISHONEST?

The man who stifles his views, who withholds his knowledge
and opinions, who conforms when he knows he should
not conform, is not honest. All men do this to some extent.
They are obliged to conform or die.

THE FORM OF THIS QUESTION IS based on the common idea that in the moral world there are straight lines and clear distinctions. It is assumed that good has no relation to bad, and right no relation to wrong. In the words of Theodore Roosevelt, "Right is right and wrong is wrong." If all questions were so simple as Mr. Roosevelt thought, it would save endless controversy, and discussions over philosophy and morals would no longer attract the interest of the intellectual world.

Theology has always held that there need be no confusion on the subject of right and wrong. If perchance here and there some weak or blind traveler could not find the road, there were always the church and theology to set him right. The fact that different churches and different theologies held more or less conflicting views seemed not to matter. Each church had its code, and every person was supposed to accept one of them for light and guidance. All these religious conceptions are now disputed. What is more important, the human machine has been tested and analyzed and its capacities appraised. The old basis of right and wrong has been found wanting, and the scientist has slowly and patiently built a new foundation which rests upon the experience, the customs, and the habits of man. That this foundation is shifting and changing in no way invalidates its verity as the criterion of right and wrong.

Aside from the religious conception of right and wrong, it was commonly supposed that all normal men were born with a conscience which automatically told them what was right and what was wrong. We now know that man has no inherited ideas on any subject. He may bring with him into the world a few life-preserving instincts, but his conscience, which was once supposed to tell him the difference between right and wrong, is acquired after birth and is formed from the ideas of right and wrong held by the parents, teachers, and others who surround him in youth. His conscience depends upon the accident of birth. Hence, in many things his moral convictions are questions of geography.

Fundamentally, man is always changing, both in structure and concepts. His mechanism and ideas are constantly acting and reacting upon each other and always reshaping the inherent man. Not only is the individual always changing, but the common concepts of morals change too. "Honesty" and "dishonesty" are very inclusive words. They carry with them so many specific ideas that no two persons would be able to classify all human conduct alike. Even though two persons could agree as to the emotions that should be classified as "honest" and "dishonest," they could never agree upon the relative importance to be attached to each. They would likewise often find themselves halting between two or more good motives which were found in conflict under certain conditions. Examples of this clash often appear between "loyalty" and "truthfulness." One of Sir Walter Scott's novels illustrates this in the suffering of a girl who was called upon to choose between telling the truth or hiding the disgrace of her sister. That this heroine chose to tell the truth simply shows that she had been brought up with an emphasized idea of truthfulness, and was really not much of a heroine. Without doubt most girls would have chosen the other course without hesitation.

It is hardly possible to discuss the question of man's integrity without stating some of the qualities that are generally understood as inherent in the word "honesty." These qualities are, of course, those which are generally recognized in the community where one lives; such qualities would include truthfulness, loyalty, frank dealing, a nice distinction as to property rights, all of which are the basis of a changing and rapidly growing conception of honesty in this materialistic age. Against these qualities can be listed lying, stealing, cheating, and overreaching. Each of these qualities can, in turn, be subdivided into many simpler ones.

No doubt the child naturally tells the truth. He tells it not because it is honorable to be truthful, but because it is easier and simpler. The child is moved in his actions by the instincts to preserve his life, to get pleasure and avoid pain. He easily learns to lie when he finds that truthfulness will bring pain.

The child knows nothing about property rights. His instinct to live leads him, as it does all other animals, to take what he wants wherever he can find it. Property rights are purely social creations, and it is a long and tedious process to teach children the constantly growing code that regulates such rights. The consciousness of the child has no ideas and conceptions to fortify this code. Violations of property rights make up most of the provisions of the criminal code. This is largely due to the fact that the distinctions are so fine that differences in the ways of securing property are hard to grasp. Then, too, the fundamental instincts of obtaining food and clothing, comfort and pleasure, are always urging the violation of some form of conventional and legal honesty.

There are no two persons who have the same conceptions of this sort of honesty. Commercial and legal honesty are far removed from ideal honesty and from the Golden Rule. In this age business seems to cover nearly the whole horizon of life. Getting money for the sake of money is the driving emotion. This tends to destroy any conception of honesty except legal and conventional honesty. One has only to look at the advertisements that fill the periodicals and deface the streets to see the universal attempt to overreach the guileless and get the public's money by false and misleading statements about wares that are for sale. Writing this sort of literature is more profitable than any other form of art. The principles of psychology are called into play to induce the public to buy. No merchant would expect to help his business by a plain statement of facts and an honest comparison of his wares with the goods that other merchants seek to sell. When the ruling instinct is to get money, there can be no idealistic conception of fair dealing.

Does this mean that men are intrinsically dishonest? The conclusion does not necessarily follow. Men possess emotions, all of which give way to the strongest. To be too idealistic would mean destruction. And after all, self-preservation is the strongest urge in life. The changes in law have followed in the wake of greed for money. Statutes against stealing have been followed by laws against obtaining property by false pretences. These have been followed by statutes forbidding the confidence game, which means almost anything that shocks the sensibilities of courts and juries. Still, in spite of all laws, cheating is a large part of trade.

All dishonesty is not confined to commercial pursuits. Just as it is almost instinctive to a child to tell the truth, so it is natural for everyone to be himself. All men have an urge to express their honest convictions on every subject that attracts their attention. Men soon learn that they cannot express honest convictions. If they would succeed they cannot get too far away from the crowd. Organized society has its rules. In most things men must conform. The wolves that run in packs must stay with the pack. If they get too far ahead or behind, too far to the right or to the left, they are lost. It is as fatal to be ahead as it is to be behind.

Men, likewise, go in packs. Everywhere there is an accepted political organization, a regular church organization, the full quota of clubs and societies. These are all a part of the social life of the community. The pressure, too, of the pack is very strong. The penalties of leaving it are severe. This means loss of business, loss of friends, the surrender of ambition. Every organization is fighting independence, courage, and real honesty.

Then, too, men take their petty affairs very seriously. The church is important. It is the preserver of the idea of immortality. One who does not believe in the tenets of the church is the bearer of evil news. He is not wanted. He cannot live a full life. He is very lonely, and no one likes to be alone. As a rule, no one can afford to be alone. The man who is hostile to the religious views of the community must suffer. The instinct to seek pleasure and avoid pain drives him to conform. He either keeps silent and stifles his honest feelings, or he pretends to believe.

The political views of the "bunch" are just as strong. Not to conform is to be marked. Something is the matter with you, or you would be like the rest. As religious ideas affect eternity, so political ideas affect the here and now. Prosperity, happiness, and the stability of the state are supposed to depend on who is president or alderman. To disagree is evidence that in some way you are wrong. The distrust and ostracism of the community is a high price to pay for political independence. The same is true of churches and clubs—all society is organized to prevent the honest expression of opinion. Everything urges conformity. To believe is to be "constructive"; to doubt is to be "destructive." So men must pretend to believe, even in matters where no one has proof. They must stultify themselves, must be dishonest in the things of life that are worth while. Few men can afford to be honest in thought and purpose—it costs too much. Such men find themselves doubted, distrusted, and outcast. They hear the hounds baying them to death.

The man who stifles his views, who withholds his knowledge and opinions, who conforms when he knows he should not conform, is not honest. All men do this to some extent. They are obliged to conform or die.

There are other reflections raised by this question, as well as all questions that assume the existence of absolute qualities and absolute values, or anything absolute in a world where everything is relative and conditioned. Under most definitions a man is dishonest when he lies. Still, there are times and circumstances when one must lie, and should lie. A lie is not necessarily wrong simply because it is a lie. One can imagine nothing more disorganizing than a universal conspiracy to tell the truth. If it is necessarily wrong to lie, it would probably follow that it is necessarily wrong to suppress the truth. It must be wrong not to tell the community all the

Is Man Dishonest?

unpleasant things you know about your neighbors and your friends and yourself. Few people could live in a community if every action and fact of this life were dragged to light. Human nature is not such that one can live in a glass house, or be always on dress parade. Every community has its sanctuaries where the individual can flee for safety. Every community has its priests, its doctors, its lawyers, its bankers, to keep the secrets of the town. Every community likewise has some rare souls to whom men and women naturally flee to unburden themselves and shift a part of the load that weighs them down.

The decent doctor does not tell his patient that his death is near; he lets him live in hope. He even lies to give him hope, unless there should be some pressing need to tell the truth. Most kindly-disposed men and women will tell the sick that they are looking well, the old that they are growing younger every day, and at least refrain from telling the plain woman that she is ugly or old. No sensitive, considerate person feels it his duty to tell another of some fact that will make him unhappy, and which he does not need to know. Such a person would much rather tell a lie that will prevent pain.

It is probably safe to say that man is fundamentally both honest and dishonest. Intelligent men know that they cannot always regulate their conduct by straight lines. The unintelligent feel this fact without knowing it. Most men are habitual liars and habitual truth tellers. They sometimes conform to severe standards of honesty, and they likewise practice deceit. Most men look for some dishonesty and deceit in the conduct of their fellows. In politics, for instance, no one expects a candidate to be straightforward and honest. All expect him to raise false issues, make absurd promises, and employ almost any means to win. The average man expects this from the highest to the lowest office-holder. It is only rarely that the straightforward and the courageous come to the top in public life, and then it is generally in some great crisis, and they disappear as suddenly as they rise.

Nearly all boys and girls are taught that honesty of conduct cannot only be determined by straight lines and fixed rules, but can be carried out in living. They may never be convinced that this is not true, but automatically they learn that life consists of adjustments, and that many of these cannot be fully figured out in advance. Life is hard enough at best, adjustments are always coming without warning, and man has little chance to do more than make them as best he can at the time. To say that all men are sometimes dishonest means only that no one can live outside of himself and those around him. He may choose what seems to him the honest way, but his nature and his life can stand only a certain pressure—when that is reached he resists no more. He may be likened to a steam boiler. Some boilers are safe at twenty pounds pressure to the square inch, but will break at forty. The boiler is neither honest nor dishonest—it stands a certain pressure, and no more. Man cannot be classified as honest or dishonest—he goes along with the game of life and can stand a certain pressure for the sake of his ideals, but at a certain point he can stand no more.

The Forum, *December, 1927.*

WHO KNOWS
JUSTICE?

If there is any way to determine what the word "justice"
means, man with his limitations has never yet found that way.

THE BLIND GODDESS, WHO IS
supposed to adorn the courthouses of the world, represents the traditional legal view of Justice. She stands erect upon a pinnacle
and holds her scales evenly balanced in her hand. Her eyes are
bandaged so that she can see no one who willingly or unwillingly
comes to her sacred temple. Sympathy and mercy, love and hate,
pride, position, and station have no weight in her scales. All of
these have nothing to do with that elusive, indefinable quality called
Justice.

The Blind Goddess is presumed to be able to appraise and determine each human being's deserts with the exactness with which the
butcher weighs a pound of beef.

When I was young I was deeply interested in the cause of labor
and all the political and social schemes looking toward the more
equal distribution of wealth. As the years have passed, I find my
zeal in this and many other causes has gradually cooled and almost
disappeared. This attitude is not due to any change of mind. Almost
instinctively I feel that my sympathies have remained constant as
time has gone by, but the zest and hope that are always associated
with a cause are not the same as in my early days.

I do not care to delude myself with the idea that this changed attitude is the result of the wisdom that old people are wont to think comes only with accumulated years. It by no means follows that men grow wiser as they grow older. It is more reasonable to believe that mental strength diminishes after maturity, and that the mind is at its best when the body is the strongest and most active. Whether the mind is only a function of the body, or something more, it at least seems clear that body and mind do not act independently of each other, and that the power of the intellect wanes as the structure fails. My zeal for the causes that once filled so much of my horizon has not diminished on account of added knowledge. The truth is, I know less about the labor question and the theories associated with that cause than I did twenty years ago.

I am quite sure that, intellectually, I can make as good an argument for private ownership of land, for unlimited individual control of business, for private monopoly—in short, for what passes as capitalism—as I can make for the socialistic view. I have little doubt that I could have done the same when I was young. Neither on these nor on other vital questions does one arrive at his conclusions through intellectual processes. Ideas upon most subjects, like personal reactions, come from likes and dislikes. These no doubt depend partly on the inherent structure of the individual, and partly on the circumstances and conditions of his life.

All men are partisans. Great emotions, or small ones, impel us to choose our sides. When once the choice is made, arguments, historical incidents, phrases, aphorisms, and half-truths are marshalled to serve us in the arena.

When as a youth I listened to the poor man's cause I was deeply impressed with the statement that "what the working man wants is not charity but justice." This slogan made a strong appeal to me. It seemed to have a significance that smacked of truth and self-respect. Since then I have heard the plea for justice instead of mercy invoked in practically every cause that found a voice.

At first glance it seems as though no one with reason and feeling could fail to respond to the sentiment that all men are at least entitled to justice. The world and its attitudes have always been powerfully moved by slogans, catchwords, and phrases. They are the food devoured by the mind, and they form the basis of opinions and convictions. These, when organized, make parties and causes and crusades, and, for a time at least, seem to change the great movements of the world.

Still, there are few words so plain and no slogans so simple that they do not call for definition. And strange to say, each man makes his definition to conform with the essence of his own being and the experiences of his life.

Are the problems of the human unit simplified by the demand for justice? In examining the dictionaries one finds many definitions of the word—but probably one will not be rewarded with any new light shed by so much as one word on the vital problems of life. Doubtless the word "justice" originally had reference to jurisprudence, but this narrow meaning was virtually abandoned long ago. No one would today pretend to say that the opinions of judges always furnish a correct conception of right and wrong. Lawyers and courts are human and have made all the mistakes that are incident to man and his institutions. Likewise, courts are bound by precedent, and interpret all words and phrases in the light of the past.

When one speaks of justice now he never uses the word in the sense of the decision of courts and juries. He has a vague sense of something that is higher and fairer and more far-seeing than established institutions—something that comes from the clouds, the institutions of man, or some source more nebulous still.

We live in a world of inharmonies. It is made up of the wise and the foolish, the strong and the weak, the rich and the poor, the fortunate and the ill-favored. Accidents of birth, health, temperament, and environment are all-powerful in settling individual destinies. What we call luck and chance is all-controlling not only in the lives of men and women but in the fate of states, the course of empires, the rise and decay of religions, and the customs, habits, and conduct of life.

By an almost universal consent justice concerns the relations of human beings to society and the individual units that compose it. How much do mortals know of this fathomless subject? We do know that whether we will or not, the fortune of each one who lives is hopelessly interwoven with the life and activities of his fellow-man. This relation does not concern alone his friends, acquaintances, neighbors, and community, but reaches out in infinite ways to the farthest limits of the earth. A pebble dropped into the ocean will stir all the waters in all the seas. Just as surely and more plainly does the activity of each individual have some effect on all who live. While those who are the nearest to him seem most influenced, still, through food and clothing, through thought and expression, through opinions and beliefs, through trade and commerce, no man lives to himself or dies to himself.

Ford cars, for instance, travel the Sahara Desert, the mountain fastnesses, and unexplored regions where only a few persons have ever been. Whether one owns a car or not, his life is more or less influenced by Mr. Ford, and in turn the influence of Mr. Ford goes back to the men in his employ and to those with whom he deals, and whoever directly and indirectly comes in contact with him. What is true of the greatest is true of the least. The difference is one of degree alone.

But not only does the activity of all the living to some extent reach all people of the earth, but the deeds and influences of all the dead reach over the conscious world and affect it even more than do those who are still clinging tenaciously to the infinitely small spark of energy that we call life.

Of the countless billions who have lived and died, and the hundreds of millions who still lie down to sleep at night and awaken in the morning, no two, in the present or past, have ever had the same kind or degree of human equipment. Some have muscle and brawn that are needful to the world and its work. Some have inventive genius, and have helped to contrive the marvelous machines that now do most of the labor of this age. Certainly these men have made a large contribution to the joint achievements of the race. Yet no one ever really invented a machine. Each man began where some other left off. Each added something to all that went before. The work of no one could have been accomplished except for the common heritage of the past.

The student of science has spent his intellect and energy to understand the operation of force and matter, and has thus made inventions possible. He, too, has had a large part in making the present world. His mind was so intent in unravelling the mysteries of life and the operation of the universe that personal reward, as men count reward, gave him slight concern. Not only has this class been an able and ready aid to the industry, trade, and commerce of the world, but it has lengthened existence, and what is more important, alleviated pain and suffering, and made it easier to live and die.

The artists, poets, and men of letters, for the most meagre wage, have promoted human happiness and brightened the lives of millions who for a time have been diverted from the misery of a sordid world. Can any conceive of any method of determining justice between all of these various units that make up society, or even between any two units who have worked for a common cause?

The written history of the race goes back but a little way. Ten thousand years would cover the whole span. The vast period of time that man has lived upon this globe has left scant evidence by which to form any correct idea of this prehistoric world. From the excavations in different portions of the earth we learn something of his existence for perhaps a hundred thousand years. This stretch of time covers the periods of stone and bronze and iron. Such remnants of his work as have found the light of day show the slow and long progress of the race. These testaments prove that a high degree of system and order must have grown as the centuries dawned and died. Even the first historical evidence shows that a very few rulers wielded absolute power over the destinies of their fellow men. Any feeling of universal rights was of the slowest growth. Every step up to the present was built upon what went before. Every age has carried into its traditions the concepts of the past. It follows that the rulers who controlled man's destiny always acted on the assumption that their ideas and ways not only were the best, but were grounded in justice and right.

The story of the conquest of one people by another, or rather of one ruler by another, is only the story of the mighty who built their empires to preserve their immortality. The stupid and silent masses that made up the conquering and defeated armies had no part in the glories of the ancient world. Whatever the pretenses may have been, there was no claim that the great had the smallest consideration for their slaves, whose part it was to live and suffer and die to satisfy the arrogance of the strong.

Very slowly some of the privileges and powers that were once the prerogative of the ruler alone were parcelled out and, in a measure, divided amongst the strongest supporters of the chiefs. The monarch thought best to grant what seemed a certain portion of authority and its perquisites rather than risk the chance of losing all. Still the belief persisted that all right rested in the king or czar, and that all authority belonged to him alone. Whatever power was conferred on retainers was derived from the king and given in payment for services to the king.

The baron retainer built his castle on the mountain, beside the highways of commerce, and levied his toll upon all who passed by. The powerless traveler was ready to give all he had, if need be, if his life and liberty were spared. The wealth gathered by these barons was so great as to induce others to ply the same trade along the same highways. This led to wars between barons who marshalled their retainers for the right to levy tribute on the commerce which passed down lakes and rivers and over the early roads. It was easy for this form of force and pillage to grow into vested rights which were defended, and in essence are still defended by the organized society of today. Of course the rulers believed that the safety of the state depended upon the preservation of these vested rights. Everyone should be rewarded for his efforts; otherwise the weak, the indolent, and the cowardly would inherit the earth.

Doubtless there are few, if any, organized governments in the world today that would permit any new right to be gained by the old means of physical force. While states would no longer recognize the justice of new robbery, most if not all of organized society validates the ancient titles founded on force and pillage.

But the ingenuity of the aggressive and dominant is untiring.

Organized society might prevent the old-time methods of building up fortunes and estates by direct violence, but there still remained cheating, deceit, shrewdness, peculiar adaptability for getting wealth, the power of combined capital, and various methods of overreaching that were equally hostile to the common good. Physical strength is no longer needful for the conquest of the world. Powerful and specialized brains that easily overcome their fellows are much more effective than brute strength. Indeed, pure physical power is now condemned to toil and to serve the intellectual, the shrewd and self-seeking in every way.

The control of finance and industry and the highways of trade and communication are now so arranged that automatically the property of the world is constantly emptied into certain pools of wealth. A very slight difference in the intelligence, the cunning, or degree of individual fitness for that purpose causes the divergence between a life of drudgery and want and the command of all the resources of the world. Does the fact that some individuals are strong and crafty mean that justice had anything to do with their inheritance of the earth? Does this sort of activity represent any greater element of justice than the methods that prevailed with primitive man? Today the captain of industry takes what he calls his because he has the power under the present rules, as did the barons of the Middle Ages under the rules of the game as it was played then. No more now than in olden time is it even intellect that brings rewards.

If there is any way to determine what the word "justice" means, man with his limitations has never yet found that way. It is evident that the rewards of this world are enjoyed by those whose strength or cleverness or greed or luck have given them the opportunity and might to take.

We think of justice in relation to the well-being of man. Justice, as generally understood, means that rewards follow from deserts. If this conception has any validity, then from what qualities, other than a certain sort of strength, does justice flow? Does justice concern virtue? Are those who control the earth better than the rest? Do the good things of the earth follow as a reward of merit for kindness, sympathy, charity, and other well-acknowledged virtues? Every one knows that these much-vaunted qualities do not bring wealth and power.

Is intellect a test of power? The wisest men of the earth have never been engaged in money-getting. What is the relative share of reward that should fall to the Newtons, Humboldts, the Darwins, the Einsteins, the Huxleys and Michelsons on the one hand, compared with the captains of industry who control the wealth of the world and the material destiny of man on the other hand? Does anyone doubt to which group belongs the highest and the greatest intelligence? If justice rules, what apportionment of reward would be made between the captains of industry and the Pasteurs, Harveys, and Oslers who have lengthened and made easier the life of man? Some of these could no doubt have turned their marvelous minds toward getting a greater share of the common bounty, but they had other and more important work to do. It will be remembered that Agassiz said that he had no time to make money.

How can any form of justice now applied by man determine what share of the common result should be taken by the brain-worker and what share doled out to the brawn-worker? How can it apportion shares between different kinds of manual labor? How can justice say what sort of brain-labor shall have the most, and what are the deserts of the various kinds?

It is obvious that no line of reasoning, no judicial process or human adjustments that the world has so far made has ever sought a solution. It is plain that justice, as it is imagined, has nothing whatever to say about the share that each one takes. The distribution is determined by the peculiar sort of mental power applied, combined with the strength or weakness of the will and the fortunes of the different lives.

Even though one may not fathom the processes by which the hideous inequalities of life are brought about, he can at least see the results that come about from our complex life.

We have made production so easy and abundant that the great concern of the state is that we produce too much. The distribution is so unequal and unfair that the laborer cannot buy and use the things he makes. The machines now yield more than our crazy system of distribution can possibly put in the hands of those whose needs are great. And their power and fecundity are growing apace.

No age in the past had even a faint conception of the enormous private fortunes that have been heaped up in every great city on the earth. And yet in America, the most favored land under the sun, the mass of our people are not far removed from want. Young boys and girls work in factories, hotels, restaurants and stores for insufficient pay. Most of these are haunted by worry lest they cannot get homes and clothes, and food and jobs. Men who reach middle life without a fortune are thrown out of employment and coldly scrapped for the virile and the young.

Great fortunes are spent for pearls and diamonds, for costly clothes, and food, and offices and habitations, for trinkets and baubles and useless things, while the workman lives in constant fear that a machine will take his job. The poor who serve in hotels and public places, who crowd streets and parks, in every nook and around every corner, hold out their hands for tips and alms.

The farmers are madly calling on the government for help because they have produced too much. Life has grown to be a bedlam where peace and quiet and comfort and ease are scarcely known. The world has learned to produce wealth almost by magic, but it knows nothing, and seems to care less, about trying to solve the problem of distributing what it makes. In the general madness lawyers and judges, and businessmen and workingmen talk of justice as if the word had some meaning which they could understand.

It should always be remembered that man's views of justice have changed as the stream of life has flowed along. It can be conceived and even hoped that the final word has not yet been said. Judges no longer sentence human beings to death for stealing a sheep or a sixpence, or for witchcraft or heresy. We no longer kill the ill or old, or imprison the unfortunate for debt.

There are men and women who have a vision of justice that, so far, the world has never yet reached.

Justice, now and always, has been based upon accepted rules, upon precedents, upon the landmarks of the past. Still, in a halting way, all old landmarks have been passed on the road, accepted rules are going out of date, and new conceptions of justice are slowly dawning upon the human mind. Might it not be possible that the world could conceive of a sense of the word "justice" where wealth and strength and intellect would call for public service, and weakness, old age, and want would be given a greater share because of its very wants? Who knows that it is just for the strong to take more than he can use, and the weak, the helpless, the unfortunate and unadjusted to take less than enough to satisfy his needs?

It is idle to expect justice and its machinery to solve any of the problems that plague and torture man. It never has and never can. Justice, at the best, is a human conception and is not a living thing. The great movements of the race have not been born of justice, but of the deep, controlling emotions that are inherent in the human structure. While we do not know and cannot possibly find out the meaning of justice, we still know that emotions have changed the conduct of men and the foundations of states. Religious feelings, wars, and the love of freedom are some of the urges that have changed and at times overturned the old civilizations of the world. The philosopher William James years ago pointed out the fact that emotions rule life, and said he hoped that the desire for the study of science might sometime become the urge which would fill the place that so long had been occupied by war. Even though at the present time science seems harnessed to machines and given to the service of producing wealth for profit, a broader conception might bring it to the service of the world.

Instead of talking vaguely of justice, while devoting their energies to getting more things that they cannot use, the organizers and captains may sometime use their intellect and power to free the world from want. An undertaking like this could easily be carried out. The machines can do the work. What is needed is the profound sympathy without which man cannot give his services to any altruistic task.

Whatever visions we may form of the word "justice," still it has never meant anything except adjusting human claims and human conduct to the established habits and customs and institutions of the world. Justice never can be a lofty ideal. It has no emotions nor passions. It has no wings. Its highest flight is to the Blind Goddess that stands on the courthouse roof. It savors of syllogisms and fine distinctions which have no meaning or value in the important matters of life. But there is no uncertainty in the meaning and effect of charity, of sympathy, of generosity, or of understanding. Without these, man is dead. With them he can create a new world where human beings may have all the happinesss that is possible for life to give. These emotions grow from his associations with his fellow-man. They are the children of imagination. They spring from sensing the weakness, the troubles, and the sorrows of all those who live. They make the whole world kin. The realization of common suffering and common needs brings no desire for the nice distinctions urged in the name of justice. It brings only the desire to help in proportion to one's strength.

Scribner's Magazine, *February, 1932.*

ATTORNEY
FOR THE
DEFENSE

Whether a jury is a good one or a bad one depends
on the point of view. I have always been an attorney
for the defense. I can think of nothing, not even war,
that has brought so much misery to the human race
as prisons. And all of it so futile!

T HE AUDIENCE THAT STORMS
the box-office of the theater to gain entrance to a sensational
show is small and sleepy compared with the throng that crashes
the courthouse door when something concerning real life and
death is to be laid bare to the public.

Everyone knows that the best portrayals of life are tame and
sickly when matched with the realities. For this reason, the
sophisticated Romans were wont to gather at the Colosseum to
feast their eyes on fountains of real blood and await breathlessly
the final thrust. The courtroom is a modern arena in which the
greatest thrills follow closely on each other. If the combat concerns human life, it presents an atmosphere and setting not unlike
those cruel and bloody scenes of ancient Rome. The judge wears
the same flowing robe with all the dignity and superiority he
can command. This sets him apart from his fellow-men, and is
designed to awe and intimidate and to impress the audience with
seeming wisdom oftener than with kindliness and compassion.

313

One cannot help wondering what happens to the pomp and pretense of the wearer while the cloak is in the wash, or while changing into a maturer, more monarchial mantle, as his bench becomes a throne, or when he strolls along the street in file with the "plain clothes" people.

When court opens, the bailiff intones some voodoo singsong words in an ominous voice that carries fear and respect at the opening of the rite. The courtroom is full of staring men and women shut within closed doors, guarded by officials wearing uniforms to confound the simple inside the sacred precinct. This dispels all hope of mercy to the unlettered, the poor and helpless, who scarcely dare express themselves above a whisper in any such forbidding place.

The stage, the arena, the court are alike in that each has its audience thirsting to drink deeply of the passing show. Those playing the parts vie for success and use whatever skill and talent they possess. An actor may fumble his lines, but a lawyer needs to be letter-perfect; at least, he has to use his wits, and he may forget himself, and often does, but never for a moment can he lose sight of his client.

Small wonder that ambitious, imaginative youths crowd the profession of law. Here, they feel, they themselves will find the opportunity to play a real part in the comedies as well as the tragedies of life. Everyone, no matter how small his chance may be, tries to hold the center of some stage where the multitudes will scan his every move. To most lads it seems as though the courts were organized to furnish them a chance to bask in the public eye. In this field the adventure of life will never pall, but prove interesting, exciting and changeful to the end. Not only will he have the destinies of men to protect and preserve, but his own standing and success to create.

If it is a real case, criminal or civil, it usually is tried by a jury with the assistance and direction of the judge. In that event, every moment counts, and neither the lawyers nor the audience, or even the court, goes to sleep. If it is a criminal case, or even a civil one, it is not the law alone or the facts that determine the results. Always the element of luck and chance looms large. A jury of twelve men is watching not only the evidence but the attitude of each lawyer, and the parties involved, in all their moves. Every step is fraught with doubt, if not mystery.

Selecting a jury is of the utmost importance. So far as possible, the lawyer should know both sides of the case. If the client is a landlord, a banker, or a manufacturer, or one of that type, then jurors sympathetic to that class will be wanted in the box; a man who looks neat and trim and smug. He will be sure to guard your interests as he would his own. His entire environment has taught him that all real values are measured in cash, and he knows no other worth. Every knowing lawyer seeks for a jury of the same sort of men as his client; men who will be able to imagine themselves in the same situation and realize what verdict the client wants.

Lawyers are just as carefully concerned about the likes and dislikes, the opinions and fads of judges as of jurors. All property rights are much safer in the hands of courts than of jurors. Every lawyer who represents the poor avoids a trial by the court.

Choosing jurors is always a delicate task. The more a lawyer knows of life, human nature, psychology, and the reactions of the human emotions, the better he is equipped for the subtle selection of his so-called "twelve men, good and true." In this undertaking, everything pertaining to the prospective juror needs to be questioned and weighed: his nationality, his business, religion, politics, social standing, family ties, friends, habits of life and thought; the books and newspapers he likes and reads, and many more matters that combine to make a man; all of these qualities and experiences have left their effect on ideas, beliefs and fancies that inhabit his mind. Understanding of all this cannot be obtained too bluntly. It usually requires finesse, subtlety and guesswork. Involved in it all is the juror's method of speech, the kind of clothes he wears, the style of haircut, and, above all, his business associates, residence and origin.

To the ordinary observer, a man is just a man. To the student of life and human beings, every pose and movement is a part of the personality and the man. There is no sure rule by which one can gauge any person. A man may seem to be of a certain mold, but a wife, a friend, or an enemy, entering into his life, may change his most vital views, desires and attitudes, so that he will hardly recognize himself as the man he once seemed to be.

It is obvious that if a litigant discovered one of his dearest friends in the jury panel he could make a close guess as to how certain facts, surrounding circumstances, and suppositions would affect his mind and action; but as he has no such acquaintance with the stranger before him, he must weigh the prospective juror's words and manner of speech and, in fact, hastily and cautiously "size him up" as best he can. The litigants and their lawyers are supposed to want justice, but in reality there is no such thing as justice, either in or out of court. In fact, the word cannot be defined. So, for lack of proof, let us assume that the word "justice" has a meaning, and that the common idea of the definition is correct, without even seeking to find out what is the common meaning. Then how do we reach justice through the courts? The lawyer's idea of justice is a verdict for his client, and really this is the sole end for which he aims.

In spite of the power that the courts exercise over the verdict of the jury, still the finding of the twelve men is very important, sometimes conclusive. It goes without saying that lawyers always do their utmost to get men on the jury who are apt to decide in favor of their clients. It is not the experience of jurors, neither is it their brain power that is the potent influence in their decisions. A skilful lawyer does not tire himself hunting for learning or intelligence in the box; if he knows much about man and his making, he knows that all beings act from emotions and instincts, and that reason is not a motive factor. If deliberation counts for anything, it is to retard decision. The nature of the man himself is the element that determines the juror's bias for or against his fellow-man. Assuming that a juror is not a half-wit, his intellect can always furnish fairly good reasons for following his instincts and emotions. Many irrelevant issues in choosing jurors are not so silly as they seem. Matters that apparently have nothing to do with the discussion of a case often are of the greatest significance.

In the last analysis, most jury trials are contests between the rich and poor. If the case concerns money, it is apt to be a case of damages for injuries of some sort claimed to have been inflicted by someone. These cases are usually defended by insurance companies, railroads, or factories. If a criminal case, it is practically always the poor who are on trial.

The most important point to learn is whether the prospective juror is humane. This must be discovered in more or less devious ways. As soon as "the court" sees what you want, he almost always blocks the game. Next to this, in having more or less bearing on the question, is the nationality, politics, and religion of the person examined for the jury. If you do not discover this, all your plans may go awry. Whether you are handling a damage suit, or your client is charged with the violation of law, his attorney will try to get the same sort of juror.

Let us assume that we represent one of "the underdogs" because of injuries received, or because of an indictment brought by what the prosecutors name themselves, "the state." Then what sort of men will we. seek? An Irishman is called into the box for examination. There is no reason for asking about his religion; he is Irish; that is enough. We may not agree with his religion, but it matters not; his feelings go deeper than any religion. You should be aware that he is emotional, kindly and sympathetic. If he is chosen as a juror, his imagination will place him in the dock; really, he is trying himself. You would be guilty of malpractice if you got rid of him, except for the strongest reasons.

An Englishman is not so good as an Irishman, but still, he has come through a long tradition of individual rights, and is not afraid to stand alone; in fact, he is never sure that he is right unless the great majority is against him. The German is not so keen about individual rights except where they concern his own way of life; liberty is not a theory, it is a way of living. Still, he wants to do what is right, and he is not afraid. He has not been among us long, his ways are fixed by his race, his habits are still in the making. We need inquire no further. If he is a

Catholic, then he loves music and art; he must be emotional, and will want to help you; give him a chance.

If a Presbyterian enters the jury box and carefully rolls up his umbrella, and calmly and critically sits down, let him go. He is cold as the grave; he knows right from wrong, although he seldom finds anything right. He believes in John Calvin and eternal punishment. Get rid of him with the fewest possible words before he contaminates the others; unless you and your clients are Presbyterians you probably are a bad lot, and even though you may be a Presbyterian, your client most likely is guilty.

If possible, the Baptists are more hopeless than the Presbyterians. They, too, are apt to think that the real home of all outsiders is Sheol, and you do not want them on the jury, and the sooner they leave the better.

The Methodists are worth considering; they are nearer the soil. Their religious emotions can be transmuted into love and charity. They are not half bad; even though they will not take a drink, they really do not need it so much as some of their competitors for the seat next to the throne. If chance sets you down between a Methodist and a Baptist, you will move toward the Methodist to keep warm.

Beware of the Lutherans, especially the Scandinavians; they are almost always sure to convict. Either a Lutheran or Scandinavian is unsafe, but if both in one, plead your client guilty and go down the docket. He learns about sinning and punishing from the preacher, and dares not doubt. A person who disobeys must be sent to hell; he has God's word for that.

As to Unitarians, Universalists, Congregationalists, Jews and other agnostics, don't ask them too many questions; keep them anyhow, especially Jews and agnostics. It is best to inspect a Unitarian, or a Universalist, or a Congregationalist with some care, for they may be prohibitionists; but never the Jews and the real agnostics! And do not, please, accept a prohibitionist; he is too solemn and holy and dyspeptic. He knows your client would not have been indicted unless he were a drinking man, and anyone who drinks is guilty of something, probably much worse

Clarence Darrow

than he is charged with, although it is not set out in the indictment. Neither would he have employed *you* as his lawyer had he not been guilty.

I have never experimented with Christian Scientists; they are much too serious for me. Somehow, solemn people seem to think that pleasure is wicked. Only the gloomy and dyspeptic can be trusted to convict. Shakespeare knew: "Yon Cassius has a lean and hungry look; he thinks too much; such men are dangerous." You may defy all the rest of the rules if you can get a man who laughs. Few things in this world are of enough importance to warrant considering them seriously. So, by all means, choose a man who laughs. A juror who laughs hates to find anyone guilty.

Never take a wealthy man on a jury. He will convict, unless the defendant is accused of violating the anti-trust law, selling worthless stocks or bonds, or something of that kind. Next to the Board of Trade, for him, the penitentiary is the most important of all public buildings. These imposing structures stand for capitalism. Civilization could not possibly exist without them. Don't take a man because he is a "good" man; this means nothing. You should find out what he is good *for*. Neither should a man be accepted because he is a bad sort. There are too many ways of being good or bad. If you are defending, you want imaginative individuals. You are not interested in the morals of the juror. If a man is instinctively kind and sympathetic, take him.

Then, too, there are the women. These are now in the jury box. A new broom sweeps clean. It leaves no speck on the floor or under the bed, or in the darkest corners of life. To these new jurors, the welfare of the state depends on the verdict. It will be so for many years to come. The chances are that it would not have made the slightest difference to the state if all cases had been decided the other way. It might, however, make a vast difference to the unfortunates facing cruel, narrow-minded jurors who pass judgment on their fellow-men. To the defendants it might have meant the fate of life rather than death.

But what is one life more or less in the general spawning? It may float away on the tide, or drop to the depths of oblivion, broken, crushed and dead. The great sea is full of embryo lives ready to take the places of those who have gone before. One more unfortunate lives and dies as the endless stream flows on, and little it matters to the wise judges who coldly pronounce long strings of words in droning cadence; the victims are removed, they come and go, and the judges keep on chanting senseless phrases laden with doom upon the bowed heads of those before them. The judge is as unconcerned about the actual meaning of it all as the soughing wind rustling the leaves of a tree just outside the courthouse door.

Women still take their new privilege seriously. They are all puffed up with the importance of the part they feel they play, and are sure they represent a great step forward in the world. They believe that the sex is co-operating in a great cause. Like the rest of us, they do not know which way is forward and which is backward, or whether either one is any way at all. Luckily, as I feel, my services were almost over when women invaded the jury box.

A few years ago I became interested in a man charged with selling some brand of intoxicant in a denatured land that needed cheering. I do not know whether he sold it or not. I forgot to ask him. I viewed the case with mixed feelings of pity and contempt, for as Omar philosophized, "I wonder often what the vintners buy one-half so precious as the stuff they sell." When I arrived on the scene, the courtroom looked ominous with women jurors. I managed to get rid of all but two, while the dismissed women lingered around in the big room waiting for the victory, wearing solemn faces and white ribbons. The jury disagreed. In the second trial there were four women who would not budge from their seats or their verdict. Once more I went back to the case with distrust and apprehension. The number of women in the jury box had grown to six. All of them were unprejudiced. They said so. But everyone connected with the case was growing tired and skeptical, so we concluded to call it a draw. This was my last experience with women jurors. I formed a fixed opinion that they were absolutely dependable, but I did not want them.

Whether a jury is a good one or a bad one depends on the point of view. I have always been an attorney for the defense. I can think of nothing, not even war, that has brought so much misery to the human race as prisons. And all of it so futile!

I once spent a winter on the shores of the Mediterranean Sea. In front of my windows, four fishermen were often wearily trudging back and forth, and slowly dragging a long net across the sand. When it was safely landed, a few small flopping fish disclosed the results of their labors. These were scattered dying on the beach, while the really worth-while fishes were left in the sea. It somehow reminded me of our courts and juries, and other aims and efforts of optimistic men, and their idle undertakings and disheartening results.

Judges and jurors are like the rest of humans. Now and then some outstanding figures will roll up their sleeves, as it were, and vigorously set to work to reform the courts and get an efficient administration of justice. This will be ably seconded by the newspapers, lashing courts and jurors, past, present and prospective, into a spasm of virtue that brings down the innocent and guilty together, assuming always that there are innocent and guilty. Then, for a time, every defendant is convicted; and soon the campaign reaches the courts; after ruining a few lives and reputations, the frenzy is over, and life goes on smoothly and tranquilly as before.

When I was a boy in the country, one of the standard occupations was whittling. It became as mechanical as breathing. Since then I have decided that this is as good a way to live as any other. Life depends on the automatic taking in and letting out of breath, but in no way is it lengthened or made happier by deep thinking or wise acting. The one big word that stands over courts and other human activities is FUTILITY.

The courts may be unavailing, lawyers stupid, and both as dry as dust, but the combination makes for something interesting and exciting, and it opens avenues that seem to lead somewhere. Liberty, lives, fortunes often are at stake, and appeals for assistance and mercy rend the air for those who care to hear. In an effort to help, often a casual remark may determine a seemingly vital situation, when perhaps the remark, of all the palaver, was the least important one breathed forth. In all questions men are frequently influenced by some statement which, spoken at the eventful time, determines fate. The most unforeseen, accidental meetings sometimes result in seemingly new and strangely fateful family lines. In fact, all that occurs in life is an endless sequence of events resulting from the wildest chance.

Amongst the twelve in a jury box are all degrees of alertness, all sorts of ideas, and a variety of emotions; and the lawyers, too, are important factors in the outcome. They are closely observed by the jurors. They are liked or disliked; mayhap because of what they say, or how they speak, or pronounce their words, or part their hair. It may be that a lawyer is disliked because he talks too little or too much, more often the latter. But a lawyer of subtlety should know when to stop, and when to go on, and how far to go. As a rule, he must not seem to be above the juror, nor below him. He must not too obviously strive for effect. He often meets baffling situations not easily explained. Sometimes it is better for him to talk of something else. Explanations must not be too fantastic or ridiculous. It does no harm to admit the difficulty of the situation, to acknowledge that this circumstance or that seems against him. Many facts point to guilt, but in another light these facts may appear harmless.

Lawyers are apt to interpret deeds and motives as they wish them to appear. As a matter of fact, most actions are subject to various inferences, sometimes quite improbable, but nonetheless true. Identifications show common examples of mistakes. Many men are in prison and some are sent to death through mistaken identifications. One needs but recall the countless errors he himself has made. How many have met some person whom they believed to be an old-time friend, and have found themselves greeting a total stranger? This is a common mistake made in restaurants and other public places. Many identifications in court are made from having seen a person but once, and under conditions not critical. Many are made from descriptions and photographs, and urged on by detectives, lawyers, and others vitally interested in the results. From all of this it is easy to see that many are convicted who are guiltless of crime. In situations of strong agitation, acquittals are rare, and sentences made long and barbarous and inhuman.

The judge is, of course, an important part of the machinery and administration of the court. Like carpenters and lawyers, brick-layers and saloon-keepers, they are not all alike. No two of them have the same fitness for their positions. No two have the same education; no two have the same natural understanding of themselves and their fellow-man, or are gifted with the same discernment and balance.

Not that judges are lacking in knowledge of law. The ordinary rules for the administration of law are rather simple and not difficult to follow. But judges should be students of life, even more than of law. Biology and psychology, which form the basis of understanding human conduct, should be taken into account. Without a fair knowledge of the mechanism of man, and the motives and urges that govern his life, it is idle to venture to fathom a situation; but with some knowledge, officers and the public can be most useful in preserving and protecting those who most need such help. The life of almost any unfortunate, if rightly understood, can be readjusted to some plan of order and system, instead of left to drift on to ruin, the victim of ignorance, hatred and chance.

If the physician so completely ignored natural causes as the lawyers and judges, the treatment of disease would be relegated to witchcraft and magic, and the dungeon and rack would once more hold high carnival in driving devils out of the sick and afflicted. Many of the incurable victims of crime are like those who once were incurable victims of disease; they are the product of vicious and incompetent soothsayers who control their destinies.

Every human being, whether parent, teacher, physician, or prosecutor, should make the comfort and happiness of their dependents their first concern. Now and then some learned courts take a big view of life, but scarcely do they make an impression until some public brainstorm drives them back in their treatment of crime to the methods of sorcery and conjury.

No scientific attitude toward crime can be adopted until lawyers, like physicians and scientists, recognize that cause and effect determine the conduct of men.

When lawyers and courts, and laymen, accept the scientific theory which the physicians forced upon the world long years ago, then men will examine each so-called delinquency until they discover its cause, and then learn how to remove the cause. This requires sympathy, humanity, love of one's fellow-man, and a strong faith in the power of knowledge and experience to conquer the maladies of men. The forum of the lawyers may then grow smaller, the courthouse may lose its spell, but the world will profit a thousandfold by a kindlier and more understanding relation toward all humankind.

Esquire Magazine, *May, 1936.*

PART FIVE

ON THE
INTERNATIONAL
SCENE

FREE TRADE
OR PROTECTION?

A PLEA FOR THE WILSON BILL

Protection appeals to the meanest sentiments of man,
to the narrowest selfishness and the most sordid greed.
It teaches that nations should be enemies instead of friends,
and that the good of one may be promoted by the
disaster and misfortune of the rest.

1894. Coxey's Army marches on Washington . . . Pullman workers strike; E. V. Debs charged with conspiracy . . . Darrow resigns as Chicago corporation counsel to defend Debs . . . Corbett defeats Mitchell . . . Sicilian revolution crushed by government troops . . . Duchess of York gives birth to a boy . . . U.S. recognizes Hawaiian Republic . . . New tariff bill becomes law without President Cleveland's signature . . . Dr. Oliver Wendell Holmes dies . . . Announce "serum cure" for diphtheria . . . $2,000,000 loss in fire at World's Fair in Chicago.

THE MC KINLEY BILL IS WITH-
out doubt the most hostile to foreign trade, the narrowest and
most reactionary of any law ever passed by an American Congress,
and probably no civilized nation in this century ever so deliberately and positively turned its face to the past, so ignored and
derided the growing sentiment of peace and universal brotherhood
which is the hope of all the progressive people and countries of
the earth.

The McKinley bill was the work of the monopolists and the
strong. It was passed at the behest of the favored few, already
wealthy and powerful through special privileges long enjoyed;
and to pass this act an appeal was made to the narrowest and
most selfish patriotism, a sentiment that is responsible for more
tyranny, bloodshed and crime than any other that has ever moved
mankind.

The McKinley bill was passed to discourage foreign trade; to
take the place of the reefs and sand bars in our oceans and our
lakes; to overcome the force and power of our great ships that
have made commerce easy and brought together the nations of
the earth; to compel "free Americans" to purchase goods of its
favored pets and to pay a higher price than they are worth in
the markets of the world.

The Wilson bill places many articles upon the free list which
have heretofore been taxed. Wool, coal, lumber, iron ore, together with many other commodities that are the raw materials

from which goods and wares are made, are left untaxed. This serves not only to make cheaper these articles and their products, but also to make it easier for our workmen to obtain them for use in their various trades and crafts. The duty on most staple manufactured articles is heavily reduced as well.

To be sure, this bill is liable to receive much amendment in the Senate at the hands of those who use their purchased seats to promote their private interests and serve their clients at the expense of the people they are sworn to represent. These senators belong to both political parties, for monopoly and greed has neither politics nor religion, particularly religion. But whatever may happen to the Wilson bill, it is still in the direction of the reduction of taxes and the freeing of trade.

The Wilson bill also largely substitutes ad valorem taxes in place of specific taxes: that is, the duty is levied on the value of the goods and not on their weight. A yard of broadcloth weighs no more than a yard of the coarsest cloth, while it is worth many times as much. Of course an ad valorem rate would tax the owner of the broadcloth most, while the specific rate would tax them just the same. This change in the interest of the poor is a grievous ground for complaint by the monopolists and their agents for whom, and by whom, all tariff laws are made.

The Wilson bill is in the direction of removing the restrictions which have been made by law, of giving more freedom to mankind, of leaving the purchaser the right to buy where and of whom he may desire. It is in the direction of restoring the laws of nature which have been repealed by the laws of man.

If the Wilson bill becomes a law, foreign commerce will grow and thrive. Many articles produced in America must be sold to consumers for a cheaper price to prevent their being purchased from abroad. Many products of American mills which have been sold heretofore because the purchaser had no right to buy elsewhere, must be produced in honest competition with the world and sold upon their merits instead of forced upon their customers by law.

The question then of the relative merits of the Wilson bill and the McKinley bill is the old question of free trade or commercial restriction.

Commerce comes from the endeavor of man to better his condition, to obtain the greatest comfort for the smallest expenditure of time and strength. The history of civilization has been the history of commerce; and the annihilation of trade would be the return of man to the barbarism of the past.

As soon as man learned to gather the fruits of the earth and make the rudest articles to satisfy his wants, he found that the power of his labor could be increased by exchanging the surplus articles he produced for other commodities made by someone else. He learned that his time and strength brought more reward when he confined his energies to some special trade or calling, and perfected himself in this, than when he sought unaided to satisfy his every want himself. For this reason, he soon learned to choose some special craft and ignore all other trades to master that. If he learned the art of making shoes he found he could get more food and clothes by "sticking to his last" and exchanging shoes for grain and cloth, than by living within himself and for himself alone. The gradual invention of machinery and the use of steam made it still more impossible for the individual to satisfy his every want himself and to live unrelated to his fellow-man. The marvelous increase of productive power that has come to the human race has only been possible by the subdivision of labor, which gives each man his trade and forces him to depend for life on all the rest. The subdivision of labor could not be, except for the power and right to buy and sell; all the wonderful machines of the present would be withdrawn from use if man could not exchange his products with his fellow-man. Beyond the subdivision of labor, which could not exist except for trade, differences of soil and climate give rise to commerce to enable each portion of the globe to participate in the advantages of all.

Foreign trade is like domestic trade. Nations as nations do not buy and sell; only individuals trade. It must also be remembered that all traffic is but exchange; whether goods are bought for cash or received direct for other goods makes no difference with the case. If cash be paid for goods, goods must first be paid for cash. Even where gold is dug and exchanged for goods, the gold is only a commodity and cannot be dug unless it is exchanged for food, clothing and other articles that are necessary to life.

Children and politicians sometimes think, 'and say, that if gold is sent out of the country in exchange for goods the gold is lost, whereas if gold is paid to another citizen of a country in exchange for goods, the nation is better off, for both remain at home. If protectionists did not persistently repeat this statement no one would think it possible that a reasoning human being would give a second thought to such a "fake," but it is persistently stated and re-stated on every hand and forms the basis of much protective talk. Gold is only valuable to exchange for goods. Suppose one-half the people in America had all the gold and the other all the goods, of equal value with the gold, the owners of the coin must exchange their cash for goods; the owners of the goods would get coin by making goods, and the owners of the coin get goods by digging gold. The same people could not at once be digging gold and making goods. Suppose America has all the gold and England has the goods, America must exchange her coin for goods, and England trade her goods for coin. If by the exchange England gets all the coin and America the goods, England must at once send back her coin for goods, for she could not live on gold. When a dollar in money is paid for a dollar in goods the purchaser has lost nothing by the trade; he cannot have his goods and money too, and each is convertible at will into the one the buyer has not got.

To purchase goods does not mean that the seller can make them more cheaply than the buyer; it means that the buyer can produce the thing he sells to better advantage than the one he buys; that he can get more of what he buys by producing what he sells. If this be true, then to produce the thing he buys would be a waste of time and strength. This must apply to foreign and domestic trade alike.

Trade is not warfare, but mutual help. A trade does not imply that one party has cheated the other, but that each has done a service to the other by giving him something that he wished for, and the other did not want. Neither does trade deprive a workman of a chance to toil. True, he does not produce the thing he buys, but he makes the thing he sells; and unless he sells, he cannot buy. Unless the people of the United States produce commodities that other nations need, they cannot buy, for foreigners will not send their goods to us unless an equivalent be given in return. The shipload of grain that leaves America is exchanged in England for a load of manufactured goods. The grain is worth more in England than in America, and the goods are worth more here than there. Thus the citizens of both nations have profited by the trade. If the American could produce woolen cloth to as good advantage as he could grain, he could not have added to his wealth by selling wheat and buying cloth. Unless he can produce the things he buys to the same advantage as the ones he sells, the law that makes him do the thing he cannot do as well is a hindrance and a cheat. And when he can produce the thing he buys more cheaply than the one he sells, it will need no law to make him do the thing that he can do the best.

Trade produces wealth, for every commodity is more valuable in the hands of the buyer than the seller, else the exchange would not be made. The right to buy and sell has evolved the mighty steamboat of today from the rude dugout of the savage tribe. It has given the railroad in place of the pack mule and ox cart of long ago. It has carried the art, letters and civilization of the earth to the remotest corners of the globe, and made all people sharers in the progress of the world.

That trade adds to wealth is as much capable of demonstration as a mathematical problem. Why then should legislation hamper and restrict?

It is true that the general good is not concerned alone with the production of wealth, but with its distribution, too; only the wilfully blind and the foolishly blind can fail to see that the wretched and unrighteous distribution of wealth today is not only a reflection on our intelligence and humanity, but a menace to such civilization as we have. And no one who has studied economics believes that free trade alone would furnish any considerable panacea for the outrageous injustice that prevails in the distribution of the products of the world, in protective and free trade lands alike.

Protection interferes with the production of wealth; how does it affect its distribution? In the first place, it must be remembered that only a small fraction of our people work in protected industries, probably not more than five or at the most ten per cent. Substantially half the people of the United States are farmers, and from the time the first bushel of grain was produced until today the American farmer has sold his product and his labor in competition with that of every other farmer on earth. About forty per cent of the staple articles the farmer sells have for years been shipped to foreign lands. He not only competes with foreign farmers, but sends his products across the seas and undersells the other farmers of the world in their own markets and their own land. True, the McKinley bill places a duty of twenty cents a bushel on foreign wheat, but as no foreign wheat ever comes to the United States, this is a reflection on the farmer's brains. It is adding insult to injury. Our mechanics, merchants, clerks, railway employees, professional men and the like are all of them engaged in non-protected industries, and work in competition with the world.

Our protected industries are the great factories and mills, forests and mines, which furnish the raw material from which our goods and wares are made. All these industries are conducted on a large scale; the plant and product belongs to corporations or individuals, and the operatives work for wages. The protective law places a tax upon foreign goods that are similar to those produced in these mills and mines, to enable the owners of these favored industries to charge more for their product than if sold in the open markets of the world, where the farmer sells his grain. This extra price, made by means of protective laws, is paid by the American consumer who is forced to buy the goods; by the farmer, the merchant, the artisan and the workingman; and goes, of course, to the one who has the goods to sell. It is obvious that every dollar of added price paid for protected goods must come from the consumers, and must go in the first instance to the sellers of the goods.

The law allows the favored owner to collect this extra toll, but it provides no way to make him pay it out in wages to his men. The rate of wages does not depend upon the amount the employer *can* pay, it has nothing to do with the wealth or poverty of the owners of the mills and mines, it depends upon the demand and supply of labor and on nothing else. The employer opens his factory or mine and offers such wages as the labor market obliges him to give, and nothing more. The workman has no tariff law to raise his wage; he sells his labor in competition with every man, native or foreign, who can do the work, and the fact that his employer has been granted special rights adds nothing to the wages he receives. The protection is on the goods, not the workman. The goods belong to the employer. The workman has nothing but his life and strength to sell, and these have never yet been considered of enough importance to warrant the protection of legislatures or the courts.

The fact that wages in most foreign lands are lower than in America has nothing whatever to do with the necessity of protective laws for the United States. This simply proves that our soil is richer and our resources greater and more undeveloped than in most countries of the world.

Goods can be produced more cheaply in America than in any other land on earth. They can be produced more cheaply because of greater natural opportunities, more skilful workmen and better machinery than can be found in other lands. That wages are lower somewhere else means that a larger portion of the product of the laborer is taken by the landowner and by the mine owner and the other parasites that live by others' toil; the difference in wages here and somewhere else is only the difference in the share that labor is able to retain for itself from the monopolist, who everywhere takes the most of what he earns. When that share is ascertained and set apart it is increased by the right to exchange for the most that it will bring.

Protection appeals to the meanest sentiments of man, to the narrowest selfishness and the most sordid greed. It teaches that nations should be enemies instead of friends, and that the good of one may be promoted by the disaster and misfortune of the rest. It is in line with the spirit of caste and exclusiveness that has ruled the world; in keeping with the camps and armies, the forts and cannons that have disgraced the earth. It is the doctrine of hatred instead of love, and at war with the rising hope and aspiration of the day "when swords shall be beaten into plough-shares and the nations of the earth shall dwell in harmony and peace."

Current Topics, *April, 1894.*

BRIEF
FOR THE WAR
(A LETTER)

*I am thoroughly convinced that not only was it right
of America to enter this war, but it was her duty,
if she recognizes duty, and that had she stayed out
she would have been so cowardly that she would have
received and deserved the contempt of all the
right-thinking people of the world.*

1917. President Wilson asks Congress for authority to declare war against Germany . . . Report of scarcity of labor in U.S. and other belligerent countries . . . Draft begins . . . Eleven-member committee of the American Institute of Criminal Law and Criminology, appointed to investigate and report on sterilization of criminals, asks to be dismissed because of lack of scientific information . . . All-Russian Congress of Workmen's and Soldiers' Delegates names Lenin premier and Trotsky minister of foreign affairs of Russia. Kerensky flees capital . . . "Indiscriminate sex relations more dangerous to the health and vigor of troops than enemy bullets" . . . Government agents raid I.W.W. halls simultaneously in twenty-four cities.

336
Clarence Darrow

My dear Kiefer:

When I told you I did not answer your first letter because I did not want to run the risk of offending a friend, I told you the truth. Now you write me, quoting what another friend has said of my position in the war, and suggest that my silence meant that I could not give my reasons for abandoning the doctrine of non-resistance and standing for the war. Well, I can give my reasons, and here are some of them which were enough for me, though they may not be for you.

I did write a book advocating non-resistance. Most of the things I said in that book, I still believe. I hated war then and I do today. My error then, as I see it now, was the belief that you could make a general rule of life that would cover every case. This, I believe, is the fundamental error of the pacifist. If the theory of non-resistance is absolutely true, then it must apply to the insane as well as the sane, to animals as well as to man. You must be willing to say that if an insane man should attack you or someone dear to you who is utterly defenseless, and the only way you can save your life or your friend's life is to kill the man, you would not do it. You have to go further and say that if a mad dog attacked you and you have a gun, you would not kill the dog, but would be bitten and die rather than take life. If you may defend yourself against a mad dog, what about a mad man or a mad nation, and what tribunal can determine whether they are mad or not? The pacifist is bound to say that this is his position. It is not and cannot be his position, because self-preservation is inherent in all life, even in the life of the pacifist; and although one might be able to construct some reason for not killing a mad dog or a mad man, his instincts would make him kill first and reason about it afterwards.

If these cases or any other cases cannot be covered by non-resistance, then non-resistance is simply a theory which is good where it is good and bad where it is bad. Ultimately, the theory of non-resistance is a religious doctrine, and as such can have no present relation to science, philosophy or life. What Jesus taught is a matter of no consequence. He did not speak as a biologist or scientist, but announced what he believed was an ideal rule of life. If you turn to nature you will find that all life is a struggle—the thriftier plant rooting out the weaker, and living from the soil that the weaker would otherwise appropriate—the strong animal destroying the weak and living from his strength.

Man is no exception to the rule, for man is not a separate creation, but a part of the whole and governed by the same laws that govern the whole. There can be no question of the attitude of nature in this matter, and it is idle to ask whether nature is right or wrong. Nature works, and her laws are immutable; and man is a part of nature, and the law that governs all other life governs man. Even conceding that some time man might develop a higher life, he has not done it; and until he does, he must accept facts as they are.

Man and all other animals are filled with instincts, and these instincts are insistent and strong. He has instincts of hatred and fear, as well as love and sympathy, and the instincts of hatred and fear do as much for the preservation of life as the instincts of love and sympathy. The animal fears something and runs away to save its life, or it fears something and kills, and thus preserves its life, and to take this instinct away would be death to the animal and the man alike. No doubt man's ignorance and timidity cause him to fear where he should not fear, and his lack of imagination makes him hate where he should not hate; but at the same time, the instinct is there and no amount of reason can overcome it. When inducing causes arouse it, he hates and he fears, he slanders and lies and kills and wars; and it is a fact of life which no logic can change.

Then we come to the present question—why do I want to see the Prussians conquered, and why do I want the United States to help? I never try to deceive myself, and I will not undertake to deceive you. I know that my first feeling against Prussia is instinctive and that I am against them because I am against them; and then I turn to my reason to justify my instincts. This is the way all men act—even pacifists, who fancy they have strangled their instincts—strangled them, I believe, to the injury of their manhood and womanhood.

The pacifists in this struggle are really with Germany. Everything they say and do helps Germany. Many of them are consciously sympathetic with Germany and against the Allies. All of them are working for Germany. All of them are doing what they can to perpetuate the medieval system of government whose root and basis is force; that believes the Kaiser takes his authority direct from God and owes nothing to his subjects, that his will is law and should be law, and that the sword is the greatest instrument for progress known to man. No other so-called civilized people hold this faith with the same crudity and simplicity as the Kaiser and his aides, and the pacifist whose every emotion should be against kaiserism and all it stands for is helping to perpetuate this doctrine and to make it the universal law of the world.

Am I right in putting down the pacifists as German sympathizers? I know what they say if not what they think—"England cannot fight"—"The French are all killed"—"The Belgians conquered the Congo"—"The submarine is starving England"—"Germany has plenty of food"—"The English are starving German women and children"—"America is too far away to make any difference"—"America was never neutral"—"We know nothing about the war, as the English send all news"—etc., etc.

Too long have I studied the human mind to be deceived. I know the pacifists are not telling us what they think, but what they wish. I know it is not their judgment but their will that is speaking. It is the pacifist's way of "doing his bit" for the Kaiser. While the German army is holding the Hindenburg line, they are "holding the thought."

I disagree with the pacifists upon another question. They tell me that this is a capitalists' war and that all its participants are equally guilty. There may be elements of truth in the statement that capitalism is one of the inciting causes of the war, but that capitalism caused the war, or that all nations are equally responsible, I utterly deny. Germany without a moment's warning, in violation of her treaty, sent millions of armed troops across Belgium, burned her cities, killed her men and women, ravished her land, and sent many of her helpless people into slavery. Pacifists say that this was only war, but the prime minister of Germany at the time said it was wrong and expressed the deepest regret that the needs of war had made Germany violate a treaty that it should have kept. She took northern France and laid it waste, stealing property, destroying cities, levying unconscionable tribute upon helpless towns and subjugating their people. She sent her army on a mad march to take Paris and was only stopped at the Marne by the French, aided by a few English soldiers, who would rather die than have their land conquered by a foreign power.

As between Germany on the one hand and Belgium and France on the other, are you without sympathy and feeling? Did you want Germany to overrun Belgium? Do you care nothing for the Belgians, or the people of northern France in their misery and desolation? Do you want the German army still to stay in

Belgium and northern France, or do you want them to return to their beloved "Fatherland"? If you want them to return, how will you get them out, by praying to their God who is a partner with the Kaiser, or by meeting them with cannons and with sword? If the pacifist has no feeling as between Belgium and Germany, then I confess I cannot understand it, excepting that some intellectual "hocus-pocus" has entirely robbed him of the human instincts upon which all life depends.

Some pacifists answered this question by saying that the Belgian government conquered the Congo and the French government conquered Morocco. To me this is no answer. I can well admit that those in authority in Belgium and France violated nations and peoples, but can find in this not the slightest justification for the violation of Belgium and France by Germany. The Belgian peasant and the French peasant, the French and Belgian women and children had no hand in the violation either of the Congo or of Morocco, and what their rulers may have done can furnish no excuse for the barbarities of the Prussian government. It is an old familiar thing to say to the helpless being who is ravished, "Your ancestors did the same to someone else." It is the excuse of the wolf for killing the lamb—that the ancestors of the lamb once muddied the stream above the place where the wolf's ancestors drank. You can carry everything back to infinity and find that all have been right and all have been wrong; but this gives no light upon the settlement of the question which is now and here.

Austria made the most intolerable and unjust demands on Serbia. Serbia accepted all demands but one, and this one involved giving up her sovereignty to Austria. Austria demanded that her requirements should be met within twenty-eight hours, or the Austrian army would be turned loose upon the people of Serbia. Every great nation in Europe, excepting Germany and Austria, at once used every effort to prevent this war. At the last moment Austria yielded, but Germany replied that it was too late; that mobilization had already begun; that they were ready to "let slip the dogs of war" that for forty years had been hungering for the sacrifice of Europe.

I believe that no human being can look at this question honestly and deny that this war was made in Germany and that all of its horrors are on the head of Germany. When I say Germany, like most every other American, I have not the slightest feeling against the German people, but only against the Prussian military clique who have made war a fine art and wholesale murder a trade.

Long ago, Wendell Phillips said, "Prussia is not a nation, but an army." It is true today Prussia is an army that sent millions singing on their road of conquest through Belgium and France, ruthlessly destroying the peace of the world and carrying death and destruction wherever they went. I cannot help rejoicing in the thought that this army is now going back to the "Fatherland" and that they are not singing as they go.

I do not believe that any right-thinking man who is not tied by blood to Germany or Austria, or moved by personal hate to some of the allied countries, can help the deep feeling which, with even the unbeliever, is almost a prayer, that Germany will be driven from France and Belgium and all the other lands which she has overrun.

If the pacifist admits that he has any feeling whatever as between Germany on the one hand and Belgium and France on the other, then the rest is easy. Of course the wise pacifists refuse to admit it, because they know that if they admit it, their cause is lost.

Then what of the United States? We are told that we will sacrifice millions of young Americans in this war. This may be true, though I hope and believe it is not, but the pacifist, first of all, is a theorist who prides himself upon the poise of his mind and the subjugation of his feelings. They should first answer this question—how much more valuable is an American life than a Belgian life, or a French life, or the life of even a despised Englishman—the Englishman whom the pacifists have learned from the politicians to hate? I have very little of what is commonly known as patriotism, and frankly confess that unless I am acquainted with the particular individual, I have as much feeling for the life of a Frenchman as I have for the life of an American; and I know what you know, that

Clarence Darrow

the entrance of this great country into this war will not destroy life, but will save life.

If the world turns loose against the conquering Germans, the war will soon be ended, to the relief of the world, including the German people themselves.

I believe that we should be in this war—first, because every feeling in me is for Belgium and France and Poland and Serbia, as against Germany and Austria. This, with me, is a real cause of war. I am willing to admit, however, that the United States would not be justified in sending her boys to France for this alone. Then where is the justification? I am thoroughly convinced that not only was it the right of America to enter this war, but it was her duty, if she recognizes duty, and that had she stayed out she would have been so cowardly that she would have received and deserved the contempt of all the right-thinking people of the world.

During this war Germany has violated nearly all the rules of war. Here again the pacifist climbs up in the clouds, the clouds which are not thick enough to obscure him, and says there are no rules for war. This is not true. Until Germany broke them, there were many rules for war. The world had thought that in the last thousand years the voice of humanity had even been heard in war, and solemn treaties had provided that certain things could not be done. For instance, prisoners could not be slain; wells and streams could not be poisoned; women and children should be protected. The right of non-combatants to travel was clearly specified. The ocean should be left free, except as to the right of belligerent nations to search vessels, take them into port, release the non-combatants, and condemn and take such goods as had been declared contraband by the contending powers.

The oceans are the highways of the nations, to which all nations whose shores touch them have equal access and use, subject only to the limitations I have stated. I believe there can be little dispute on this proposition. Germany in her frenzy manufactured submarines, sent them out in the ocean, not to capture ships and take them into port and search them for contraband goods, but to blow up ships without notice, and destroy the lives of combatants and non-combatants alike. For this there can be no justification. The military powers of Germany deliberately contrived to send a torpedo into the *Lusitania* and kill hundreds of people, many of whom were citizens of the United States, without giving them a chance to escape. More than this, the Germany Embassy at Washington gave notice to the American people not to sail on that ship. Had the American Ambassador to Germany given similar notice to the Germans, he would not have been dismissed from Germany—he would most likely have been hanged or shot.

The *Lusitania* is but one ship. A number of others were torpedoed in violation of the laws of war and the rights of America. Finally Germany promised that no more ships should be torpedoed unless the people on board were given a safe place to land. But finally in their desperation, on the first of February they announced to America and the world that after that date all ships within a certain zone should be torpedoed without notice and without a chance for any person to save his life. To this the pacifist said that an American who would venture on a boat under those circumstances would deserve to lose his life, and that every American should keep off a boat when they knew there was danger. This depends upon what kind of an American he is. I fancy that if there was a street fight with pistols and guns and I wanted to pass down the street, I would go around several blocks to seek my safety and avoid trouble; but if somebody stood on the street and gave me notice that I could not pass, I hope I would have the courage to go down the street regardless of the notice, or even go out of my way that I might settle the question with him. If I did not have that courage, I would scarcely have the right to live. At least a country could not be made up of people who are lacking in that much courage and self-assertion.

It is no reply to say that England may have held up boats to search them for contraband and thus delay a letter for a week. This is a trivial matter and can be easily settled without war; at its best it amounts to little; but taking life under these circumstances cannot be settled, and the government that has the power and would not defend its people in the assertion of their clear rights, on sea and on land, can neither command nor deserve the respect of the people of the world, and cannot survive.

Everyone knows of the innumerable plots that have been executed in the United States to destroy munition plants, and with them the lives of American citizens. It will not do to say that these citizens were in the business of furnishing munitions to the Allies. Every country has a clear right to manufacture munitions and to sell them to whatever country will buy, and Germany is the last nation that has a right to object, as she has sold munitions to every land on earth. We have never made munitions for the Allies. We have made munitions to sell. If Germany wanted them she could buy them. Whether they ever reach their destination is not a question for America, but a question between England and Germany.

Again, we are told that the submarine is necessary because England is seeking to starve German women and children. Since war began, starvation has been a legitimate method of warfare, always with one exception, that the people of a starving nation shall have the right to surrender and will then be fed. If the German people are starving, they can be fed when they go back to the "Fatherland" and lay down their arms. The North starved the South, and were within their rights. Germany drew its armies around Paris in 1871 and waited for the people to starve. They were asked to let the women and children go out of the gates so that they might be fed, and answered, "Let Paris fry in its own fat." Paris was starved, and surrendered; and her people were then fed. In this Germany was well within its rights, as the Allies are now within theirs, in preventing food reaching the Central Powers.

Neither can you overlook the fact that before Germany and America were at war, the German government deliberately plotted with Japan and Mexico to invade the United States; and still we are asked to stay out, and our President is condemned for doing not only what he had the right to do, but doing what he must do, if he obeyed his oath and was loyal to his trust.

I believe that neither in logic, philosophy, law nor, what is more, the commonest instincts of humanity, have the pacifists a chance to make a case. I respect them as I respect everyone who stands for his honest convictions, but in this I believe they are wrong—woefully wrong; and that while they are professing to believe in democracy, they are giving all the strength of their character and their mind to autocracy, force, violence and war. As ever,

Your friend,

CLARENCE DARROW.

From a letter to Daniel Kiefer of Cincinnati, Ohio, dated June 28, 1917, which appeared in The Liberal Review, *July, 1917.*

THE
FOREIGN DEBT
AND AMERICA

*As a man needs the friendship of his neighbors,
so nations need the good will of other nations. The least
we can do to get that is to cancel the bonds incurred
for our help in the late war.*

1927. Lindbergh flies non-stop New York to Paris, 3,610 miles in 33½ hours . . . U.S. intervenes in Nicaraguan Civil War . . . Office of World War Foreign Debt Commission expires . . . France expresses willingness to make periodic payments to U.S.; says she can continue to pay her war debts only as long as Germany continues to pay reparations . . . Judge Elbert H. Gary dies . . . Hemingway's *Men Without Women* published . . . Sen. Capper of Kansas introduces joint resolution calling for the "general renunciation of war as an instrument of policy" and asking the nation "to adjust and settle its international disputes by mediation, arbitration and conciliation."

For a number of years the United States has been growing rich at an amazing rate. We are now very fat. In fact, we are obsessed of our lard. When we think of ourselves we think about our fat, and when we talk, we talk about our fat. The national urge is for more fat. Nothing else counts, unless it is the desire to brag about it. We have most of the gold in the world. We are the financial center of the earth.

All the people of the world come to America to borrow money. We are glad to loan this cash at exorbitant rates and unconscionable commissions. We are fat all over, but especially we have fatty degeneration of the heart. This is a dangerous disease. As a nation we have made the same sacrifices that individuals make in growing obese rapidly. We have lost all our friends. We know that when any nation speaks a good word for us, it is a sign that they want to borrow money.

This is a ticklish position for a nation, exactly as it is for an individual. Still, why should we care? We can lick the world! We have more iron and coal and other raw material than all of Europe put together. We have more machinery than the others. We have more brains applied to production than all the rest. In fact, all our brains are applied to production. To what other use could real brains be applied? No one stops to inquire why we should want to lick the world—or what good it would do us to thrash it. Neither do they inquire why we want to be so "fat."

Of course our fatness is not very evenly distributed. Many of our people are lean; but lumping us all together, and designating the lump as "we," the world has never before witnessed such obesity. This condition has come about very quickly. Strange to say, we were accumulating our fat while the rest of the world was growing poor. Our great financial corpulency grew out of the late war. The impoverishment of Europe likewise grew out of the late war. We were a comparatively new country before the war. England was the financial center of the world. England was the financial center because she was older and nearer the center of the world's population. England still is older and nearer the center of population, but she is now very poor, while we are very rich. If abundant fat is a good thing, then the war was a godsend for America.

Every European state is now close to bankruptcy. The immediate future of all Europe is a serious question. Her people are over-taxed and idle and in want—meanwhile we are rich. Is their poverty any concern of ours? Our politicians seem to think that it is not. They think it is not, because they believe that their constituents feel that way.

The United States was involved in the European war long before we openly took sides; we sold everything that we could spare to the warring countries. We sold at exorbitant prices. We were able to get these prices because our customers were in dire need.

After two years of carnage in Europe we went into the war. We had no right to take sides for any reason other than that our national interests were involved. From the beginning many of our people considered that our rights were invaded. It is not necessary to discuss whether we did right or wrong in going in. At least we *thought* that the rights of America were involved, and we went in on the side of the Allies. We had no army and only a small navy. We had no munitions of war. We had one thing needful to war—cash. We also had the food and material that our allies needed for carrying on the war.

Our soldiers reached the front only in the closing days of the contest. Our money and food reached it long before. As soon as we entered the war we began to furnish cash and supplies to our allies. The armies of Europe were in the field and had been for two long years. True, their ranks were depleted by shot and shell, and disease and famine. Still, in spite of that they were holding the line. By the time we entered they were hanging on in grim despair, willing that every man should die, if need be, in the cause.

Not only the most fitting of the Allies' soldiers had gone down to death, but a large part of their property had been destroyed. Hundreds of cities and villages had been riddled with cannonballs and desolated with flame. All the Allies had contracted debts without limit wherever they could sell their bonds, and at whatever price. The United States had stayed out of the war, but we had sold supplies at exorbitant rates, for cash, from the first.

When we finally went in, we gave our allies cash to buy supplies, mostly in America—some ten billions of dollars altogether. We furnished them no money until we went in. Up to that time we had taken their money for the stuff that we had to sell. Our soldiers were ready for war only in the closing days. The United States lost some fifty thousand dead, while the Allies lost ten millions, at least. How many millions of American lives were saved by the cash we gave our allies?

The war was won by the help of American money and by the lives of the Allies. Our money was furnished after the Allies had poured in all that they could give or borrow from every other source. The war was won. Our dead numbered fifty thousand; theirs, at least ten million. The money we gave was about ten billion. They gave all that they had, which was vastly more. We are now rich. Too rich, in fact. So rich that we are in danger of death from fatty degeneration of the heart. When I say in danger of death, I mean the death of all that once was the finest and the bravest and the truest in American character.

After we got in, and growing out of the general effort to win the war, America received war bonds of the allied countries for this ten billion dollars. We are told that the Allies should pay; that they "hired the money." Did they "hire the money," and should they pay the bonds?

The Congress and Senate who voted this money to help the common cause did not expect it to be returned. The leaders in both houses made this plain when the money was appropriated. The people did not expect it to be repaid, nor did they want it to be. They were thankful that the Allies could shorten the war by sending their remaining men to death, while we furnished the supplies. Who had the best of this bargain, our allies or ourselves? Every American soldier who returned from the shambles of Europe knows what it meant that the war was prosecuted with our money before our soldiers reached the front. Every American father and mother whose sons returned alive knows how little was our contribution compared with the lives sacrificed by Britain, France, Italy and the rest, during the long months while their sons were dying and America was furnishing the supplies.

It is true that many of our people did not believe in the war; the justice or injustice of our entrance is no longer a matter worth discussing. For myself, I believed we should go in. At any rate, we did go in. And pledged ourselves to fight it to the end. And, of course, whether men believed in it or not, they were compelled to go. It is not now a question of whether we were right or wrong, but whether a nation as corpulent as ours should take money from nations that were our allies in this common world disaster; and nations that did infinitely more to bring victory than we ever dreamed of doing.

The bonds of our allies lack every element that is necessary to make a valid obligation. America gave the money to save herself, and for two years before that time the Allies were fighting without our help. We never expected it back, nor even wanted it to be returned. The Allies who gave their bonds could do nothing else. They were in a death grapple, and of course they were heartened and jubilant when at last we went in. They could do nothing else but pledge their people with their bonds; neither America nor the Allies expected it to be anything but a small contribution on our part to a common cause.

These bonds are not such obligations as call for the strict rules of legal construction. They are rather instruments that should be determined in the light of equity. They have not been transferred before due to an innocent holder for value. They are still in the hands of the United States. Besides this, it is a question only of what the people of the United States think should be done.

Every principle of equity is against us. Rather should we contribute still larger sums to our allies. If we were ever justified in entering this war, it was in equity our war from the beginning. The need for the defeat of Germany was just the same when the war opened as it was when we went in. For two terrible years our allies fought this war without our aid. More than that, every American was greedily gathering every dollar of profit possible to be garnered on account of the holocaust in Europe. We sold our stuff at the most exorbitant prices and demanded cash or good security for our wares. America as a nation would doubtless be vastly ahead in a financial way, even though we never collected a single penny on our European bonds. Does this mean nothing to a people who are at heart really big and generous and fair?

Let us think, too, of who must pay these bonds. First, England, who practically endorsed all the war obligations of the Allies; England, who risked her empire and the fortunes of every Briton in the contest. I am aware that many Americans do not like the English. I am not of that number. I know too much of the history of civilization not to recognize the debt of the world to England. Great Britain is now staggering under an appalling load of debt. Her industries are languishing. Her people are suffering. She is willing to cancel her debts against France and Italy and the other Allies whose obligations she underwrote.

After Great Britain, France is the next who must pay. France was the first nation to suffer from the German attack. Many of her cities were ruined and her country laid waste. A generation of men were killed and hopelessly maimed in the carnage. Her country is small and her population large. Her people are excessively poor and over-burdened with taxes. Where is the American who wants her money? It is not even needful to call attention to the fact that but for France our American Revolution would have been only a rebellion.

Italy, too, made great sacrifices in the war. She is very poor. Her national resources are small and her people over-burdened. What is true of these countries is even truer of the still smaller countries from whom we are demanding money that was used to help us as well as them, and money, moreover, that we do not need.

Nothing further than this demand upon our allies is needed to stamp us in the eyes of the world as *Shylocks*, devoid of sentiment and a sense of justice. If anything more is needed, it is shown by our attitude toward the world in reference to trade. How are our former allies to pay what we demand? They have no gold; all of this is in America. They can give new bonds for old, but this only postpones the payment and adds to the obligation. There is but one way, and that is by the products of the European people. For two or three generations, at least, the poor of Europe must work to pay us money that we do not need and should not take. Have we no feeling for the unborn children who must bear this load incurred in a common cause?

But even this will not satisfy America. We will not buy from Europe. Our tariff wall is so high that we keep out foreign goods so that our "market-mongers" can fix the prices of their wares. We want the money which we should not have, and will give them no chance to pay. I know of only one parallel for our attitude, and that was the demand of the Egyptians on the Hebrews to make bricks without straw. The Hebrews did not comply.

The world (outside of America) is in dire want, growing out of the World War. Its civilization is in danger. Anything may happen in any European country. Does not human feeling and fellowship call on the richest country on earth to help? No man can live to himself alone, and still less can any nation live to itself alone. We have made all the people of the world our enemies. We are strong, but not so strong that we want the world against us. As a man needs the friendship of his neighbors, so nations need the good will of other nations. The least we can do to get that is to cancel the bonds incurred for our help in the late war. This simple act of justice would bring hope and courage to our allies. For one, I should be glad if it were done on condition that the allies should forgive the indemnities from the Central Powers, but we at least should cancel our allies' bonds; and eventually it will be done. It should be done now. America should do something to raise the gloom and despair that overhangs Europe. She should do something to make friends with the world. She should do something to redeem herself from her reputation of a *Shylock* and a usurer. This is the least she can do, and it really will cost us nothing. The cancellation of foreign indebtedness growing out of the war will bring us, collectively and individually, more return for a smaller outlay than anything else can bring. Surely that should commend it to our people even if nothing else does.

Vanity Fair, *February, 1927.*

PART SIX

ON THE PRESS
AND LITERATURE

REALISM IN
LITERATURE

*The true artist has no right to choose the lovely spots alone
and make us think that this is life. He must bring the
whole world before our eyes and make us read and learn.*

MAN IS NATURE'S LAST AND
most perfect work; but however high his development or great
his achievements, he is yet a child of the earth and the rude forces
that have formed all the life that exists thereon. He cannot separate
himself from the environment that gave him birth, and a thousand
ties of nature bind him back to the long-forgotten past and prove
his kinship to all the lower forms of life that have sprung from
that great universal mother, Earth.

As there is a common law of being which controls all living
things, from the aimless motions of the mollusk in the sea to the
most perfect conduct of the best-developed man, so all the activities of human life, from the movements of the savage digging
roots to the work of the greatest artist with his brush, are controlled
by universal law, and are good or bad, perfect or imperfect, as they
conform to the highest condition nature has imposed.

The early savage dwelt in caves and cliffs and spent his life in
seeking food and providing a rude shelter from the cold. He looked
upon the earth, the sun, the sea, the sky, the mountain peak, the
forest and the plain, and all he saw and heard formed an impression
on his brain and aided in his growth. Like a child he marvelled at

the storm and flood; he stood in awe as he looked upon disease and death; and to explain the things he could not understand, he peopled earth and air and sea with gods and demons, and a thousand other weird creations of his brain. All these mysterious creatures were made in the image of the natural objects that came within his view. The gods were men grown large and endowed with marvelous powers, while tree and bird and beast alike were used as models for a being far greater than any nature ever formed.

An angry god it was that made the rivers overrun their banks and leave destruction in their path; an offended god it was that hurled his thunderbolts upon a wicked world, or sent disease and famine to the sinning children of the earth; and to coax these rulers to be merciful to man, the weak and trembling children of the ancient world turned their minds to sacrifice and prayer. And the first clouded thoughts of these rude men that were transcribed on monument and stone, or carved in wood, or painted with the colors borrowed from the sun and earth and sky; in short, the first rude art was born to sing the praise, and tell the fame, and paint the greatness of the gods. But all of this was natural to the time and place; the graven images, the chiseled hieroglyphics and all this rude beginning of literature and art were formed upon what men saw and heard and felt, enlarged and magnified to fit the stature of the gods.

As the world grew older, art was used to celebrate the greatness and achievements of kings and rulers as well as gods, and their tombs were ornamented with such decorations as these early ages could create; and yet all literature and art were only for the gods and rulers of the world. Then, even more than now, wealth and power brought intellect to do its will, and all its force was spent to sing the praises of the rulers of the earth and air. The basis of all this art of pen and brush was the reality of the world, but this was so magnified and distorted for the base use of kings and priests that realism, in the true sense, could not exist. It would not do to paint a picture of a king resembling a man of flesh and blood, and of course a god must be far greater than a king. It would not do to write a tale in which kings and princes, lords and ladies should act like men and women, else what difference between the ruler

Clarence Darrow

and the ruled? The marvelous powers that romance and myth had given to gods and angels were transferred to those of royal blood. The wonderful achievement of these kings and princes could be equalled only by the gods, and the poor dependents of the world, who lived for the glory of the great, were fed with legends and with tales that sang the praises of the strong.

Literature, sculpture, painting, music and architecture, indeed all forms of art, were the exclusive property of the great, and the artist then, like most of those today, was retained to serve the strong and maintain the status of the weak. No one dreamed that there was any beauty in a common human life or any romance in a fact. The greatest of the earth had not yet learned to know that every life is a mystery and every death a tragedy; that the spark of the infinite, which alone transforms clay to life, animates alike the breast of the peasant and the soul of the prince. The world had not yet learned that the ant-hill is as great as Mont Blanc, and the blade of grass as mysterious as the oak. It is only now that the world is growing so delicate and refined that it can see the beauty of a fact; that it is developing a taste so rare as to distinguish between the false and true; that it can be moved by the gentle breeze as well as by the winter's gale; that it can see greater beauty in a statement true to life, than in the inflated tales which children read.

Most of the art and literature the world has known has been untrue. The pictures of the past have been painted from the distorted minds of visionists, and the pliant brains of tools. They have represented impossible gods and unthinkable saints; angels and cherubs and demons; everything but men and women. Saints may be all right in their place, but a saint with a halo round his head was born of myth and not of art. Angels may be well enough, but all rational men prefer an angel with arms to an angel with wings.

When these artists were not drawing saints and madonnas, they were spending their time in painting kings and royal knaves; and the pictures of the rulers were as unlike the men and women that they were said to represent as the servile spirit of the painter was unlike that of the true artist today. Of course an artist would not paint the poor; they had no clothes that would adorn a work of art, and no money or favors that could remunerate the toil. An ancient artist could no more afford to serve the poor than a modern lawyer could defend the weak.

After literature had so far advanced as to concern other beings than gods and kings, the authors of these ancient days told of wondrous characters endowed with marvelous powers: knights with giant strength and magic swords; princes with wondrous palaces and heaps of gold; travelers that met marvelous beasts and slew them in extraordinary ways; giants with forms like mountains and strength like oxen, who could vanquish all but little dwarfs. Railroads were not invented in those early days, but travel was facilitated by the use of seven-league boots. Balloons and telescopes were not yet known, but this did not keep favored heroes from peering at the stars or looking down from on high upon the earth; they had but to plant a magic bean before they went to bed at night, and in the morning it had grown so tall that it reached up to the sky; and the hero, although not skilled in climbing, needed simply to grasp the stalk and say, "Hitchety, hatchety, up I go. Hitchety, hatchety, up I go," and by this means soon vanish in the clouds. Tales of this sort used once to delight the world, and the readers half believed them true. We give them to children now, and the best of these view them with a half contempt.

The modern man does not enjoy these myths. He relishes a lie, but it must not be too big; it must be so small that, although he knows in his inmost soul that it is not true, he can yet half make himself believe it is not false. Most of us have cherished a pleasing waking dream, and have fondly clung to the sweet delusion while we really knew it was not life. The modern literary stomach is becoming so healthy that it wants a story at least half true; should the falsehood be too strong, it acts as an emetic instead of food. These old fairy tales have lost their power to charm, as the stories of the gods and kings went down before. They have lost their charm, for as we read them now, they wake no answering chord born of the experiences that make up what we know of human life.

When the beauty of realism shall be truly known, we shall read the book, or look upon the work of art, and in the light of all we know of life shall ask our beings whether the picture that the author or the painter creates for us is like the image that is born of the consciousness that moves our soul and the experiences that have made us know.

Realism worships at the shrine of nature; it does not say that there may not be a sphere in which beings higher than man can live, or that some time an eye may not rest upon a fairer sunset than was ever born behind the clouds and sea, but it knows that through countless ages nature has slowly fitted the eye of man to the earth on which we live and the objects that we see; and the perfect earthly eye must harmonize with the perfect earthly scene.

To say that realism is coarse and vulgar is to declare against nature and her works, and to assert that the man she made may dream of things higher and grander than nature could unfold. The eye of the great sculptor reveals to him the lines that make the most perfect human form, and he chisels out the marble block until it resembles this image so completely that it almost seems to live. Nature, through ages of experiment and development, has made this almost faultless form. It is perfect because every part is best fitted for the separate work it has to do. The artist knows that he could not improve a single organ if he would, for all the rest of nature must be adjusted to the change. He has the skill to reproduce this shape in lasting stone, and the human brain could not conceive a form more beautiful and fair. Here is a perfect image of the highest work that countless centuries of nature's toil has made, and yet some would seek to beautify and sanctify this work by dressing it in the garb that shifting fashion and changing fancy makes for man.

Only the vulgar superstition of the past ever suggested that the reproduction of human forms in stone was an unholy work. Through long dark centuries religion taught that the flesh was vile and bad, and that the soul of man was imprisoned in a charnel house, unfit for human sight. The early Christians wounded, bruised, and maimed their house of clay; they covered it with skins, which under no circumstances could be removed, and many ancient saints lived and died without ever having looked upon the bodies nature gave. The images of saints and martyrs, which in the name of religion were scattered through Europe, were covered with paint and clothes and were nearly as hideous as the monks that placed them there.

When the condition of Europe and its religious thought are clearly understood, it is not difficult to imagine the reception that greeted the first dawn of modern realistic art. Sculpture and painting defied the material. They told of beauty in the human form which hundreds of years of religious fanaticism had taught was bad and vile. If the flesh was beautiful, what of the monks and priests, who had hidden it from sight, who had kept it covered night and day through all their foolish lives, who maimed and bruised, cut and lacerated for the glory of the spirit, which they thought was chained within? The church had taught that the devil of the flesh was the birth of the soul, and they therefore believed that the artist's resurrection of the flesh was the death of the soul.

The old religious prejudice, born of a misty, superstitious past, has slowly faded from the minds of men, but we find its traces even yet. The origin of the feeling against realistic art has well nigh been forgot, but much of the feeling still remains. No one would now pretend to say that all the body was unholy or unfit for sight, and yet years of custom and inherited belief have made us think that a part is good and the rest is bad: that nature, in her work of building up the human form, has made one part sacred and another vile. It is easy to mistake custom for nature, and inherited prejudice for morality. There is scarcely a single portion of the human body but that some people have thought it holy, and scarcely a single portion but that some have believed it vile. It was not shame that made clothing, but clothing that made shame. It we would eradicate from our beliefs all that inheritance and environment have given, it would be hard for us to guess how much should still remain. Custom has made most things good and most

Clarence Darrow

things bad, according to the whim of time and place. To find solid ground we must turn to nature and ask her what it is that conduces to the highest happiness and the longest life.

The realistic artist cannot accept the popular belief, whatever that may be, as to just where the deadline on the human body should be drawn that separates the sacred and profane. There are realists that look at all the beauty and loveliness of the world, and all its maladjustments too, and do not seek to answer the old, old question whether back of this is any all-controlling and designing power; they do not answer, for they cannot know; but they strive to touch the subtle chord that makes their individual lives vibrate in harmony, which they love; and they cannot think but that all parts of life are good, and that while men may differ, nature must know best.

Other realists there are that believe they see in nature the work of a divine maker who created man in his own image as the last and highest triumph of his skill; that the minutest portion of the universe exists because he wished it thus. To the realist that accepts this all-controlling power, any imputation against a portion of his master's work must reach back to the author that designed it all.

We need not say that the human body might not be better than it is; we need only know that it is the best that man can have, and that its wondrous mechanism has been constructed with infinitely more than human skill; that every portion is adapted for its work, and through the harmony of every part the highest good is reached; and that all is beautiful, for it makes the being best adapted to the earth. Those who denounce realistic art deny that knowledge is power and that wisdom only can make harmony, and they insist instead that there are some things vital to life and happiness that we should not know, but that if we must know these things, we should at all events pretend that we do not know. One day the world will learn that all things are good or bad according to the service they perform. One day it ought to learn that the power to create immortality, through infinite succeeding links of human life, is the finest and most terrible that nature ever gave to man; and that to ignore this power or call it bad, or fail to realize the great responsibility of this tremendous fact, is to cry out against the power that gave us life, and commit the greatest human sin, for it may be one that never dies.

The true artist does not find all beauty in the human face or form. He looks upon the sunset, painting all the clouds with rosy hue, and his highest wish is to create another scene like this. He never dreams that he could paint a sunset fairer than the one which lights the fading world. A fairer sunset would be something else. He sees beauty in the quiet lake, the grassy field, and running brook; he sees majesty in the cataract and mountain peak. He knows that he can paint no streams and mountain peaks more perfect than the ones that nature made.

The growth of letters has been, like the growth of art, from the marvelous and mythical to the natural and true. The tales and legends of the ancient past were not of common men and common scenes. These could not impress the undeveloped intellect of long ago. A man of letters could not deify a serf, or tell the simple story of the poor. He must write to maintain the status of the world, and please the prince that gave him food; so he told of kings and queens, of knights and ladies, of strife and conquest; and the coloring he used was human blood.

The world has grown accustomed to those ancient tales, to scenes of blood and war, and novels that would thrill the soul and cause the hair to stand on end. It has read these tales so long that the true seems commonplace and unfit to fill the pages of a book. But all the time we forget the fact that the story could not charm unless we half believed it true. The men and women in the tale we learn to love and hate; we take an interest in their lives; we hope they may succeed or fail; we must not be told at every page that the people of the book are men of straw, that no such beings ever lived upon the earth. We could take no interest in men and women that are myths conjured up to play their parts, and remind us in every word they speak that, regardless of the happiness or anguish the author makes them feel, they are but myths and can know neither joy nor pain.

It may be that the realistic tale is commonplace, but so is life, and the realistic tale is true. Among the countless millions of the earth it is only here and there, and now and then, that some soul is born from out of the mighty deep that does not soon return to the great sea and leave no ripple on the waves.

In the play of life each actor seems important to himself; the world he knows revolves around him as the central figure of the scene; his friends rejoice in all the fortune he attains and weep with him in all his grief. To him the world is bounded by the faces that he knows and the scenes in which he lives. He forgets the great surging world outside, and cannot think how small a space he fills in that infinity which bounds his life. He dies, and a few sorrowing friends mourn him for a day, and the world does not know he ever lived or ever died. In the ordinary life nearly all events are commonplace; but a few important days are thinly sprinkled in amongst all of those that intervene between the cradle and the grave. We eat and drink, we work and sleep, and here and there a great joy or sorrow creeps in upon our lives, and leaves a day that stands out against the monotony of all the rest, like the pyramids upon the level plains. But these events are very few and are important only to ourselves, and for the rest we walk with steady pace and slow along the short and narrow path of life, and rely upon the common things alone to occupy our minds and hide from view the marble stone that here and there gleams through the overhanging trees just where the road leaves off.

The old novel which we used to read, and to which the world so fondly clings, had no idea of relation or perspective. It had a hero and a heroine, and sometimes more than one. The revolutions of the planets were less important than their love. War, shipwreck, and conflagration all conspired to produce the climax of the scene, and the whole world stood still until the lovers' hearts and hands were joined. Wide oceans, burning deserts, arctic seas, impassable jungles, irate fathers, and even designing mothers were helpless against the decree that fate had made, and when all the barriers were passed and love had triumphed over impossibilities, the tale was done; through the rest of life nothing of interest could occur. Sometimes in the progress of the story, if the complications were too great, a thunderbolt or an earthquake was introduced to destroy the villain and help on the match. Earthquakes sometimes happen, and the realistic novelist might write a tale of a scene like this, but then the love affair would be an incident of the earthquake, and not the earthquake an incident of the love affair.

In real life the affections have played an important part, and sometimes great things have been done and suffered in the name of love, but most of the affairs of the human heart have been as natural as the other events of life.

The true love story is generally a simple thing. "Beside a country road, on a sloping hill, lives a farmer, in the house his father owned before. He has a daughter who skims the milk, and makes the beds, and goes to singing school at night. There are other members of the household, but our tale is no concern of theirs. In the meadow back of the house a woodchuck has dug its hole, and reared a family in its humble home. Across the valley only a mile away, another farmer lives. He has a son who plows the fields and does the chores and goes to singing school at night. He cannot sing, but attends the school as regularly as if he could. Of course he does not let the girl go home alone, and in the spring, when singing school is out, he visits her on Sunday eve without excuse. If the girl had not lived so near, the boy would have fancied another girl about the same age, who also went to singing school. Back of the second farmer's house is another woodchuck hole and woodchuck home. After a year or two of courtship the boy and girl are married as their parents were before, and they choose a pretty spot beside the road, and build another house nearby, and settle down to a common life; and so the world moves on. And a woodchuck on one farm meets a woodchuck on the other, and they choose a quiet place beside a stump, in no one's way, where they think they have a right to be, and dig another hole and make another home." For after all, men and animals are much alike; and nature loves them both and loves them all, and sends them forth to drive the loneliness from off the earth, and then takes them back into her loving breast to sleep.

It may be that there are few great incidents in the realistic tale, but each event appeals to life and cannot fail to wake our memories and make us live the past again. The great authors of the natural school—Tolstoy, Hardy, Howells, Daudet, Ibsen, Flaubert, Zola, and their kind—have made us think and live. Their words have burnished up our minds and revealed a thousand pictures that hang upon the walls of memory, covered with the dust of years and hidden from our sight. Sometimes, of course, we cry with pain at the picture that is thrown before our view, but life consists of emotions, and we cannot truly live unless the depths are stirred. These great masters, it is true, may sometimes shock the over-sensitive with the tales they tell of life, but if the tale is true, why hide it from our sight?

There is nothing more common than the protest against the wicked stories of the realistic school, filled with tales of passion and of sin; but he who denies that passion, denies all the life that exists upon the earth, and cries out against the mother that gave him birth. And he that ignores this truth passes with contempt the greatest fact that nature has impressed upon the world. Those who condemn as sensual the tales of Tolstoy and Daudet still defend the love stories of which our literature is full—those weak and silly tales that make women fit only to be the playthings of the world, and deny to them a single thought or right except to serve their master, man. These objectors do not contend that tales dealing with the feelings and affections shall not be told, they approve these tales; they simply insist they shall be false instead of true. The old novel filled the mind of the schoolgirl with a thousand thoughts that had no place in life—with ten thousand pictures she could never see. It taught that some time she should meet a prince in disguise to whom she would freely give her hand and heart. So she went out upon the road to find this prince, and the more disguised he was, the more certain did she feel that he was the prince for whom she sought.

The realist paints the passions and affections as they are. Both man and woman can see their beauty and their terror, their true position, and the relation that they bear to all the rest of life. He would not beguile the girl into the belief that her identity should be destroyed and merged for the sake of this feeling, which not once in ten thousand times could realize the promises the novel made; but he would not leave her as an individual to make the most she can, and all she can, of life, with all the hope and chance of conquest, which men have taken for themselves. Neither would the realist cry out blindly against these deep passions which have moved men and women in the past, and which must continue fierce and strong as long as life exists. He is taught by the scientist that the fiercest heat may be transformed to light, and is taught by life that from the strongest passions are sometimes born the sweetest and the purest souls.

In these days of creeds and theories, of preachers in the pulpit and preachers out, we are told that all novels should have a moral and be written to serve some end. So we have novels on religion, war, marriage, divorce, socialism, theosophy, woman's rights, and other topics without end. It is not enough that the preachers and lecturers shall tell us how to think and act; the novelist must try his hand at preaching too. He starts out with a theory, and every scene and incident must be bent to make it plain that the author believes certain things. The doings of the men and women in the book are secondary to the views the author holds. The theories may be true, but the poor characters that must adjust their lives to these ideal states are sadly warped and twisted out of shape.

The realist would teach a lesson, too, but he would not violate a single fact for all the theories in the world—for a theory could not be true if it did violence to life. He paints his picture so true and perfect that all men who look upon it know it is a likeness of the world that they have seen; they know that these are men and women and little children that they meet upon the streets; they see the conditions of their lives, and the moral of the picture sinks deep into their minds.

There are so-called scientists that make a theory and then gather facts to prove their theory true; the real scientist patiently and impartially gathers facts, and then forms a theory to explain and harmonize these facts. All life bears a moral, and the true artist must teach a lesson with his every fact. Some contend that the moral teacher must not tell the truth; the realist holds that there can be no moral teaching like the truth. The world has grown tired of preachers and sermons; today it asks for facts. It has grown tired of fairies and angels, and asks for flesh and blood. It looks on life as it exists, both its beauty and its horror, its joy and its sorrow; it wishes to see it all; not the prince and the millionaire alone, but the laborer and the beggar, the master and the slave. We see the beautiful and the ugly, and with it know what the world is and what it ought to be; and the true picture, which the author saw and painted, stirs the heart to holier feelings and grander thoughts.

It is from the realities of life that the highest idealities are born. The philosopher may reason with unerring logic, and show us where the world is wrong. The economist may tell us of the progress and poverty that go hand in hand. But these are theories, and the abstract cannot suffer pain.

Dickens went out into the streets of the great city and found poor little Jo sweeping the crossing with his broom. All around was the luxury and the elegance which the great have ever appropriated to themselves: great mansions, fine carriages, beautiful dresses; but in all the great city of houses and homes, poor little Jo could find no place to lay his head. His home was in the street, and every time he halted for a moment in the throng, the policeman touched him with his club and bade him "move on." At last, ragged, wretched, almost dead with "moving on," he sank down upon the cold steps of a magnificent building erected for "The Propagation of the Gospel in Foreign Parts." As we think of wretched, ragged Jo in the midst of all this luxury and wealth, we see the tens of thousands of other waifs in the great cities of the world, and we condemn the so-called civilization of the earth that builds the mansions of the rich and the great upon the rags and miseries of the poor.

The true realist cannot worship at the shrine of power, nor prostitute his gifts for gold. With an artist's eye he sees the world exactly as it is, and tells the story faithful unto life. He feels for every heart that beats, else he could not paint them as he does.

It takes the soul to warm a statue into life and make living flesh and coursing blood; and each true picture that he paints or draws makes the world a better place in which to live.

The artists of the realistic school have a sense so fine that they cannot help catching the inspiration that is filling all the world's best minds with the hope of greater justice and more equal social life. With the vision of the seer they feel the coming dawn when true equality shall reign upon the earth; the time when democracy shall no more be confined to constitutions and to laws, but will be a part of human life. The greatest artists of the world today are telling facts and painting scenes that cause humanity to stop, and think, and ask why one should be a master and another be a serf; why a portion of the world should toil and spin, should wear away its strength and life, that the rest should live in idleness and ease.

The old-time artists thought they served humanity by painting saints and madonnas and angels from the myths they conjured in their brains. They painted war with long lines of soldiers dressed in uniforms, and looking plump and gay; and a battle scene was always drawn from the side of the victorious camp, with the ensign proudly planting his bright colors on the rampart of the foe. One or two were dying, but always in their comrades' arms, and listening to shouts of victory that filled the air, and thinking of the righteous cause for which they fought and died. In the last moments they dreamed of pleasant burial yards at home, and of graves kept green by loving, grateful friends; and a smile of joy shone on their wasted faces that was so sweet that it seemed a hardship not to die in war. They painted peace as a white-winged dove settling down upon a cold and fading earth. Between the two it was plain which choice a boy would make, and thus art served the state and king.

But Verestchagin painted war; he painted war so true to life that as we look upon the scene, we long for peace. He painted war as war has ever been, and will ever be—a horrible and ghastly scene, where men, drunk with blind frenzy which rulers say is patriotic pride, and made mad by drums and fifes and smoke and shot and shell and flowing blood, seek to maim and wound and kill, because a ruler gives the word. He paints a battlefield, a field of life and death, a field of carnage and of blood; and who are these that fight like fiends and devils driven to despair? What cause is this that makes these men forget that they are men, and vie with beasts to show their cruel thirst for blood? They shout of home and native land, but they have no homes, and the owners of their native land exist upon their toil and blood. The nobles and princes, for whom this fight is waged, are far away upon a hill, beyond the reach of shot and shell, and from this spot they watch their slaves pour out their blood to satisfy their rulers' pride and lust of power. What is the enemy they fight? Men like themselves; who blindly go to death at another king's command; slaves, who have no land, who freely give their toil or blood, whichever one their rulers may demand. These fighting soldiers have no cause for strife, but their rulers live by kindling in their hearts a love of native land, a love that makes them hate their brother laborers of other lands, and dumbly march to death to satisfy a king's caprice.

But let us look once more after the battle has been fought. Here we see the wreck and ruin of the strife; the field is silent now, given to the dead, the beast of prey and night. A young soldier lies upon the ground; the snow is falling fast around his form; the lonely mountain peaks rise up on every side; the wreck of war is all about. His uniform is soiled and stained, a spot of red is seen upon his breast. It is not the color that his country wove upon his coat to catch his eye and bait him to his death; it is hard and jagged and cold. It is his life's blood, which leaked out through a hole that followed the point of a saber to his heart. His form is stiff and cold, for he is dead. The cruel wound and icy air have done their work. The government that took his life taught this poor boy to love his native land; as a child he dreamed of scenes of glory and of power, and the great wide world just waiting to fall captive to his magic strength. He dreamed of war and strife, of victory and fame; if he should die, kind hands would smooth his brow, and loving friends would keep his grave and memory green, because he died in war. But no human eye is there at last, as the mist of night and mist of death shut out the lonely mountains from his sight. The snow is all around, and the air above is gray with falling flakes which soon will hide him from the world; and when the summertime shall come again, no one can tell his bleaching bones from all the rest. The only life upon the scene is the buzzard slowly circling in the air above his head, waiting to make sure that death has come. The bird looks down upon the boy, into the eyes through which he first looked out upon the great, wide world, and which his mother fondly kissed; upon these eyes the buzzard will commence his meal.

Not all the world is beautiful, and not all of life is good. The true artist has no right to choose the lovely spots alone and make us think that this is life. He must bring the world before our eyes and make us read and learn. As he loves the true and noble, he must show the false and bad. As he yearns for true equality, he must paint the master and the slave. He must tell the truth, and tell it all, must tell it o'er and o'er again, till the deafest ear will listen and the dullest mind will think. He must not swerve to please the world by painting only lovely tales. He must think, and paint, and write, and work, until the world shall learn so much and grow so good, that the true will all be beautiful and all the real be ideal.

From A Persian Pearl and Other Essays, *1899.*

Clarence Darrow

THE
BREAKER
BOY

*He never had a great deal of imagination, and what
he had was buried long ago in the deep, black mine.*

J OHNNY MC CAFFERY WAS ELEVEN
years old when he became a man.

Five years before this his father and mother with their four
children and steerage tickets sailed out of the Queenstown Harbor,
bound for the United States. They had heard of America—all
Irishmen had—they knew that America had no English landlords,
no rack-rented tenants, no hopeless men and ragged women and
hungry boys and girls. So, as they stood on the steerage deck
and looked through the wire netting at the fading white houses
and green fields of their native land, Owen and Bridget were
light of heart. Beyond the great turbulent oceans were contentment, equality and wealth; a home for themselves and a brilliant
future for the four children who, half in fear and half in wonder,
were looking out at the white gulls and the white-crested waves.

Two weeks later they landed in New York, were rushed
through Castle Garden and hurried to the railway train, where
they set out for Scranton, Pennsylvania.

Within a few days Owen had found a job in the mines and
had opened an account with a "company" store, and rented a
"company" house, with a kitchen and parlor below and two

little bedrooms above. Down under the kitchen floor was a hole in the ground which was called a cellar, and some rough wooden steps led down to the bottom from the side of the house. The hut was closed with boards which ran up and down, and the inside was without paper or even plaster, while here and there the cracks let in the daylight and, through the winter, the wind and sifting snow.

Owen and Bridget were a little disappointed at their home. In their little stone hut in their far-off island they had never dreamed that a house like this could be found in a land so rich and free. But they were starting life in a strange new world, and with strong hopes and brave hearts they set to work to make the best of what they had, never doubting but what the looked-for mansion would soon be theirs.

Owen went to work in the coal mines—down five hundred feet beneath the ground. Every morning he stepped on board a car, holding his dinner pail in one hand while he grasped the iron rail in his other hand, and held his breath until it dropped him to the bottom; and then at night he went back to the foot of the pit and boarded the car to be taken again to the top of the earth.

But this story is about Johnny, so we have no time to tell more of Owen, except that one day a great piece of rock broke off from the roof of the chamber where he worked and fell squarely upon him, crushing him to death.

The miners took him to the top of the shaft and back to the little hut, and consoled the helpless widow and children the best they could, and then followed him to the grave. The story of his hopes and struggles was told.

Johnny was almost eleven when they laid his father in the little consecrated ground and put the white wooden cross above his head. He was at school the day the rock came down, and had done so well that he was already in the third reader and had reached division in the arithmetic.

Johnny's older brother was already tending a door in the mine, and his sisters were in school with him. Luckily, some years before, a wise, good man, seeing how scant was the miner's income, had built a lace mill so that his girls could earn something to help the family along. So one night when the older sister left the school she carefully packed up her books and slate and took them home, and the next day went to the mill.

Bridget planned and saved the best she could. She had great hopes for little Johnny. He would surely be a scholar and make famous the McCaffery name. But all her hopes and struggles went for naught. Owen's funeral had left them hopelessly in debt, and the earnings of the boy and girl could not keep the family alive. There was really nothing left to do but send Johnny to the breaker. The law had humanely said that a child should be spared from the mine until he was twelve years old, but Bridget soon saw that this law was no protection against poverty and want; so she went to a justice of the peace and swore that Johnny's age was twelve, and sent him to the breaker. She somehow did not think much about this oath. In fact, she almost felt that Johnny was twelve years old. She knew of other boys of the same age who were at work.

Well, Johnny went to the breaker. He was halfway pleased to be released from school. If there is any place for a boy more cruel and hopeless than the breaker it is the ordinary public school.

Johnny lived about half a mile from the breaker where he went to work. Over and over again he had seen the huge rough black building standing up against the sky, and just beyond, the great pile of refuse which they called "culm" that loomed up higher still; especially at night, they rose up somber and black like the mountains just behind. The front of the building was a hundred feet high. It sloped slowly and evenly down to about twenty-five feet in height at the rear. Its great sides were dotted with windows, little gray spots in the vast surface of black weatherbeaten boards. Johnny had never seen a cathedral, but from the stories his teacher told at school he thought this building was about the size of one of those medieval temples—but it was a temple built not to God but to mammon.

Along the side of the great building ran the zigzag stairs, and in the early morning light, sometimes before the gloom had been fairly driven away, little boys tugged up the hundred steps to the breaker's top. Here the cars of coal were raised in an elevator and then dumped into a chute; the coal went sliding and scattering down through a myriad of sieves and chutes and turning wheels and the jaws of the great iron rolls which crushed the large lumps into little blocks, on, down, down, down from the place where it started a hundred feet above, until it landed in the huge iron pocket at the back of the breaker, twenty feet from the ground and just above the railroad track, ready for a gate to be opened to be let into the waiting car.

All the way down these long slanting chutes the lumps of coal tumbled and slid and fell. The clatter and shuffle of the endless rushing black stone over the sheet-iron lining of the long trough drowned even the sound of the whirling machinery and the crunching of the mighty iron teeth as they ground the large blocks into little bits, while above all an overhanging black cloud of dust from the sliding coal covered the black building and the black young children with an everlasting pall.

Over the top of the slanting chutes was nailed a row of little planks like wide steps upon a mighty ladder. Johnny was told to sit upon one of these little planks and put a foot on each side of the chute, and then as the lumps of coal ran swiftly down between his legs to snatch at the pieces of slate as fast as his hands and arms could move, and throw them into another pitching trough at his side. From the top of the great breaker down almost to the bottom sat this stairway of little boys, each grabbing at a chunk of slate as the coal rushed madly by, until it passed the last boy and tumbled clean and free from slate into the iron pockets above the tracks.

It took Johnny but a little time to become a breaker boy. He only had to learn the difference between slate and coal, and he had known this from a child. True, it took some skill to snatch the stone from the madly rushing black flood covered with its dense black cloud of dust; but little eyes are sharp and little fingers are nimble, and it was really remarkable to see how this long line of little hands would unerringly grasp the slate and let the coal pass by. The rich man who owned the breaker, whose name was Fox, used sometimes to stand and watch these little hands, lost in admiration of their dexterity and skill—their rapid movements and machine-like precision seemed to him the beauty and rhythm of a poem.

Mr. Fox had a daughter whom he dearly loved. He fancied that she had musical talent, and he got her the most skillful teacher that money could procure. Sometimes he stood by the piano and watched the girl take lessons in finger development, and he marvelled at her dexterity and skill; but when he paused for a few moments beside the great long chutes and saw the black diamonds rushing down into his great iron pockets, and watched the little deft hands of the breaker boys, he could not help thinking that the piano was not the only place to develop finger movement. Still, that was about all he thought. Mr. Fox was not a bad man. He was really good. He loved his daughter, and he intended to send her to Paris and Vienna to complete her studies when she was old enough. Really, every lump of coal that rolled down the chutes proved how fondly he loved the girl.

In a few weeks Johnny was a full-fledged breaker boy. His mother woke him at six in the morning. He put on his oldest clothes, ate his breakfast and went to the breaker. Morning after morning he climbed the long flight of stairs to the top of the breaker. Morning after morning he went down the ladder until he found his little flat seat, nailed across the chute. Then he sat down on the rough board, placed one foot on each side of the trough and waited for the flood of coal to come rattling down. In front of him and behind him and at the side of him were other little boys covered with the same black pall that ever hung above his head. No one spoke or looked up in the gloom. They simply picked, picked, picked, while the black flood moved down. The constant stooping made his back very lame and sore. And often in the night his mother was awakened with his crying and left her bed to rub his little back.

Then, too, in the winter when the frost was in the air and

on the black lumps his hands grew cold and numb, and he felt that he picked the coal with wooden prongs instead of flesh and blood. The nails of his fingers were worn; often he bound them with rags to protect them from the cold, or to save some bleeding wound made by the quickly rushing coal. His face was always as black as the coal that tumbled down the chute, and the dust filled his nose and lungs, and the flakes and splinters sometimes flew into his eyes, but still he worked away. Of course, he did not know why he worked. There was no more reason why he sat on the chute day after day than why Mr. Fox's daughter took "finger practice" on the piano in her luxurious home.

Not much happened to Johnny while he sat upon the hard, rough board. Not much can happen to a boy of this sort; and if it did, why should it matter? One day his little companion who always sat beside him leaned too far over as he picked the slate. He lost his balance and fell into the trough where the lumps of coal ran down. He plunged madly along with the rushing flood into the iron teeth of the remorseless breaker. Johnny shouted, but no one heard him in the din. Then he ran up the ladder and gave the signal to stop the great engine below, but of course it was too late. It took a long while to stop the mighty machine, and then it was almost an hour before the boy could be put together into one pile. Several days thereafter a man in a little town in Massachusetts thought that he saw blood on some lumps of coal that he was pouring into the top of his fine nickel-plated stove —but still there is blood on all our coal—and for that matter on almost everything we use, but a man is a fool if he looks for other people's blood.

It will not do to imagine that Johnny had no fun. He learned to chew plug tobacco and often went to the saloon at night. Of course he was pretty young for this—still, a boy who is old enough to go to a breaker is old enough to go to a saloon. When one is old enough to do manly work he is old enough to have manly sport. He used to go home at night so black that his closest friends could not have told his name. Then he washed himself in a tub

Clarence Darrow

of water in the parlor, changed all his clothes, got his supper and went out with the rest of the boys to play. There were the ordinary games for boys; there were cats to stone; there was a great cave where a house had gone down into an old worked-out mine and where the boys gathered at night and built a fire from old rubbish. One boy who had gone as far as the fourth grade read to the rest, wonderful stories from the nickel novels that they managed somehow to get. Then there was the night school kept up for miners' boys and girls—of course they could not be expected to study much after the day's work at the mill. Sometimes Johnny went to the night school, but he often fell asleep when he tried to study, and he never got past the third reader after all.

So Johnny went on until his fourteenth year. There was really nothing to tell after that time, and very little before it. In fact, it is rather absurd to write a story about a breaker boy. There must be some dramatic situation to make a story, and there is nothing dramatic in a life of endless toil. Strange as it may seem, Johnny never had an unknown uncle who died and left him a fortune. Mr. Fox never looked down at his swiftly moving fingers and took a fancy to him and invited him to his home and married him to his daughter. In fact, Mr. Fox never even saw him in the dust and gloom.

Almost all his life must be skipped because it is so dull. In writing biography you cannot dwell long on the parts that are very dull, and you must entirely omit the parts that are very interesting—and so biography is not biography after all. Anyhow, Johnny left the breaker when he was fourteen and was promoted to the place of door-keeper in the mine.

Somehow I forgot to state that all of this was forty years ago.

Forty years makes a great change in anyone who lives upon the earth—but it makes a greater change in the miner than in most other men. Fifty-four is not very old, so at least most of us think who cling tenaciously to the forties, and still more those who watch anxiously while the fifties are checked off. But at fifty-four the man who has money and can have leisure still feels that he is young. He can eat and drink; he can laugh and dance and play; he can marry and travel and write; in fact, can still chase all the phantasies and bubbles that make us forget the waiting open grave.

Forty years entirely transformed Johnny. Even his name was changed: he was now John; generally Uncle John. He had been a door boy, a driver, a helper, a miner, and he had now come up out of the earth to spend his last few years above the ground. His face was scarred and one ear was missing. This came not from war, but from powder all the same. A belated fuse exploded when he thought it had gone out. But still he counted this as luck, for his life was saved. One arm was crippled from a fallen rock and his right hip was never free from pain, but this was only the rheumatism that he caught while working in the ground. Except for the asthma he could still have stayed a number of years inside the earth before the last time that he should be lowered, to come up no more. But his old valves were growing more and more rusty every year. He wheezed instead of breathing, and he could walk but a very little way and could stand upon his feet only a few minutes at a time. His strength was almost gone. Some doctors would have advised rest and travel and a higher altitude, but his did not. In fact, he had no doctor. Everyone in the mine knew all about asthma, the black shadow that hangs ever above a miner's life.

John did not live in the same house where his father first placed him when he came from Ireland so long ago, but he lived very near the spot, still in a "company" house. The miners, and the mules, and machinery, had changed from time to time, but the breaker, the black culm pile, and the "company" houses still remained.

In forty years John had buried his mother, had married, raised a family, and traveled back and forth along the short path from his hut to the open mouth of the mine day after day; and this was all. As the years passed his one ambition had been to go back to Ireland, even for a short time, as his father's had been to come to the United States, but this ambition he had buried in the mines long years ago. He had left the valley once in forty years. He had gone to Philadelphia to the Centennial, and his ticket had cost him $5.40. This was a quarter of a century ago, but he remembered the exact money that he gave in exchange for the little pasteboard at the station window.

John really had earned the right to rest, but then, he and his family must live—at least he thought they must, and so they must, else the coal could never be dug up. The mine boss was really not unkind, so when John told him that he could not go down the shaft again, he promised him an easier job. The boss took him to the breaker, up the long flight of stairs, down the ladder of little boards nailed across the chute, and sat him down on the old board that he had left forty years ago.

John was not a poet or a dreamer. In fact, he never had a great deal of imagination, and what he had was buried long ago in the deep, black mine. He did not seem to think of the strange fate that sat him down on the narrow board after the circle of his life was done. He thought no more about it than do the rest of us of the everlasting turning of the great wheel to which all of us are strapped.

This is about all of John's story. It is really up to date. The other morning he walked up the slope to the great black mill. As he went up the hill his wheezing could be heard a hundred feet away. Every few rods he stopped to rest. In his right hand he carried the everlasting dinner pail. In his mouth was a black briar pipe. Thank God, he could smoke. He reached the breaker and started up the steps. At the first landing he stopped to rest. The boys rushed past, calling out, "Hello, Uncle John!" At the second landing he stopped again, and so on at each landing to the top. Then he took a good long wait until he finally got his breath before he started down the ladder to his seat. Slowly and deliberately he sat down upon the rough, hard board. Mechanically he took his tobacco pouch from his pocket, knocked the ashes from his pipe, filled it full of fresh tobacco, put it in his mouth, struck a match upon the sheet-iron lining of the chute, drew in his wheezy breath and commenced to smoke. Then he took his rheumatic leg in his hand, raised his foot until it rested on the right side of the long chute; then he raised his left foot to the other side, bent over and looked down at the black, iron trough, and waited for the coal to tumble down.

From "Easy Lessons In Law," Chicago Evening American, *1902.*

LITTLE
LOUIS
EPSTINE

*He did not know that the man who is born in poverty
and misfortune almost always grows very hard,
unless he keeps his poverty and misfortune.*

T HIS STORY IS ABOUT LITTLE
Louis Epstine, aged nine years. As might be guessed, Louis was
a Jew. But there are different kinds of Jews. There are Jews
who live on Grand Boulevard, and Jews who live on Maxwell
Street. For the most part, the Jews on Grand Boulevard own
wholesale clothing stores, and for the most part, the Jews on
Maxwell Street work in the stores. Louis Epstine lived on Maxwell Street.

When this tale began, he had only one hand. How he lost
the other is a matter quite outside of this story. It seems he was
run over by a beer wagon when he was a baby. His nurse—or,
no, it was an older sister, just past five—left him for a moment
alone on the street, and the wagon came along. But he had long
since forgotten all about this, if indeed he ever knew.

When Louis Epstine was nine years old, he went to a Jewish
charity school. This was kept up by the wealthy Jews, who
wished to do something for the poor. The fathers and mothers
and brothers and sisters of the little fellows worked for the men
who paid for the charity school. The patrons of the school never

asked why their employees had to use the charity school. People do not get rich by asking foolish questions of this sort.

Louis was not the only child in the family. His mother had five more besides him, and they all lived together in two large rooms back of a bakery. They had lived a whole year without moving. The rent was five dollars a month. Louis had plenty of playmates when he was a child, for Maxwell Street is full of houses and shops and flats, and even then there is not room for all the children. Some of them live in the basements. Over on Grand Boulevard there are great houses and big yards, and the people fancy it is a good place for children, but Maxwell Street is a much better place. Either poverty makes large families, or large families make poverty; at least there are a hundred children on Maxwell Street to every one on Grand Boulevard.

When Louis was nine years old, he helped the family by selling papers. He got up at five o'clock in the morning and went over to Newspaper Alley and bought his papers, and then stood on the corner until about eleven o'clock, and sold them; then he went to school in the afternoon. In this way he managed to make three or four dollars a week, sometimes even five. Once in a while a good man would come along and give him a nickel for a paper, and now and then some kind-hearted fellow would give him a paper which he had read, and then Louis would sell it again. He never took a nickel from a customer and then ran to a corner to get it changed and forgot to come back, although he knew some boys who did. Louis' mother had told him that this was not honest and that he would never get rich if he got money that way, although the boys who did it always seemed to get along as well as the others, sometimes better. But Louis' mother had taught him to be honest, and he had heard of a man who once sold papers and who always gave the change, and he was now a floorwalker in a department store. Louis had seen the man himself.

Louis' mother was a good woman, and she loved her child and he loved her, although he never said anything about it to anyone. She kept him and the other children as clean as she possibly could, and they almost always had something to eat. It is not necessary here to tell how she managed to get it; indeed, perhaps we could not tell. Really, the mother hardly knew herself, but if anyone doubts the fact, let them visit Maxwell Street. No one can tell how all the children are fed, but all the same they live. True, some of them do not grow to be very old, but there are always plenty of new ones to take their places if they die.

Well, Louis got along fairly well up to his ninth year. Nothing serious happened to him, barring the loss of his hand, and this never bothered him a great deal; in fact, he never thought anything about it. If boys had three hands, they would doubtless use them, but one is really quite enough. Louis could do almost anything that the other boys could do. Of course, he could run as fast, he could play all sorts of games, he could throw stones at cats, he never had any trouble to eat everything his mother gave him, and even his stub of a left arm was quite useful; he could hold papers under it and fix his hat on his head and use this stub in connection with his right hand to do almost anything he wished to do. He really felt quite lucky to think that only his hand was gone. He knew a boy who had lost his whole arm, and it was his right one, too.

One day, Louis' mother had been better to him than usual. She had bought him a nice warm cap that pulled down over his ears, and cost twenty-five cents at the department store. He had never seemed to know how good she was before, and then suddenly in his boyish mind he commenced to think how hard she worked, what poor clothes she had, how she never went to a circus or killed a rat in the gutter, or had any kind of fun; how she got up every morning and fixed his breakfast before he was out of bed; and how she washed the dishes after he had gone to sleep. He felt very tenderly toward her. It was really more pity than love. And then he remembered a string of great red glass beads that he had seen hanging in the department store on the corner where he sold his papers, and which were marked forty-eight cents, and he thought how happy his mother would be if he could buy this string of beads. He was only a boy, and did not know why the beads were not as valuable as a string of pearls, and perhaps they were. So in his foolish, boyish mind he conceived the thought of saving enough money to buy the beads and giving them to his mother at Christmas time. He kept out a penny or two each day and carefully hid it away until he had thirty-five cents that no one but himself knew anything about. Every morning when he took his stand before the great store he looked in through the polished window to see that the beads were still hanging in their place. As Christmas time drew on, he always looked with quaking heart, for he felt almost sure that some rich lady would buy them before he had saved enough.

The eighteenth of December came around. The day can easily be remembered, because it was so very cold. This morning was far the coldest of the winter, and all through the night Louis had kept waking up because there were not enough quilts on the bed. In the morning he was ready to get up and go after his papers before the usual time. His mother urged him not to go, telling him it was too cold, but Louis would not hear to this; it was only a week till Christmas time, and, besides, if it was cold he could sell more papers, for some of the other boys would stay away. So his mother got him a cup of coffee and a big slice of black bread with some yellow stockyard butter— not a bad breakfast for a poor child in the Ghetto. In fact, some-how he had been getting pretty well fed this fall and winter. He still had the memory of a nice turkey that the alderman had sent them on Thanksgiving, and there was a rumor in the ward that this year another one would be sent on Christmas. Some of the boys said that the alderman wanted to be assessor in the spring. Louis did not know what this was. He had never even seen an assessor, but then he had never seen a king.

Well, on this morning, after breakfast, Louis' mother bundled him up the best she could. His shoes were not very good. He had bought them "second hand," or whatever it is with shoes. And they were really not mates, but neither were his feet exactly, for that matter. One shoe had a hole on the side and was ripped down the back, but otherwise was pretty good. The other was worn through in one place on the bottom and his old stocking stuck out at the toe. Both of them were pretty large, but his mother had always told him that large shoes were the best and would wear the longest and would not make corns. As he understood it, only rich people wore shoes that were too small, and then mostly ladies. His pants had most likely been made from gray cloth, and certainly for someone else. These, too, were quite large, and had a number of patches scattered around in various places like sores. There was one on each leg about the knee and quite a large one in the back, and a few more besides. Then there were several places where there was no patch. The cloth did not seem to hold the thread very well, and anyhow Louis expected a new pair—or, rather, another pair—this winter. He could have had them long ago only for the beads. His pants were held up by a black strap, just like the swells that he had seen on State Street; well, not just like them, but still with a black strap.

His coat was really a prize affair. It was the best garment he had, except a woolen comforter which we have not yet reached. This coat had been given to him two years before by a charity society. It is not sure where it came from, but it must have been from some rich people on the North Side. There was not much wrong with the coat. The lining, of course, was torn, and when Louis put his hand into the sleeve he had to grasp hold of the wristband of his shirt, and hold it until his hand came out at the bottom of the sleeve, but this was partly because the buttonhole of the shirt was broken out. This was his right hand. He always put his left stub down through the arm very carefully, as a navigator would steer a ship through the shoals. He put this arm through first.

Then his mother wound a wool comforter around his neck. This was really a grand affair, or had been once. Now so many threads had been broken that it was getting pretty ragged, and it seemed to be about the same color all the way through, although it would be hard to tell what that was. His mother often told Louis how it looked years ago. It had been given to her by a rich uncle in Russia who was a peddler, but it really was very warm.

Then on top of his head, best of all, was the new cap, the cause of all his trouble. This he pulled clear down over his face so that only his eyes could be seen. There is no use to describe his shirt and things like that. Even poor boys ought to have some privacy, and besides you could only see his shirt in one place, down below his coat, and not then unless his back was turned. Of course, he had no overcoat. None of the boys had these, except some of the little dudes that he had seen their mothers leading into the department stores on State Street.

When Louis went to get his papers, he was in the habit of going down Van Buren Street and then along Franklin Street. The buildings on these streets were so big that they kept the wind away. When he would go down on the cold mornings, he would meet men and boys with great stacks of overcoats on their heads and in their arms. They were carrying them in and out of the great stores; none of the men and boys wore over-coats, except now and then one that was very old and poor; and then he would pass great rows of clothing stores—miles and miles of this kind of stores—and he looked in through the great square windows and saw endless heaps of overcoats, and other nice new coats and pants, too, piled up in great high heaps and long rows as far as he could see. There was not much else the whole line of Franklin Street, except these clothes, and now and then a great building full of shoes, and Louis used to think that there were more coats than all the boys on the whole West Side could wear, more than all the boys he ever heard of could possibly use; and then in his foolish way he wondered why these were locked up all the cold winter when none of the little boys had coats; but Louis was not a statesman or a political economist, he was only a poor little Jew boy, nine years old.

On this morning, Louis' mother opened the door and started him out. She did not kiss him good-by. This is no use when a mother has any other way of showing her love. She just opened the door and let him out. She told him to be sure and keep his coat buttoned up. He sang out, "Gee, ain't this cold!" And that was all that was said as he went away. He walked down the street to Jackson Boulevard, and then crossed to the south side. He always liked to cross on the Boulevard. The buildings were so grand, and the walk so smooth. He went on down to Franklin Street, and turned north past the great clothing stores. The coats and pants and vests seemed to be piled up higher than ever. He looked at them and said, "Gee, I wish I had one o' dem." But he never thought of going in and getting it; poor people never do. In this way he got down to Newspaper Alley, where the boys were trying hard to trade their pennies for papers. There were fewer there this morning than before. He got his bundle of papers, thrust them under his stub arm and started off. Besides the cold, there was a cutting wind, and as he came north it was all he could do to walk, but when he turned south with his papers it was easier, though the drifting snow bothered him quite a bit.

He darted along one or two alleys, and in one place walked through an arcade. These made him a little warmer than before. Finally, he got down to the department store and took his stand just in front of the great red beads and began to call off something that they had told him was in the papers, something about some grand affair, a charity ball, or an inaugural, or something of the sort. Anyhow, he didn't know what it was. On the corner he missed the man who usually sold lead pencils and the boy without any legs, who always sat with his cap in his hand and raked out the pennies as fast as the people put them in.

Louis did not stand there very long until he began to get cold, so he commenced walking up and down the block and calling his papers whenever anyone passed. There were not many people out on the street that morning and they all hurried pretty fast, most of them not stopping long enough to buy a paper. Along toward eight o'clock, his hand had begun to get very cold. He couldn't put it in his pocket and use the other one.

Little Louis Epstine

He was obliged to make all the change with this one, and could only use his stub to hold the papers. Two or three times he stepped into the outside doorway of the store for a minute, but he could not sell papers there, and then the last time the floor-walker drove him out. The floorwalker had once sold papers, but this was long ago. He was now a self-made man. Louis had not yet learned never to expect anything from a self-made man. He did not know that the man who is born in poverty and misfortune almost always grows very hard, unless he keeps his poverty and misfortune. Indeed, he is obliged to grow hard to get over his poverty and misfortune.

Two or three times in the morning Louis thought he would give it up and go home, but then there were the glass beads, and besides he had the papers and could not afford to get "stuck" with them on his hands; so he stayed at his post. It is possible he might have gone away anyhow, except that along about nine o'clock or half-past, his hand began to get warmer, and although his feet and body were pretty cold, he could move around and manage to stand this. So he stayed and sold out his papers and went back home about the usual time. Soon after he got into the house his hand commenced to feel queer—it was all prickly and numb, and seemed to burn. He told his mother, and she had him put it in cold water; still it ached so bad that she finally sent over to the corner for a doctor. He looked the hand over carefully, and then shook his head. The doctor finally said that the hand was badly frozen, and he did not know whether Louis could ever use it again or not. But he put some stuff on it and wound it up in a cloth and went away.

In a few hours he came back. The hand did not pain as much as before, but it felt numb and queer. The doctor took off the bandage and shook his head again. It was red and purple clear up to the wrist. The doctor told Louis and his mother that he must go to the hospital, and he was afraid they must cut off the hand, but they would ask the doctor at the hospital first. Louis and his mother had no time to cry—they had to start at once. They went in to the great big building. Louis thought it smelled pretty badly, although he was used to all kinds of smells in the Ghetto.

They found the big doctor, and he looked at Louis' hand and said it must be amputated at once. Louis did not know exactly what that was, but of course he made no objection and his mother made none. It had all come so suddenly that neither of them fully realized what it meant, and then poor people never do object to anything that the rich say must be done. The doctor told Louis that it would not hurt, and this was the main thing at the time. They took him into a great long bedroom, where there were dozens of little white cots all the same size, and most of them with a child lying on top. They told him that they would give him something which would put him to sleep, but that he would wake up all right, and it would be all over without his knowing it.

There is no need to tell about the operation. If anyone really has a taste for that sort of thing he can visit a hospital any day in the week. Most people stay away as long as they possibly can, and of course they would not like to read about it—for that matter, they do not like to see how poor people live.

Well, Louis went to sleep, and the next thing he knew he was lying in one of the little cots, and his mother, the doctor and a girl with a striped blue and white dress were standing by the bed. His hand was tied up in a cloth and was aching pretty bad. It took him some time to remember where he was, and then he asked them about his hand, why it was hurting so much. Then his mother told him all about it, although it was almost as hard for her as for Louis. But the little fellow was rather dazed at first, and did not seem to think much about his hand.

Then Louis lay still for quite a while. He was looking at the ceiling and the walls, and following the zigzag pattern of the paper up and down. Finally, he turned away from his mother, and pretty soon they heard a sob. The poor woman went around to the other side of the cot, and stroked Louis' face and hair gently, and asked him not to cry. She told him that he would be well again before long, and that she and his brothers and sisters would always be good to him and take care of him as long as he lived. Louis told her that he knew this, but it was so near Christmas and he couldn't get the rest of the money. She asked him what he meant, and then between his sobs he told her about the beads.

The Pilgrim, *1903.*

CHILDHOOD
SURROUNDINGS

*The difference between the child and the man lies chiefly
in the unlimited confidence and buoyancy of youth.*

T HE LIFE OF THE CHILD IS NOT
the life of the man, and the town of the child is not the town
of the man.

I can never see Farmington except through my boyhood's eyes,
and no doubt the town and its people were not at all the same
to the men and the women that they were to me. Every object
meant one thing to them and quite a different thing to our
childish minds. As I grew to boyhood, the mill-pond was only a
place where I could fish and skate and swim, and the great
turning wheel served only to divert my wondering eyes and
ears as it kept up its noisy rounds. The old mill furnished us
boys a place to hide and run and play our games. The whole
scheme of things was ours, and was utilized by a boy's varying
needs to help fill up his life.

To the kind old miller the condition of the water in the
pond was doubtless quite another thing, and every revolution of
the groaning wheel must have meant bread to him—not only
bread for the customers whose grain he ground, but sorely-needed
bread for the hungry mouths of those who had no thought or
care whence or how it came, but only unbounded faith that it
would always be ready to satisfy their needs.

It is only by imagination, through the hard experience life

has brought, that I know these familiar things had a different meaning to the old miller and to me. Yet even now I am not sure that they had for him a deeper or more vital sense. Perhaps the water for my swimming-hole was as important as the water for his bread. For after all, both were needed, in their several ways, to make more tolerable the ever-illusive game of life.

But I must describe Farmington and its people as they seemed to me—as in fact they were according to their utility in the small schemes of a little child.

The world seems to take for granted that every parent is a hero to his children, and that they look to the father and mother as to almost superhuman beings whose power they cannot understand, but can rely upon with implicit faith. Even the street-car signs tell this old tale, and advertise "pies like mother used to make." No doubt the infant looks with perfect confidence into the eyes of the mother who gave it birth, and in its tender years the child has the utmost trust in the wisdom and protection of the parent to whom it has always looked to satisfy its needs. But I cannot remember that in my youth either I, or any of my companions, had the feeling and regard for our parents that is commonly assumed. In fact, we believed that, as to wisdom and general ability to cope with the affairs of life, we were superior to them; and we early came to see their shortcomings rather than their strength. I cannot say that I looked upon my mother even as a cook exactly in the light of the street-car advertisements, but I distinctly recall that often when I visited the woodsheds of neighboring children and was kindly given a piece of pie or cake, I went back home and told my mother how much better this pie tasted than the kind she baked, and asked her why she did not make pies and cakes the way the neighbors did. To all these suggestions I ever got the same reply—if I did not like her cooking I could go elsewhere to board. Of course this put a stop to all discussion. I am quite certain that it is only after long years of absence, when we look back upon our childhood homes, the bread and pies are mixed with a tender sentiment that makes us imagine they were better than in fact they really were. I rather fancy that if our mother's cooking were set before us once again, we should need the strong primitive appetite of our youth to make it taste as our imagination tells us that it did.

As to my father, I am sure I never thought he was a man of extraordinary power. In fact, from the time I was a little child I often urged him to do things in a different way—especially as to his rules about my studies and my schooling. I never believed that he ran the mill in the best way; and I used to think that other men were stronger or richer, or kinder to their children, than my father was to us. It was only after years had passed, and I looked back through the hazy mist that hung about his ambitions and his life, that I could realize how great he really was. As a child, I had no doubt that any man could create conditions for himself; the copybooks had told me so, and the teachers had assured us in the most positive way that our success was with ourselves. It took years of care and toil to show me that life is stronger than man, that conditions control individuals. It is with this knowledge that I look back at the old miller, with his fatal love of books; that I see him as he surveys every position the world offers to her favored sons. He knows them all and understands them all, and he knows the conditions on which they have ever been bestowed; yet he could bury these ambitions one by one, and cover them so deep as almost to forget they had once been a portion of his life, and in full sight of the glories of the promised land could day by day live in the dust and hum of his ever-turning mill, and take from the farmers' grist the toll that filled the mouths of his little brood. To appreciate and understand the greatness of the simple life, one must know life; and this the child of whatever age can never understand.

After my father and mother—whom I did not appreciate, and who, I am bound to think, but half understand me—no other men or women came very near my life. My relations were with the boys and girls, especially the boys. The men and women were there only to board and clothe the children, and furnish them with a place to sleep at night. To be sure, we knew something of all the men and women in the town, but we saw them only through childish eyes. There was the blacksmith, who was very strong, and whom we liked and called "clever" because he sometimes helped us with our games. There was one old farmer in particular, who had a large orchard and a fierce dog, and who would let his apples rot on the ground rather than give us one to eat. We hated him and called him stingy and a miser. Perhaps he was not that sort of a man at all, and the dog may not have been so very fierce. No doubt someone had given them bad names, and the people preferred to believe evil of them instead of good.

Then there was the town drunkard, whom all of us knew. We liked him when he was sober, although we were told that he was very bad; but he always laughed and joked with us, and watched our games in a friendly way, but when we heard that he was drunk we were all afraid of him and ran away. Then there was another man who kept a little store, and we knew he was very rich; we had no idea how much he was really worth, but anyhow we knew he was rich. And so on, through all the neighborhood, we knew something of the men, and classified them by some one trait or supposed fact—just as the grown-up world always persists it has a right to do.

The women, too, we knew even better than the men, for it was the mothers who controlled the boys, and in almost every case it depended on them alone whether or not the boys might go and play. Still, we children only knew and cared about the grown-up people in a remote secondary way. Every home was full of boys, and by common affinity these boys were always together—at least, as many of them as could get away from home. As a rule, the goodness and desirability of a parent were in exact proportion to the ease with which the children could get away from home. I am afraid that in this child's world my good parents stood very low upon the list—much lower than I wished them to stand.

We children had our regular season's round of games and sports. There was no part of the year in which we could not play, and each season had its special charm. There might not have been much foundation for the custom, but somehow certain games always came at certain times. When the season was over the games were dropped unceremoniously and left for another year.

Of course the little creek and the great millpond and the river were sources of never-failing delight. I cannot remember when I learned to swim, but I learned it very young and very well; and it was lucky that I did, for I have been in deep water many times since then. The boys seemed to prefer water to land—that is, water like a pond or a stream. We did not care for the kitchen tub and the wash-basin. It was the constant aim of our parents and teachers to keep us out of the water for at least a portion of the time, and they laid down strict rules as to when and how often we should go swimming. But when boys are away from home they are apt to forget what teachers and parents say; and we always contrived to get more swimming than the rules prescribed. This would have been easier except for the fact that it generally took us so long to dry our hair, and our teachers and parents could often detect our swimming by simply feeling of our heads. I shall always remember that a boy was never supposed to be a complete swimmer until he could swim the "big bend." There was a bend in the river which was wide and deep, and a favorite swimming-place for the larger boys. I well remember the first time I swam across, and I have accomplished few feats that compared with this. All my life I had supposed that the big bend was very broad and deep, until I made a special examination of the place on my last visit, a little time ago, and really it was so changed that I could almost wade across. Still, at that very time there were little boys in the stream just getting ready to perform the same feat that I had accomplished long ago.

The same water that served us in summertime delighted us equally in the winter months. We learned to skate as early as we learned to swim. Our skates were not the fancy kind that are used today, but were made of steel and wood, and were fastened to our boots with straps. Few boys could skate long without the straps coming loose; but then, a few difficulties more or less have little terror for a boy. It would be hard to make a town better fitted for boys than Farmington; even the high hills were made for coasting in the wintertime. In fact, nothing was lacking to us except that our parents and teachers were not so kind and considerate as they should have been.

In the summertime we often climbed to the top of the hills and looked down the valley to see the river winding off on its everlasting course. Then we would fancy that we were mountaineers and explorers, and would pick our way along the hills with the beautiful valley far beneath. I do not know why we climbed the hills in the summertime. It could not have been for the scenery, which was really fine, for boys care little for this sort of thing. The love of nature comes with maturing years and is one of the few compensations for growing old. More and more as the years go by we love the sun and the green earth, the silent mountains and the ever-moving sea. It seems as if slowly and all unawares our Mother Nature prepares and ripens us to be taken back to her all-embracing breast.

But boys like hills and animals and trees, not so much because they are part of nature as for the life and activity they bring. So we climbed the hills and the trees, and went far down the winding stream for no purpose except to go, and when we reached the point for which we started out we turned around and came back home. Still, since I have grown to man's estate I do the self-same thing. I make my plans to go to a foreign port, and with great trouble and expense travel halfway round the earth, and then, not content with the new places I have found, and longing for the old ones once again, I turn back and journey home.

Since the days when we children followed the crests of the hills along the valley, this lovely scene has fallen under the notice of a business man. He has built a hotel on the top of the highest hill, overlooking the valleys and the little town, and in the summertime its wide verandas are filled day after day with women, young and old, who sit and swing in hammocks, and read Richard Harding Davis and Winston Churchill, and watch for the mail and wait for the dinner-bell to ring.

With what never-ending schemes our youth was filled, and in what quick succession each followed on the others' heels! Our most cherished plans fell far short of what we hoped and dreamed. Somehow everything in the world conspired to defeat our ends, and most of all, our own childish nature, which jumped from fad to fancy in such quick succession that we could never do more than just begin. Even when we carried our plans almost to completion, their result was always far short of the thought our minds conceived.

With what infinite pains and unbounded hopes we prepared to go nutting in the woods! How many bags and sacks we took, and how surely these came back almost empty with the boys who started out with such high hopes as the sun rose up! How often did we prepare the night before to go blackberrying in the choicest spots, but after a long day of bruises and wasp-bites and scratches, come back with almost empty pails! Still, our failures in no way dampened the ardor of any new scheme we formed.

We could run and jump and throw stones with the greatest ease; but when we put any of our efforts to the test, we never ran so fast or jumped so high or threw a stone so far as we thought and said we could—and yet our failures had no effect in teaching us moderation in any other scheme. I well remember one ambitious lad who started out to make a cart. He planned and worked faithfully, until the wonderful structure took on the semblance of a cart. Then his interest began to flag, and the work went on more slowly than before. For days and weeks we used to come to his shop and ask, "Will, when are you going to finish your cart?" We asked this so often that finally it became a standing joke, and the cart was given up in shame and chagrin.

When the snow was soft and damp, we often planned to make a giant snow-man or an enormous fort. We laid out our work on a grand scale, and started in with great industry and energy to accomplish it. But long before it was finished, the rain came down or the sun shone so hot that our work and schemes melted away before our eyes.

So, too, the grown-up children build and build, and never

complete what they begin. When the last day comes, it finds us all busy with unfinished schemes—that is, all who ever try to build. But this is doubtless better than not to try at all.

The difference between the child and the man lies chiefly in the unlimited confidence and buoyancy of youth. The past failure is wholly forgotten in the new idea. As we grow older, more and more do we remember how our plans fell short; more and more do we realize that no hope reaches full fruition and no dream is ever quite fulfilled. Age and life make us doubtful about new schemes, until at last we no longer even try.

Well, our youth brought its mistakes and its failures, its errors of judgment and its dreams so ·hopeless to achieve. But still it carried with it ambition and life, a boundless hope, and an energy which only time and years could quench. So, after all, perhaps childhood is the reality, and in maturity we simply doze and dream.

From Farmington, *1904.*

Clarence Darrow

THIS IS WHAT
I DON'T LIKE
ABOUT THE
NEWSPAPERS

*We are always crucifying some people and adopting
their theories later, after it is too late to do them any good.*

Gentlemen, THIS IS THE first time I have heard the subject of this talk. As I haven't been able to specially prepare, it may be all right. I asked one of the men here what they wanted me to do this afternoon, and he said, "They want you to abuse the newspapers." I can't do it adequately. So perhaps I had better not undertake it at all. I don't propose to tell you how good you are, what a great institution this is, or anything like that. I will tell you frankly, so you can roast me the next day, some of the things that I don't approve of. But I don't know just how you can change them, even if you want to, which you probably do not.

In the first place, a newspaper today is purely a commercial enterprise. There was a time in the history of this country, long ago, when people had ideas—even newspapers—and when they were interested in something, or things. But those days are gone. There are very few of them now, and nobody knows about those, because they haven't much of a circulation. You cannot get a circulation by publishing ideals, or by stating cold matters of fact. That doesn't make newspaper circulation.

The newspapers do not own themselves. Of course, if they did, they might be worse than they are. But anyhow, they do not own themselves. They have little to do with themselves. When you can take five or ten cents worth of white paper and spoil it by news (if it is) and advertising (which it surely is) and sell it for two or three cents, somebody has to pay for it. I am not telling you anything new—but that is one of the fundamental troubles with the newspaper business.

The newspapers aren't the only sinners in this respect. This is an age in which people think of nothing but money, and the newspapers are just like all the rest. A newspaper today costs so much money and sells so cheaply that the advertisers are the first thing they are bound to look for. In supporting your newspaper, it isn't a question of how many readers you can get, except incidentally, but what kind of advertising you can get. Readers are all right incidentally, because if you didn't have readers, they couldn't get swindled on the advertising the next day and therefore you couldn't get higher advertising rates.

I don't know how it is possible to run a newspaper for any idealistic purpose under the present scheme of things. If I owned one, I would go broke quickly or else I would be obliged to conform. The thing is, I don't think anybody has much to do with it himself. I think our work is cut out for us, and it is something that I see no remedy for at this time, until this fever of money-getting dies, if it ever does die. It doesn't look very hopeful now.

It is absolutely certain that a newspaper must have its eye first of all to advertising, and it can't offend the advertisers, no matter how much they should be offended. For instance, the advertisers get the cleverest ad writers there are to help pick people's pockets, to write up alluring and false statements to induce some person to buy something that he doesn't need and can't afford, and the newspapers have to publish them. They might not publish them if they are too raw, and they certainly wouldn't publish them if the advertisers are petty larceny fellows, but when it comes to big fellows who have the money and sell their goods, of course they must publish them, and newspapers are really published for the purpose of sending out advertising, as you know better than I do. There is where the proceeds come from.

At various times, I have been interested in certain enterprises. If I can get interested in something respectable enough (which I seldom can), something which will command the respect of an advertiser, that is—if I do something wrong, or promote something wrong, I always get the advertisers to go to the newspapers and get publicity. Nobody else can get it, that is, pleasant publicity. You can get unpleasant publicity without any help, but the kind you want you really can't get except through these chosen channels. You know that. I know it. Everybody knows it. It isn't a secret any more.

People say they do not believe the newspapers, but they all do believe them. That is the trouble. You know that also. I have heard men over and over talk about how unreliable they are in their statements about everything, and still we get all our information from them. Preachers pray from them. If they get up a crusade of virtue in a town, why, of course, all the clergymen take their statements to be absolutely true. If they get up stories about the crime wave—which is always popular, except that it sometimes gets a little overworn—everybody believes them and pays no attention to facts or figures, or statements, or logic, or reason. They just get angry all at once.

First of all, then, I don't see how anything like rendering a public service can be done by the newspapers under the present way of living, and that doesn't apply to the newspapers alone. Nobody ever dreamed of starting a newspaper, especially in a big town, a daily newspaper, except to get advertising. The news is a minor thing. Of course it has to be such news, written in such a way, that people will read it and accidentally read the advertising which is scattered all over the place. That is true not only of the newspapers but the magazines as well. They start a story on Page 1 and then put down in a footnote, "Turn to Page 972." In between is advertising, or the beginning of another story, and so on.

The art that is employed in these advertisements is crazy work.

Nobody likes to see his own stuff spread out that way, but perhaps it catches people for the big stores. Probably it does help the chewing gum business, and all that sort of thing—but it shows how absolutely commercialized the whole business is. And it must be so long as newspapers are made as they are. A man who would publish a paper not devoted to advertising would be obliged to charge a very high rate for it, and of course that paper wouldn't reach the common people, and the common people are the victims all over the world. They are the ones who are lured by these ads and things that are carried in the newspapers. Of course, once in a while the newspapers get good, and when they get good they won't publish any advertisements of patent medicines, but it never goes any further than that. Their goodness doesn't put them in an attitude so they won't help swindle the public by these alluring ads that are written for the purpose of swindling.

I am not blaming you seriously. You all have the modern itch of money. Of course, the owners haven't anything to say about it, and least of all have the men who make up the papers and run them anything to say about it. They know just what is wanted.

They always carry a list, as I have been informed by newspaper men, of what they call "sacred white cows," whom you mustn't say anything about. It "kills" the Catholic Church and "kills" all the denominations, even down to the Christian Scientists, as some of them read the newspapers, and they must be left alone. What it means, in the end, is that you mustn't say anything against any organization or body of people who are numerous. Of course, I can't get into that list. I have never done anything to get me in. I never was on that list and never expect to be on it, and never tried to get on it. I never behaved myself badly enough to get on it. But there is that list, and they are always safe, no matter what happens.

Another thing about it—I couldn't begin to tell everything in the whole afternoon, but I am not going to take the whole afternoon—a newspaper must come out immediately. It has to be done "on the dot." A man will come and interview you and say, "I must get this quickly because our deadline is 2:15." (Whether

A.M. or P.M. doesn't make any difference.) Everything is done with haste. It can't be done with deliberation. If some newspaper wanted to do it with deliberation, there would be headlines on some other newspaper down the street before they ever got started, and it is utterly out of the question to get good results in great haste. Necessarily, therefore, even where it isn't desired, papers are filled with erroneous statements, and very unsatisfactory ones, but the intelligent public make up their minds from them—the very intelligent, the moronistic element, which is the element, after all, to be served, because there are more of them.

Of course, the newspapers are wise on every question. I have been more or less interested in crime, as you know. I am not employed by any syndicate, but I am interested in the subject as the manifestation of human beings, and I am interested in the causes that conduce to it. Newspapers aren't. I am interested in the question of how it can be prevented. They know only one thing: get the public angry so they will kill somebody or increase the term of servitude. That resulted the other day in the state of Michigan in sending a man to the penitentiary for life for having a pint of whiskey in his possession. That was a terrible crime. But this fellow had been convicted once before on the ground of carrying whiskey, and another time on some other count, and this happened to be the fourth time. So he finds himself in prison for life for having a pint of whiskey in his possession.

Some of the newspapers did everything they could to bring about prohibition, because it was good news, I suppose, and as soon as they got it they began doing everything they could to knock it and prevent its operation. They don't know how to get rid of it exactly now. That is good news, anyhow. Of course, I have known many newspaper people who really were not pro-hibitionists. In fact, I have seldom found a city editor who was. But it makes good reading for certain kinds of people, and there you are.

Then they have talk about the crime question. They have gotten some statistics, which aren't true, like all statistics, about the number of arrests and the number of times justice has been cheated—and whenever a fellow gets in trouble and he doesn't get into the penitentiary justice has been cheated. Of course, nobody knows the meaning of justice, but cheating justice means getting somebody acquitted, or not hanged. Of course, they are crazy about hangings. The crueller it is, the better, because the public must have a kick, especially since prohibition. Somebody getting killed is a very important thing, especially if he is killed by the state.

When something happens, if it is at all sensational, the reporters are sent out on the job to get every kind of statement, relevant or irrelevant, and keep it up, to never stop until everybody's opinion is made up—and you know how hard it is to change anybody's opinion when it is made up. It can't be changed if it is made up. It is pretty easy to make up the opinion of a newspaper's reading public. They saw it in the paper, therefore, and therefore. . . . Then when they talk about it they say, "Well, one trouble is they don't get criminals killed quickly enough. There are too many delays in the courts."

I suppose most of you people have put out that stuff, too, about there being too many delays in the court. Well, now, what are the facts about it? When there is a serious crime committed that is important enough to interest the state's attorney, everything else is sidetracked in court, and the wheels are greased to get an early trial, because the thing to do is to strike while the iron is hot, that is, while everybody has an opinion that will cause the jury to bring in a verdict of guilty, and the prisoner can get a severe penalty.

You can't talk about justice and quick justice at the same time.

They get an earlier trial in England, but there is no newspaper in England that ever says a word about the case at the time of the arrest; there isn't a stickful about it, and then there is no reflection on anybody. A man can go into court the day after and he can get a trial that is fair, so far as the opinions of the jurors are concerned.

Most young people act from suggestion. All education is suggestion. I have seen the same type of crimes repeated over and over again in the city of Chicago.

I remember the carbarn murders which occurred several years ago, which were rather strange and fantastic. They hanged the fellows. Very soon after another gang of boys repeated it in substance, just the same as it has been done over and over again.

Take, for instance, the case in Michigan, where a man was sent to the penitentiary for copying the crime of the youth in Los Angeles. It had been spread over the papers with all the horrible details, and here was a moronistic man who went out and killed a young girl, and within forty-eight hours of the time he was arrested he was in the penitentiary with a life sentence. The only complaint the people had about it was that they couldn't hang him, because Michigan has no hanging law.

There isn't anybody who thinks who doesn't know the power of suggestion. It reaches the old and the young, but especially the young. We forbid certain pictures being shown on the screen on account of the power of suggestion, but that doesn't prevent the printing in the newspapers of all the horrible details of these crimes, and pointing out the way in which they were committed, thus stimulating many uneducated minds and untrained boys to do the same thing.

That is the truth, as everybody knows. I am not here to advertise any newspaper, but I wish more of them would follow the policy of the *Christian Science Monitor*. I think it is absolutely right. I don't agree with them on their religious policies. I don't agree with them on their attitude on the "dry" question—I don't mean the paper is so dry, but that is what they advocate. I don't agree with them on a whole lot of things, but I do think that they are absolutely sound upon that question, in that they do not play on the passions and the feelings of men, which I think is one of the worst things that has befallen the newspaper business in the last twenty or twenty-five years.

There are not only certain people on the sacred list, but there are certain people on some other list. I am not personally complaining, because I have gotten by with murder, and I always think when they roast me that they could have done more, which they could, if they started out deliberately to do so. But if they happen to run on to something through some obscure policeman, or some obscure minister, whether it is true or not true, they publish it—about anybody that they want to. They spread the story, and it doesn't make any difference how many denials there are, you never can catch up with it. The best policy, I have found, is to keep still about it, let it run its course, and that isn't very good either. Once in a while an enthusiastic friend says to me, "All right, you have done a good deal while you were alive. You are honest, independent, and courageous, and history will take care of you," but that won't do me any good. History is not what you want. History is what you make every day. So far as I get into anything after I am dead, my story will be what the newspapers and the public have already made it, true in some cases, untrue in others.

Another thing that "gets" you is the imputations as to the reasons one does certain things. If he is a lawyer, he did it for a big fee, utterly regardless of the fact that he takes more cases for which he gets nothing than cases for which he gets paid. They always read into whatever is done their own motives about it and the motives that the public wants.

Newspapers, as I have said, are in business to sell their advertising. They have got to be good, and being good means to conform to existing things, because there have always been these people who live on the outer edges, decrying the injustices of the day. They may be wrong, too. But we are always crucifying some people and adopting their theories later after it is too late to do them any good. Then we settle down to those theories, until something new comes along.

Newspapers are not alone in this. We are all natural joiners. I never joined anything except the Elks. I joined the Elks because in the early days it was about the only place where you could get a drink in a small town. But I no sooner joined them than they passed the prohibition law, and I haven't been back since. There is no reason for going back.

But the thing that is good is the thing that is done. When I was a boy it used to be all right to eat with your knife. I got along all right doing it. I never cut myself, or anything, but along came a fellow who told me I had to eat with my fork, that it is wrong to eat with your knife, because it isn't being done, that is all. And our whole code of morals and of right and wrong is made up of customs and habits of the time.

So the person who wants to be right and respectable has to do what other people do, say what they say, and think what they think, if anything. And that prevents any change; it prevents what we call progress. Whether there is any such thing in the world, I haven't time to discuss this morning. It is conforming to the mores, the habits. The things that are right are the Rotary Clubs and the Kiwanis Clubs, and the Elks, and the Lions, and the Owls, and all the rest of the animals, and the Ku Klux Klan, the Knights of Columbus, the Masons—everything that is organized —the Monday Morning Ministerial Association. Everything that is supposed to represent people is right. That is good citizenship.

Of course, it is foolish, idle perhaps, to point out where it could be bettered, or to criticize. Today it is one hundred per cent Americanism, with the D.A.R.s and things like that, whose ancestors were rebels—but they are not. They would be crucifying their own ancestors, if their ancestors were living now and did now as they did then. But that doesn't make any difference. It is fashionable now. It wasn't fashionable then. One hundred per cent Americanism is the fashion today.

I never was more than ninety-eight per cent, and hardly that. I have traveled some. I have read some. I have been over the world. I prefer to live in this country to any other country in the world. In the first place, I can understand what people are talking about. I might many times like it better if I couldn't. But, after all, I want to. There are many things in England that I think are superior to the things we have. There are many attitudes of life in England that I admire tremendously. I think there is more tolerance there. And there are many things on the Continent that I admire. For instance wine and beer.

Of course, there are all grades of newspapers—you will all admit that. I won't specify, I don't dare here, but there are all grades of papers, and the tendency for one is to be just as bad as the other, just as quick in their judgments, just as stern in their demands, just as unthinking and unreasoning.

Take the city of Chicago, where I live when I am at home. We have a pretty bad name, haven't we? People ask me about it in Europe. They say, "What kind of savages live in Chicago?" Of course, they ask you about it in New York. They ask you about it everywhere. They ask, "How do you account for all your crimes?"

Well, I account for them, first of all, by saying it isn't true. Not long ago I very carefully and painstakingly wrote up a magazine article, published in *Harper's Monthly*, analyzing and criticizing the figures of the Crime Commission upon which the newspapers base their statistics of crime, and I found out that they reported six times as many murders as ever occurred in Chicago.

I think I have told you about more things than you will correct, a good many more, but they are all things that you yourselves know are true. I haven't much complaint, personally. I haven't conformed. I have never found any organization which was intelligent enough to conform to. Of course, if I got one up, that would be all right, but I couldn't find anybody to join it. What am I going to do standing out all alone, a safe target for everybody?

It is this idea of conforming that gets us. When you ask most people what they mean by "morals," they will say, "We know what it means." Everybody knows what it means. Do they? They don't know anything about it. Morals means habits, customs, folk play. A thing is right today and wrong tomorrow. What is wrong today may be right tomorrow. All the man means is that he is taking the standards of his time, that is what morals have always meant.

In spite of that there have always been a few fellows, crazy of course, who couldn't conform and wouldn't. After awhile, now and then, the world comes to their viewpoint, and they create more hard and fast rules, so you aren't much better off than you were before, but always on the outskirts there are these fellows who won't conform and can't conform but who, after all, carry the banner of civilization, if there is any such thing as a banner of civilization. I don't know whether there is or not.

I got quite excited over the last war, it so happened. I can't see that the world is any safer for democracy today as a result of it than it was before. It probably is not nearly as safe. Newspapers and orators busied themselves talking about German atrocities. One well-known preacher exhibited moving pictures of Germans cutting off the hands of Belgian children. It made a profound impression. Of course, they must have cut off the hands of those Belgian children in the presence of a camera. Otherwise, they couldn't have had those pictures.

I don't know that there is anything to do about it. I suppose we expect too much of human beings. We don't know what they are. A human being is nothing but an organism that acts and reacts according to the stimuli applied. You can't make anything but a human being out of him. Many, many people have the idea that the mind can control the body. It can't. In fact, the mind is the body. It consists of the reactions of the whole organism, and when a man is angry, he will fight.

Let me say just one word more about newspapers. I want to close with something that is a little bit different. There are some things you can say in favor of the newspaper men. First, they are clever. I don't mean you; I mean the others. The way to get an education is to be a reporter. They know what is going on. They are sophisticated. They are a little too sophisticated. They always think. What the devil is he doing it for? If he is rescuing somebody that is drowning, he must be going to run for office. If he is founding an orphan asylum, what is he doing it for? Has he got a lot of orphans around the country? There must be something back of it. Almost none of them ever think that he might have a sincere motive of an idealistic kind.

Well, of course, if I was to make any criticism on most of the fellows individually, I would say they are too sophisticated.

Of course, they have a right to be. Everybody is trying to work them. Everybody is lying to them. Everybody is seeing what he can get out of them, and they know it pretty well, and they sometimes, many of them, think that there isn't anybody on the square. I think about the only way to fool a newspaper man is to tell him the absolute truth. He is never looking for that, and if you can't tell him the truth don't tell him anything. Then you have a chance.

Newspaper men are very intelligent. Many, many of them see things way beyond the paper. Many of them are humane and kindly. I have never had any more loyal friends than some of the newspaper men.

The newspaper business is a good business for a man who has the stuff in him. It is full of temptations to tell things that are not true, to write sensational stories for the public to read, but every once in a while you will find one with noble purpose and high ideals. They are there, doing the best they can, and caught like everybody else; the great machine is sometimes too strong for them.

I have never been given to complaining about myself. I have intelligence enough to know how to get along and conform, but I can't do it. I wasn't made that way. I have always enjoyed the opportunity of expressing my opinions pretty nearly the way I hold them, and there have always been men of that kind, and they have all had the same luck or lack of luck. Perhaps I have gotten through easier than most of them, but one can't keep his pie and eat it too. If he wants to be a Congressman, he can't be a fearless man or anything approaching it. If he wants to be a Congressman, he can't have opinions. If he wants office or favor with the public, he has got to think what they think, if they think, which they don't. I know it as well as everybody knows it, but with me, as well as with thousands of other people, due to the way we are made, with our eyes wide open, we have been willing to live out on the edges in no man's land. It isn't an easy place to live, but it does often bring you loyal friends. Amongst newspaper men, the same as anywhere else, it brings some men that will stay with you and help you and try to encourage you in doing what you really think you ought to do.

I wish it was easier. If it was easier, there would be more men to follow it. I wish I knew how to tell you people to change it, for I haven't any doubt of your sincerity. Of course, you wouldn't have invited me if you hadn't been sincere, you wouldn't have dreamed of it. I haven't any doubt that all of you know the shortcomings of papers better than I know them. The trouble with the newspaper as against all the rest of the world is that it is so much more powerful. It is pretty nearly the whole thing. It is the only means of information of the people, and regardless of what we know about it, we make up our minds upon the stories that they carry day by day in all the details of life. No matter how intelligent people are, they make up their minds upon the stories.

I know there are men in the business that are honestly trying to do the best they can toward giving real service to the world, but I suppose as long as the world lives, the humane, the idealistic, those who are cursed with a purpose and those who follow it, will find the world a rather hard place to live in, and they would find it so even if there were no such things in the world as newspapers.

Chairman: I am glad Mr. Darrow didn't go into this assignment deliberately. I think he did rather a deft and thorough job of hide-lifting extemporaneously. If anyone were to ask me tonight what Clarence Darrow did to us this afternoon, I think I could say, like the small, freckle-faced boy in his discourse about God and his testimony as to what God had done to him, that Clarence Darrow almost ruined us this afternoon.

Address at the Sixth Annual Meeting, American Society of Newspaper Editors, Washington, D.C., April 20, 1928.

PART SEVEN

ON RELIGION

THE MYTH
OF THE SOUL

*Upon what evidence, then, are we asked to believe
in immortality? There is no evidence. One is told to rely
on faith, and no doubt this serves the purpose so long
as one can believe blindly whatever he is told.*

T HERE IS, PERHAPS, NO MORE
striking example of the credulity of man than the widespread
belief in immortality. This idea includes not only the belief that
death is not the end of what we call life, but that personal
identity involving memory persists beyond the grave. So determined is the ordinary individual to hold fast to this belief that,
as a rule, he refuses to read or to think upon the subject lest it
cast doubt upon his cherished dream. Of those who may chance
to look at this contribution, many will do so with the determination not to be convinced, and will refuse even to consider the
manifold reasons that might weaken their faith. I know that this
is true, for I know the reluctance with which I long approached
the subject and my firm determination not to give up my hope.
Thus the myth will stand in the way of a sensible adjustment to
facts.

Even many of those who claim to believe in immortality still
tell themselves and others that neither side of the question is
susceptible of proof. Just what can these hopeful ones believe
that the word "proof" involves? The evidence against the per-

sistence of personal consciousness is as strong as the evidence of gravitation, and much more obvious. It is as convincing and unassailable as the proof of the destruction of wood or coal by fire. If it is not certain that death ends personal identity and memory, then almost nothing that man accepts as true is susceptible of proof.

The beliefs of the race and its individuals are relics of the past. Without careful examination, no one can begin to understand how many of man's cherished opinions have no foundation in fact. The common experience of all men should teach them how easy it is to believe what they wish to accept. Experienced psychologists know perfectly well that if they desire to convince a man of some idea, they must first make him *want* to believe it. There are so many hopes, so many strong yearnings and desires attached to the doctrine of immortality that it is practically impossible to create in any mind the wish to be mortal. Still, in spite of strong desires, millions of people are filled with doubts and fears that will not down. After all, is it not better to look the question squarely in the face and find out whether we are harboring a delusion?

It is customary to speak of a "belief in immortality." First, then, let us see what is meant by the word "belief." If I take a train in Chicago at noon, bound for New York, I believe I will reach that city the next morning. I believe it because I have been to New York. I have read about the city, I have known many other people who have been there, and their stories are not inconsistent with any known facts in my own experience. I have even examined the timetables, and I know just how I will go and how long the trip will take. In other words, when I board the train for New York, I believe I will reach that city because I have *reason* to believe it.

But if I am told that next week I shall start on a trip to Goofville; that I shall not take my body with me; that I shall stay for all eternity: can I find a single fact connected with my journey—the way I shall go, the part of me that is to go, the time of the journey, the country I shall reach, its location in space, the way

Clarence Darrow

I shall live there—or anything that would lead to a rational belief that I shall really make the trip? Have I ever known anyone who has made the journey and returned? If I am really to believe, I must try to get some information about all these important facts.

But people hesitate to ask questions about life after death. They do not ask, for they know that only silence comes out of the eternal darkness of endless space. If people really believed in a beautiful, happy, glorious land waiting to receive them when they died; if they believed that their friends would be waiting to meet them; if they believed that all pain and suffering would be left behind: why should they live through weeks, months, and even years of pain and torture while a cancer eats its way to the vital parts of the body? Why should one fight off death? Because he does *not* believe in any real sense: he only hopes. Everyone knows that there is no real evidence of any such state of bliss; so we are told not to search for proof. We are to accept through faith alone. But every thinking person knows that faith can only come through belief. Belief implies a condition of mind that accepts a certain idea. This condition can be brought about only by evidence. True, the evidence may be simply the unsupported statement of your grandmother; it may be wholly insufficient for reasoning men; but, good or bad, it must be enough for the believer or he could not believe.

Upon what evidence, then, are we asked to believe in immortality? There is no evidence. One is told to rely on faith, and no doubt this serves the purpose so long as one can believe blindly whatever he is told. But if there is no evidence upon which to build a positive belief in immortality, let us examine the other side of the question. Perhaps evidence can be found to support a positive conviction that immortality is a delusion.

The belief in immortality expresses itself in two different forms. On the one hand, there is a belief in the immortality of the "soul." This is sometimes interpreted to mean simply that the identity, the consciousness, the memory of the individual persists after death. On the other hand, many religious creeds have formulated a belief in "the resurrection of the body"—which is something

The Myth of the Soul

else again. It will be necessary to examine both forms of this belief in turn.

The idea of continued life after death is very old. It doubtless had its roots back in the childhood of the race. In view of the limited knowledge of primitive man, it was not unreasonable. His dead friends and relatives visited him in dreams and visions and were present in his feeling and imagination until they were forgotten. Therefore the lifeless body did not raise the question of dissolution, but rather of duality. It was thought that man was a dual being possessing a body and a soul as separate entities, and that when a man died, his soul was released from his body to continue its life apart. Consequently, food and drink were placed upon the graves of the dead to be used in the long journey into the unknown. In modified forms, this belief in the duality of man persists to the present day.

But primitive man had no conception of life as having a beginning and an end. In this he was like the rest of the animals. Today, everyone of ordinary intelligence knows how life begins, and to examine the beginnings of life leads to inevitable conclusions about the way life ends. If man has a soul, it must creep in somewhere during the period of gestation and growth.

All the higher forms of animal life grow from a single cell. Before the individual life can begin its development, it must be fertilized by union with another cell; then the cell divides and multiplies until it takes the form and pattern of its kind. At a certain regular time the being emerges into the world. During its term of life millions of cells in its body are born, die, and are replaced until, through age, disease, or some catastrophe, the cells fall apart and the individual life is ended.

It is obvious that but for the fertilization of the cell under right conditions, the being would not have lived. It is idle to say that the initial cell has a soul. In one sense it has life; but even that is precarious and depends for its continued life upon union with another cell of the proper kind. The human mother is the bearer of probably ten thousand of one kind of cell, and the human father of countless billions of the other kind. Only a very small fraction of these result in human life. If the unfertilized cells of the female and the unused cells of the male are human beings possessed of souls, then the population of the world is infinitely greater than has ever been dreamed. Of course no such idea as belief in the immortality of the germ cells could satisfy the yearnings of the individual for a survival of life after death.

If that which is called a "soul" is a separate entity apart from the body, when, then, and where and how was this soul placed in the human structure? The individual began with the union of two cells, neither of which had a soul. How could these two soulless cells produce a soul? I must leave this search to the metaphysicians. When they have found the answer, I hope they will tell me, for I should really like to know.

We know that a baby may live and fully develop in its mother's womb and then, through some shock at birth, may be born without life. In the past, these babies were promptly buried. But now we know that in many such cases, where the bodily structure is complete, the machine may be set to work by artificial respiration or electricity. Then it will run like any other human body through its allotted term of years. We also know that in many cases of drowning, or when some mishap virtually destroys life without hopelessly impairing the body, artificial means may set it in motion once more, so that it will complete its term of existence until the final catastrophe comes. Are we to believe that somewhere around the stillborn child and somewhere in the vicinity of the drowned man there hovers a detached soul waiting to be summoned back into the body by a pulmotor? This, too, must be left to the metaphysicians.

The beginnings of life yield no evidence of the beginnings of a soul. It is idle to say that the something in the human being which we call "life" is the soul itself, for the soul is generally taken to distinguish human beings from other forms of life. There is life in all animals and plants, and at least potential life in inorganic matter. This potential life is simply unreleased force and matter—the great storehouse from which all forms of life emerge and are constantly replenished. It is impossible to draw

The Myth of the Soul

the line between inorganic matter and the simpler forms of plant life, and equally impossible to draw the line between plant life and animal life, or between other forms of animal life and what we human beings are pleased to call the highest form. If the thing which we call "life" is itself the soul, then cows have souls; and, in the very nature of things, we must allow souls to all forms of life and to inorganic matter as well.

Life itself is something very real, as distinguished from the soul. Every man knows that his life had a beginning. Can one imagine an organism that has a beginning and no end? If I did not exist in the infinite past, why should I, or could I, exist in the infinite future? "But," say some, "your consciousness, your memory may exist even after you are dead. This is what we mean by the soul." Let us examine this point a little.

I have no remembrance of the months that I lay in my mother's womb. I cannot recall the day of my birth nor the time when I first opened my eyes to the light of the sun. I cannot remember when I was an infant, or when I began to creep on the floor, or when I was taught to walk, or anything before I was five or six years old. Still, all of these events were important, wonderful, and strange in a new life. What I call my "consciousness," for lack of a better word and a better understanding, developed with my growth and the crowding experiences I met at every turn. I have a hazy recollection of the burial of a boy soldier who was shot toward the end of the Civil War. He was buried near the schoolhouse when I was seven years old. But I have no remembrance of the assassination of Abraham Lincoln, although I must then have been eight years old. I must have known about it at the time, for my family and my community idolized Lincoln, and all America was in mourning at his death. Why do I remember the dead boy soldier who was buried a year before? Perhaps because I knew him well. Perhaps because his family was close to my childish life. Possibly because it came to me as my first knowledge of death. At all events, it made so deep an impression that I recall it now.

"Ah, yes," say the believers in the soul, "what you say confirms our own belief. You certainly existed when these early experiences took place. You were conscious of them at the time, even though you are not aware of it now. In the same way, may not your consciousness persist after you die, even though you are not now aware of the fact?"

On the contrary, my fading memory of the events that filled the early years of my life leads me to the opposite conclusion. So far as these incidents are concerned, the mind and consciousness of the boy are already dead. Even now, am I fully alive? I am seventy-one years old. I often fail to recollect the names of some of those I knew full well. Many events do not make the lasting impression that they once did. I know that it will be only a few years, even if my body still survives decay, when few important matters will even register in my mind. I know how it is with the old. I know that physical life can persist beyond the time when the mind can fully function. I know that if I live to an extreme old age, my mind will fail. I shall eat and drink and go to my bed in an automatic way. Memory—which is all that binds me to the past—will already be dead. All that will remain will be a vegetative existence; I shall sit and doze in the chimney corner, and my body will function in a measure even though the ego will already be practically dead. I am sure that if I die of what is called "old age," my consciousness will gradually slip away with my failing emotions; I shall no more be aware of the near approach of final dissolution than is the dying tree.

In primitive times, before men knew anything about the human body or the universe of which it is a part, it was not unreasonable to believe in spirits, ghosts, and the duality of man. For one thing, celestial geography was much simpler then. Just above the earth was a firmament in which the stars were set, and above the firmament was heaven. The place was easy of access, and in dreams the angels were seen going up and coming down on a ladder. But now we have a slightly more adequate conception of space and the infinite universe of which we are so small a part. Our great telescopes reveal countless worlds and planetary systems which make our own sink into utter insignificance in comparison.

We have every reason to think that beyond our sight there is endless space filled with still more planets, so infinite in size and number that no brain has the smallest conception of their extent. Is there any reason to think that in this universe, with its myriads of worlds, there is no other life so important as our own? Is it possible that the inhabitants of the earth have been singled out for special favor and endowed with souls and immortal life? Is it at all reasonable to suppose that any special account is taken of the human atoms that forever come and go upon this planet?

If man has a soul that persists after death, that goes to a heaven of the blessed or to a hell of the damned, where are these places? It is not so easily imagined as it once was. How does the soul make its journey? What does immortal man find when he gets there, and how will he live after he reaches the end of endless space? We know that the atmosphere will be absent; that there will be no light, no heat—only the infinite reaches of darkness and frigidity. In view of modern knowledge, can anyone *really believe* in the persistence of individual life and memory?

There are those who base their hope of a future life upon the resurrection of the body. This is a purely religious doctrine. It is safe to say that few intelligent men who are willing to look obvious facts in the face hold any such belief. Yet we are seriously told that Elijah was carried bodily to heaven in a chariot of fire, and that Jesus arose from the dead and ascended into heaven. The New Testament abounds in passages that support this doctrine. St. Paul states the tenet over and over again. In the fifteenth chapter of First Corinthians he says: "If Christ be preached that he rose from the dead, how say some among you that there is no resurrection of the dead? . . . And if Christ be not risen, then is our preaching vain. . . . For if the dead rise not, then is not Christ raised." The Apostles' Creed says: "I believe in the resurrection of the body." This has been carried into substantially all the orthodox creeds; and while it is more or less minimized by neglect and omission, it is still a cardinal doctrine of the orthodox churches.

Two thousand years ago, in Palestine, little was known of man, of the earth, or of the universe. It was then currently believed that the earth was only four thousand years old, that life had begun anew after the deluge about two thousand years before, and that the entire earth was soon to be destroyed. Today it is fairly well established that man has been upon the earth for a million years. During that long stretch of time the world has changed many times; it is changing every moment. At least three or four ice ages have swept across continents, driving death before them, carrying human beings into the sea or burying them deep in the earth. Animals have fed on man and on each other. Every dead body, no matter whether consumed by fire or buried in the earth, has been resolved into its elements, so that the matter and energy that once formed human beings has fed animals and plants and other men. As the great naturalist, Fabre, has said: "At the banquet of life each is in turn a guest and a dish." Thus the body of every man now living is in part made from the bodies of those who have been dead for ages.

Yet we are still asked to believe in the resurrection of the body. By what alchemy, then, are the individual bodies that have successfully fed the generations of men to be separated and restored to their former identities? And if I am to be resurrected, what particular *I* shall be called from the grave, from the animals and plants and the bodies of other men who shall inherit this body I now call my own? My body has been made over and over, piece by piece, as the days went by, and will continue to be so made until the end. It has changed so slowly that each new cell is fitted into the living part, and will go on changing until the final crisis comes. Is it the child in the mother's womb or the tottering frame of the old man that shall be brought back? The mere thought of such a resurrection beggars reason, ignores facts, and enthrones blind faith, wild dreams, hopeless hopes, and cowardly fears as sovereign of the human mind.

Some of those who profess to believe in the immortality of man —whether it be of his soul or his body—have drawn what comfort they could from the modern scientific doctrine of the indestructibility of matter and force. This doctrine, they say, only confirms in scientific language what they have always believed. This, however, is pure sophistry. It is probably true that no matter or force has ever been or ever can be destroyed. But it is likewise true that there is no connection whatever between the notion that personal consciousness and memory persist after death and the scientific theory that matter and force are indestructible. For the scientific theory carries with it a corollary, that the forms of matter and energy are constantly changing through an endless cycle of new combinations. Of what possible use would it be, then, to have a consciousness that was immortal, but which, from the moment of death, was dispersed into new combinations so that no two parts of the original identity could ever be reunited again?

These natural processes of change, which in the human being take the forms of growth, disease, senility, death, and decay, are essentially the same as the processes by which a lump of coal is disintegrated in burning. One may watch the lump of coal burning in the grate until nothing but ashes remains. Part of the coal goes up the chimney in the form of smoke; part of it radiates through the house as heat; the residue lies in the ashes on the hearth. So it is with human life. In all forms of life nature is engaged in combining, breaking down, and recombining her store of energy and matter into new forms. The thing we call "life" is nothing other than a state of equilibrium which endures for a short span of years between the two opposing tendencies of nature —the one that builds up, and the one that tears down. In old age, the tearing-down process has already gained the ascendency, and when death intervenes, the equilibrium is finally upset by the complete stoppage of the building-up process, so that nothing remains but complete disintegration. The energy thus released may be converted into grass or trees or animal life; or it may lie dormant until caught up again in the crucible of nature's laboratory. But whatever happens, the man—the *You* and the *I*—like the lump of coal that has been burned, is gone, irrevocably dispersed. All the King's horses and all the King's men cannot restore it to its former unity.

The idea that man is a being set apart, distinct from all the rest of nature, is born of man's emotions, of his loves and hates, of his hopes and fears, and of the primitive conceptions of undeveloped minds. The *You* or the *I* which is known to our friends does not consist of an immaterial something called a "soul" which cannot be conceived. We know perfectly well what we mean when we talk about this *You* and this *Me:* and it is equally plain that the whole fabric that makes up our separate personalities is destroyed, dispersed, disintegrated beyond repair by what we call "death."

Those who refuse to give up the idea of immortality declare that nature never creates a desire without providing the means for its satisfaction. They likewise insist that all people, from the rudest to the most civilized, yearn for another life. As a matter of fact, nature creates many desires which she does not satisfy; most of the wishes of men meet no fruition. But nature does not create any emotion demanding a future life. The only yearning that the individual has is to keep on living—which is a very different thing. This urge is found in every animal, in every plant. It is simply the momentum of a living structure: or, as Schopenhauer put it, "the will to live." What we long for is a continuation of our present state of existence, not an uncertain reincarnation in a mysterious world of which we know nothing.

All men recognize the hopelessness of finding any evidence that the individual will persist beyond the grave. As a last resort, we are told that it is better that the doctrine be believed even if it is not true. We are assured that without this faith, life is only desolation and despair. However that may be, it remains that many of the conclusions of logic are not pleasant to contemplate; still, so long as men think and feel, at least some of them will use their faculties as best they can. For if we are to believe things that are not true, who is to write our creed? Is it safe to leave it to any man or organization to pick out the errors that we must accept? The whole history of the world has answered this question in a way that cannot be mistaken.

And after all, is the belief in immortality necessary or even desirable for man? Millions of men and women have no such faith; they go on with their daily tasks and feel joy and sorrow without the lure of immortal life. The things that really affect the happiness of the individual are the matters of daily living. They are the companionship of friends, the games and contemplations. They are misunderstandings and cruel judgments, false friends and debts, poverty and disease. They are our joys in our living companions and our sorrows over those who die. Whatever our faith, we mainly live in the present—in the here and now. Those who hold the view that man is mortal are never troubled by metaphysical problems. At the end of the day's labor we are glad to lose our consciousness in sleep; and intellectually, at least, we look forward to the long rest from the stresses and storms that are always incidental to existence.

When we fully understand the brevity of life, its fleeting joys and unavoidable pains; when we accept the fact that all men and women are approaching an inevitable doom: the consciousness of it should make us more kindly and considerate of each other. This feeling should make men and women use their best efforts to help their fellow travellers on the road, to make the path brighter and easier as we journey on. It should bring a closer kinship, a better understanding, and a deeper sympathy for the wayfarers who must live a common life and die a common death.

The Forum, *October, 1928.*

WHY I AM
AN AGNOSTIC

*The modern world is the child of doubt and inquiry,
as the ancient world was the child of fear and faith.*

A<small>N AGNOSTIC IS A DOUBTER.</small>
The word is generally applied to those who doubt the verity of
accepted religious creeds or faiths. Everyone is an agnostic as
to the beliefs or creeds they do not accept. Catholics are agnostic
to the Protestant creeds, and the Protestants are agnostic to the
Catholic creed. Anyone who thinks is an agnostic about something, otherwise he must believe that he is possessed of all knowledge. And the proper place for such a person is in the madhouse
or the home for the feeble-minded. In a popular way, in the
western world, an agnostic is one who doubts or disbelieves the
main tenets of the Christian faith.

I would say that belief in at least three tenets is necessary to
the faith of a Christian: a belief in God, a belief in immortality,
and a belief in a supernatural book. Various Christian sects require
much more, but it is difficult to imagine that one could be a
Christian, under any intelligent meaning of the word, with less.
Yet there are some people who claim to be Christians who do not
accept the literal interpretation of all the Bible, and who give
more credence to some portions of the book than to others.

I am an agnostic as to the question of God. I think that it is
impossible for the human mind to believe in an object or thing

unless it can form a mental picture of such object or thing. Since man ceased to worship openly an anthropomorphic God and talked vaguely and not intelligently about some force in the universe, higher than man, that is responsible for the existence of man and the universe, he cannot be said to believe in God. One cannot believe in a force excepting as a force that pervades matter and is not an individual entity. To believe in a thing, an image of the thing must be stamped on the mind. If one is asked if he believes in such an animal as a camel, there immediately arises in his mind an image of the camel. This image has come from experience or knowledge of the animal gathered in some way or other. No such image comes, or can come, with the idea of a God who is described as a force.

Man has always speculated upon the origin of the universe, including himself. I feel, with Herbert Spencer, that whether the universe had an origin—and if it had—what the origin is will never be known by man. The Christian says that the universe could not make itself; that there must have been some higher power to call it into being. Christians have been obsessed for many years by Paley's argument that if a person passing through a desert should find a watch and examine its spring, its hands, its case and its crystal, he would at once be satisfied that some intelligent being capable of design had made the watch. No doubt this is true. No civilized man would question that someone made the watch. The reason he would not doubt it is because he is familiar with watches and other appliances made by man. The savage was once unfamiliar with a watch and would have had no idea upon the subject. There are plenty of crystals and rocks of natural formation that are as intricate as a watch, but even to intelligent man they carry no implication that some intelligent power must have made them. They carry no such implication because no one has any knowledge or experience of someone having made these natural objects which everywhere abound.

To say that God made the universe gives us no explanation of the beginning of things. If we are told that God made the universe, the question immediately arises: Who made God? Did he always exist, or was there some power back of that? Did he create matter out of nothing, or is his existence co-extensive with matter? The problem is still there. What is the origin of it all? If, on the other hand, one says that the universe was not made by God, that it always existed, he has the same difficulty to confront. To say that the universe was here last year, or millions of years ago, does not explain its origin. This is still a mystery. As to the question of the origin of things, man can only wonder and doubt and guess.

As to the existence of the soul, all people may either believe or disbelieve. Everyone knows the origin of the human being. They know that it came from a single cell in the body of the mother, and that the cell was one out of ten thousand in the mother's body. Before gestation the cell must have been fertilized by a spermatozoön from the body of the father. This was one out of perhaps a billion spermatozoa that was the capacity of the father. When the cell is fertilized a chemical process begins. The cell divides and multiplies and increases into millions of cells, and finally a child is born. Cells die and are born during the life of the individual until they finally drop apart, and this is death.

If there is a soul, what is it, and where did it come from, and where does it go? Can anyone who is guided by his reason possibly imagine a soul independent of a body, or the place of its residence, or the character of it, or anything concerning it? If man is justified in any belief or disbelief on any subject, he is warranted in the disbelief in a soul. Not one scrap of evidence exists to prove any such impossible thing.

Many Christians base the belief of a soul and God upon the Bible. Strictly speaking, there is no such book. To make the Bible, sixty-six books are bound into one volume. These books were written by many people at different times, and no one knows the time or the identity of any author. Some of the books were written by several authors at various times. These books contain all sorts of contradictory concepts of life and morals and the origin

Why I Am an Agnostic

of things. Between the first and the last nearly a thousand years intervened, a longer time than has passed since the discovery of America by Columbus.

When I was a boy the theologians used to assert that the proof of the divine inspiration of the Bible rested on miracles and prophecies. But a miracle means a violation of a natural law, and there can be no proof imagined that could be sufficient to show the violation of a natural law; even though proof seemed to show violation, it would only show that we were not acquainted with all natural laws. One believes in the truthfulness of a man because of his long experience with the man, and because the man has always told a consistent story. But no man has told so consistent a story as nature.

If one should say that the sun did not rise, to use the ordinary expression, on the day before, his hearer would not believe it, even though he had slept all day and knew that his informant was a man of the strictest veracity. He would not believe it because the story is inconsistent with the conduct of the sun in all the ages past.

Primitive and even civilized people have grown so accustomed to believing in miracles that they often attribute the simplest manifestations of nature to agencies of which they know nothing. They do this when the belief is utterly inconsistent with knowledge and logic. They believe in old miracles and new ones. Preachers pray for rain, knowing full well that no such prayer was ever answered. When a politician is sick, they pray for God to cure him, and the politician almost invariably dies. The modern clergyman who prays for rain and for the health of the politician is no more intelligent in this matter than the primitive man who saw a separate miracle in the rising and setting of the sun, in the birth of an individual, in the growth of a plant, in the stroke of lightning, in the flood, in every manifestation of nature and life.

As to prophecies, intelligent writers gave them up long ago. In all prophecies facts are made to suit the prophecy, or the prophecy was made after the facts, or the events have no relation to the prophecy. Weird and strange and unreasonable interpre-

Clarence Darrow

tations are used to explain simple statements, that a prophecy may be claimed.

Can any rational person believe that the Bible is anything but a human document? We now know pretty well where the various books came from, and about when they were written. We know that they were written by human beings who had no knowledge of science, little knowledge of life, and were influenced by the barbarous morality of primitive times, and were grossly ignorant of most things that men know today. For instance, Genesis says that God made the earth, and he made the sun to light the day and the moon to light the night, and in one clause disposes of the stars by saying that "he made the stars also." This was plainly written by someone who had no conception of the stars. Man, by the aid of his telescope, has looked out into the heavens and found stars whose diameter is as great as the distance between the earth and the sun. We now know that the universe is filled with stars and suns and planets and systems. Every new telescope looking further into the heavens only discovers more and more worlds and suns and systems in the endless reaches of space. The men who wrote Genesis believed, of course, that this tiny speck of mud that we call the earth was the center of the universe, the only world in space, and made for man, who was the only being worth considering. These men believed that the stars were only a little way above the earth, and were set in the firmament for man to look at, and for nothing else. Everyone today knows that this conception is not true.

The origin of the human race is not as blind a subject as it once was. Let alone God creating Adam out of hand, from the dust of the earth, does anyone believe that Eve was made from Adam's rib—that the snake walked and spoke in the Garden of Eden—that he tempted Eve to persuade Adam to eat an apple, and that it is on that account that the whole human race was doomed to hell—that for four thousand years there was no chance for any human to be saved, though none of them had anything whatever to do with the temptation; and that finally men were saved only through God's son dying for them, and that unless human beings believed this silly, impossible and wicked story they were doomed to hell? Can anyone with intelligence really believe that a child born today should be doomed because the snake tempted Eve and Eve tempted Adam? To believe that is not God-worship; it is devil-worship.

Can anyone call this scheme of creation and damnation moral? It defies every principle of morality, as man conceives morality. Can anyone believe today that the whole world was destroyed by flood, save only Noah and his family and a male and female of each species of animal that entered the Ark? There are almost a million species of insects alone. How did Noah match these up and make sure of getting male and female to reproduce life in the world after the flood had spent its force? And why should all the lower animals have been destroyed? Were they included in the sinning of man? This is a story which could not beguile a fairly bright child of five years of age today.

Do intelligent people believe that the various languages spoken by man on earth came from the confusion of tongues at the Tower of Babel, some four thousand years ago? Human languages were dispersed all over the face of the earth long before that time. Evidences of civilizations are in existence now that were old long before the date that romancers fix for the building of the Tower, and even before the date claimed for the flood.

Do Christians believe that Joshua made the sun stand still, so that the day could be lengthened, that a battle might be finished? What kind of person wrote that story, and what did he know about astronomy? It is perfectly plain that the author thought that the earth was the center of the universe and stood still in the heavens, and that the sun either went around it or was pulled across its path each day, and that the stopping of the sun would lengthen the day. We know now that had the sun stopped when Joshua commanded it, and had it stood still until now, it would not have lengthened the day. We know that the day is determined by the rotation of the earth upon its axis, and not by the movement of the sun. Everyone knows that this story simply is not true, and not many even pretend to believe the childish fable.

Clarence Darrow

What of the tale of Balaam's ass speaking to him, probably in Hebrew? Is it true, or is it a fable? Many asses have spoken, and doubtless some in Hebrew, but they have not been that breed of asses. Is salvation to depend on a belief in a monstrosity like this?

Above all the rest, would any human being today believe that a child was born without a father? Yet this story was not at all unreasonable in the ancient world; at least three or four miraculous births are recorded in the Bible, including John the Baptist and Samson. Immaculate conceptions were common in the Roman world at the time and at the place where Christianity really had its nativity. Women were taken to the temples to be innoculated of God so that their sons might be heroes, which meant, generally, wholesale butchers. Julius Caesar was a miraculous conception—indeed, they were common all over the world. How many miraculous-birth stories is a Christian now expected to believe?

In the days of the formation of the Christian religion, disease meant the possession of human beings by devils. Christ cured a sick man by casting out the devils, who ran into the swine, and the swine ran into the sea. Is there any question but what that was simply the attitude and belief of a primitive people? Does anyone believe that sickness means the possession of the body by devils, and that the devils must be cast out of the human being that he may be cured? Does anyone believe that a dead person can come to life? The miracles recorded in the Bible are not the only instances of dead men coming to life. All over the world one finds testimony of such miracles; miracles which no person is expected to believe, unless it is his kind of a miracle. Still at Lourdes today, and all over the present world, from New York to Los Angeles and up and down the lands, people believe in miraculous occurrences, and even in the return of the dead. Superstition is everywhere prevalent in the world. It has been so from the beginning, and most likely will be so unto the end.

The reasons for agnosticism and skepticism are abundant and compelling. Fantastic and foolish and impossible consequences are freely claimed for the belief in religion. All the civilization of any period is put down as a result of religion. All the cruelty and error and ignorance of the period has no relation to religion. The truth is that the origin of what we call civilization is not due to religion but to skepticism. So long as men accepted miracles without question, so long as they believed in original sin and the road to salvation, so long as they believed in a hell where man would be kept for eternity on account of Eve, there was no reason whatever for civilization: life was short, and eternity was long, and the business of life was preparation for eternity.

When every event was a miracle, when there was no order or system or law, there was no occasion for studying any subject, or being interested in anything excepting a religion which took care of the soul. As man doubted the primitive conceptions about religion, and no longer accepted the literal, miraculous teachings of ancient books, he set himself to understand nature. We no longer cure disease by casting out devils. Since that time, men have studied the human body, have built hospitals and treated illness in a scientific way. Science is responsible for the building of railroads and bridges, of steamships, of telegraph lines, of cities, towns, large buildings and small, plumbing and sanitation, of the food supply, and the countless thousands of useful things that we now deem necessary to life. Without skepticism and doubt, none of these things could have been given to the world.

The fear of God is not the beginning of wisdom. The fear of God is the death of wisdom. Skepticism and doubt lead to study and investigation, and investigation is the beginning of wisdom.

The modern world is the child of doubt and inquiry, as the ancient world was the child of fear and faith.

From a symposium with three other speakers: a rabbi, a Protestant bishop and a Catholic judge, in Columbus, Ohio, March 12, 1929.

Clarence Darrow

EPILOGUE

IF DARROW WERE ALIVE TODAY, WHAT WOULD HE SAY, WHAT would he do, how would he act in the issues confronting mankind?

These are mere speculations, mere observations based on his life, his philosophy. No individual can prophesy how another will act given certain conditions. No individual can always predict how he himself would act in a situation until he is confronted by it. But the makeup, the psychological orientation, the background of a life, can give a clue.

Based on these, the editors have attempted to recreate Darrow in our modern world: confronted by the atom bomb, by United States Supreme Court decisions, Congressional investigations, immigration restrictions, civil rights demands, capital punishment, the right of counsel in criminal cases, and labor unions.

Darrow was deeply troubled with humanity and its plight during his lifetime. He would still be seeking and searching for the answers. His underlying concern would be for the individual: for his rights, whenever or wherever challenged.

There is nothing in Darrow's life or writings which would indicate a lessening of interest in labor unions. But Darrow would insist on the individual's rights through a democratic union. His energies would be directed to the protection of the member in a strong union, as it was in defending the right of the citizen against a strong government.

Darrow believed that "the man who works in a mill or on a railroad is as vitally interested in its management and should have as much to say about hours, conditions, and terms of labor as the one who has nothing but money invested in the plant."

As a lawyer, Darrow would be ready to defend the unpopular today as he was during his lifetime. He would feel that all are entitled to the best defense obtainable. He would decry attempts to smear defense lawyers with the onus of their clients whether the defendant be a criminal, a labor leader, a Communist or a fascist. "When every other man has turned against him, the law provides that he should have a lawyer," he said, "one who cannot only be his lawyer, but his friend."

In civil liberties Darrow would insist, as he did in his defense of the Communists in 1920, that "I know that the humblest and the meanest man who lives, I know that the idlest and the silliest man who lives, should have his say. I know he ought to speak his mind. And I know that the Constitution is a delusion and a snare if the weakest and the humblest man in the land cannot be defended in his right to speak and his right to think as much as the greatest and the strongest in the land. I am not here to defend their opinions. I am here to defend their right to express their opinions."

The growing awareness of the Negro, his move to take his place as an equal with his white fellow-man, would be applauded by Darrow, for all his life he had fought for the rights of the Negro. He would applaud the Freedom Riders and the sit-ins in the efforts to break the hold of segregation. "I do not believe in the law of hate. I may not be true to my ideals always, but I believe in the law of love, and I believe you can do nothing with hatred," he had said.

"The law has made him [the Negro] equal, but man has not. And, after all, the last analysis is, what has man done?—and not, what has the law done?" Darrow told the jury in the Sweet housing segregation case in Detroit.

In the area of separation of school and state, there is no doubt where Darrow would stand on the United States Supreme Court decision declaring unconstitutional the reading of a prescribed prayer in schools. Darrow, as an agnostic, did not want to suppress the teaching of religion, but he would not want it exercised as a requirement in a school curriculum.

The continued restricted and prejudiced immigration standards in effect in the United States—pinpointed by the McCarran-Walter Act—would be opposed by Darrow. As he said in a debate on the 1924 Immigration Act when the restrictive law was passed: "It is hard for me to forget that there are other people on earth besides the stock I came from."

As for capital punishment, Darrow's consistency cannot be questioned in this area. He was to state it time and again to juries, on lecture platforms, in writing and in debate: "I do not believe in man taking away the life of his fellow man." He would have to decry capital punishment today, whether the "criminal" be the architect of genocide—Adolf Eichmann—or the poor, uneducated, deprived black or white man.

He would have been particularly happy in early March of 1963, when one of his most celebrated clients, Nathan Leopold, was released from parole. Five years earlier, Leopold was paroled from the Illinois penitentiary after spending thirty-three years in prison for the kidnapping and murder of Bobby Franks. Leopold with his friend, Richard Loeb, had been sentenced to life plus ninety-nine years for the crime. Loeb was killed in a prison fight in 1936. Leopold, after his parole March 13, 1958, on the twentieth anniversary of Darrow's death, went to work in the hospital of the Brethren Service Commission in Puerto Rico.

Darrow in his plea to Judge Caverly in 1924, asking for "mitigation of the punishment," said that the boys "may have hope that as the years roll around they might be released. I do not know. I will be honest with the court as I have tried to be from the beginning. I know that these boys are not fit to be at large. I believe they will not be until they pass through the next stage of life, at forty-five or fifty."

Leopold was fifty-three when he was released from Stateville penitentiary. Today he is a respected citizen living in Puerto Rico.

Perhaps the one area where Darrow was most inconsistent was that of international affairs. A long-time pacifist, a believer in non-violence, Darrow abandoned his pacifism during World War I, and undoubtedly would have for World War II. But he unequivocally opposed the witchhunts created by the first war and its aftermath. He would have been just as ready to decry the McCarthy era after World War II and defend its victims as he did during the Palmer raids after the first World War.

"I am always watchful of anybody when he overdoes patriotism," Darrow commented during the twenties.

Where would Darrow stand today with the threat of nuclear war?

The smallness of the planet which man inhabits compared to what it was even during the last days of Darrow's life, would probably have shifted the isolationism expressed by him after World War I to an internationalist position. The destructiveness of the atom bomb would probably have reverted him back to his pacifist philosophy. The present era would find him a nuclear pacifist renouncing the use of the bomb.

He might still feel that "man can never reach a state of non-violence." But he would proclaim: "Resist not evil? Yes, I will resist evil. But with non-violent means."

For as he wrote in his autobiography: "What we know as moral forces are even more important than guns and battleships. These forces would constantly grow stronger if nations relied upon them and cultivated them instead of the munitions of warfare. It may be that the world will never be at peace, and that liberty will never be secure in any land. If liberty and 'peace on earth, good will to men' shall ever prevail it will be after forts and arsenals and hatreds have disappeared."

SOURCE

MATERIALS

THE RIGHT OF REVOLUTION, *Everyman*, August-September, 1914.

THE PROBLEM OF THE NEGRO, *International Socialist Review*, November, 1901.

THE OPEN SHOP, The Hammersmark Publishing Company, 1904.

IF MAN HAD OPPORTUNITY, *Everyman*, January-February, 1915.

RESOLVED: THAT THE UNITED STATES CONTINUE THE POLICY OF PROHIBITION AS DEFINED IN THE EIGHTEENTH AMENDMENT, League for Public Discussion, December 23, 1924.

IS THE U.S. IMMIGRATION LAW BENEFICIAL?, Haldeman-Julius, Girard, Kansas, copyright April 23, 1929.

ROBERT BURNS, WALT WHITMAN, REALISM IN LITERATURE, THE SKELETON IN THE CLOSET, from *The Persian Pearl*, Roycroft Shop, 1899, copyright Clarence S. Darrow.

LEO TOLSTOY, *The Rubric*, January 1902, published and copyrighted by the Rubric Studios, Chicago, 1901.

FACING LIFE FEARLESSLY, Haldeman-Julius, Girard, Kansas, copyright March 11, 1929.

THE HOLDUP MAN, *International Socialist Review*, copyright Charles H. Kerr and Company, February, 1909.

CONDUCT AND PROFESSION, *The Rubric*, Vol. 2, No. 2, 1901.

THE THEORY OF NON-RESISTANCE, Worker's University Society, February, 1910.

BIRTHDAY RESPONSE, the Walden Book Shop, April 18, 1918.

THE CONSOLATIONS OF PESSIMISM, John F. Higgins, printer and binder, 1920.

FREE TRADE OR PROTECTION? *Current Topics*, 1894.

BRIEF FOR THE WAR, *Liberal Review*, Liberal Review Company, Chicago, July, 1917.

THE BREAKER BOY, *Chicago Evening American*, 1902.

LITTLE LOUIS EPSTINE, *The Pilgrim*, 1903.

CHILDHOOD SURROUNDINGS, from *Farmington*, Charles Scribner's Sons, copyright Clarence S. Darrow, 1904, 1932.

WHY I AM AN AGNOSTIC, Haldeman-Julius, Girard, Kansas, copyright December 5, 1929.

SELECTED
BIBLIOGRAPHY

ADAMIC, LOUIS. *Dynamite*, 1931.

ALTGELD, JOHN P. *Live Questions*, 1899.

BARNARD, HARRY. *Eagle Forgotten*, 1938.

BUSCH, FRANCIS. *Prisoners at the Bar*, 1952.

CRANDALL, ALLEN. *The Man From Kinsman*, 1933.

GIESLER, JERRY. *The Jerry Giesler Story*, 1960.

GINGER, RAY. *The Bending Cross*, 1949.

————. *Altgeld's America: The Lincoln Ideal versus Changing Realities*, 1958.

————. *Six Days or Forever: Tennessee versus John T. Scopes*, 1958.

GOLDMAN, ERIC. *Rendezvous With Destiny*, 1952.

HALDEMAN-JULIUS, MARCET. *Darrow's Two Great Trials*, 1927.

HARRISON, CHARLES YALE. *Clarence Darrow*, 1931.

MASTERS, EDGAR LEE. *Across Spoon River*, 1936.

MORDELL, ALBERT. *Clarence Darrow, Eugene V. Debs and Haldeman-Julius*, 1950.

RAVITZ, ABE C. *Clarence Darrow and the American Literary Tradition*, 1962.

ST. JOHN, ADELA ROGERS. *Final Verdict*, 1962.

STEFFENS, LINCOLN. *Autobiography*, 1931.

STONE, IRVING. *Clarence Darrow for the Defense*, 1941.

WEINBERG, ARTHUR. *Attorney for the Damned*, 1957.

YARROS, VICTOR S. *My 11 Years with Clarence Darrow*, 1950.

INDEX

Gertz, Elmer, 11
Giesler, Jerry, 21, 34
God, concepts of, 280-292, 294
Gogol, Nikolai, 189
Gompers, Samuel, 106

Hardy, Thomas, 367
Harvey, William, 309
Haymarket massacre, 23
Haywood, Moyer and Pettibone case, 19, 20, 32-33
Hearst, William Randolph, 27
Heine, Heinrich, 274
Hemingway, Ernest, 347
Henley, W. E., 202, 204
Heroes: discrepant with popular morality, 248-250; dualism in, 246-247, 253-258; free will in, 248-249, 251; nature of, 250-253; popular concept of, 246-247; religious origin of, 247-248
Hillman, Sidney, 102
Hillquit, Morris, 49
Hirohito, Emperor, 224
Holdups, holdup man: economic factors in, 221-223; emigration affecting, 222-223; historical parallels, 223; religion and, 224; seasonal factors, 220-221
Holmes, Dr. John Haynes, 45, 106ff
Holmes, Oliver Wendell, 273, 327
Homicide, 227-229
Honesty: ambivalence of human nature regarding, 300-301; circumstances altering, 299-300; commercial and legal, 297; conclusions on, 300-301; group pressures on, 289-290; in children, 297; legal concept of, 297; mechanistic concept of, 296; moral concept of, 295; religious concept of, 295, 298; social concept of, 298; traditional standards of, 296-297
Hoover, Herbert, 225
Housman, A. E., 101; free will, 207, 211; pessimist, 214-215
Howells, William Dean, 367
Hughes, Charles Evans, 49
Humboldt, Friedrich von, 309
Huxley, Thomas Henry, 309

Ibsen, Henrik, 367
Identification, error in, 322-323
Immigration, 20, 132, 437, 439; arguments for control of, 135-136, 142; brotherhood and, 145, 146; discrimination in, 142-143; future of, 143-144, 146; historical background of, 137-138, 139, 140-141; labor and, 138, 139, 144; National Origins Act, 136, 137; prosperity affecting, 138-139
Independent, The, 34
Industrial Workers of the World (I.W.W.), 336
Infidels and Heretics, 51
Insanity, 263

International Socialist Review, 224
Irish National Convention, 57

Jails, 263; seasonal factors, 221
Japan, earthquake in, 106
Javits, Jacob K., 48
Johnston, Mrs. Jessie, 11
Judges, 323
Jungle, The, 28
Jurors: choice of, 315ff; prohibitionists as, 318-320; racial factors, 317-318; religious factors, 318-319; variety in, 322-323; women as, 319
Jury trial, 136, 138
Justice: ambiguities in, 308-312; arts and, 306; based on emotion, 311; contemporary view of, 308-309; courts as setting for, 313-315; definitions of, 304; errors in, 322-324, 406; historical development of, 306-308; legal concept of, 304; popular concept of, 304-305; social application of, 302-303; social concept of, 304-305; social impacts on, 305-306; traditional view of, 302

Kant, Immanuel, 274
Kerensky, Alexander, 336
Kidd, Thomas I., 21, 23
Kiefer, Daniel, 337, 346
Kiwanis, 409
Knights of Columbus, 409
Knuti, Ernest L., 11
Ku Klux Klan, 409

Labor, 51, 61, 138, 144
Labor Temple School, 45
Labor unions (*see organized labor*)
Landis, Kenesaw Mountain, 101
Landru, "Bluebeard," 101
Law, 27; courts as setting for, 313; nature of, 27; prone to error, 322-324
Lawyers, 102
Lenin, Nikolai, 336
Leopold, Nathan Jr., 20, 36, 38-41, 106, 439
Lewis, Arthur M., 267
Lincoln, Abraham, 67, 70
Lindbergh, Charles A. Jr., 347
Lions Club, 409
Literary Review, 39
Lloyd, William Bross, 38
Lloyd George, David, 101
Loeb, Richard, 20, 36, 38-41, 106, 439
Los Angeles Times bombing, 19
Lowell, Abbott Lawrence, 219
Lusitania, sinking of, 344
Lynching, 65

MacDonald, J. Ramsay, 134
Mahler, Gustav, 219